Office 2000
Made Easy

Office 2000
Made Easy

ALAN NEIBAUER

Osborne McGraw-Hill

Berkeley New York St. Louis San Francisco
Auckland Bogotá Hamburg London Madrid Mexico City Milan Montreal
New Delhi Panama City Paris São Paulo Singapore Sydney Tokyo Toronto

Osborne McGraw-Hill
2600 Tenth Street
Berkeley, California 94710
U.S.A.

For information on translations or book distributors outside the U.S.A., or to arrange bulk purchase discounts for sales promotions, premiums, or fund-raisers, please contact Osborne/**McGraw-Hill** at the above address.

Office 2000 Made Easy

1234567890 AGM AGM 90198765432109

ISBN 0-07-882585-7

Publisher
Brandon A. Nordin

Associate Publisher and Editor-in-Chief
Scott Rogers

Acquisitions Editor
Joanne Cuthbertson

Project Editor
Cynthia Douglas

Editorial Assistant
Stephane Thomas

Technical Editor
Terrie Solomon

Copy Editor
Jan Jue

Proofreaders
Jeff Barash
Mike McGee
Pat Mannion

Indexer
Valerie Robbins

Computer Designers
Roberta Steele
Gary Corrigan

Illustrators
Beth Young
Robert Hansen

Series Design
Peter F. Hancik

To Barbie

Contents at a Glance

Part I
Welcome to Microsoft Office

Part II
Word for Windows

Part III
Working with Excel

Part IV

Presenting with PowerPoint

Part V

Managing Data with Access

Part VI

Microsoft Outlook

Contents

Acknowledgments

My thanks to everyone who worked on this project, especially acquisitions editor Joanne Cuthbertson for sticking with this project, project editor Cynthia Douglas, editorial assistant Stephane Thomas, copy editor Jan Jue, proofreaders Jeff Barash, Mike McGee and Pat Mannion, and indexer Valerie Robbins

Thanks also to the Osborne production team of Roberta Steele, Beth Young, Gary Corrigan, and Robert Hansen, all of whom worked marvelously on this project.

A special thanks to a real live doll of a wife and woman, my own Barbie. Through good times and bad, she's always ready to perk me up or calm me down, make me laugh, or just be there with a supporting hand.

Introduction

Sometimes it is not easy to improve on a standard, but Microsoft has done just that with Microsoft Office 2000, a new standard in office productivity. Here is a suite of programs designed to create and publish documents and information of all types—on paper, on screen, as electronic mail or faxes, and for the world to see on the Internet. The professional edition of Office 2000 includes these powerful programs:

- Microsoft Word 2000
- Microsoft Excel 2000
- Microsoft PowerPoint 2000
- Microsoft Access 2000
- Microsoft Outlook 2000
- Microsoft Internet Explorer 5
- Outlook Express

This book covers all of the suite's key features with enough detail and illustrations so you'll be using the software almost as fast as you can install it. You get all of the basics of the suite, and then go beyond the basics to learn special techniques to take full advantage of its power, with plenty of clearly labeled and annotated illustrations to make learning easy. You'll also find some helpful elements along the way, such as notes, tips, and cautions. In special sections titled Putting It To Work, you'll learn practical methods to increase productivity, and each chapter ends with a handy section of tips to use a reference for power-user techniques.

In the first five chapters you will learn to use the common elements that run through Office's major applications—including the Address Book, Office Templates and Wizards, the Office Shortcut Bar, and the Binder. You'll learn how to save and print documents, get online help, check your spelling and grammar, and improve your vocabulary. You'll also learn how to automatically enter text, work with multiple documents, and track changes to documents.

Because Office is integrated with the Internet, in Chapter 3 you will learn how to use Office applications to send e-mail, browse the Internet, and to create Web documents. In Chapter 4, you will learn how to personalize Office to your own tastes, and in Chapter 5 you'll learn how to share information between Office applications.

Chapters 6 through 12 are all about Word 2000, the powerhouse word processing program praised by millions of devoted users around the world.

In Chapter 6 you will learn how to create and edit documents, as well as how to insert special characters, use bookmarks, and track versions of documents. Formatting characters, lines, and paragraphs is covered in Chapter 7. You'll also learn how to add background colors and borders, print envelopes, and dress up documents with drop capitals. Chapter 8 is all about setting and using tabs, creating tables, and dividing your pages into columns for newsletters and other documents. In Chapter 9, you'll learn how to work with long documents by adding headers and footers, numbering pages, displaying a document map and creating outlines. That chapter also covers inserting footnotes, recording voice comments, adding cross-references, and numbering lines.

You'll learn all about Word's graphics features in Chapter 10, which includes information on adding pictures and charts and creating special effects with text. Chapter 11 is all about formatting shortcuts to streamline even the most complex document. You'll learn how to create your own templates and how to format with themes and styles. Creating form documents and macros is covered in Chapter 12.

Excel 2000 is the focus of Chapters 13 through 19. This powerful program lets you create worksheets, graphs and maps, and databases. After learning how to create worksheets in Chapter 13, you will learn how to format and print Excel information in Chapter 14. Chapter 15 explains how to work with multiple windows and worksheets, how to prevent information from scrolling off the screen, and how to protect your work from unauthorized changes.

In Chapter 16 you'll learn how to work with formulas and functions. Adding maps, charts, and graphics to worksheets is discussed in Chapter 17. Using the map feature, for example, you can show a map of the United States, along with major highways, illustrating the geographic distribution of your company's sales or organization's membership.

In Chapter 18 you will learn how to use Excel as a database management tool, and in Chapter 19 you'll learn how to use sophisticated but easy tools to analyze information and solve problems.

Microsoft PowerPoint 2000 is covered in Chapters 20 and 21. You will learn how to create slides of all types in Chapter 20, and how to add graphics and sound effects, work with tables, and how to play and save slide shows. In Chapter 21 you'll learn techniques for creating eye-catching presentations, such as adding slide transitions, advancing slides, animating text and graphics, creating action buttons, and broadcasting shows over a network.

In Chapters 22 through 25, you'll learn how to manage information using Microsoft's world-renowned database program, Access 2000. Chapter 22 covers creating complete databases with the Database Wizard, using forms and reports, and customizing tables. In Chapter 23, you'll learn how to create custom databases and tables, including powerful relational databases using lookup tables.

Finding information in a database is covered in Chapter 24, along with queries and filters, while Chapter 25 discusses creating forms and reports, and designing data access pages to share your information in the Internet.

Finally, Chapters 26 through 28 are all about communication and organization with Microsoft Outlook and Outlook Express. In Chapter 26, you'll learn to use Outlook to send and receive e-mail. In Chapter 27, you'll learn how to manage your schedule with Outlook, including scheduling appointments and meetings, tracking tasks and phone calls, and conducting meetings online and over a network. Outlook Express is the focus of Chapter 28. In this chapter, you'll learn how to use Outlook Express to send and receive e-mail, and to communicate with newsgroups.

Because this book is organized by Office 2000 application, you do not have to read it from cover to cover. You should read the first five chapters to get acquainted with the suite, but then you can jump ahead to the section or chapter you are most interested in. You can read the other sections later to learn how the remaining applications and features work, so you can take full advantage of Office. You'll find easy-to-follow, step-by-step instructions and clear but complete details on the features that you'll want to use.

Office 2000 is perfect for use in the office, home, classroom, or dorm. The more you use it, the more features you'll find, and you'll grow to love its ease and versatility. You will especially like its integration with the Internet and the many ways that you can take advantage of the vast world of resources on the World Wide Web. In fact, once you get on-line, drop me a line describing what you like best about Office. You can reach me at alann@att.net.

Welcome to Microsoft Office

1

Microsoft Office 2000

BASICS

- Parts of Microsoft Office 2000
- Installing Office Components
- Office Templates and Wizards

BEYOND

- The Office Shortcut Bar
- Using the Binder
- The Office Address Book

The Microsoft Office 2000 Suite is a complete set of desktop applications and tools for creating, publishing, and distributing documents of all types. The applications are integrated to provide stand-alone and workgroup solutions as well as easy access to the Internet and online services.

Because the applications are integrated, you can move conveniently from one application to another. It also means that you can use the best features of each program to build *compound documents*—documents that can combine text, tables, charts, and graphics—without worrying about compatibility between file types and program features.

While there are different flavors of the suite available, with different combinations of programs, the applications discussed in this book are the following:

- Microsoft Word
- Microsoft Excel
- Microsoft PowerPoint
- Microsoft Access
- Microsoft Outlook
- Microsoft Internet Explorer
- Outlook Express
- Microsoft Clip Gallery

To make the Office Suite easy to use, the applications are installed directly on the taskbar, and you can access them from the Start menu. Click the Start button, and point to Programs to see the applications that you've installed. You'll also see a listing for Microsoft Office Tools, which contains some useful accessory programs.

To start an Office application, just click the program name in the Start menu.

Installing Office Components

Installing Microsoft Office is easy. Just insert your Office CD and follow the instructions that appear onscreen. Once you install Office, however, keep the CD handy when you work. Unless you perform a complete custom installation of every Office component, some Office features are held in reserve and not copied onto your hard disk. Be warned—a complete installation of Office requires over 300 megabytes (MB) of space on your hard disk.

Some features, for example, are designated to be installed the first time you use them. In this case, you'll see a message asking if you want to install the feature. Insert the Office CD in your CD drive, and then click Yes to the message.

N O T E : If the setup program does not start automatically, select Run from the Windows Start menu, type **D:/Setup** (using the letter of your CD drive) and click OK.

In some other cases, a message will appear reporting that you have to install the feature yourself. If this happens, exit the Office program you are using and insert the CD labeled "CD 1." The setup routine will start automatically, and you'll see this dialog box:

Click Add Or Remove Features to see the Update Features dialog box in Figure 1-1.

Click the plus sign next to the component that contains the feature you want to install. You will see a list of features that are part of the component. In this example, the Microsoft Excel For Windows option was expanded. The icons next to each feature indicate its status:

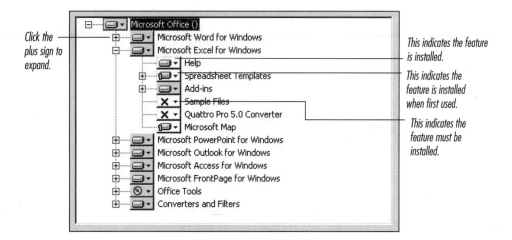

Click the plus sign to expand.

This indicates the feature is installed.

This indicates the feature is installed when first used.

This indicates the feature must be installed.

To install an option, click the down arrow next to the icon to display the choices shown in the following illustration.

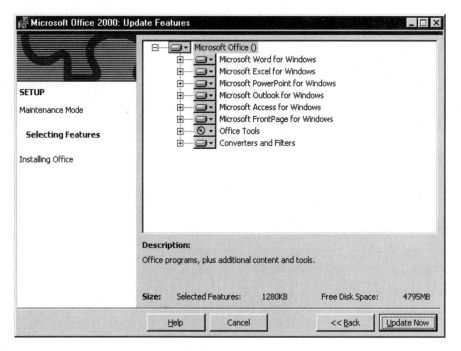

FIGURE 1-1 Installing an additional Office function

Select an option from the menu. When you've chosen options for all the features you want, click the Update Now button to complete the process.

Office Templates and Wizards

In the remaining chapters of this book, you will learn how to create and open Office documents. You'll learn how to start new documents from scratch, and how to use *templates* and *wizards* to create documents.

Options for creating and opening Office documents are also available directly from the Start menu:

Click here to start a new Office document from scratch or by using a template.

Click here to open an existing Office document.

If you click Open Office Document, a dialog box appears in which you can locate an existing document that you want to continue to work on. You'll learn how to use this dialog box in Chapter 2.

If you click New Office Document, you'll see the dialog box shown in Figure 1-2.

Use the General tab of the dialog box to start a new blank document. Use the other tabs of the dialog box to create a new document using a template or a wizard. A *template* is a sample document complete with text, formatting, or other items appropriate to the Office application. Templates for faxes in the Letters & Faxes tab, for example, start a new Word document with a completed

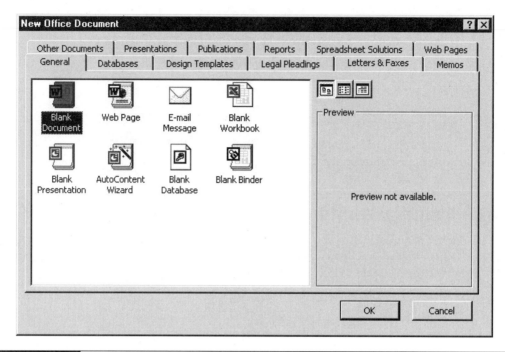

FIGURE 1-2 Creating a new Office document from the Windows desktop

fax cover sheet. The Invoice template in the Spreadsheet Solutions tab contains a complete invoice form that you complete in Microsoft Excel using the techniques that you will learn in this book.

Wizards, on the other hand, are a series of dialog boxes that take you step-by-step through creating a document. After you select options or enter information in the dialog boxes, the completed document appears in the application for you to fine-tune.

The Office Shortcut Bar

To make it even easier to work with Office applications, you can use the Office Shortcut bar. In fact, when you start your computer, you may see the Office Shortcut bar somewhere on your screen, as shown in Figure 1-3. As you can see in Figure 1-3, the default Office Shortcut bar contains buttons for starting and opening Office documents, as well as several common Microsoft Outlook functions.

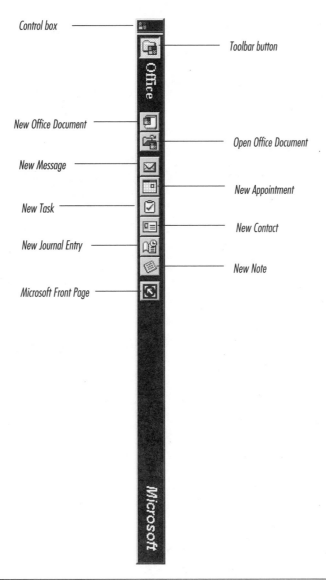

Control box — Toolbar button

New Office Document — Open Office Document

New Message — New Appointment

New Task — New Contact

New Journal Entry — New Note

Microsoft Front Page —

FIGURE 1-3 Office Shortcut bar

N O T E : The icons on your bar may be different, depending on your version of Microsoft Office 2000 and the installed components. If the Accessories bar appears, right-click on a blank area of the bar and choose Office from the shortcut menu.

If the bar does not appear automatically on your screen, and you want it to, click Start | Programs | Microsoft Office Tools | Microsoft Office Shortcut bar. Office displays this dialog box:

 NOTE: If the Office Shortcut bar is not yet installed, you will be prompted to insert your Office CD so the feature can be installed.

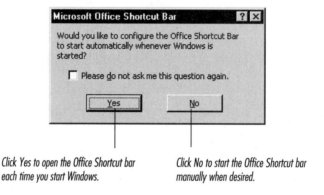

Click Yes to open the Office Shortcut bar each time you start Windows.

Click No to start the Office Shortcut bar manually when desired.

When you run a program, the Office Shortcut bar remains displayed onscreen so you can always access its features. As with all toolbars, just click the button for the function you want to perform. To create an e-mail message, for example, just click the New Message button.

Changing Toolbars

The default Office Shortcut bar is one of six shortcut bars that Office makes available. To select another bar, right-click any blank area of the bar to see this shortcut menu:

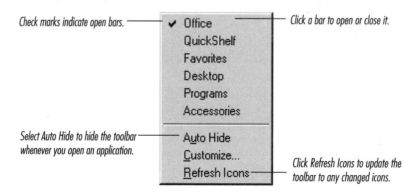

Check marks indicate open bars.

Click a bar to open or close it.

Select Auto Hide to hide the toolbar whenever you open an application.

Click Refresh Icons to update the toolbar to any changed icons.

The toolbars offer these features:

- **Quick Shelf** This starts out as an empty toolbar to which you can add your own items.
- **Favorites** This displays buttons to access the web sites and documents in your Favorites folder.
- **Desktop** This displays icons for each item on your Windows desktop.
- **Programs** This displays icons for the items on the Programs menu.
- **Accessories** This displays icons for the items on the Accessories menu.

When you choose to display a toolbar from the menu, that toolbar appears over the current toolbar. The new Toolbar button appears below the default Office Toolbar button. To redisplay the default toolbar, click its Toolbar button. Office hides the currently open bar and moves that toolbar's Toolbar button to the end of the bar. Click that Toolbar button to open the toolbar. This way, you can have many of the bars open and switch among them.

In this example, here is what appears if you turn on the Accessories bar:

Display the Office Shortcut bar
Accessories Bar Toolbar button

You can also switch toolbars and perform other functions by right-clicking on the Toolbar button to see these options:

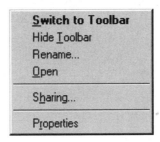

Clicking on Open in the menu opens a window showing shortcuts for every item on the bar.

Customizing Toolbars

You can change the appearance of toolbars, and even add and remove programs, to customize them to your taste.

Right-click any blank area of a toolbar, and choose Customize from the shortcut menu to see the Customize dialog box, shown in Figure 1-4.

- Use the *View* tab to change the color of the bar and its appearance.
- The *Buttons* tab lets you add or remove buttons from the bar. There will be check boxes for most Office programs and common functions. Select the check boxes for the items to add to the bar. You can also add a button that represents a specific file or folder of your choice.
- The *Toolbars* tab lets you display additional toolbars. Select the check boxes for the bars to display.
- The *Settings* tab of the Customize dialog box lets you set the default location for files.

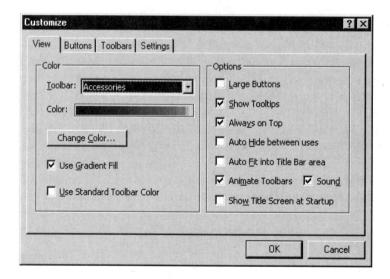

FIGURE 1-4   Customizing the Office Shortcut bar

Address Book

Use the *Address Book* to store names, addresses, telephone numbers, e-mail addresses, and other useful information about the people you contact. You can also store information about organizations, grouping your contacts according to their company or other affiliation. How the address book appears, however, depends on how your system is set up.

If you use the Corporate/Workgroup installation of Outlook, you will probably have two address books. One, referred to as the MAPI Address Book, is used to record your Outlook contacts as well as addresses of persons attached to your network, such as a Windows peer-to-peer network using a Microsoft Mail Postoffice, or Microsoft Exchange running on Windows NT. You will learn how to use this address book in Chapter 26. The other address book is used with Outlook Express and may also be the Windows Address Book accessible from the Start | Programs | Accessories | Windows Address Book command. You will learn how to use this address book in Chapter 28.

If you are using the Internet Only setup of Microsoft Outlook, there may only be one address book shared by Outlook, Outlook Express, and your Office applications.

The address book is fully integrated into Office. For example, in Word you can select addresses for envelopes and labels by clicking on this icon in the Envelopes And Labels dialog box:

If you are using the Corporate/Workgroup installation of Outlook, a dialog box may appear asking you to select a profile. A *profile* contains information about your mail services and other files used by Microsoft Outlook. You create and edit profiles using the Mail feature in the Windows Control Panel. A typical address book using this setup is shown in Figure 1-6.

Pull down the Show Names From The list to choose the address list that contains the addresses you want to use. Depending on Outlook and your network connections, you may have several lists available. You can select a name from the list, add a new address book entry, or display an item's properties (the details of the listing).

 N O T E : If the New button is dimmed, you have chosen a list to which you cannot add addresses. These usually are lists that contain the names of network users and that can only be changed by the network administrator.

Some projects include more than one document, and even documents created by more than one Office application. To organize such a project, you could save all the related files in a special folder on your disk. Even so, each document is a separate file, and you'd have to switch back and forth between applications to display or print each part of the project.

Microsoft Binder lets you collect the related documents into one group, regardless of the application used to create them. From one location, you can then review, edit, or even create new documents, and print them using a common heading and consecutive page numbers.

 NOTE: If Microsoft Binder is not available, you have to rerun Office Setup and choose it from the Office Tools category.

To create a binder, choose Start | Programs | Microsoft Office Tools | Microsoft Binder. To add an existing file to the binder, drag it from the desktop to the pane on the left side of the binder window, or select Section | Add From File and choose the file in the dialog box that appears. You can also create a new Office document from the Binder. Just select Section | Add, and choose the type of document or template from the dialog box that appears.

A binder with a number of documents is shown in Figure 1-5. The documents, called *sections*, are shown in the section bar on the left, with the selected document open in the binder window. The window contains the menu and toolbars of the application used to create the selected document, so you can edit and format it just as if you were working in the program itself.

Use the File menu to open, save, or start a new binder, and to print or preview the current binder. You can use the File | Binder Page Setup command to create a header and footer, to determine which documents they apply to, and to number the pages consecutively

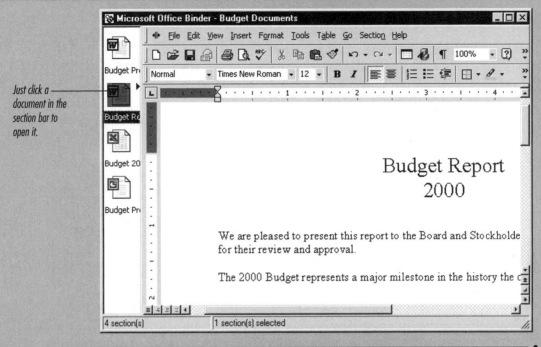

Just click a document in the section bar to open it.

FIGURE 1-5   Sample binder

or starting with each document. Use the Section menu to add, delete, duplicate, rename, hide, or rearrange the order of documents in the binder, as well as to print, preview, and set up individual documents.

Adds an address
book entry

Displays details of
the selected entry

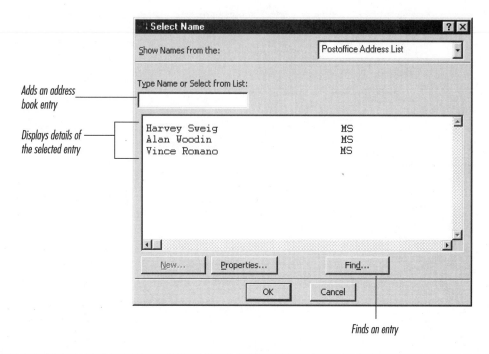

Finds an entry

FIGURE 1-6   Address Book using Microsoft Outlook

If you are sharing one address book between Outlook and Outlook Express, the address book appears as in Figure 1-7. This address book is described in detail in Chapter 28.

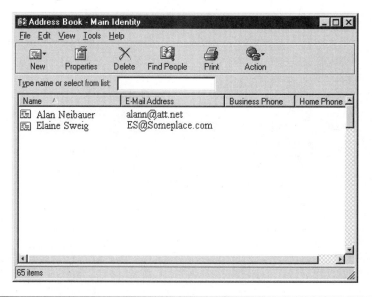

FIGURE 1-7   Address Book using Outlook Express

- Don't bother installing everything at once. Use the typical installation and then add components as you use them. Just make sure to have your Office CDs available as you work.

- There is a lot of integration between the Office applications, including Microsoft Outlook and Internet Explorer. Install Outlook and the version of Internet Explorer provided with Office, and do not delete them, to take advantage of all of Office's potential. You can continue to use another browser and e-mail program for non-Office work.

- After installing an Office component, save your work and restart your computer even if you are not prompted to do so. This ensures that all the installed components are fully registered in Windows and available for use.

- Remember, there are several varieties of Microsoft Office 2000. Your own version may have additional programs besides those discussed in this book, or may lack a program or feature described here.

- When you have time, experiment with the templates and wizards that are available. You may have to install some, along with sample files, from the Office CD.

- You can drag the Office Shortcut bar to other locations on the screen— drag it by the Control box or by a blank area of the bar. Positioning the bar along an edge of the screen, however, lets you take advantage of the Auto Hide feature.

- If you do not want the Office Shortcut bar to appear all the time, yet want it available when you need it, right-click its Control box and choose Auto Hide from the shortcut menu. The bar will disappear when you are working in an application but reappear when you point to the edge of the screen where the bar appeared.

- Microsoft Binder is often overlooked because it is not automatically installed, but it is worth investigating. The Binder is particularly useful if you have several documents that relate to the same job, event, or task.

- If you set up and administer a Windows workgroup, consider using Microsoft Outlook as the network mail client.

- While there are six Office Shortcut bars available, and you can create your own, having too many open can be confusing. Using Windows 98, you can always switch to the desktop using the Show Desktop button in the taskbar, or run applications from the Start menu.

Using Common Office Techniques

2

Office 2000 provides a set of features and tools that you can use in its major programs. Once you learn how to use a feature in one program, you know how to use it in all the others. In this chapter, we'll look at some of these tools so you're prepared to learn Word, Excel, PowerPoint, and Access in the chapters to come.

Starting an Office Application

It's easy to start an Office program.

2 *Point to the word "Programs."*

3 *Click on the program name you want.*

1 *Click the Start button.*

NOTE: You can also start an Office program by clicking on its button on the Office Shortcut toolbar, if it appears on your screen.

When you are done using the program, you should exit it to return to the Windows desktop. To exit the program, select File | Exit or click on the Program Close box. You'll be given a chance to save any unsaved work.

WEBLINK: Get the latest Office 2000 information at *http://office.microsoft.com/office/enhoffice.asp.*

Understanding the Application Window

All applications have certain elements in common. While we'll look at each application in detail in later chapters, Figure 2-1 shows the standard elements

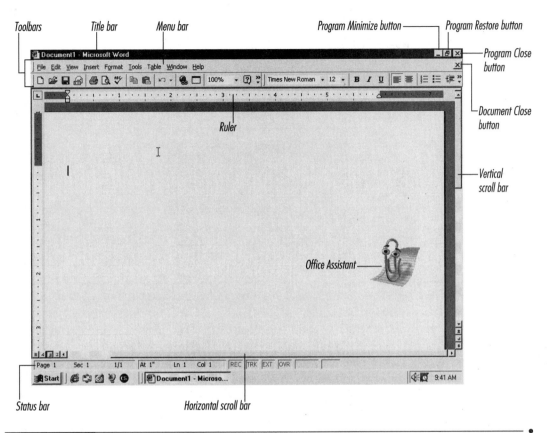

Toolbars Title bar Menu bar Program Minimize button Program Restore button Program Close button Document Close button Ruler Vertical scroll bar Office Assistant Status bar Horizontal scroll bar

FIGURE 2-1 The Word screen

that you'll find on the Word screen. You'll learn how to use all these features throughout this book. And, yes, the little character moving on your screen is part of Office.

Using the Menu Bar and Toolbar

The main difference between Office and other Windows programs is that Office learns about your work habits. It starts by displaying a basic set of commands, and then adjusts the menus and toolbars to include the commands you use most often. To use a menu, click on it with the mouse to display a *drop-down list* of operations that you can perform.

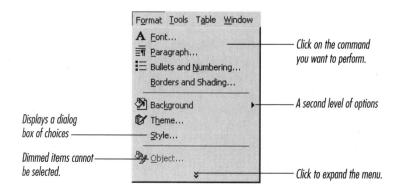

Click on the command you want to perform.

A second level of options

Displays a dialog box of choices

Dimmed items cannot be selected.

Click to expand the menu.

 N O T E : Office organizes menus to show recently used commands first.

If you don't see the command you want to perform, just hold the mouse pointer over the menu a few seconds or click the down arrows at the bottom of it. Office expands the menu to show additional items. If you choose an item from the expanded menu, Office figures you'll be using it again and automatically displays it on the unexpanded menu.

 T I P : Office also offers shortcut menus that appear at the mouse pointer when you press the right mouse button. The options listed on the shortcut menu depend on where you are pointing to when you click the mouse button.

To use a toolbar, simply click on the button for the task you want to perform. The picture on the button indicates its function. When you point to a button with the mouse, you'll see a *ToolTip*—a small box with the button's name. Here are some other features of toolbar buttons:

Type your choice in the text box.

Click the arrow to display additional choices.

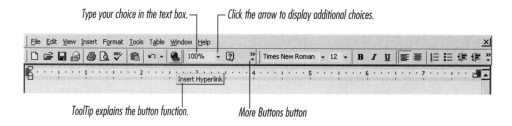

ToolTip explains the button function.

More Buttons button

In Word, Excel, and PowerPoint, two toolbars are displayed side-by-side on one line, so you can't see all their buttons. Click on the toolbar More Buttons button to see additional choices, similar to this:

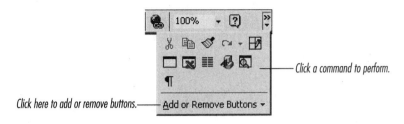

Click here to add or remove buttons. ——— *Click a command to perform.*

When you select a button from this additional list, Office assumes you'll be using it again and adds it to the toolbar.

 N O T E : You'll learn more about toolbars in Chapter 4, including how to reset toolbars and menus to their original contents.

Office automatically displays specialized toolbars for the task you are performing. To hide or display other toolbars, right-click on any toolbar to see a list of the available toolbars, and then click the name of a bar to toggle it on or off.

If you want to see all the toolbar buttons at one time, move one of the toolbars to a separate row:

Move a toolbar by dragging this line.

Working with Dialog Boxes

Choosing some commands displays a *dialog box* of additional options. Many dialog boxes look like a series of index cards; at the top of each card is a tab naming the category of options that the card contains. Click a tab to display its options.

When you save or open a file, Office displays a dialog box such as the one shown in Figure 2-2. Use the Folder icons on the left to quickly open popular folders or to display the contents of your Windows desktop.

The Look In box shows the name of the current folder—where a new document will be saved or that contains documents to open. Documents and other folders in that location are displayed in the large box below it. To choose

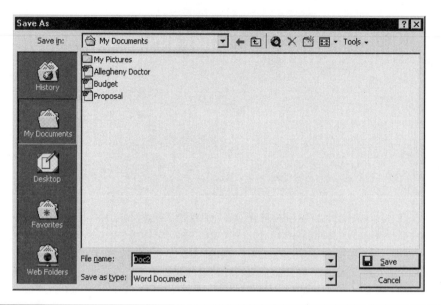

FIGURE 2-2   The Save As dialog box

another disk or folder, click on the down arrow to the right of the list, and choose from the items that appear. To open a subfolder listed in the large window, double-click in it. You can also use the buttons on the dialog box's toolbar as shown in Table 2-1.

You can either click on the Views button to cycle between different views, or pull down the list to choose from these options:

- **List**   Displays only filenames
- **Details**   Displays the filename, type, size, and the date the item was last modified
- **Properties**   Displays information about the selected item
- **Preview**   Displays the selected item

In Details view you can change the order in which items appear by clicking on the Name, Size, Type, or Modified column heading. You can also pull down the Views list, and choose from the Arrange Icons submenu.

BUTTON	NAME	FUNCTION
←	Back	Moves to the previous open folder
⬆	Up One Level	Displays the next highest directory level
🔍	Search The Web	Launches your web browser
✕	Delete	Deletes the folder or document selected in the window
🗀	New Folder	Creates a new folder
▦ ▾	Views	Changes the way items are displayed
Tools ▾	Tools	Lets you find, delete, rename, and print files, add a file to the Favorites folder, map a network drive, and display a file's properties

TABLE 2-1 Options in the Open and Save As Dialog Boxes

Saving and Printing a Document

By saving a document, you can complete or print it later. To save a document, click on the Save button in the toolbar to see the Save As dialog box.

1. Type a new name if you do not want to use the suggested one.
2. Select the location for the file by using the Look In list.
3. Click Save.

Once you edit a saved document, you must save it again to record your changes. When you click Save, however, the document will be saved without displaying a dialog box, because it already has a name. If you want to save it under a different name or in a new location, choose File | Save As.

Printing a document is just as easy—just click on the Print button in the toolbar. Office prints your document while you continue working in the program.

You can also select printing options before you print your document. To set printing options, select File | Print to display the Print dialog box. Make your selections from the dialog box and click on Print. The options that you can select depend on the program. We'll look at these in later chapters.

Closing Your Document

Saving a document does not clear it from the screen, so you can save your document and then print it or continue working on it. When you are done working with the document, choose File | Close or click on the Document Close icon.

If you've changed the document since you last saved it, you'll be asked if you want to save it before closing. Select Yes to save the document, select No to discard your changes, or select Cancel to leave the document on the screen.

Starting a New Document

To start a new document once the program is open, click on the New button in the toolbar. Word and Excel open and display a blank document window; PowerPoint and Access display a dialog box of options. You can also start a new document by selecting File | New to display a dialog box like the one shown in Figure 2-3. This dialog box lets you start with a new blank document, or choose a template for a completely formatted document, such as a letter or budget.

 TIP: You can also create and open an Office document directly from the Start menu. Click Start and then choose New Office Document or Open Office Document.

1 *Click the tab for the type of document to create.*

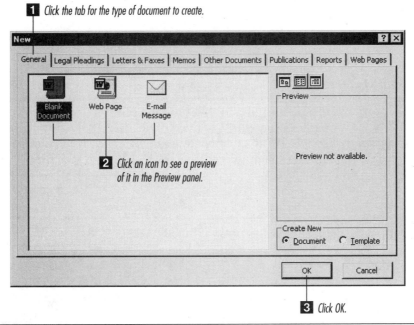

2 *Click an icon to see a preview of it in the Preview panel.*

3 *Click OK.*

FIGURE 2-3 Starting a new document

Opening Existing Documents

To edit an existing document that is not already on the screen, you must first *open* it. If it is a document you recently worked on, pull down the File menu. At the bottom you'll see up to the last four documents that you've opened or saved; just click on the one you want to open.

Otherwise, click on the Open button in the Standard toolbar to display the Open dialog box. Office lists document files that have the extension for the current application, such as DOC and HTM files in Word, and XLS files in Excel. If the document you want is not listed, navigate to its location by using the Look In list and toolbar buttons. Then double-click on the document you want to open, or highlight its name and then click on Open.

N O T E : You can also pull down the Open list and choose Open Read Only so it cannot be modified, Open As Copy to make a copy of the selected file, or Open In Browser to display a web page in Internet Explorer.

Using Undo

 Don't worry if you delete characters you really want, or type characters and then change your mind about them. Just click on Undo. Each time you click on the button, Office reverses the last change you made to the document.

 T I P : Not every action that you perform can be undone.

Notice the down arrow next to the Undo button. Click on the arrow to display a list of your actions, with the most recent on top. Clicking on the item at the top of the list will undo your last action. Clicking on an item not on top undoes *every* action from there to the top of the list.

 If you undo something and then change your mind, use the Redo button or its Redo list to cancel what you just "undid." You'll have to choose Redo by expanding the Edit menu or Standard toolbar.

Scrolling in Your Document

Office documents can be much larger than the screen. To display parts of the document you can't see, you have to scroll them into view.

The simplest way to scroll the window is to use the *arrow keys*. When the insertion point is at the top line of the document window, pressing UP ARROW scrolls a new line into view—if there are any. When the insertion point is on the last line in the window, pressing DOWN ARROW scrolls a new line into view—again, if there are any.

If you have to move a great distance through a long document, however, use the *scroll bars*. Use the scroll bar on the right of the window—the *vertical scroll bar*—to scroll up and down, and the scroll bar at the bottom of the window—the *horizontal scroll bar*—to scroll left and right.

To scroll through your document line by line, just as you would by pressing an arrow key, click on the up or down triangles on the ends of the scroll bar.

To scroll screen by screen, click above or below the *scroll box*—the box within the bar.

You can also drag the scroll box to scroll to a relative position in the document. For example, if you were to drag the box to the middle of the scroll bar, Office would display page 5 of a nine-page document. As you drag the box in Word, Office displays the number of the page next to the scroll box.

There is one important point to keep in mind when using the scroll bar: it does *not* move the insertion point. The insertion point remains where it was. Scrolling only changes the portion of the document being displayed on the screen. If you want to edit or insert text in the area displayed, you must first click where you want to type. If you do not click the mouse, the screen scrolls back to its previous location when you begin typing.

Selecting Things

When you want to perform a function on text or a graphic, you first have to select the text or graphic. Selecting lets Office know what you want it to perform an action on. To select a graphic, click on it. You use the same technique to select a single cell in Excel, or to select a heading or other object on a PowerPoint slide. A selected object appears surrounded by a border, with eight small boxes called *handles*.

The easiest way to select text in Word is by dragging. Point the mouse at one end of the text that you want to select. It can be at either end—in front of the first character or following the last character. For example, here I'm preparing to select the word "computer":

Regardless of your level of computer literacy, anyone can use Microsoft Office.

Hold down the left mouse button as you drag the mouse to the other end of the text, then release the mouse button. The selected text will appear *highlighted*—that is, light letters over a dark background.

Click the mouse anywhere except on a menu or toolbar button to deselect the object or text.

C A U T I O N : Selected text will be deleted if you press any number, letter, punctuation key, the SPACEBAR, or the ENTER key.

TIP: To select the entire Word document or Excel worksheet, press CTRL-A.

To simulate dragging with the keyboard, hold down the SHIFT key or press the F8 key. Now text becomes selected as you move the insertion point by using the arrow keys, other key combinations, and even by clicking the mouse. Release the SHIFT key or press ESC to stop simulating dragging.

Moving and Copying Text with Drag and Drop

Sometimes you type text or insert an object only to discover it would be better in another location. With Office, you can easily move text from one place to another. You can even copy something, placing a duplicate of it at another location.

You can easily copy and move things using a method called *drag and drop*. This means that you drag the selected item to where you want to insert it, and then release the mouse button to drop it into place.

Start by selecting the text or object. Point anywhere in the selected area in Word, or to the borderline line around a selected cell or group of cells in Excel, so the mouse pointer is shaped like this:

To drag an object, such as a selected graphic, point to the object until the pointer is shaped like a four-directional arrow.

Next, press and hold down the mouse button, and then drag the pointer to where you want to insert the text or object. Release the mouse button when the text or object is where you want to drop it.

NOTE: If you want to copy text rather than move it, press and hold down the CTRL key while you release the mouse button.

If you change your mind about moving the text while you are dragging, just move the pointer back to the selected text and then release the button. If you've already dropped the text and then change your mind, click on Undo.

Moving and Copying Text Through the Clipboard

If you have to move something a long distance or from one document to another, you might use the *Clipboard* instead of dragging. The Clipboard is an area in the computer's memory where Windows temporarily stores information. When you move text by using the Clipboard, it's called *cut and paste*. When you copy text with the Clipboard, it's called *copy and paste*.

To move text by using cut and paste, first select what you want to move, and then click on the Cut button in the Standard toolbar (use More Buttons to access it). Click on the Copy button (use More Buttons to access it) if you want to make a copy of the item in a new location. Next, point the mouse where you want to place the object, and then click on the Paste button in the Standard toolbar.

Office lets you store up to 12 items in the Clipboard. When you cut or copy the second item to the Clipboard, Office displays the Clipboard toolbar. You can also display it by right-clicking on any toolbar and choosing Clipboard from the shortcut menu. You can then add selected text to the Clipboard, paste one or more items, or empty the Clipboard, as shown here:

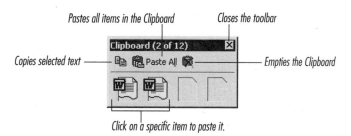

Pastes all items in the Clipboard

Closes the toolbar

Copies selected text

Empties the Clipboard

Click on a specific item to paste it.

 N O T E : The same Clipboard is available to all Office programs, so you can use it to paste information from one application into another.

Getting Help from Office

Because no one, not even an Office guru, can remember every program feature, Office includes a help system on each command, function, and technique that the program can perform.

Certainly one of the most entertaining ways to get help is to use the Office Assistant, a cute animated graphic that appears onscreen. If the Assistant is not already displayed, select the first option on the Help menu or just press F1.

 N O T E : You can drag the Assistant to any location on the window.

Sometimes, the Assistant comes to life automatically, asking if you want help with a function you are performing. A balloon appears with a list of possible help subjects. Click on a subject to read detailed information about it. Other times, a light bulb appears over the Assistant—click on it to read a helpful tip about the task you are performing.

To find help on a specific subject, just click on the Assistant to display a balloon like the one shown here:

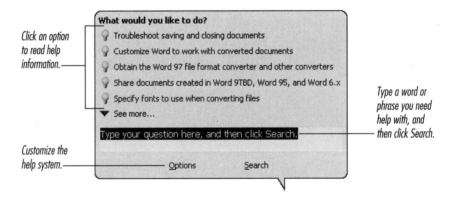

Click an option to read help information.

Customize the help system.

What would you like to do?
- Troubleshoot saving and closing documents
- Customize Word to work with converted documents
- Obtain the Word 97 file format converter and other converters
- Share documents created in Word 9TBD, Word 95, and Word 6.x
- Specify fonts to use when converting files
- See more...

Type your question here, and then click Search.

Options   Search

Type a word or phrase you need help with, and then click Search.

Once you locate the information you need help with, a box of information appears on the right of the window, as shown in Figure 2-4. Read the information, following any links that appear to additional help sources.

To locate additional information, click on Show to expand the box as shown in Figure 2-5. The three dialog box tabs offer you different ways to find information.

The Contents tab displays a list of general topics. Next to each topic is an icon of a book. To find information, double-click on a topic to display subtopics, which may be additional books or icons representing specific information. Continue "opening books" until you see the information icon for the subject you want help on, and then double-click on the icon.

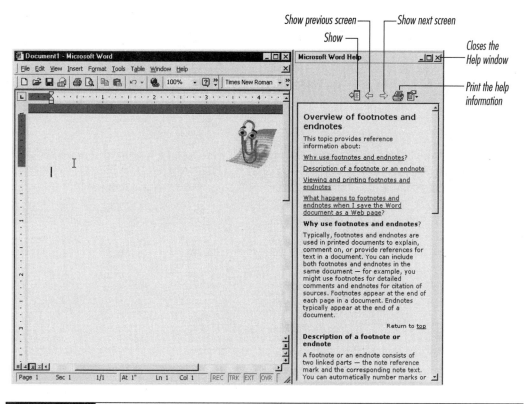

FIGURE 2-4 Help dialog box

The Index tab displays an alphabetic list of help topics. In the text box, type a word or phase that describes the topic you need help on. Word scrolls the list to display help words or phrases that match your entry. When you select an item from that list, Word displays in the second list box all the help windows containing that word or phrase. Double-click on an item in the second list to display the help window.

On the Answer Wizard tab, type a word or phrase, and click on the Search button. Office displays a list of subjects containing that text—double-click on the one you want to read.

To learn how any toolbar or menu button works, click Help | What's This?, and then click on the button. Choose Help | Office On The Web to get current information and help directly from Microsoft on the Internet.

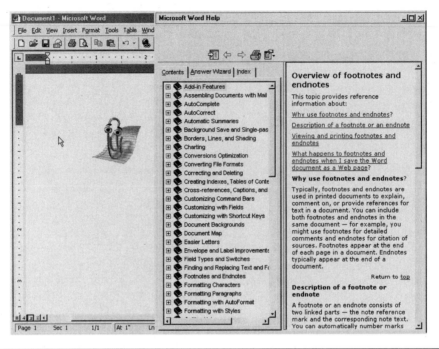

FIGURE 2-5 Finding help information

Proofing Your Documents

Office provides three powerful tools to improve your work: the *spelling checker* to check spelling, the *thesaurus* to find synonyms, and the *grammar checker* to check for grammatical mistakes. First, let's take a look at a special feature in Word.

Checking Documents as You Type

Word actually checks your spelling and grammar as you type. In fact, if you misspell a word and Word only has one alternative in its dictionary, it corrects the word for you automatically. Otherwise, Word places a wavy line under misspelled words and grammatical errors. You can correct the error yourself to remove the wavy line, or click the right mouse button on the word to see a shortcut menu of options, such as this:

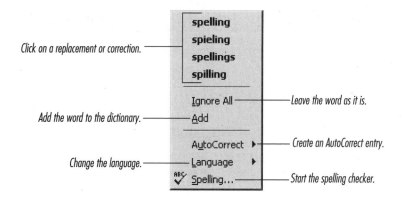

Click on a replacement or correction. — spelling / spieling / spellings / spilling

Ignore All ——— Leave the word as it is.

Add the word to the dictionary. ——— Add

AutoCorrect ▶ ——— Create an AutoCorrect entry.

Change the language. ——— Language ▶

Spelling... ——— Start the spelling checker.

N O T E : If you right-click on a grammatical error, you can choose to correct or ignore it, or to start the grammar checker. Choose About This Sentence from the shortcut menu to read about the grammatical rule being violated.

Interactive Spelling and Grammar

Rather than catch each error as you type it, you can check the entire document at one time. This is the only way to check spelling in Excel, PowerPoint, and Access.

T I P : To spell-check a single word or portion of text, select the word or the text before starting the spell check.

In Word, spelling and grammar checking are combined, although you can turn off grammar checking if you like. You'll see how this combination works in Word, but keep in mind that only spell checking is available in Excel, PowerPoint, and Access.

To begin checking your document, click on the Spelling and Grammar button in Word's Standard toolbar. (In the other applications, click on the Spelling button on the toolbar or choose Tools | Spelling.) When Office finds a word that is not in its dictionary, or a grammatical problem, it shows the offending word or phrase and its surrounding text in the Spelling and Grammar dialog box, as shown in Figure 2-6.

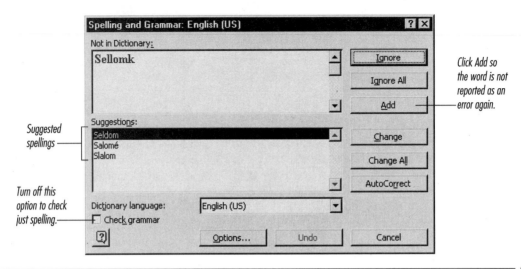

FIGURE 2-6 Checking spelling

Double-click on the correct word in the Suggestions list, or select it and then choose either Change or Change All. Office inserts the correctly spelled word and then searches for the next error. If you choose Change, Office will report the next occurrence of the word as a possible error; when you choose Change All, Office automatically replaces other occurrences of the same misspelling. If you do not see the correct spelling, or if no suggestions are listed, type another spelling for the word in the text box with the insertion point, and then click Change or Change All.

If the word is indeed spelled correctly, click on either Ignore or Ignore All to leave the word as you typed it and continue the spell check. When you choose Ignore, Office stops at the next occurrence and reports it as a possible error. When you choose Ignore All, Word skips over all occurrences of the word in the document.

Now let's look at some other options in the Spelling dialog box.

- Click on the Undo button if you select Change or Ignore by mistake.
- When you know it's a word that you frequently misspell, click on the correct spelling in the list and then click on the AutoCorrect button. Office makes the replacement in your document and creates an AutoCorrect entry. Now whenever you type the incorrectly spelled word, AutoCorrect will replace it with the correct spelling.

When Office detects a grammatical error, it shows the offending text with the rule of grammar being violated, such as Subject-Verb Agreement, and a description may appear with the Assistant. Double-click on the suggested replacement in the Suggestion box, or choose to ignore the error.

 N O T E : Use the Options button, or the Spelling And Grammar tab of the Options dialog box (from the Tools menu) to turn off spelling or grammar as you type and set other options.

Improving Your Vocabulary

With the thesaurus, you can look up a word because it doesn't quite convey the correct meaning, because you've repeated the same word several times already, or just to understand its meaning, such as distinguishing "cloth" from "clothe," and "whether" from "weather."

 N O T E : The first time you use the thesaurus, Office may install it from the CD. Have the CD handy—you'll be prompted to insert it.

To look up a synonym, right-click on the word and point to Synonyms to see other possible words:

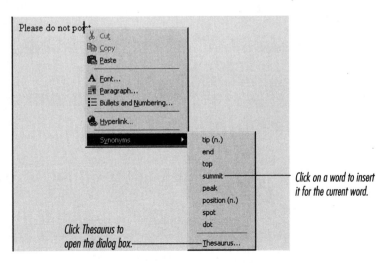

Click on a word to insert it for the current word.

Click Thesaurus to open the dialog box.

TIP: To look up a phrase containing more than one word, such as "over the top," select the entire phrase first.

You can get even more help with your vocabulary by choosing Tools | Language (you may have to expand the menu first) and then clicking Thesaurus to display the Thesaurus dialog box, such as the one shown in Figure 2-7 for the word "point." The word you are looking up appears in the Looked Up box, and one or more meanings for the word appear in the Meanings box. More than one meaning will appear when the word has several connotations.

Select the meaning that best represents what you are trying to say, and Word lists synonyms in the Replace With Synonym list. Choose the synonym that you want to insert in your document and then select Replace.

If none of the synonyms is quite right, select the word that has the closest meaning and choose Look Up. Word will find meanings and synonyms for it. Continue selecting meanings and looking up suggested synonyms until you find just the right word.

TIP: To return to a word that has already been looked up, pull down the Looked Up list and click on the word.

The Meanings box may also list the options Related Words and Antonyms. Select Related Words to show the root of the word, such as "point" for "pointing." Selecting Antonyms lists words with the opposite meaning.

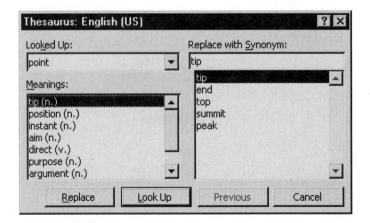

FIGURE 2-7 Looking up synonyms for the word "point"

Your version of Word will include a dictionary in your language. When you purchase Word in France, for example, your dictionary will contain French words. If you type documents using words from another language, Word will not find them in the dictionary, will report them as possible errors, and will list no suggested alternatives.

You can purchase another dictionary in the language that you use, but if your document contains sections of text in a language other than the default, you must tell Word which dictionary to use for which text. To designate a language other than the default for a section of text, select the text and then choose Tools | Language (you'll have to expand the menu first); then click on Set Language to see this dialog box:

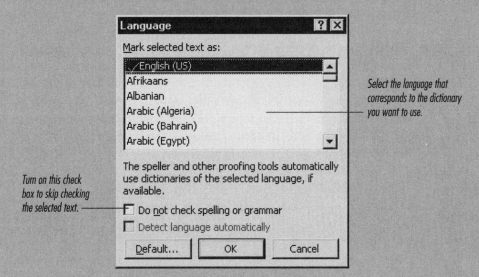

Select the language that corresponds to the dictionary you want to use.

Turn on this check box to skip checking the selected text.

If Word cannot find your word in the thesaurus, an alphabetical listing of words and phrases will appear in the Meanings box. Double-click on a word or phrase in the list that has the same meaning that you want to convey—Word will use it for the lookup, displaying related meanings and synonyms.

Streamline Your Work with AutoCorrect

Not only will Office check your spelling as you type, but it also can correct mistakes and insert special symbols and characters as you type. AutoCorrect actually watches as you work, correcting common spelling mistakes and typographical errors on the fly when you press SPACEBAR, ENTER, or TAB after the error. If you accidentally press CAPS LOCK and start typing a sentence using the SHIFT key for the first character, AutoCorrect even turns off CAPS LOCK and corrects the case of the text.

You can add your own AutoCorrect entries for words that you frequently misspell, or to insert text when you type an abbreviation. Select Tools | AutoCorrect to display the dialog box shown in Figure 2-8.

The checked items on the top of the dialog box show the defaults for general corrections. Deselect the check boxes for the corrections you do not want Office to make.

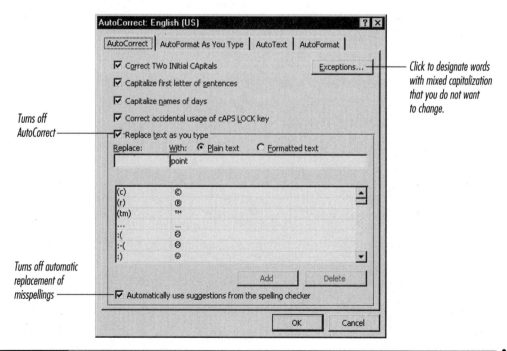

Click to designate words with mixed capitalization that you do not want to change.

Turns off AutoCorrect

Turns off automatic replacement of misspellings

FIGURE 2-8   The AutoCorrect dialog box

The two-column list box shows AutoCorrect entries that Office has already defined for you. In the Replace box, you type the abbreviation for an automatic entry, or the way you normally misspell a word. In the With box, type the full text you want displayed with the abbreviation, or type the correct spelling of the word that you misspell. Choose Add to create the entry, and then close the dialog box.

To create an AutoCorrect entry from text that you've already typed, select the text and then choose Tools | AutoCorrect. The selected text automatically appears in the With text box, and you can select either the Plain Text or Formatted Text option button. In the Replace box, type the way you normally misspell the word or the abbreviation you want to enter for it, and click on Add.

Working with Multiple Documents

You can have multiple documents open, switch back and forth between them, even see them all onscreen at the same time. Open the second, third, or any other document just as you opened the first. You can also start a new document when one is already open, by clicking on the New button or by using File | New. The name of each document appears on the Windows taskbar. To switch documents, just click on its name.

 N O T E : With Access, you can only have one database open at a time.

While switching between windows is easy, wouldn't it be even easier to refer to a document as you type if you could see both documents at the same time? You're in luck because Office lets you divide the screen into more than one document window.

The method varies with the application:

- With Word, choose Window | Arrange All. Word *tiles* (arranges so they do not overlap) the open windows.
- With Excel, choose Window | Arrange. In the dialog box that appears, choose if you want the windows tiled or cascaded. *Cascaded* windows are neatly overlapped so you can see the title bar of each.
- With PowerPoint, choose Window | Arrange All to tile the windows, or choose Cascade.

Now that the windows are displayed, you can switch between them by clicking on the document you want to work with.

When you have multiple documents open in Excel and PowerPoint, each will have its own document Minimize, Restore, and Close buttons. To close one document, click on its Close button or choose File | Close. Clicking on the Program Close button in the title bar closes the entire program.

Word is different. When you have multiple documents open in Word, the Document Close button no longer appears. Click on the Program Close button to close just the open document.

Magnification

When you start a program, text and graphics appear about the same size onscreen as they do on the printed page. You can change the magnification to display your document larger or smaller than it will be when printed.

 N O T E : Changing magnification does not actually change the font size; it just changes how it appears onscreen.

If you have trouble reading small characters, as I do, you can enlarge the display. For example, set magnification at 200% to display your document at twice the printed size. You can also reduce magnification to display more text on the screen than normal, and you can display a full page or more at one time.

To change magnification from the toolbar, click on the down arrow next to the Zoom Control and choose the display desired.

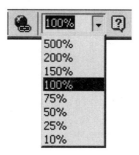

 N O T E : You can access more zoom options if you use the Zoom dialog box. To display the box, select View | Zoom. In Access, you can only zoom the display in Print Preview.

You can also change the look of the application window by hiding and displaying other elements, or by displaying the document full screen. The choices available in the View menu depend on the program. In Word, for example, you can choose to hide or display the ruler. In Excel, you can hide or display the status bar and something called the Formula bar.

The View | Full Screen command hides everything but the document, displaying a small button labeled "Close Full Screen." Click on that button or press ESC to restore the hidden elements.

Tracking Changes

If you're collaborating on a Word document or Excel worksheet with other persons, it is easy to get confused between changes. What did they add or delete? Who made that change? How can I restore what someone else erased?

Rather then waste your time making these decisions, let Office indicate each change made to the document, and who made it. You can then easily review the document, accepting or rejecting the changes. Rejecting a deletion, for example, restores the original text.

The first step is to tell Word or Excel to start keeping track of your changes. Start by choosing Tools | Track Changes, and clicking on Highlight Changes. In Word, you can select these options:

If you turn on tracking, Office marks the changes you and others make to the document. In Word, for example, text you add will be displayed in a different color, and deleted text appears in strikeout. The text and strikeout color used changes for each person. In Excel, a colored border with a triangle will surround changed cells:

Point to the cell to see the name of the person who made the change, and how the cell was altered.

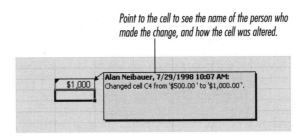

When you are ready to review the document, select Tools | Track Changes, and click on Accept Or Reject Changes. You can then choose to accept or reject individual changes, or accept or reject them all.

- If a ToolTip doesn't appear immediately, just wait.
- Drag side-by-side toolbars to separate lines to see all their buttons.
- Store frequently used documents in the Windows 98 My Documents folder for easy access.
- To find out about a dialog box option, click on the Help button (?) in the title bar and click on the option.
- Remember to turn off document tracking when you do not want to mark changes.
- If you have an IntelliMouse, click the wheel and then scroll by moving the mouse.
- Stop scrolling with the IntelliMouse by clicking the wheel again.
- If Office 2000 is not working correctly, choose Help | Detect and Repair.
- Choose File | Print Preview to see how your document looks before you print it.
- Don't type when something is selected unless you want to delete the selected part.

Microsoft Office and the Internet

The Internet is an informal network of computers around the world. Millions of individuals, companies, and institutions are connected to "the Net" in some way. The World Wide Web is one interface to the Net. Think of the web as a series of linked documents spread across the globe that can be reached simply by clicking the mouse, or by typing the document's name and address.

The address of a computer on the web is referred to as the computer's *web site*. Again, you don't have to worry about the geographic location of the site, just its address. As far as you are concerned, you can be connected to a site on the other side of the world or across the street with equal ease.

Connecting with Internet Explorer

Office's primary tool for connecting to the Internet is Microsoft Internet Explorer, the web browser that comes with Office. A *web browser* is a program that communicates with the Internet, letting you move about the web, send and receive messages, and search for information.

To connect to the Internet, however, you will also need an account with an *Internet service provider* (ISP). If you work somewhere where you have access to your company's network, you might be able to use the network to connect to the Internet. Otherwise, you'll need a *dialup account* that connects to the Internet through your phone line. You can access the Internet with a local service provider (your area probably offers several), or through a nationally based ISP like America Online or AT&T WorldNet.

Office's Internet features are designed to work with Microsoft Internet Explorer, the web browser that comes bundled with the Office software. However, if you want to use another browser (for example, Netscape Navigator), you'll be able to install that browser on your desktop and use most of the features discussed in this chapter. Don't be surprised, however, if some features don't work exactly as described here.

To connect to the web, use any of these techniques:

- Click the Launch Internet Explorer Browser icon in the Windows 98 taskbar.

- Open the Internet Explorer icon on the Windows desktop.

Internet
Explorer

What happens when you first make a connection to the Internet depends on your system and your ISP. If you have a dialup account and you're not yet online, you may see the Windows Dial-Up Networking Connect To dialog box. Make sure the information in this box is correct—it should be if you set up everything correctly—and then click Connect. Your modem will dial your ISP, and your browser will download and display a web page.

It takes some time for information from the Internet to be displayed on your monitor. Sometimes text appears first with icon boxes showing where graphics will appear, and then the graphics are downloaded and displayed. As the information is being transferred to your computer, you'll see a message in the progress bar at the bottom of the browser window reporting the percentage of the information that has been transmitted, and perhaps the speed at which it is being accepted. You may also see an animated icon on the top right of the screen, an indicator bar at the bottom of the screen, or some messages that the browser is waiting for a connection to take place—just be patient. Most pages will be too large to appear on the screen, so you'll see a vertical scroll bar. The information is both displayed and saved into a temporary file on your disk called a *cache*. The cache enables the browser to quickly redisplay the information without having it transmitted all over again.

Web pages can contain several types of elements—text, links, inline images, and frames. You already know that a link lets you move to another location. A *frame* is a smaller, independent section within the window. Sometimes the contents of a frame can change automatically as you are connected to the site. A web page may also have *inline images*—graphics that are dynamically linked to locations on the page and that are transmitted separately. In many instances, the text of the page will appear first, so you can start reading and clicking on links right away, with the inline images being added after.

Internet Explorer Basics

A typical web page displayed in Internet Explorer is shown in Figure 3-1, using AT&T WorldNet as the ISP and connecting to the AT&T WorldNet home page.

The purpose of most of the toolbar buttons, shown in Table 3-1, is relatively straightforward, but the Refresh button may need clarification. This button tells Internet Explorer to redisplay the current page. If you view a page long enough, the computer that generated it may make changes to the page. When you click Refresh, Internet Explorer determines if any changes were made; if so, it asks the server to transmit the entire page again. If no changes were made to the page, then Internet Explorer reloads the image from the temporary cache file on your disk.

NOTE: To learn how to send and receive e-mail, see Chapter 26, "Microsoft Outlook," and Chapter 28, "Working with Outlook Express."

You use the Address box to move to a specific location on the web, and to see the address of the web site being displayed.

The buttons below the Address box are called the Link buttons. Clicking on these takes you to sites on the Internet that Microsoft considers entertaining, interesting, or informative. If the Links toolbar is not displayed, select View |

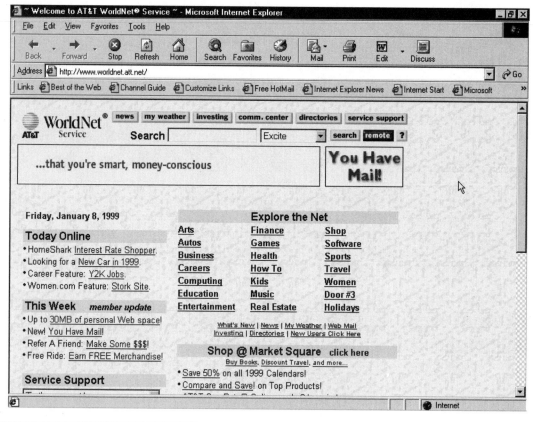

FIGURE 3-1 Typical web page

Toolbars | Links. You may have to move the Links toolbar to its own line on the screen to display it.

With Internet Explorer 5, you can also display the Radio toolbar, shown here. You use the Radio toolbar to play music or listen to news or other live radio broadcasts. To display the Radio toolbar, select View | Toolbars | Radio. To locate a station you want to listen to, click on Radio Stations and choose Radio Station Guide from the drop-down menu. The browser will take you to a web site that offers a wide range of links for all music tastes.

BUTTON	FUNCTION
Back	Redisplays the previous web page
Forward	Returns to the previous page after using the Back command
Stop	Stops the transmission of the page to your computer
Refresh	Redisplays the current page
Home	Displays the designated home page
Search	Displays a page of search engines to find information on the Internet
Favorites	Displays sites you've designated as favorites in a pane on the left of the screen
History	On the left of the screen, displays recently visited sites
Mail	Launches your e-mail program to read messages, create a new message, send a message with a link to the current site, send a message that contains the current site as its text, or launch your news reader program
Print	Prints the displayed page
Edit	Lets you display and change security settings
Discuss	Connects to a group discussion server sending and receiving messages

TABLE 3-1 Internet Explorer Toolbar Buttons

Using the QuickMenu

One other way to control Internet Explorer is by using the shortcut menu that appears when you click the right mouse button on an object. As with all shortcut menus, the items on it depend on the object you click on. For example, here are the shortcut menu items when you right-click a graphic image:

- **Open This Link**   Displays a specified page.
- **Open in New Window**   Opens the page into another window.
- **Save Target As**   Opens the linked document, but saves it on your disk rather than displaying it onscreen.
- **Print Target**   Prints a copy of the object.
- **Show Picture**   Displays a specified image onscreen.
- **Save Picture As**   Opens an image but saves it on the disk rather than displaying it onscreen.

- **Set as Wallpaper** Uses the graphic as the wallpaper on the Windows desktop.
- **Set as Desktop Item** Adds the graphic as an Active Desktop item—double-click the item to launch your browser and jump to the site.
- **Cut** Removes the graphic and places it in the Clipboard, although this command is dimmed for sites you are viewing.
- **Copy** Places the address of the link into the Clipboard.
- **Copy Shortcut** Creates a shortcut to the current web page.
- **Paste** Inserts a copy of the item from the Clipboard. Again, this item is dimmed when you're viewing others' web pages.
- **Add to Favorites** Creates a bookmark of the address of the link being clicked on.
- **Properties** Displays information about the graphic.

Navigating the Web

The process of moving from one place to another on the Internet is called *navigating* or *surfing*.

The easiest way to navigate around the web is to click *hypertext links*. These may be underlined words, text in a different color than other text, or even icons, buttons, and graphics. When you point to a hypertext link, the mouse pointer will appear like a small hand. Just click the link to connect to another location in the same document, another document on the same computer, or another location in the world. You don't have to worry about where it takes you, because you can always return to your previous location by clicking on the Back button in the toolbar.

If you return to the previous page, you'll notice that the color of the link that you've used has changed. This indicates that you have already used the link, but you can still click it again to return to the page.

If you know the address of the web site, you can go directly to it. Web pages are identified by a *uniform resource locator* (URL) address. An URL (pronounced "Earl") is much like your own street address in that it tells the browser exactly where to locate the information. You'll find lists of useful or interesting addresses in magazines, newspapers, advertisements—almost anywhere these days. Type the address in the Address box at the top of the window and press ENTER or click Go.

| Address | http://www.microsoft.com | ▼ | ⟳ Go |

N O T E : When you start typing an address, a drop-down list may appear showing recently visited sites starting with the same characters you've typed. Click a site in the list to go to it.

The syntax of the URL depends on the type of protocol it uses for its interface. Some of the most common are these:

- **http**   for web pages that use Hypertext Transfer Protocol.
- **ftp**   for transferring files through the File Transfer Protocol.
- **news**   for Usenet newsgroups.
- **gopher**   for a menu-driven interface.

Following the protocol is the identifier of the computer system that contains the information. For example, the URL for AT&T WorldNet is *http://www.worldnet.att.net/*. If the site you want to go to uses the http protocol, you can start typing with "www." When you press ENTER or click Go, Internet Explorer automatically inserts "http://" for you.

T I P : Use the pull-down list on the right of the Location box to select from your recently used sites.

You can also view a history of the locations you visited. Click the History button in the Internet Explorer toolbar to see the names of the sites that you've recently visited, as shown in Figure 3-2. Click a day to see the sites you visited that day, or click Today to see the sites you visited today. To determine how the sites are listed, pull down the View list and choose from these options:

- By Date
- By Site
- By Most Visited
- By Order Visited Today

Printing Web Pages

In addition to saving a web page, you can also print it. Click the Print button on the toolbar, or choose File | Print to see a dialog box and then click Print.

Click Search to find a site in the History list.

Click a folder icon to see pages of the site.

Click a page to open it.

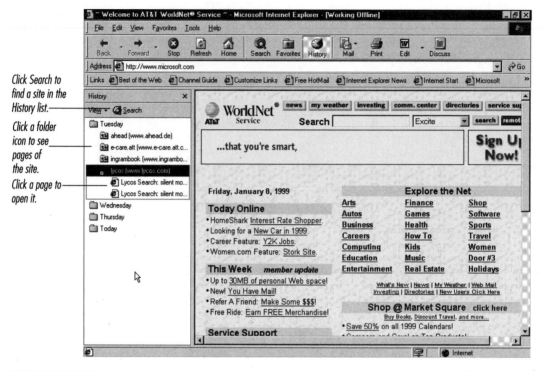

FIGURE 3-2 Using the History list

To adjust the format of the printout, choose File | Page Setup to see the Page Setup dialog box. Select options from the box and click OK.

Searching for Information

One way to locate information is to follow the trail of links, clicking on them to move from site to site on the Internet until you find the information you are looking for. You can also search for the information using a keyword or phrase. You will be amazed at the breadth of information and services available on the Internet.

When you find a web page that you are interested in, you can save it on your disk. You can even save a page before you display it, either as a formatted HTML file or as plain text. To do so, follow these steps:

1. Choose File | Save As to open the Save Web Page dialog box.
2. Pull down the Save As Type list and select either of these options:
   - Web Page, Complete (*.htm, *.html)
   - Web Page, HTML only (*.htm; *.html)
   - Text File (*.TXT).
3. Type a name for the file.
4. Click Save.

If you save the page as a complete web page, Internet Explorer saves all the text and graphics displayed. You'll find a web page file in the location where you saved it containing the text and format of the site, along with a folder containing its graphics and other associated files. Double-click the web page on your Windows desktop to open the page in Internet Explorer without having to connect to the Internet.

 NOTE: You can also open an HTML-formatted file directly into Office applications.

If you save the page using the Text File option, you can open the file into any word processing program. It won't have any of the formats or graphics—just the text of the page.

Before you go surfing around the Internet using search tools, however, keep in mind that much of the information there may not be useful, valuable, accurate, or socially acceptable. The Internet is just a ragtag network of millions of computers. No one controls, polices, or censors it—which is actually one of its greatest strengths. Searching for something on the Internet using a word or phrase may reveal a list of hundreds of locations, some of which may have little or nothing to do with the subject you had in mind.

Chances are, your ISP will have search options available in its home page. You can also initiate a search from the Internet Explorer toolbar by following these steps:

1. Click the Search button in the toolbar. Internet Explorer displays search tools on the left of the window, as shown in Figure 3-3.
2. Select the type of search you want to perform.

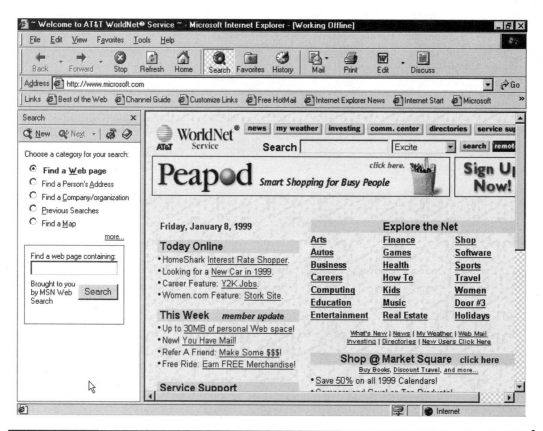

FIGURE 3-3   Searching for information

3. Enter a keyword or phrase to search for.

4. Click Search.

Internet Explorer will then display links for the results of the search, as shown in Figure 3-4.

 TIP: The Customize button lets you choose default search engines.

Choose the number of items to display.

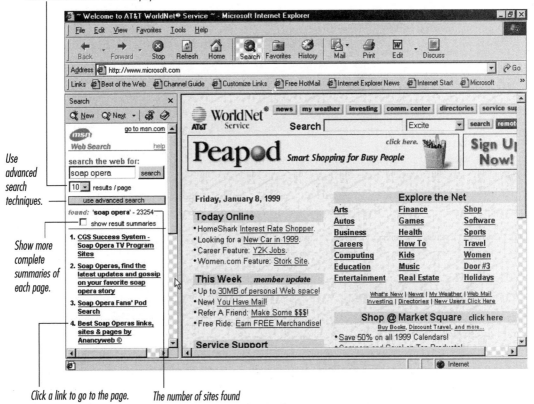

Use advanced search techniques.

Show more complete summaries of each page.

Click a link to go to the page.

The number of sites found

FIGURE 3-4 Results of a search

Accessing Favorite Web Sites

Once you find an interesting site, you want to be able to find it again quickly. You could write down the URL address that appears in the Address box. Better yet, save the address as a favorite site. This means that you can quickly return to the site by clicking on its name in a list of favorites, either from Internet Explorer, within an Office application, or from any open Windows 98 folder.

You can also *subscribe* to a web site. This means that Internet Explorer periodically checks the site to determine if it has changed since you last viewed it. You can then *synchronize* the site so the most recent version of it is available to you offline without even connecting to the Internet.

To add a favorite site, follow these steps:

1. Start Microsoft Internet Explorer.
2. Go to the web page you want to add as a favorite.
3. Choose Favorites | Add To Favorites to see the dialog box shown here:

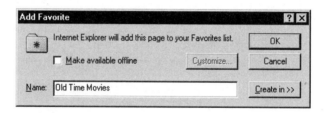

4. In the Name text box, you can modify the default title of the page if you want something different to appear in the Favorites folder.
5. If you want to save the page in a subfolder of Favorites, click Create In >>. The dialog box expands so you can choose an existing subfolder or create a new one.
6. Click OK. (If you want to make a page available offline, do not click OK. Refer to "Making Web Pages Available Offline" later in this chapter.)

Using Favorites

You can access your favorites from within Internet Explorer, the Windows desktop, or any Office 2000 application.

From Internet Explorer, pull down the Favorites list and click the site you want to display. If you don't want to pull down the Favorites menu all the time, click the Favorites button in the toolbar to open a favorite panel on the left of the screen. Use the panel to jump to a web site or to add a new favorite.

You can also access your favorite sites when Internet Explorer isn't even open, by using any of these techniques:

- Click Start on the Windows taskbar, point to Favorites on the Start menu, and then click the site.
- From any open Windows 98 folder, pull down the Favorites menu and click the site.
- From an Office 2000 application, display the web toolbar and pull down the Favorites menu.

You'll notice that the Favorites list may contain subfolders. Subfolders let you group related favorite sites in one location. To display the sites contained in a subfolder, just point to the subfolder in the Favorites list.

To create new subfolders, move sites to groups, or delete sites from the Favorites list, choose Favorites | Organize Favorites from the Internet Explorer menu bar to display the dialog box shown in Figure 3-5.

Making Web Pages Available Offline

If you want to subscribe to the web site so you can look at it when you are offline, don't click OK in step 6 in the preceding "Accessing Favorite Web Sites"

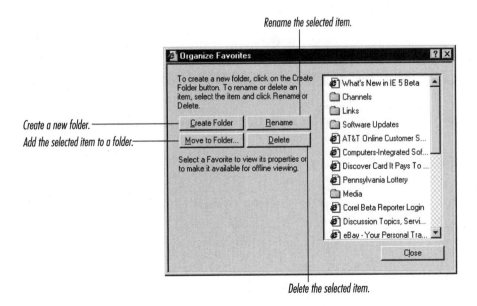

Rename the selected item.

Create a new folder.
Add the selected item to a folder.

Delete the selected item.

FIGURE 3-5 Organizing favorites

section. Instead, enable the Make Available Offline check box and then follow these steps:

1. Click the Customize button in the Add Favorite dialog box to start the Offline Favorite Wizard.

2. Read the information in the dialog box and then click Next. The dialog box that appears asks if you also want to make available offline any pages that are linked to the web site you are viewing.

3. Choose No if you do not want to make linked pages available, Yes if you do. If you choose Yes, you can also designate the number of levels of links. Just be aware that choosing Yes takes up more disk space and takes pages longer to synchronize.

4. Click Next to see the Offline Favorite Wizard shown in Figure 3-6.

5. Choose when you want to synchronize the page. You can select to synchronize manually from the Tools menu, to create a new schedule for automatic synchronization, or to use an existing schedule for automatic synchronization. Existing schedules are daily, weekly, and monthly.

6. Click Next.

7. If you chose to create a new schedule, the next page of the wizard lets you designate the number of days between synchronization, the time to synchronize, and a name for the schedule. Then click Next.

8. In the final Wizard dialog box, enter your user name and password if the site requires one for you to log on.

9. Click Finish to complete the wizard.

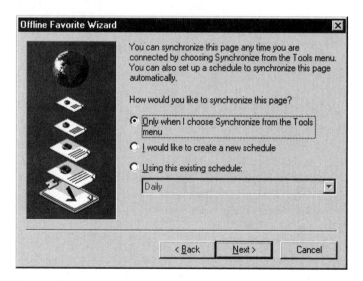

FIGURE 3-6   The Offline Favorite Wizard

10. Click OK to close the Add Favorite dialog box.

If you selected to make the page available offline, Internet Explorer now downloads the latest version of the site to your computer, dialing your ISP if you are not yet connected.

 TIP: If you want to make a site available offline that is already listed in your Favorites, right-click the item, and then choose Make Available Offline from the shortcut menu to start the Offline Synchronization Wizard.

Synchronizing Web Pages Manually

If you did not choose to automatically synchronize your web sites, you have to do so manually. To synchronize a single offline web page, locate the page in the Favorites list or folder, right-click it, and then choose Synchronize from the shortcut menu that appears.

To update multiple sites at one time, use Tools | Synchronize from within Internet Explorer to see the dialog box in Figure 3-7. Select the check boxes for the sites you want to synchronize, and then click Synchronize.

To change synchronization settings for a specific site, select the site in the Name list, and click the Properties button to open a dialog box like the following:

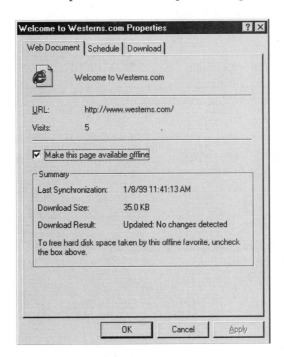

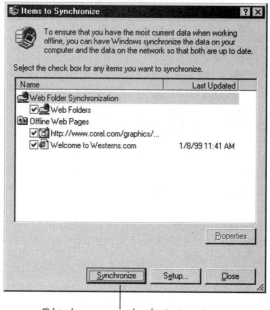

Click to change your general synchronization settings.

FIGURE 3-7 Synchronizing offline web pages

Clear the Make This Page Available Offline check box to no longer synchronize the page.

Use the Schedule tab to synchronize the page manually or on an automatic schedule.

Use the Download tab to specify the number of links to download, how much hard disk space is used, to receive an e-mail when the site has changed, and to limit which elements of a web site are stored on your hard disk.

Using Integrated Internet Access

Internet access is integrated directly into the major applications of Microsoft Office. You can send e-mail, launch your browser and go to a specific site, work with favorites, and create and open web pages.

Sending E-Mail and Attachments

While Office 2000 includes two powerful e-mail programs—Outlook and Outlook Express—you can initiate e-mail from within any Office program. When you want to send e-mail, just type an e-mail address in the format *xxx@xxxx.xxx* as in "alann@compuserve.com," and press SPACEBAR or ENTER. Office converts the address into an underlined link; clicking on it will launch your e-mail program and display a mail window already addressed. Office will also create a link when you type any web site URL, such as *www.microsoft.com.*

 NOTE: To set the default e-mail program, open Internet Options in the Windows Control Panel, click the Programs tab, and select the program in the E-Mail list.

 Sharing your work with someone over the Internet is even easier. Just click the E-Mail button, shown to the left, in the Word, Excel, or PowerPoint toolbar.

 NOTE: You can also use the File | Send To | Mail Recipient and File | Send To | Mail Recipient (As Attachment) commands to send documents as the text of the message or as an attachment.

If you are in Word, an e-mail window opens with the current document as the text of the message. Just enter the recipient and a subject, and click Send in the message window toolbar.

In Excel, clicking on the e-mail button lets you choose from these options:

- **Send the Entire Workbook as an Attachment**   Adds the workbook as the message attachment. Specify the recipient and subject, enter a message, and then click the Send button.
- **Send the Current Sheet as the Message Body**   Adds the worksheet as the actual text of the message. If you are using Microsoft Outlook or Outlook Express as your e-mail program, the mail window appears directly on your Excel window, as shown in Figure 3-8. Use Excel's features to create or edit the worksheet, specify the recipient and subject, and then click the Send This Sheet button.

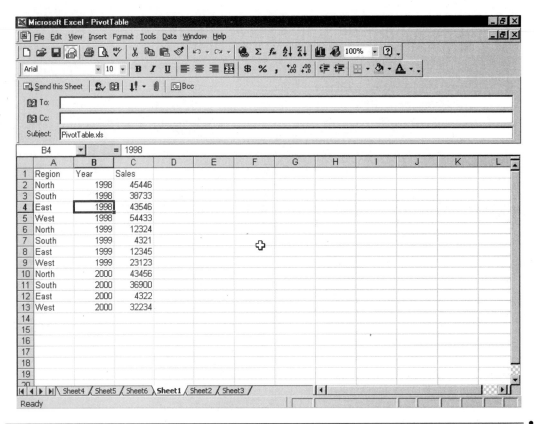

FIGURE 3-8 Sending an Excel worksheet as an e-mail message

In PowerPoint, clicking on the E-Mail button gives you the options to send the entire presentation as an attachment or the current slide as the message body.

 NOTE: Depending on your e-mail program, the message may be transmitted immediately, or placed in your Outbox. You may have to start your e-mail program and initiate the send process from there.

Creating and Using Hyperlinks

Hyperlinks are the engine that makes the web work because they enable you to quickly move to a location on the Internet or on an intranet.

The easiest way to create a hyperlink is just to type the address. When you use the format www.*something.something* (as in *www.microsoft.com*), Office automatically converts it into a link—underlined and in blue. When you point to the link, the mouse cursor appears as a small hand. Just click the link to launch your web browser, dial up your ISP, connect to the Internet, and go to the site.

You can also use the dialog box shown in Figure 3-9 to create a link. If you want the reader to see something other than the actual address of the link, type and select some text that you want the reader to click on. For example, you could select the phrase "Click here for more information" to use as the link. Otherwise, just place the insertion point where you want the link to appear. Next, click the Insert Hyperlink button on the Standard toolbar, or choose Insert | Hyperlink, to display the dialog box.

If the URL begins with "http:\\www," you can leave off the "http:\\" designation; Office will add it for you automatically. If you are unsure of the address, click the Web Page button to launch your browser. Navigate to the site and then switch back to the dialog box. Click OK to accept the address, and then close your browser.

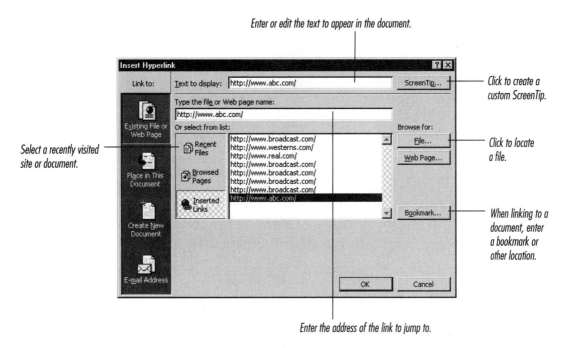

Enter or edit the text to appear in the document.

Click to create a custom ScreenTip.

Select a recently visited site or document.

Click to locate a file.

When linking to a document, enter a bookmark or other location.

Enter the address of the link to jump to.

FIGURE 3-9   Inserting a hyperlink

TIP: To create a link to another Office document—such as a Word document or Excel worksheet—copy text from the document and then use Insert | Paste As Hyperlink to place it into the field. Clicking on the hyperlink opens the document, letting you easily move between related documents.

Changing a Link

Unlike other text in a document, a hyperlink cannot be clicked to edit it, since clicking jumps immediately to the site of the link. To change either the address of a link or the link text, right-click it and point at Hyperlink to display these options:

Your choices are

- **Edit Hyperlink**   Displays the Edit Hyperlink dialog box, which is the same as Insert Hyperlink except for the title.
- **Open**   Jumps to the hyperlink, replacing the site currently in the browser if it is already open.
- **Select Hyperlink**   Selects the hyperlink so you can format its text or delete it.
- **Open in New Window**   Jumps to the site and opens it in a second window.
- **Copy Hyperlink**   Copies the hyperlink address to the Clipboard so you can paste it in another location.
- **Add to Favorites**   Adds the hyperlink to the Favorites folder.
- **Remove Hyperlink**   Converts the hyperlink to regular text.

The Web Toolbar

Office gives you several ways to access the Internet, but one of the most versatile ones to use from Office's applications is the Web toolbar, shown in Figure 3-10. If you're on a network or already connected to the Net, use the

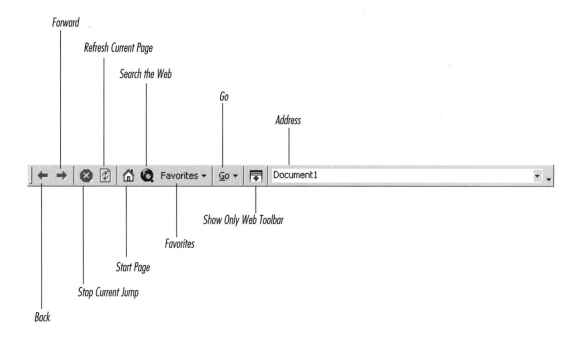

FIGURE 3-10 The Web toolbar

toolbar just as you would your browser. If you are not connected, selecting a site with the toolbar launches your browser and makes the connection for you. For example, click Start to go to the home page set in Internet Explorer, or to the Microsoft Corporation home page if you are using another browser.

In all Office's applications, you can display the Web toolbar by right-clicking on any toolbar and choosing Web from the shortcut menu that appears. The Web toolbar appears automatically when you open an Access table or form containing a hyperlink field, or click a hyperlink in any Office application. The functions of the toolbar buttons are explained in Table 3-2.

Using Go

The Go list on the Web toolbar gives you another way to navigate the Internet. It lets you open a document, move to a web site, go to the start page, search the web, or make the current document the start page or search page.

When you make a document the Start Page, it is opened automatically when you launch your web browser or click the Start button in the Web toolbar or the Home button in Internet Explorer.

To make a document the start page, open the document and display the Web toolbar. Pull down the Go list and choose Set Start Page. Click Yes in the dialog box that asks if you want to change your start page to the current page.

To set a web page as the start page, start Internet Explorer, choose View | Internet Options, and display the General tab. Type the address of the site in the Address text box in the Home Page section. You can also use the Use

BUTTON	FUNCTIONS
Back	Moves back through the list of previously opened web pages
Forward	Moves forward through the list of previously viewed web pages
Stop Current Jump	Stops loading the web page being transmitted to your computer
Refresh Current Page	Reloads the currently displayed page
Start Page	Jumps to your selected home page
Search the Web	Lets you search the Internet
Favorites	Lets you create bookmarks for or jump to frequently used or specific sites
Go	Lets you jump to a site, navigate through recently used sites, or set the Start Page and Search Page
Show Only Web Toolbar	Toggles off and on the display of other toolbars
Address	Lists recently visited sites

TABLE 3-2 The Web Toolbar

Current, Use Default, and Use Blank buttons to use the currently open page, the default page, or a blank page as the start page.

Publishing Your Work on the Web

Web pages are formatted using special codes called *HTML* (Hypertext Markup Language) *tags*. The tags tell your web browser how to display the information on the screen. You can manually construct a web page by writing tags, but they can be rather obscure and require quite a bit of learning. Office saves you from all that trouble. With Office, you use the program's own formatting commands to create your document, then have the program convert the formats into the HTML tags automatically. You get a complete web page without the worry.

 N O T E : The information presented here requires some knowledge of the Office applications discussed. Review this section to learn about Office's capabilities, but return to it after you've read the rest of this book.

Saving and Opening Web Pages

All Office applications can open and save web pages. This means, for example, that you can create a document in Microsoft Word or a worksheet in Microsoft Excel and save it in HTML format, so you can publish to a web site and make it available to others on the Internet. You can also open HTML documents in your application.

 N O T E : Most web sites contain copyrighted information, so you may not be allowed to use the content and design of another web page without getting permission.

When you look at these files on the Windows desktop, they have the familiar HTML file icon. Opening the file from the desktop launches your web browser offline with the document displayed as a web page.

With the exception of files saved in Access, when you look at these files from a File Option dialog box within an Office application, however, their icons indicate the program you use to create it, as shown next. So when you open the file from within any Office program, it opens in its original program.

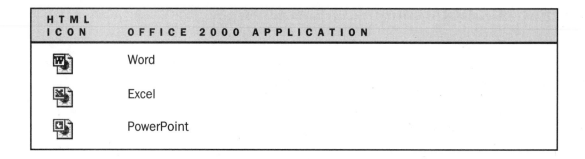

HTML ICON	OFFICE 2000 APPLICATION
	Word
	Excel
	PowerPoint

Creating Web Pages with Word

Word gives you two ways to create web pages. You can convert an existing document to a web page, or select from complete designs using the Web Page Wizard.

To convert a document, first create it using Word's standard techniques. Some Word formats, however, cannot be converted to HTML codes, so you should first save the document in Word format. When you save the document as a web page, Office will let you know which formats cannot be converted. Next, convert the Word file to an HTML document using File | Save As Web Page to see this dialog box:

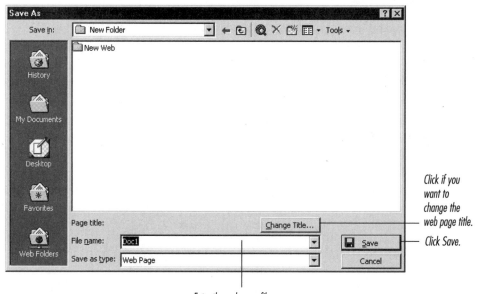

Click if you want to change the web page title.

Click Save.

Enter the web page filename.

N O T E : The web page *title* appears in the title bar of the Browser; the web page *name* is the filename on your disk.

Word converts the document to web page format and changes to Web Layout view. If any formats cannot be converted to HTML, however, you'll see a dialog box such as the one shown here:

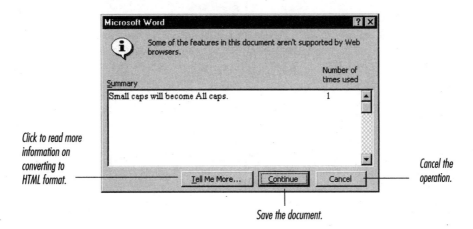

Click to read more information on converting to HTML format.

Save the document.

Cancel the operation.

In Web Layout view, your document appears just as it will when displayed in a web browser, and all Word's formatting commands are available. For example, use Format | Theme to select from layouts that apply a background, set the colors of links, add a graphic bullet character, and use custom heading styles. Then to see how it will actually appear on the Internet, choose File | Web Page Preview. Office will launch your web browser without logging you on to the Internet, and display the document as it would be seen if it were published on the web. Close the browser to return to Word. Because the document is already in HTML format, just click Save to save it—you do not have to select Save To HTML.

Working with Frames

Most modern web browsers can handle *framed* pages. The example shown in Figure 3-11 shows a web page that is divided into two frames, but a web page can have more than two frames. Each frame scrolls separately, and each one has its content and links. Creating a frames page in Word is easy by use of the Format | Frames command. The command displays a submenu that offers two options. Choose Format | Frames | Table Of Contents In Frame if your document includes a table of contents. Word places the table in a separate frame on the left. Each entry in the Table Of Contents frame has a hyperlink to the section of the document that appears in the right frame.

You can also choose Format | Frames | New Frames Page to open the Frames toolbar shown in the following illustration:

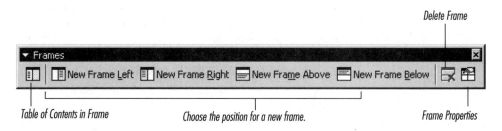

Delete Frame

Table of Contents in Frame   Choose the position for a new frame.   Frame Properties

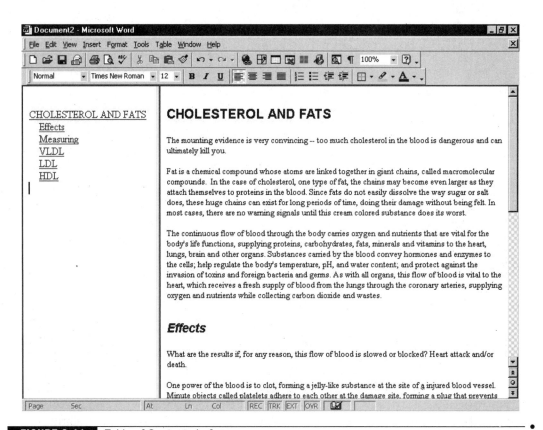

FIGURE 3-11   Table of Contents in frame

N O T E : After you create a frame, all the features in the Frames toolbar are also available in the Format Frames submenu.

When you are ready to enter and format text, click the frame where you want the material to appear. If you need to resize the frames, you can resize them by dragging the lines between the frames, as you would adjust column widths in Word's table feature. You can use the Frame Properties button on the toolbar to insert or link a file into the frame, change the frame size, set the width and color of the border, turn off the borders between frames, and determine when scroll bars appear in frames in your browser.

When you save the document, several files are created. Then each frame's content is saved in a separate file, with one additional file that saves how the frames should be arranged.

 T I P : You can use frames in any Word document; this feature is not exclusive to web pages.

Web Page Wizard

In Word, you can also use the Web Page Wizard to create one or more linked web pages. Word will display a formatted page ready for you to enter text. Choose File | New and then click the Web Pages tab.

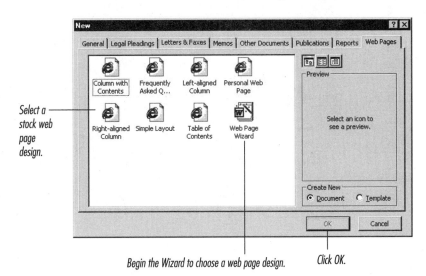

Select a stock web page design.

Begin the Wizard to choose a web page design.   Click OK.

When you double-click the Web Page Wizard, Word presents a series of dialog boxes. The first just tells you a little about the Wizard, so after you have read this information, click Next to proceed to the next dialog box. In the second box that Word presents, enter a title for the web page and the location where you want it stored (where on your hard disk you want the folder stored). Then click Next to see the options shown in Figure 3-12.

Word's Web Page Wizard offers three basic ways to arrange material for navigation in your web page: two vertical frames that link to other pages, two horizontal frames that link to other pages, and a series of web pages linearly linked to other pages with navigation buttons.

When you select a layout and click the Next button to proceed to the next dialog box, you can then add more pages. The Web Page Wizard's default option is a configuration called Personal Web Page and two blank pages—Page 1 and Page 2. You can add blank pages, or add pages using templates provided by the Wizard. Click Add Template Page to see the possible options, as shown in Figure 3-13. When you click an option from the Web Page Templates list, a sample of the page appears in the background.

Click the option button for the layout you want.

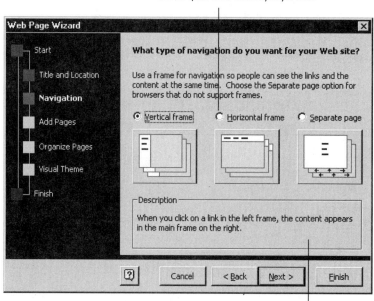

Read a description of the layout here.

FIGURE 3-12   Select an overall layout for your web page

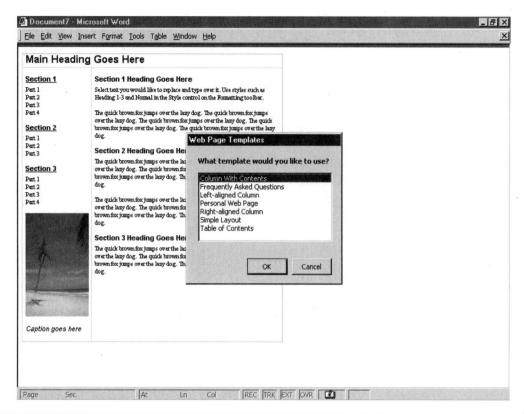

FIGURE 3-13 Click a template to see a sample of it in the background

Once your site is constructed by selecting all the pages you want it to contain, click Next. With the page of the Wizard that appears, you can change the position of pages by selecting one you want to change and then clicking on the Move Up or Move Down button. Click Next to move to the Web Page Wizard's fourth dialog box, the Theme box, when the pages are in the desired order.

In the Themes Web Page Wizard dialog box, you can choose to add a visual theme to the pages. Click the option button labeled "Add A Visual Theme," and then click Browse Themes to see the options shown in Figure 3-14. As you scroll through the theme options listed in the Theme window, the template of the theme appears in the window on the right.

After you have clicked OK in the Theme dialog box, click Finish in the Web Page Wizard's final dialog box to display the web page on the screen, as shown in Figure 3-15. Word adds sample text as placeholders for where you will insert

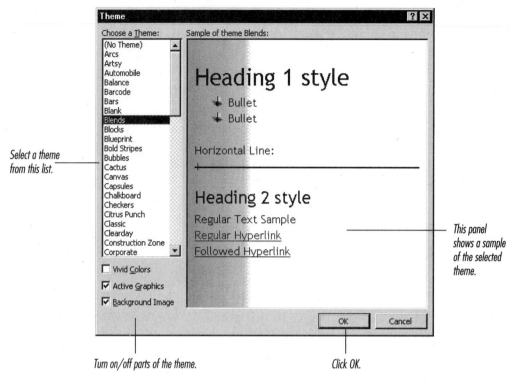

Select a theme from this list.

Turn on/off parts of the theme.

Click OK.

This panel shows a sample of the selected theme.

FIGURE 3-14 Adding a theme to your web site

your web material. Now all you have to do is fill in the sample text areas. Click a link to one of the other pages to open and edit it. (You may have to click twice on a link to open the page.) Click a link to a topic to move to the linked section of the page.

Web Pages with Excel

Saving an Excel worksheet as a web page couldn't be any easier, but you have several options. Start by choosing File | Save As Web Page to see the Save As dialog box (Figure 3-16).

If you choose the Entire Workbook option button, enter a filename and then click Save. When you open the file in your browser, all the workbook pages will be available. You'll see sheet tabs at the bottom of the window—just click the tab to open the web page for that sheet.

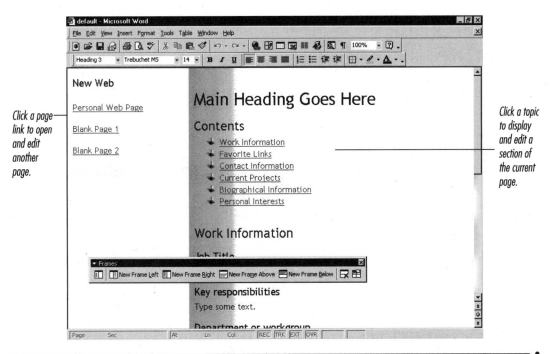

Click a page link to open and edit another page.

Click a topic to display and edit a section of the current page.

FIGURE 3-15 Web page created by Web Page Wizard

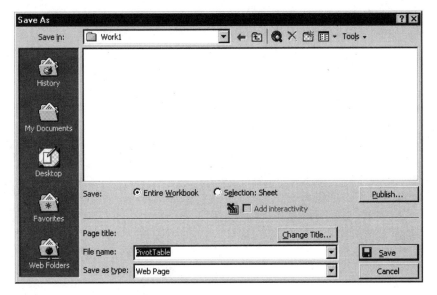

FIGURE 3-16 Save As dialog box for creating web pages with Excel

N O T E : Click the Publish button in the Save As dialog box to see options for selecting a specific sheet or range of cells to save, and to open your web browser after the information has been saved.

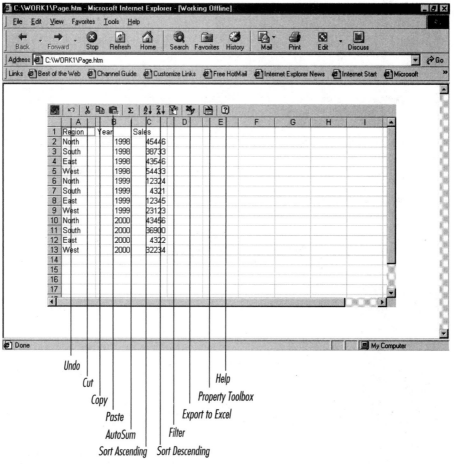

FIGURE 3-17 Excel web page with interactivity

If you choose the Selection: Sheet option button, only the current worksheet is saved as an HTML file. However, you can also enable the Add Interactivity check box. With this option the worksheet appears with an Excel toolbar when the worksheet is displayed in a web browser, as shown in Figure 3-17. Having the Excel toolbar available to anyone who accesses the web page lets that person do some basic Excel operations on the web page. You can use the toolbar to sort columns, click AutoSum to total values, and perform other Excel functions. You can even add and edit information. To save your changes to the worksheet, however, you have to click the Export To Excel button to open Excel with the worksheet displayed.

To format cells and perform other Excel functions, click the Property Toolbox button to display the Spreadsheet Property toolbox, as shown:

Click a header to hide or display its options.

With this toolbox, you'll be able to select from these options:

- **General**   Lets you undo your last changes.
- **Format**   Lets you format text, change the font and font size, format the appearance of cells, set the column width and row height, set the horizontal and vertical alignment, and change the number format.
- **Show/Hide**   Lets you hide or display the toolbar, gridlines, title bar, and column and row headers.
- **Calculations**   Determines when the sheet is recalculated and displays the formula in the active cell.
- **Find**   Lets you search the worksheet for specific text.

Web Pages with Access

Access lets you save web pages in three formats:

- HTML Document
- Microsoft IIS 1-2
- Microsoft Active Server Pages

N O T E : Access also lets you create Data Access Pages that you can use like forms in both Access and on the web. See Chapter 25 for additional information.

With the HTML document format there is no link between the HTML page and the data itself. Once you create the page and upload it to the Net, any changes to the information in the database will not be reflected in the web page.

N O T E : Dynamic web pages are very advanced, so don't be surprised if you do not understand the discussion in this section of the book. If you are not a web page designer or database administrator, just scan this section for a general understanding of its concepts.

The other two options create dynamic pages so Net users will always see the most current information in the database. The information on the page will be updated each time it is accessed. The dynamic options are designed for users of the Microsoft Internet Information Server (IIS).

The Microsoft IIS (also known as HTX/IDC) creates two files that tell the Internet Server how to use Open Database Connectivity (ODBC) to access the database information and how to format it as an HTML document. The IDC file tells the server the names of both the data source and the HTX file, and includes an SQL statement to access the information from the file. The HTX file serves as a template to specify how to format the data as an HTML document. When a user accesses the web page, the files retrieve the information from the database and display it on the screen.

> **N O T E :** ODBC (Open Database Connectivity) is a set of standards for working with information in SQL database servers. It allows various programs to access the same information.

The Microsoft Active Server Pages option is for use with the ActiveX component of the Microsoft Internet Information Server 3.0 or later. The ASP file contains HTML formatting commands as well as SQL statements needed to access the information, along with Visual Basic code that references ActiveX Server Controls.

Click the name of the item you want to save in the Access database window, and then choose File | Export. Pull down the Save As Type list and choose the format. For Reports, HTML is the only option available.

If you selected a dynamic type of web page, the next dialog box asks you to specify information the server needs to access and update the information. You'll need to enter the Data Source Name, User Name, and Password. If you choose the ASP type, you'll also have to specify the Server URL and the Session Timeout options.

Creating Data Access Pages

When you use the Export command, Access creates a page that can be opened and accessed by your web browser. As an alternative, you can create a data access page that can be used both from within Access and on the Internet.

A typical data page is shown in Figure 3-18. It displays fields with text boxes in which you can view, edit, and add information. At the bottom of the form is a special toolbar containing the familiar navigation, add record, and delete record buttons as well as buttons to save and undo record changes, sort the table, and create and apply a filter.

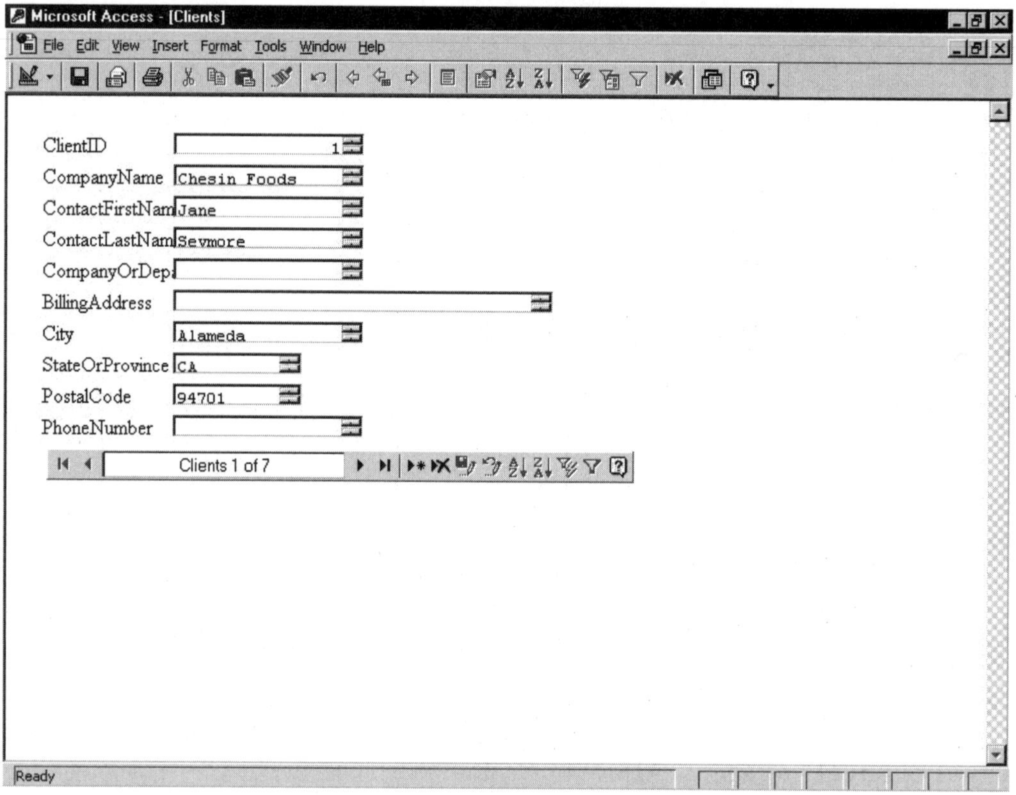

FIGURE 3-18   Data access page

When you open a data access page, you are actually looking at a web page. Right-clicking on the page displays your browser's shortcut menu rather then Access' shortcut menu.

To create a data access page in as few steps as possible, click Pages in the database window, and then double-click Create Data Access Page By Using Wizard.

In the first Wizard dialog box, shown in Figure 3-19, you select the fields that you want to add to the web page, including fields from related tables. To create a data access page using multiple tables, pull down the table list and select the "one" table in a one-to-many relationship; then add the fields that you want from the table to the form. Next, pull down the table list and select the next table, the "many" side of the relationship, and add fields from it. You can then repeat the process for any other tables that have one-to-many relationships.

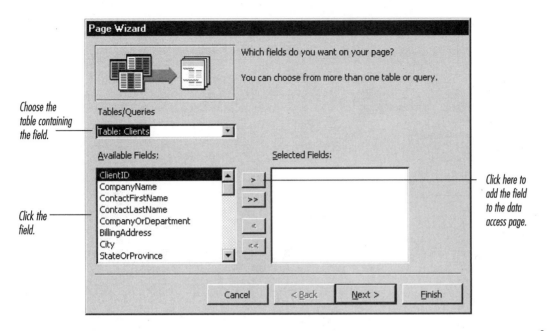

FIGURE 3-19 Selecting fields for a data access page

The next Wizard dialog box, shown in Figure 3-20, lets you choose the way fields are grouped. A grouping level will organize the information according to the fields that you designate. However, it will also make the page read-only, so the information cannot be changed using the data access page.

The next dialog box lets you choose if you want to sort the detail information by any other field. You can choose up to four fields, each in either ascending or descending order.

In the last Wizard dialog box, type a name for the page and select if you want to choose a theme, and then click Finish.

Choosing a theme lets you format the data access page with a background and other graphic elements. If you chose to apply a theme, you can select the theme desired, enable the boxes for the theme elements to apply, and then click OK.

You will then see the data access page in Design view. To save the data access page at this time, however, select File | Close, and then click Yes to the message that appears asking if you want to save the page. To view a data access page on your web browser, right-click it in the Database window and choose Web Page Preview from the shortcut menu.

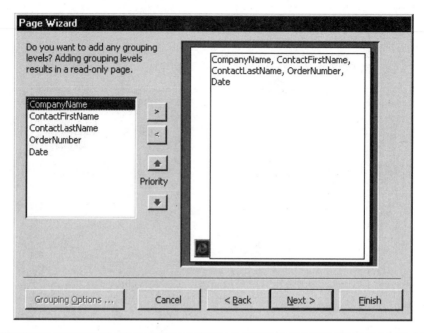

FIGURE 3-20 Selecting a grouping level

Web Pages with PowerPoint

One of the easiest ways to create a web site is to do so as a PowerPoint Presentation. Create the slide show as you would any other presentation, and then choose File | Save As Web Page. In the dialog box that appears, enter a filename and click Save. PowerPoint creates an HTML file with the name you designate as well as a separate folder of supporting files. The folder has the same name as the web page but with "_files" appended to the name.

When you open the resulting HTML file in your browser, there will be an index frame on the left showing the presentation outline. The entries in the outline serve as hyperlinks to move from slide to slide, with each slide serving as another web page. As seen in Figure 3-21, PowerPoint also features a navigational bar at the bottom of the web page to let the viewer page through the PowerPoint presentation.

To customize the web presentation, click Publish in the Save As dialog box to see the Publish As Web Page dialog box, shown in Figure 3-22. In this dialog box, you can choose which slides to publish, whether you want to display speaker notes along with your slides, and the type of browser for which to create the web page.

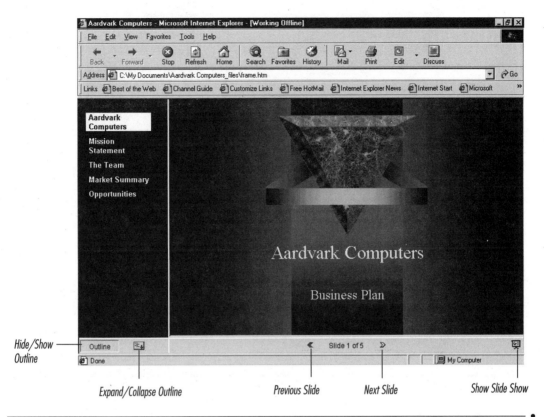

Hide/Show Outline

Expand/Collapse Outline

Previous Slide

Next Slide

Show Slide Show

FIGURE 3-21   PowerPoint presentation saved as web page

The Web Options button lets you determine these settings:

- Show navigation controls
- Animate slides in the browser
- How and where files are saved
- Default web page editor
- Type of graphic format
- Target monitor size

Putting Your Page on the Web

The techniques you learned in this chapter create documents with HTML tags that can be displayed on the web. To actually make these documents available

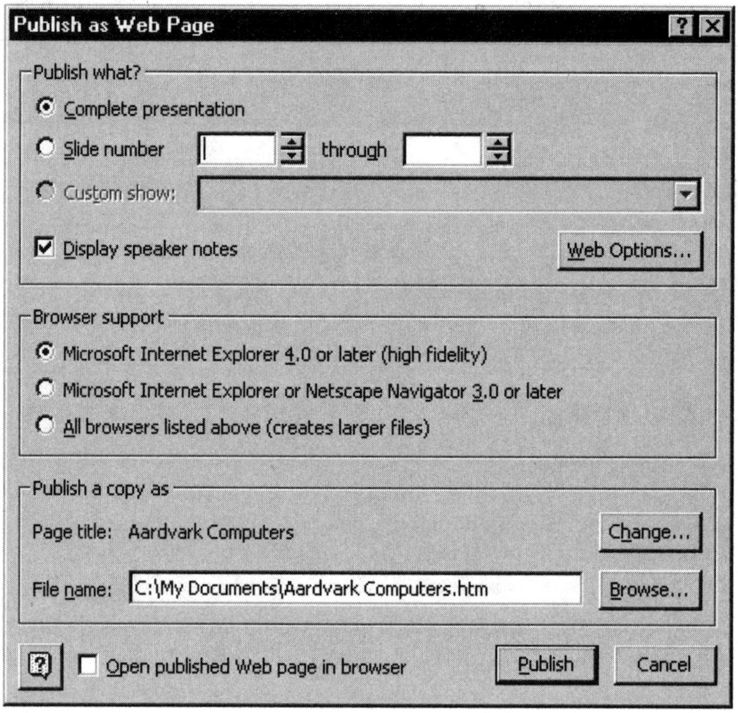

FIGURE 3-22 Customizing web pages in PowerPoint

on the Internet, however, you have to upload them to your web server. This means placing the files created by the application on a specific folder on your network or on your hard disk.

If you are on an intranet or Internet server, check with your system administrator to learn how to upload the files and where to locate the files on your system. If you connect to the web through an ISP, such as America Online, CompuServe, or AT&T WorldNet, check with its customer service department. In some cases, you have to use a program called FTP (File Transfer Protocol) to upload the files. FTP is provided as part of the Windows operating system. Many Internet service providers, however, have special programs that will help you upload the files without trouble.

Using Web Folders

In addition to publishing your web pages on the Internet, you can use a web site to store documents. Office 2000 offers a special feature called Web Folders, in which a web site can be treated just like a folder on your disk. You can save documents to the site and open them at any time. This is particularly useful if you travel. Once you save a document to the web site, you can open it using any computer that is connected to the Internet.

To create a Web Folder, open the My Computer icon on the desktop and then open Web Folders. Double-click Add Web Folder. In the box that appears, enter the address of the site and then click Next. Office 2000 connects to the web site, dialing in to your ISP if you are not already connected. If you need authorization to access the site, a box appears asking for your user name and password. Once your access is verified, a box appears in which you enter a name for the folder. Enter a name that you can easily identify when saving or opening files, and then click OK.

You can now access the web site by double-clicking its name in the Web Folders window or by selecting Web Folders in any file management dialog box.

- The first time you fill out an online form, Internet Explorer will ask if you want to use AutoComplete. This feature saves your entries of web address, information in forms, and user names and passwords. Select Yes only if you do not share your computer with someone else. If you select Yes and do share your computer, other users will be able to access confidential information using your user name and password. The next time you start to enter the information on the same form, a menu of choices appears for you to select.

- While you can install and use another web browser (such as Netscape Navigator), do not uninstall Internet Explorer. Some features of Microsoft Outlook and Access require Internet Explorer to be installed on your system.

- When you display a web page from within an Office application or open an HTML file from the Windows desktop, your browser opens with the page but does not connect to the web. Use this technique to review web pages saved on your disk without going online.

- You can also publish your web pages with the Microsoft Web Publishing Wizard that comes with Microsoft Internet Explorer. Use Tools | Internet Options to customize Internet Explorer, such as changing your home page and setting Internet security options.

- You can use hyperlinks to move to a location in the current document, another document on your computer, or another computer on your network.

- You can use the View Channels button on the Windows 98 desktop to open popular web sites directly from your Windows desktop.

- Use the File | Edit With Microsoft Word For Windows command in Internet Explorer to transfer a web page to Microsoft Word. In Word, you can then edit and save the web page as desired—being mindful of copyrights, of course.

- Always save your documents before converting them to web pages or publishing them to the web. While glitches in the process are rare, it pays to have copies of documents stored on your disk in case your Office application accidentally closes.

- In addition to using Web Page Wizard, you can select a template for a specific type of page by choosing File | New and then clicking on the Web Pages tab of the New dialog box.

- ISPs offer a variety of services and tools for creating and publishing web pages. Check with your ISP before creating any complex web sites to make sure it will be compatible with their service.

Personalizing Office

4

If you don't like something about the way Office works, don't despair—you can customize Office to suit your tastes and work habits.

There are two general ways to customize Office—by use of Tools | Options and Tools | Customize.

The Tools | Options command displays a dialog box with multiple tabs. Each tab contains a series of settings that you can use to modify what appears on the screen or how your Office application operates. You can also customize menus and toolbars for the Office features you use most often.

Some of the options are for advanced or specialty users, and a few are seldom changed. It is best to use a program a little before customizing it, so you have a better understanding of the option you're changing. This chapter concentrates on the options that the average Office user might want to change.

N O T E : Your settings may differ from these, depending on how you set up Office.

The Tools | Customize command lets you modify the toolbars and menus. You can add and remove commands from toolbars and menus, and even create your own.

Let's take a look at the Options command first.

Customizing Word

The Options dialog box in Word offers ten tabs of choices. Probably the first options you should consider are those for opening and saving documents. Start with where your files are saved, and where Word expects to find documents you want to open. The default setting for documents is the MY FILES folder, but suppose, for instance, that you are working on a series of files in the BUDGET folder. To save time, set Word to use that folder as the default by using the File Locations tab of the Options dialog box, as shown in Figure 4-1. You can change the default folder for documents, as well as for graphics, templates, and other Word files.

In the dialog box that appears when you click Modify, type the folder name or select it from the Look In list, and then select OK.

In the General tab of the Options dialog box, set the number of recently used documents that you want listed at the bottom of the File menu. Increase the setting from the default 4 if you want to quickly access a larger number of documents.

Next, consider how your files are saved by use of the Save tab of the dialog box, shown in Figure 4-2. By default, Word saves a temporary copy of your

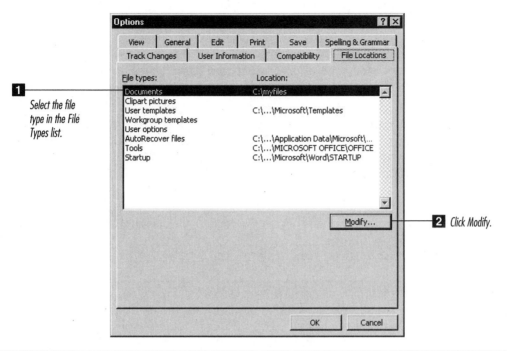

1
Select the file type in the File Types list.

2 Click Modify.

FIGURE 4-1 Setting the default location for files

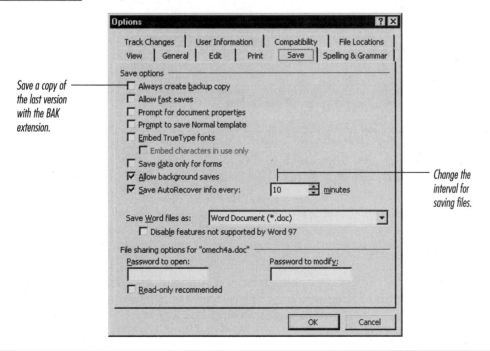

Save a copy of the last version with the BAK extension.

Change the interval for saving files.

FIGURE 4-2 Save options

work every 10 minutes. If your machine crashes before you've had a chance to save your work, a special recovered copy of your document will appear the next time you start Word. If you're working on an important document, you may want to reduce the amount of time between AutoRecover saves. You can also automatically save a copy of the last version of each document you save.

The Allow Fast Saves option lets Word speed up the saving process. When this option is turned on, Word adds the edited material to the current version when you save the document. This reduces the time it takes to save documents, but can greatly increase their size. For example, rather than actually incorporating changes into the saved text of the document, it adds a special section to the file just showing where the changes have been made. When you next open the document, Word incorporates the changes into the document as it is displayed. Turn off the option for smaller file sizes and maximum compatibility with other word processing programs.

 TIP: The Save tab also lets you set a password to access or share the current document. Just remember that passwords are case-sensitive.

Changing the Look of Word

The View tab of the Options dialog box, shown in Figure 4-3, lets you change what appears on the Word screen.

Edit and Printing Options

You can also change the way Word works when you edit and print documents. The options on the Edit tab let you customize some of Word's editing features, such as turning off drag and drop. The two options to consider are Typing Replaces Selection and Use Tab And Backspace Keys To Set Left Indent.

By default, Word replaces selected text with what you type when it is selected. This makes it all too easy to select text, then accidentally delete it. If you find this annoying, turn off the Typing Replaces Selection option.

The Use Tab And Backspace Keys To Set Left Indent option changes a tab that starts a paragraph into a first line indentation. If you decide not to indent the first line, you won't be able to remove the indentation by simply deleting the tab—you'd have to adjust the format by using the ruler or a dialog box. Turn off this option when you want a tab to stay a tab.

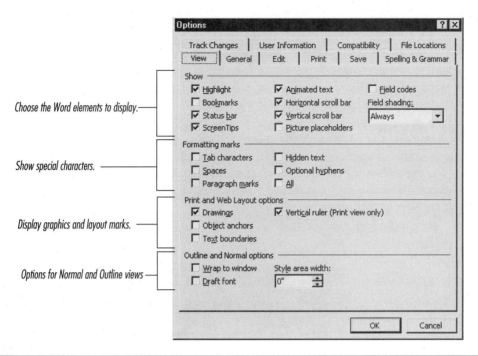

Choose the Word elements to display.

Show special characters.

Display graphics and layout marks.

Options for Normal and Outline views

FIGURE 4-3 The View options

The Print tab lets you control how and what Word prints when you print your document. Some of the more useful settings are as follows:

- **Draft Output**   Switches on your printer's draft mode, if it has one, so pictures and drawings may not print, and all text appears in one font. Use this option when you want a quick printout of a complex document, for just checking the text, for example.
- **Reverse Print Order**   Prints your document from the last page to the first. Use this option if you have a laser printer that outputs pages face up, so the document will be in the correct order when printed.
- **Update Fields**   Automatically updates field codes, such as dates and caption numbers, before the document is printed.
- **Update Links**   Automatically retrieves the current version of linked files.

Use the Include With Document section on this tab to determine what Word prints. You can choose to print just the document or the document along with summary information, field codes, annotations, hidden text, and drawing objects.

Spelling and Grammar Options

On the Spelling & Grammar tab, you can turn off and on spelling-as-you-type and grammar-as-you-type. These features are good to use, but can slow down your system. Turn them off if you want to check spelling and grammar when you're done rather than as you work.

Educators, editors, and others who rely on the grammar checker will appreciate the wide range of options for customizing how Word checks for grammatical errors. First, you can select to apply rules based on an overall writing style—the choices are Casual, Standard, Format, and Technical. You can even create your own set of rules for a custom style. For each style, you can choose specific rules.

Click the Settings button on the Spelling & Grammar tab to display the options shown here:

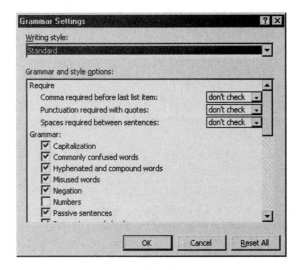

Choose the writing style whose rules you want to customize, and then go through the list specifying options. You can, for example, determine when to check the items listed in the Require section of the dialog box, and select check boxes for rules of grammar and style to be applied.

Other Word Options

Check out the User Information tab for your name, initials, and mailing address. Word inserts this information into certain templates, so it pays to make sure it is correct.

The Track Changes tab lets you set the style and color used to mark edited text when you've turned on the Track Changes feature. Normally you only need to change these when you want to indicate changes you make to your own work or when you're working with a number of reviewers.

Customizing Access

Because of the possible intricacies of database management, Access offers a lot of advanced options. Most of these options are used for special purposes. The settings on the Tables/Queries, Forms/Reports, Module, and Advanced tabs of the Options dialog box, for example, won't make a lot of sense to you until you learn how to create your own tables, queries, and other objects. So take a look at them only after you've had a chance to read the Access section of this book.

Changing How Access Looks

There are several ways to control the way Access appears. You can set options for what appears, how datasheets look, and how hyperlinks look before and after you use them.

The options on the View tab of the dialog box set what Access elements are displayed on the screen, as shown in Figure 4-4.

The Datasheet tab lets you set the default appearance for datasheets. A *datasheet* displays information in rows and columns like a spreadsheet does. While you can change the look of a datasheet as you use it, you can take advantage of the options on this tab when you have a special combination of effects that you want applied to every datasheet in a database.

Use the Hyperlinks/HTML tab to customize the way links appear when you're creating documents for the World Wide Web. A *hyperlink* is text you click to move to a site on the Internet. By default, hyperlink text will be underlined, and when you point to the link, its address will appear on the status bar.

Adjusting How Access Works

There's another whole set of options for customizing how Access works. The General tab is a good place to start. On that tab, for example, set the default margins for printed forms, reports, and datasheets. Use the Default Database Folder to determine where Access saves and expects to find your databases. You may want to save all your databases in a folder separate from Word

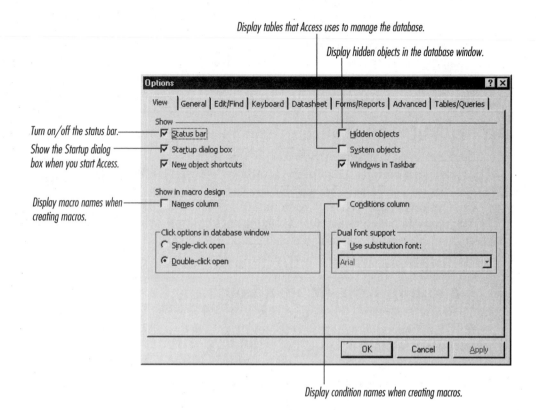

Display tables that Access uses to manage the database.

Display hidden objects in the database window.

Turn on/off the status bar.

Show the Startup dialog box when you start Access.

Display macro names when creating macros.

Display condition names when creating macros.

FIGURE 4-4 The View tab of the Options dialog box

documents and Excel worksheets to help you organize your work or to make backups easier.

The options on the Edit/Find tab are a little esoteric, but they are useful if you use the Find, Replace, and Filter By Form commands a lot. Refer to these options after reading Chapter 24.

If you use the TAB, ENTER, or arrow keys to move around a datasheet or form, then you'll find the Keyboard tab (see Figure 4-5) can be your best friend. The options in the Move After Enter section, for example, determine what happens when you press the ENTER key. You can choose to have Access stay where it is, move to the next field, or move to the next record.

You can also set what happens when you press the arrow key when a field is selected (the Arrow Key Behavior section) and what happens when you press TAB, ENTER, or an arrow key to move to a field (the Behavior Entering Field section). The Cursor Stops At First/Last Field option determines what happens

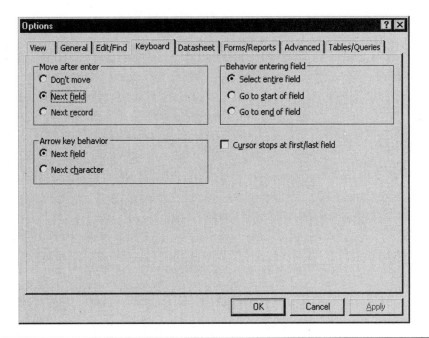

FIGURE 4-5   Keyboard options

when you reach the first or the last field. You can choose to stay on the record, or move to the next or previous record depending on the key you press.

Customizing Excel

Excel offers eight tabs of options that you can set to customize it for the way you work. Some of the options are only for advanced users, and a few are probably hardly ever changed.

Changing How Excel Looks

Most of the options for changing how Excel looks are on the View tab of the Options dialog box. You can choose to display the Formula bar and status bar, and how comments, charts, text boxes, buttons, and drawing objects appear. As with Word, you can choose to show just placeholders if graphics, charts, and text boxes seem to slow down scrolling.

There are individual check boxes for all of Excel's elements. Turn on the boxes for the items you want to appear. Commonly, users turn off the gridlines—the default lines that appear around cells—once they add their own custom gridlines. A useful option to turn off is Formulas. This will display the formulas you enter into a worksheet rather than the calculated results of the formula. Use this to print a reference copy of a worksheet to use for a backup.

 TIP: Since formulas can be long, you may have to widen the columns to see them on the screen and printout.

Setting How Excel Works

The General, Edit, and Calculation tabs of the Options dialog box contain most of the settings you'll use to customize how Excel works.

On the General tab, for example, you set the number of recently used files shown on the File menu, the number of worksheets in new workbooks, and the default location for files.

In the Edit tab you control what happens when you press the ENTER key. By default, pressing ENTER accepts your entry in a cell and moves down to the next row. You can also choose to move up, to the right, to the left, or not at all—just accept the entry and stay where you are. Other options on that tab let you turn off drag and drop, the ability to edit within a cell, and the ability to cut or copy objects within cells.

When you change a value in a worksheet that is referenced in a formula, Excel automatically recalculates the results. Automatic recalculation might slow down your system somewhat if you have a very large worksheet and a very slow computer. You can change to manual recalculation on the Calculation tab of the Options dialog box. To recalculate formulas manually, press the F9 key.

Customizing PowerPoint

Customizing PowerPoint is remarkably easy. Most of the choices in the Options dialog box are self-explanatory once you're familiar with the program.

Changing How PowerPoint Looks

Use the View tab of the PowerPoint Options dialog box to choose what appears onscreen. You can choose, for example, to display a Startup box each time you start PowerPoint. The box lets you create a new presentation using a wizard or template, or lets you start with a blank presentation. Other options let you display a box to insert a new slide, or display the status bar and vertical ruler.

Changing How PowerPoint Works

The other tabs of the Options dialog box let you customize how PowerPoint works:

- Use the *General* tab to set the number of recently used files on the File menu, and to set your user name and initials.
- On the *Edit* tab, you can choose to use smart quotes, allow drag-and-drop editing, and specify the maximum number of undos allowed.
- The *Print* tab lets you turn off background printing, print TrueType fonts as graphics, and print inserted objects at your printer's resolution.
- The *Save* tab lets you control fast saves, specify when AutoRecover information is saved, and set the default format for saved files. You can choose to use the current PowerPoint format, or choose previous versions to share files with users of older versions.
- The *Spelling* tab turns on or off spell checking as you type, or lets you ignore uppercase characters or words with numbers.
- The *Advanced* tab determines how 24-bit bitmaps are printed, the default location for files, and how pictures are exported.

Customizing Toolbars and Menus

While Office will adjust the toolbars and menus for you automatically as you work, you may want to customize them yourself. You can set how toolbar buttons and menus appear, change the options on them, and even create new ones.

Setting Toolbar and Menu Options

First, however, take a quick look at how you can change the appearance of the toolbar, as well as how the pull-down menus appear. Select Tools | Customize | Options to see choices for customizing the toolbar and menus. You can also right-click any toolbar and then select Customize to access the same customization menu. Select options from the dialog box, shown in Figure 4-6.

The options in the Personalized Menus And Toolbars section of the dialog box control the dynamic nature of Office's toolbars and menus. Click Reset My Usage Data, and then click Yes on the message that appears, to restore the

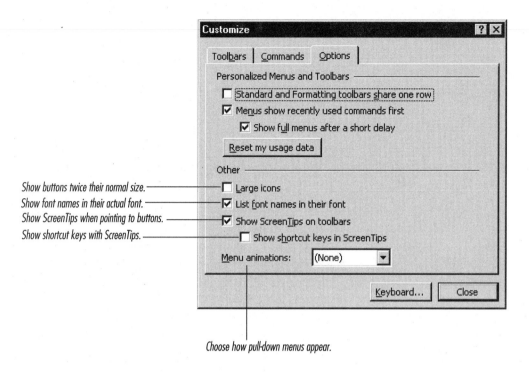

Show buttons twice their normal size. ——————

Show font names in their actual font. ——————

Show ScreenTips when pointing to buttons. ——————

Show shortcut keys with ScreenTips. ——————

Choose how pull-down menus appear.

FIGURE 4-6   Customizing toolbar and menu options

toolbars and menus to their original abbreviated versions. Buttons that were added when you selected them, the More Buttons list, and items added to menus when you expanded them, will be removed.

You can also choose to display the Standard and Formatting toolbars in one row, to display the most recently used commands first in a menu, and to expand menus after a delay when you point to them.

The Menu Animations option controls the way menus appear when you click the menu bar. By default, a menu just pops up when you click a menu item. You can also choose to have menus slide down like a window shade, unfold at an angle, or appear using random angles.

Creating Your Own Custom Toolbars

Suppose you find yourself changing the tab layout frequently in Word, or manually recalculating in Excel. Neither function is on the Standard toolbar.

Luckily, Office 2000 applications let you modify the toolbars by adding other buttons to them. First, make sure that the toolbar you want to add a button to is displayed on the screen. To display the toolbar you want to customize, follow these steps:

1. Pull down the View menu.
2. Select Toolbars.
3. Click on the toolbar you want to modify.

Next, right-click any toolbar, choose Customize from the shortcut menu, and click the Commands tab. Then use the steps shown here:

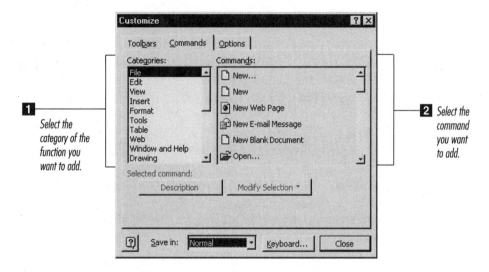

1 Select the category of the function you want to add.

2 Select the command you want to add.

3 Drag the button from the list to the toolbar.

To add a command to a menu, click the menu so the pull-down list appears and stays down. Then drag the item from the Commands tab to the position on the menu where you want the command to appear.

TIP: To move a menu item to a toolbar, choose the item from the menu, hold down CTRL, and drag the item to the toolbar. If you do not hold down the CTRL key, you will remove the item from the menu, rather than copy it to the toolbar.

To remove a button from a toolbar or a command from a menu, display any tab of the Customize dialog box, and then drag the button down off the toolbar, or drag the menu item down into the window. When you release the mouse, the button or menu command will be gone. You can also drag a toolbar button to a menu.

If you mess up one of the default toolbars, such as deleting or adding buttons by mistake, display the Toolbars dialog box, click the name of the toolbar, and then click Reset. The original settings will be restored.

Creating a New Toolbar

You use the New button in the Toolbars tab of the Customize dialog box to create your own toolbar. Click New, and then enter a name for the toolbar in the dialog box that appears. A small blank toolbar will appear onscreen. Use the Customize dialog box to add buttons to it. If you decide to later delete the entire toolbar, click its name, not its check box, in the Toolbars dialog box and select Delete. Use the Rename option in the Toolbars dialog box to change the name of the selected toolbar.

Creating New Menus

Menus are easy to create and use, and you can add menus to either the menu bar or a toolbar.

On the Commands tab of the Customize dialog box, scroll the Categories list to the end and choose New Menu. The Commands list shows one item, New Menu. Drag New Menu to the toolbar where you want to add it. A menu appears labeled "New Menu."

Change the menu name by right-clicking the new menu. In the shortcut menu that appears, delete the text in the Name box and type your own menu name.

Finally, add items to the menu—drag commands or built-in menus to it.

Customizing Buttons

Once you insert a button on a toolbar or menu, you can customize it. Right-click the item to see this shortcut menu:

You can reset the button to all its default settings or delete the button. To change the name of the button that appears in the ScreenTip, change the text in the Name box. Use the ampersand (&) to indicate the underlined (shortcut) character in menus.

Copy Button Image moves the image to the Clipboard so you can use it for another button with the Paste Button Image command. Reset Button Image restores the original icon, while Change Button Image lets you choose from a menu of icons like this:

You can select to display the default style (which shows the icon), to display just the name of the button (such as the word "New" for the New button), or to display both text and the icon. The Begin Group option inserts a vertical line before the button or a horizontal line before the menu item to organize items in groups.

If you do not like any of the icons shown, you can create your own or edit one of those suggested by Office. When the Customize dialog box is displayed, right-click the button you want to change, and choose Edit Button Image from the shortcut menu to display the Button Editor shown in Figure 4-7.

The Picture section is a grid with each square representing another dot of color—called a *pixel*—in the icon. The squares with the gray diagonal lines will appear as the gray background around the icon. In the Colors section, select the color of the pixel you want to insert, and then click the square in the grid. To erase a dot, click it again when using the same color, or click Erase and then on the square. To erase the entire icon, click Clear. Use the arrows in the Move section to shift the entire drawing up, down, left, or right one column or row at a time. The arrows will not move individual pixels. As you draw the icon, a sample of it in its actual size will appear in the Preview pane. When you're done, click OK and then close the Customize dialog box.

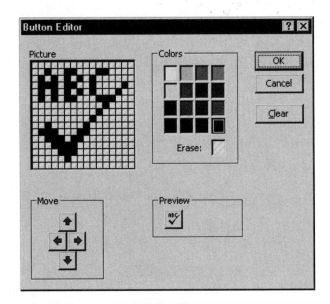

FIGURE 4-7   Creating a custom button with the Button Editor

- Outlook and Outlook Express have a wide range of options that you can set, but it's better if you learn these programs before trying to customize them.
- For more information about an option, click the What's This button (the question mark in the dialog box title bar), and then click the option.
- There are many options common to all applications, but they are not always on the same tabs of the Options dialog box. Review all the tabs in each application.
- In Word, use the E-Mail Options button in the General tab of the Options dialog box to select a stationery design and signature to use for mail created with Word.
- Use the Web Options button in the General tab of the Options dialog box in Word, Excel, PowerPoint, and Access to control how web pages are created, displayed, and edited.
- Use the same custom dictionary (accessed in the Spelling tab of the Options dialog box or from the Spelling dialog box) for all applications.
- The Show Shortcut Keys With ScreenTips setting on the Options tab of the Customize dialog box is not available in Excel—shortcut keys cannot be displayed with ScreenTips in that program.
- In Excel, use the Transition tab of the Options dialog box if you want to automatically save workbooks in a format other than Excel. Use the other settings on that tab if you are switching to Excel from Lotus 1-2-3.
- In Word, you can also use templates to customize how documents appear. Refer to Chapter 11 for more information.
- You can customize the Help system by selecting a Microsoft Assistant. Right-click the assistant and select Choose Assistant Or Options from the shortcut menu.

Sharing Information

5

As you've seen, Office applications share a lot of features. Information you enter in one program can often be used in another. You can use your Access database to prepare form letters in Word or to perform statistical analysis in Excel. In this chapter, we'll take a look at how Office programs can share information.

N O T E : This chapter refers to techniques and procedures that you will learn more about in later chapters. You may want to review this chapter now to see the types of features that are available, then return to it after you've read the appropriate chapters.

Sharing Worksheets

Both Excel and Word let you prepare *tables*—information in rows and columns. Excel's analysis capabilities and its ability to manage and print large worksheets, however, make it the program of choice when you're working with important data. What if you want to include a worksheet, or a portion of it, in a document that you're preparing in Word? You can always print the worksheet in Excel, and then add the pages to the document. But if you want to incorporate a section of a worksheet directly into a document page, you don't have to type the information into Word all over again.

Office gives you a number of ways to add a range of worksheet cells to a Word document. The method you select depends on how you want to use and update the information.

Making a Static Copy of Cells

If you simply want to duplicate a section of a worksheet as a Word table, you can either open the worksheet directly into Word, or copy it from Excel and paste it into the document. The worksheet is inserted as a Word table, which you can then edit and format using any of Word's table commands, as shown in Figure 5-1.

The cells are inserted as a *static copy*. This means that there is no connection between the Excel worksheet and the table in the document. If you change the worksheet in Excel, for example, the change does not appear in the Word document table. In addition, only the results of formulas are inserted, not the formulas themselves. If you want to use formulas in the resulting Word table, you have to add them using Word's Table | Formula command.

To start a new Word document that will contain an existing worksheet, choose File | Open, and then open the Excel file just as you would any Word document. You'll see this dialog box that asks if you want to open the entire workbook or a selected sheet:

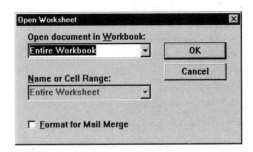

If you choose a specific worksheet, you can also designate the entire sheet or a named cell range. You can format the result to use for a mail merge, too. When you choose to mail merge, the information in the cells will be aligned on the left rather than the alignment that appears in Excel. You can then save the table and use it as a data source for a mail merge.

If you selected to use the entire workbook and there is more then one worksheet, each sheet will be inserted as a separate Word table.

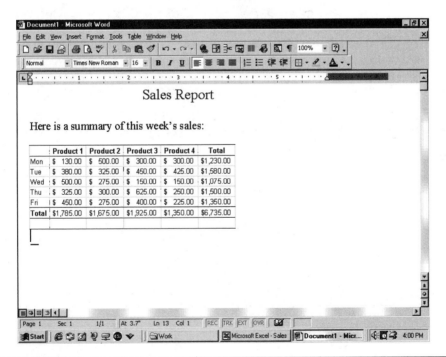

FIGURE 5-1   Excel cells pasted into Word

To use just a portion of a worksheet, copy and paste it. In Excel, select the cells that you want to insert as a Word table and click the Copy button. Then open or switch to the Word document and click the Paste button, or choose Edit | Paste Cells.

Creating a Hyperlink

Another way to insert a group of cells is to insert them as a hyperlink. A *hyperlink* is an object that the reader clicks on in Word to open Excel. Select and copy the cells in Excel, switch to the Word document, and then choose Edit | Paste As Hyperlink.

 N O T E : Paste As Hyperlink will be dimmed in the Word Edit menu if the Excel worksheet has not yet been saved.

The pasted cells appear in a Word table as a series of links, underlined as shown in the following illustration, and in blue. Unlike when you simply paste the cells, you cannot edit or format the links. To change the contents of any part of the table, click any cell in the table. Office then starts Excel and opens the workbook from which you pasted the cells. The information is still static, however. Changing the data in the worksheet does not affect the table in Word. To update the information in Word, you have to copy the edited cells and paste them in Word as a hyperlink again.

Sales Report

Here is a summary of this week's sales:

	Product 1	Product 2	Product 3	Product 4	Total
Mon	$ 130.00	$ 500.00	$ 300.00	$ 300.00	$1,230.00
Tue	$ 380.00	$ 325.00	$ 450.00	$ 425.00	$1,580.00
Wed	$ 500.00	$ 275.00	$ 150.00	$ 150.00	$1,075.00
Thu	$ 325.00	$ 300.00	$ 625.00	$ 250.00	$1,500.00
Fri	$ 450.00	$ 275.00	$ 400.00	$ 225.00	$1,350.00
Total	$1,785.00	$1,675.00	$1,925.00	$1,350.00	$6,735.00

Using Paste Special

For more choices in sharing a worksheet, including linking the cells so they can be updated automatically, copy the cells and select Edit | Paste Special. You'll have several options, shown in Figure 5-2, including buttons to Paste and Paste Link. Let's look at the Paste options first.

N O T E : You can only choose Paste Special if you copy—not cut—the cells.

When you turn on the Paste option button, which Office has on by default, you can paste the cells in any of these formats:

- **Microsoft Excel Worksheet Object** This inserts the worksheet as an object that you cannot edit in Word.
- **Formatted Text (RTF)** This inserts the worksheet as a Word table, but using the text formats that it has in Excel.
- **Unformatted Text** This simply inserts the text from the worksheet, not as a table but with each cell's contents separated by tabs.
- **Picture and Bitmap** These insert the cells as a graphic object, with the option to float the graphic over text. You can also use the Picture toolbar to customize its appearance. With Bitmap, you'll see the same gridlines as in Excel.
- **Picture (Enhanced Metafile)** This also inserts it as a graphic object but one that cannot float over text.
- **HTML Format** This inserts the information retaining any applied HTML formats.

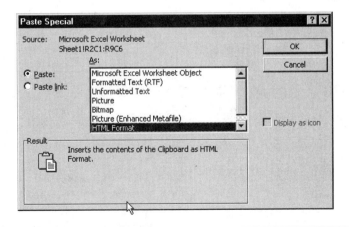

FIGURE 5-2 Paste Special dialog box

If you paste the worksheet as an object, picture, or bitmap, you can drag handles to change its size and position.

Sales Report

Here is a summary of this week's sales:

	Product 1	Product 2	Product 3	Product 4	Total
Mon	$ 130.00	$ 500.00	$ 300.00	$ 300.00	$1,230.00
Tue	$ 380.00	$ 325.00	$ 450.00	$ 425.00	$1,580.00
Wed	$ 500.00	$ 275.00	$ 150.00	$ 150.00	$1,075.00
Thu	$ 325.00	$ 300.00	$ 625.00	$ 250.00	$1,500.00
Fri	$ 450.00	$ 275.00	$ 400.00	$ 225.00	$1,350.00
Total	$1,785.00	$1,675.00	$1,925.00	$1,350.00	$6,735.00

Pasting the object using the Microsoft Excel Worksheet Object option creates an embedded object. This means that along with the worksheet, Windows also stores the name of the program used to create it—Microsoft Excel. You can't edit or format the information in Word itself, but if you double-click the object, Windows opens Excel and transmits the data from the object in Word to the Excel window.

Excel is opened, however, for *in-place editing*. You'll see a miniature version of the Excel worksheet right on the Word window, with Word's menus and toolbars replaced by those of Excel, as shown in Figure 5-3. This way, you can edit the worksheet data while seeing the document in which it will be printed.

Keep in mind that there is no link between the worksheet in Word and the actual worksheet file from which the data was copied. What Word contains is a copy of the data linked to Excel as its program of origin. If you change the information in the original disk file, the data in Word will not change.

Creating Dynamic Links with Cells

Now what happens if you paste cells into a Word document, then later change the information in Excel? The Word document and Excel worksheet will have different information. When you want both the document and worksheet to always contain the same information, use the Paste Link option in the Paste Special dialog box, as shown in Figure 5-2. When you turn on the Paste Link option in the Paste Special dialog box, the inserted worksheet is actually linked to the original file, regardless of your choice in the As box. Now if you change the information in the worksheet file, you can update the information in Word.

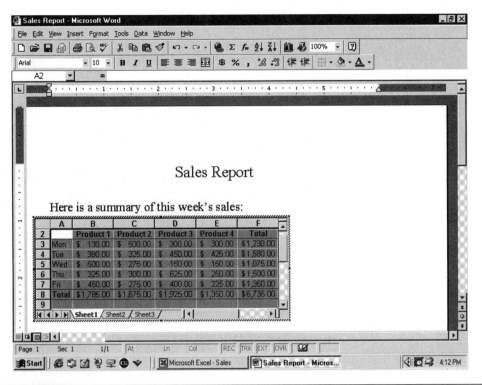

FIGURE 5-3 Editing an embedded object in place

N O T E : When you select Paste Link, the Picture (Enhanced Metafile) option is replaced with Word Hyperlink. This inserts the cells as a hyperlink, but not as a dynamic link that is updated with changes to the Excel file.

When you double-click the object, Windows opens Excel and the associated file, not in-place but in an Excel window. When you edit and save the worksheet, the changes are also shown in the Word document.

T I P : To open Excel when you paste link the worksheet using the Formatted Text or Unformatted Text options, right-click any text in the object, point to Linked Worksheet Object in the shortcut menu, and click either Edit Link or Open Link.

Normally, Word automatically updates links—retrieves the current version of the information—when you open a file. You can also set Word's options to update the link when you print the document. To update the link at any time yourself, select the object and press F9. To update every link in a document, choose Edit | Select All before you press F9.

You can also update and change links by choosing Edit | Links to see the dialog box shown in Figure 5-4. Select the link you want to update, and then click Update Now. Update several links at once by holding down the CTRL key when you select them.

In the Update section of the dialog box, choose Automatic to update the object every time you open the document or choose Manual. With manual update, you have to select the object and press F9, or update it in the Links dialog box.

Here is a summary of other options in the box:

- **Locked**   This prevents the objects from being updated.
- **Open Source**   This opens the object in the program used to create it.
- **Change Source**   This lets you relink the file if you changed its name or location.
- **Break Link**   This disconnects the link so the object is no longer linked with the file.
- **Save Picture In Document**   This stores a copy of a linked graphic file with the document.

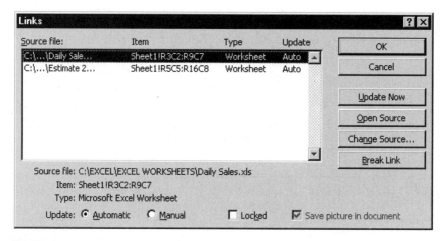

FIGURE 5-4   Working with links

When you open an Excel table into Word, you can use it for creating form letters, as you'll learn in Chapter 12. When you open the worksheet in this way, however, you are making a static copy of the information. The data source may contain out-of-date information if you later change data in the worksheet.

You can also link an Excel worksheet and an Access database as a data source to create form letters and other merge documents. You can send letters to persons in a client database, or print a catalog from inventory information in an Excel table. When you merge the main document with a linked data source, the resulting documents will contain the most up-to-date information.

When you are creating the merge file in Word, select Get Data in Mail Merge Helper and then choose Open Data Source. In the Open dialog box that appears, pull down the Files Of Type list and select either MS Access Databases or MS Excel Worksheets.

If you select MS Excel Worksheets, locate the worksheet file you want to use and then double-click it. You'll see a dialog box asking if you want to use the entire worksheet or just a named range, if there are any. When you make your choice and click OK, the columns of the worksheet will be treated as the data fields and used to create the form document. The data fields will be shown when you pull down the Insert Merge Fields list.

If you select to use an Access database, you'll see a dialog box listing the tables and queries in the database, as shown here:

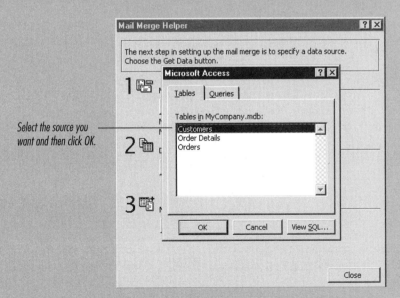

Select the source you want and then click OK.

Sharing Databases

You can also share a database when you're working with it in Access. Select the table you want to share in the Database window, pull down the OfficeLinks button in the Access toolbar, and select from these options:

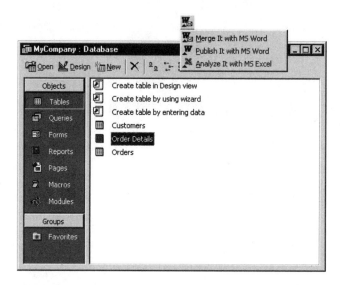

Choose Merge It With MS Word from the OfficeLinks options when you want to use the table as a data source for a mail merge. You can choose to link the database with an existing form document or to open Word and create a new merge document.

If you want to print a formatted copy of the table in Word, choose the Publish It With MS Word option. This saves the database as a Word document with the RTF (Rich Text Format) extension and opens it in Word, as shown in Figure 5-5.

To perform statistical analysis on the data in the table, choose Analyze it With MS Excel from the OfficeLinks options. Access saves the database as an Excel worksheet and opens it in Excel. This option is useful when you want to quickly calculate row or column totals, or to group or filter the information in the table.

Creating Slides from Outlines

PowerPoint can be an effective program for getting your points across in a presentation. If you've already outlined your presentation in a Word document,

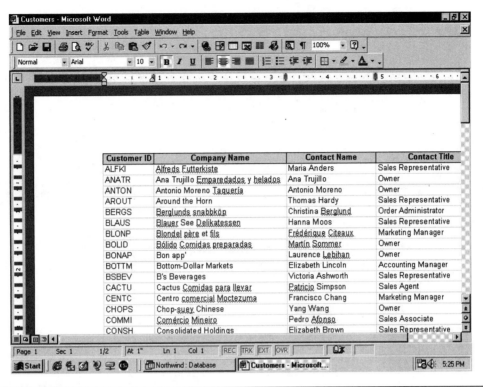

FIGURE 5-5 Database opened in Word as a document

you don't have to retype it in PowerPoint. You can convert a Word outline into a series of PowerPoint bullet list slides.

First, when you create the Word document, make sure it is in outline format. It doesn't have to actually be a Word outline, but should include headings and subheadings. Either use the Heading styles to indicate levels, or just use the TAB key to create indentations. When you create slides from the outline, each heading-1 level will be used for a slide title, with the subheadings as the bullet items.

To create a new presentation using the open document, display the document onscreen in Word, choose File | Send To from Word, and choose Microsoft PowerPoint. Office opens PowerPoint, creating a series of bullet list slides.

You can also add the outline as a series of slides to an existing presentation. Open the presentation in PowerPoint, and then from PowerPoint choose Insert | Slides From Outline. In the dialog box that appears, select the Word file containing the outline and click OK.

Sharing with Open and Save

Not everyone uses Office. If you have to share your files with those who don't use Office, you can make it easier on them by saving your files in a format their program understands. You might even be able to open their files in your Office applications in the format they give it to you.

You should first save your document normally, in Word's own format. Then follow these steps:

1. Select File | Save As.
2. Pull down the Save As Type list. You'll see a list of formats that Word can save your documents in:

3. Scroll the list and click the format that you want to use.
4. Enter a filename and then click Save.

In addition to all previous Word formats, you can select from several versions of WordPerfect, a few varieties of text files, Rich Text Format (RTF), HTML, Unicode, Microsoft Works, and Windows Write. If you don't see the format you want, try Rich Text Format if the other person uses some other Windows word processing program. This file type will retain as much formatting as possible. If the RTF option doesn't work, try the Text Only or MS-DOS Text options. You'll lose your formatting, but chances are the other person will be able to open the file.

If another person gives you a file that is not in Word format, start by trying to open it into Word just as you would any other document. The file may or may not open. If it does open, it will either be converted and displayed as text so you can read it, or appear like meaningless characters. Ask the person to save the file in one of the formats that Word can read (basically the same formats it can save in).

Use the same principle to open and save worksheet files in the formats. Excel can save any open files in a variety of formats, including Lotus 1-2-3, Quattro Pro, SYLK, DIF, and even dbase files created by some database programs.

Access will not directly open files except those in its own format, but you can import files in Excel, Exchange, Lotus, dBASE, Paradox, ODBC, and HTML formats. It will also let you export a file as a Word merge file, in Rich Text Format, Excel, Lotus, dBASE, Paradox, Microsoft IIS, Microsoft Active Server Pages, and as an ODBC database.

Working with Objects

The most common way to share information between Office applications is to copy and paste. Most programs let you copy information to the Clipboard, then paste it elsewhere. Sometimes, however, this method isn't convenient or possible. For example, it assumes that you have to open the program containing the information you want to use, copy the information, and then change programs and paste it.

There may be times when you want to create a new file and insert it into a document in one step, or when you're working with a file that cannot be copied and pasted. When there is no direct way to open, import, or paste the information, deal with it as an embedded object. You can click an embedded object to edit it in its source program, and even link the information so it can be updated automatically.

Inserting an object also lets you manipulate some items in ways you could not if you simply pasted it. For example, you can insert an object from Microsoft Photo Editor and be able to keep Photo Editor's added textures and other special effects.

Start by opening the program where you want to insert the file. If you already created the file, choose Insert | Object, and then click the Create From File tab to see these options:

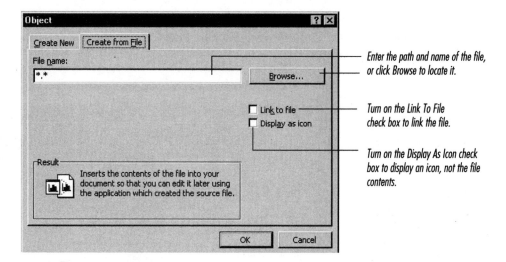

Enter the path and name of the file, or click Browse to locate it.

Turn on the Link To File check box to link the file.

Turn on the Display As Icon check box to display an icon, not the file contents.

Objects are inserted like pictures, with handles for changing the size and position. If you turn on the Display As Icon option, you'll see just an icon representing the file in the document:

MEMO

To:	Adam Chesin
From:	Barbara Elayne
Subject:	Sales
Date:	Jan 19, 2000

Open this file for a summary of the week's sales.

"Sales Report.doc"

I

To edit the contents of the object, double-click it. Office opens the program that you used to create it with the file displayed.

You can also create a new file to insert as an object. In the Object dialog box, display the Create New tab:

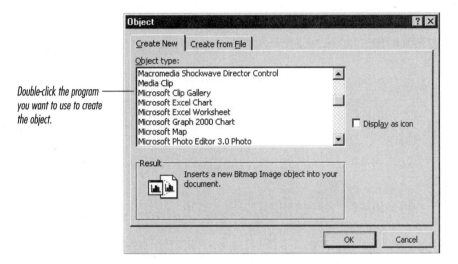

Double-click the program you want to use to create the object.

NOTE: You cannot link a new file that you create when using the Create New tab of the Object dialog box.

Office opens the program so you can create the file. In some cases, as with a bitmap image or Paint file, the program opens for in-place editing, as shown in Figure 5-6. Create the object, and then click outside of the in-place window to insert it into the document. In other instances, the program opens in its own window. In these cases, create the file and then choose File | Exit And Return.

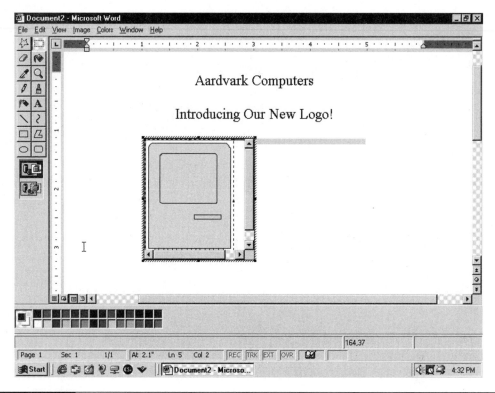

FIGURE 5-6 Bitmapped image opened for in-place editing

- Remember, all Office 2000 programs can save and open (or import) files in web page (HTML) format.
- The Paste Special and Paste As Hyperlink commands discussed for Word are also available in Excel, PowerPoint, and Access. Use the dialog box to paste and link copied information from another Windows application.
- In Access, you can choose Edit | Paste Append to paste information as a new record at the end of a table. Use this command, for example, to paste a row copied from Excel into an Access datasheet.
- If you link worksheet cells in a Word document, the linked file must always be available in its original location to be updated, unless you change the location of the file in the Links dialog box.
- Save a document before making major changes to it by inserting links and other objects.
- Rich Text Format is a widely available format in Windows programs. If you need to share a file with a person and you're not sure what software he or she has available, save the file twice. Choose the program's native format (such as a Word document or an Excel workbook) and Rich Text Format.
- Performing in-place editing on large files requires a lot of computer resources. If you do not have enough memory, in-place editing may be slow and cumbersome. It can also cause your computer to lock up or not respond, losing your work. If this problem occurs, create and edit the file in its native program, and then paste it into the document.
- The techniques you learned in this chapter apply to most Windows programs. You can use Paste and Paste Special, for example, to share text between Office and other Windows suites and stand-alone applications.
- Before printing a document that contains linked information, you may want to manually update all the links to assure that up-to-date data is printed. In Word, for example, select the document and press F9. In other programs, choose Edit | Links | Update Now.
- If the Paste Link button is dimmed in the Paste Special dialog box, you may have cut rather than copied the file, the source document is not saved, or the source is from a document that is not registered in Windows for sharing.

Word for Windows

Creating and Editing Word Documents

B A S I C S

- The Word Screen
- Changing Views
- Typing in Word
- Inserting the Date
- Changing Case
- Searching Your Document
- Replacing Text Automatically
- Highlighting Text

B E Y O N D

- Automating Your Work
- Inserting Special Characters
- Using Bookmarks
- Tracking Document Versions

Microsoft Word is the flagship program of the Office suite and for good reason. Word is a powerful and versatile program for creating documents of all types. Whether you're writing a one-page letter or a 500-page book, sending form letters, or printing mailing labels—Word has just the features you need.

WEBLINK: Get the latest information in Microsoft Word at
http://office.microsoft.com/office/enhWord.asp.

The Word Screen

Word contains all the typical Windows elements, as shown in Figure 6-1. As with all Office programs, the shape of the mouse pointer depends on its location. When the pointer is in the typing area, for example, it appears as a large letter "I," sometimes called the *text select point* or the *I-beam.*

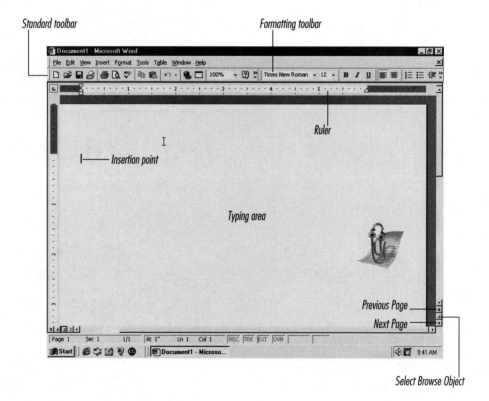

Standard toolbar

Formatting toolbar

Ruler

Insertion point

Typing area

Previous Page

Next Page

Select Browse Object

FIGURE 6-1   The Word screen

To change the actions of the Next Page and Previous Page buttons, click the Select Browse Object button and choose from the box that appears. If you choose Heading, for example, clicking Next moves to the next heading in the document, not to the next page.

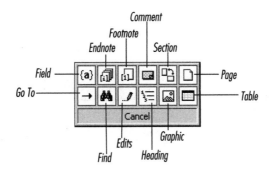

You'll find information about your document, the location of the insertion point, and the status of the Word program in the status bar:

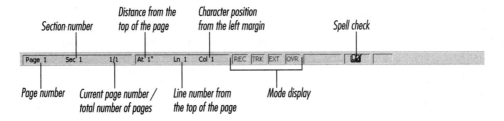

Characters in gray in the mode display indicate that a mode is currently turned off. To turn a mode on or off, or to activate a dialog box of options, double-click on the characters in the status bar.

- **REC** Reports whether the Record macro function is on or off
- **TRK** Reports whether tracking changes to the document is on or off
- **EXT** Indicates if text selection is on or off
- **OVR** Shows if Overtype mode is on or off

When you start Word, it uses default settings for text format and page size. Text will usually be 12 point New Times Roman, with a one-inch top and bottom margin and 1.25-inch right and left margins. Tabs are set every 0.5 inch. You will learn how to change all these settings in Chapter 7.

Views

Not every document you create will use the same format or overall design. Because documents can vary, Word gives you several *views,* or ways to display documents on the screen. You can change views using the buttons above the Page indicator in the status bar or by selecting options from the View menu.

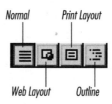

Normal   Print Layout

Web Layout   Outline

 N O T E : Figure 6-1 shows the Normal view; Figure 2-1 shows the Print Layout view.

VIEW	DESCRIPTION
Normal view	You'll see text in the typeface and size it will be when printed, but not headers, footers, page numbers, and other elements that are not part of the body of your text. Graphics appear at the left margin, not in their exact placement. Page breaks appear as lines across the screen.
Web Layout view	Lines wrap to fit on the window so you can see without scrolling horizontally. Graphics and backgrounds appear just as they will when displayed on a web browser.
Print Layout view	Graphics and all page elements appear exactly where they belong. There will also be a ruler down the left side of the screen.
Outline view	You use Outline view to create and organize outlines. An Outline toolbar replaces the ruler.

If you are creating a document designed for the web, you can see how it looks in your browser. Choose File | Web Page Preview to open the browser with the current document displayed. Refer to Chapter 3 for more information about using Word to create web pages.

TIP: Another way to change the appearance of the document is to click the Show/Hide button, shown next, on the Standard toolbar. This displays special symbols for spaces, tabs, and paragraph breaks. You may have to click More Buttons to access this tool.

Typing in Word

Typing in Word for Windows is easy. Just type as you would using a typewriter or any computer program. Instead of pressing the ENTER key at the right margin, however, just continue typing until the end of the paragraph. Word senses when the word you are typing will not fit in the line, and it moves the word to the next line automatically. Press ENTER only to end a paragraph or to insert a blank line between paragraphs. Word also automatically starts a new page when one becomes filled. To end one page manually before it becomes full, press CTRL-ENTER.

If you make a mistake as you type, press the BACKSPACE key. Each time you press BACKSPACE, Word deletes a character to the left of the insertion point. You can also press the DEL key to erase a character to the right of the insertion point.

 TIP: Make sure you've read Chapter 2 to learn how to move through a Word document, how to move and copy text, and how to perform other common Office functions.

Inserting and Replacing Text

You can insert characters anywhere on the page by moving the insertion point.

As long as you're within text, above the endmark, just place the mouse pointer where you want the insertion point to appear, click the left mouse button, and start typing. If the characters "OVR" are dimmed in the status bar, then, as you type, characters to the right shift over or down to the next line to make room. To replace existing characters as you type, double-click on the dimmed characters "OVR" so they appear bold.

In Print Layout and Web Layout views, you also place the insertion point in blank areas of the page, even below the last text in the document—but not in the margin areas. In those views, point to where you want to start typing and then double-click. Double-clicking actually inserts a tab at that location so you can start typing. In fact, if you pause slightly when moving the mouse, you'll see an icon with the pointer showing the type of tab.

When you're pointing at the center of the screen, for example, the icon appears like this, indicating that double-clicking will insert a center tab.

As you type, characters shift left and right to remain centered on the screen. Point and double-click at the right margin to insert a right tab—characters will shift to the left so they are aligned at the right margin. Double-clicking at any other location inserts a normal left tab.

Selecting Text in Word

Word uses the selection methods described in Chapter 2, with a few extra twists thrown in. Word uses *intelligent selection*. If you drag to select the space between words, for example, Word automatically selects the whole word to the left or right, depending on the direction you are dragging. If you don't want to select the entire word, keep the mouse button down and drag back toward the starting position.

Here are some other ways to select text in Word:

- Double-click on a word to select it.
- Click three times to select the entire paragraph.
- Hold down the CTRL key when you click to select the entire sentence.
- Click the mouse once in the left margin to select the line of text to the right of the pointer, click twice to select the entire paragraph, and click three times to select the entire document.
- Drag in the left margin to select multiple lines.

Automating Your Work

As you learned in Chapter 2, Word checks your spelling and grammar as you type, and corrects typos with AutoCorrect. But, depending on what you type, you'll also see AutoComplete and AutoFormat in action. AutoComplete lets you quickly enter common words and phrases, while AutoFormat formats your text as you type it.

Using AutoComplete

Word knows the days of the week, the months of the year, and the current date, as well as a whole list of commonly used words and phrases, such as Sincerely, Thanks, Personal, and Dear Mom and Dad. When you type the first few letters of one of these entries, you'll see a small box suggesting the word:

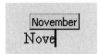

Press ENTER or F3 to accept the word. To reject it, just keep on typing. If you type a space after the name of the current month, Word suggests the current date.

To see the words and phrases that Word can insert for you, or to insert one into a document, choose Insert | AutoText:

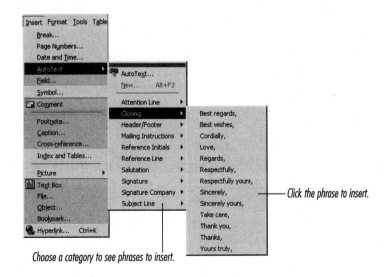

Choose a category to see phrases to insert.

Click the phrase to insert.

Inserting with AutoText

AutoComplete is part of a general feature call *AutoText*. AutoText lets you insert a word, phrase, or entire section of text by typing an abbreviation for it. AutoText is similar to AutoCorrect, except that the phrase appears in an AutoComplete box and it will not be inserted until you accept it.

To use AutoText, you first link a word or phrase with its abbreviation. Type and select the text you want to assign to an abbreviation. Then choose Insert | AutoText, and click New to display this dialog box.

1 Type the abbreviation here.

2 Click OK.

 N O T E : You can type a shorter abbreviation, but then the entry may not appear in an AutoComplete box.

The next time you need to insert the text into a document, type the abbreviation, followed by a space or carriage return, and press F3.

If you forget what abbreviations you used, or you want to delete an AutoText entry, choose Insert | AutoText and click AutoText. The dialog box appears as in Figure 6-2.

Using AutoFormat As You Type

This powerful Word feature formats text as you type it. If you surround a word in quotes, for instance, Word automatically changes straight quotes into "smart quotes," like this:

He said "Your money or your life".

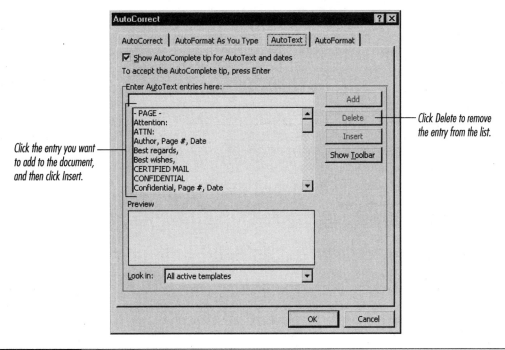

Click the entry you want to add to the document, and then click Insert.

Click Delete to remove the entry from the list.

The AutoText dialog box for inserting an AutoText entry

AutoFormat will also format ordinal numbers as superscripts (such as 1st to 1st), change fractions to fraction characters (such as 1/2 to ½), and change two hyphens (--) to an em dash (—). The feature can also insert lines, format headings, and create bulleted and numbered lists as you type.

You can control what formats this feature applies by choosing Tools | AutoCorrect, then clicking on the AutoFormat As You Type tab.

Inserting the Date and Time

To quickly insert the date, type the month and then press the SPACEBAR to display the date in an AutoComplete box. Then press ENTER or F3 to insert it.

If you want to control the format of the date, however, Select Insert | Date And Time to display the dialog box shown in Figure 6-3.

When you insert the date as a *field,* you will *see* the date on the screen, but Word actually entered a code called a field. When you later open the document, you can update the field so the current date appears. Select the date (it will appear in a gray box), and then press F9 to update it.

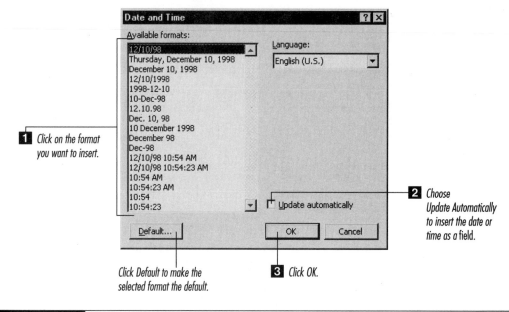

1 *Click on the format you want to insert.*

2 *Choose Update Automatically to insert the date or time as a field.*

Click Default to make the selected format the default.

3 *Click OK.*

FIGURE 6-3 The Date And Time dialog box

 N O T E : Use the Print page of the Options dialog box to update field codes automatically when you print a document. See Chapter 2.

Changing Case

To quickly change case, select the text and press SHIFT-F3. Each time you press SHIFT-F3, the case rotates through uppercase, lowercase, and title case. For more options, select the text and choose Format | Change Case to display this dialog box.

Click on the case you want, and then click OK.

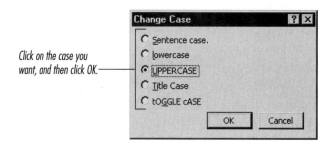

Inserting Special Characters and Symbols

When you want to insert an international character or a symbol in your document, select Insert | Symbol, and then click the Symbols tab to see the dialog box shown in Figure 6-4. To insert an accented character—to use with French or Spanish documents, for example—choose "(normal text)" from the Font list.

 T I P : If you want to insert a character in another typeface, pull down the Font list and make a new selection. Choose Symbol from the list for Greek and mathematical characters.

Special characters appear in the size and style of the characters at the insertion point. So, if you insert a character into a phrase that is bold and underlined, the character will be bold and underlined.

Click here to insert typographical characters. Double-click a character to add it to a document.

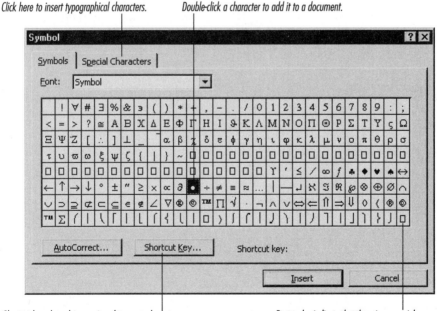

Shortcut keys have been assigned to some characters.

Rectangles indicate that there is no special character at that position in the font.

FIGURE 6-4 Insert special characters by using the Symbol dialog box.

N O T E : The Shortcut Key command button at the bottom of the dialog box lets you customize the keyboard so you can designate a key combination that will insert the character you have selected.

Searching Your Document

Suppose you're looking for a specific reference in your document. You know it's there, but you don't know exactly where. Instead of reading the entire document looking for the reference, use the Find command. The Find command scans your document starting at the location of the insertion point looking for the first occurrence of the word or phrase that you specify, and highlights it. You can repeat the command to find the next occurrence, and so on.

To search your document, select Edit | Find, or press CTRL-F to display the dialog box shown in Figure 6-5.

 T I P : If you cannot see the highlighted found word in your document, move the Find dialog box to the bottom of the window by dragging its title bar.

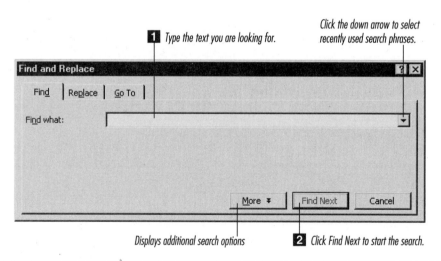

1 Type the text you are looking for.

Click the down arrow to select recently used search phrases.

Displays additional search options

2 Click Find Next to start the search.

FIGURE 6-5 The Find dialog box

To find the next occurrence, click Find Next again or press ENTER. When Word reaches the end of the document, it starts over at the beginning until it reaches the insertion point where it started the find operation. A message appears if Word cannot find the text.

TIP: If you close the Find dialog box and decide you want to continue searching for the same text, press SHIFT-F4. Word begins the search without displaying the Find dialog box.

By default, Word looks for the characters that you type wherever they are, even if they are part of another word. So searching for "ever" will also stop at words such as "forever" and "every."

If you click More in the Find dialog box, you'll be able customize the search with these options:

- **Search**   Lets you scan through the entire document (All), or Down or Up through the document until it reaches the end or start.
- **Match Case**   Determines whether Word pays attention to the case of characters.
- **Find Whole Words Only**   Determines whether Word finds text that is part of another word.
- **Use Wildcards**   Lets you use the character ? to represent any single character in the search phrase. Searching for "m?l", for example, will locate the letters *m* and *l* with any other letter between them, such as the *mil* in "family," and *mel* in "limelight."
- **Sounds Like**   Lets you search for words that sound like the Find What text. For instance, searching for "kranberi" will locate "cranberry."
- **Find All Word Forms**   Locates all tenses of a word. For example, searching for "sing" with this option selected will locate "sing," "sang," and "sung."

Replacing Text Automatically

To err is human, to make the same mistake more than once is downright annoying. Have you ever typed a document only to discover that you've made the same mistake several times? The Replace command searches your document to find text automatically and replace it with something else.

TIP: If you select text first, Word will only make replacements in the selected area.

To start a replace operation, select Edit | Replace. Word displays the dialog box shown in Figure 6-6.

 CAUTION: If you leave the Replace With entry blank, Word will delete every occurrence of the Find What text when you select Replace All.

If you do not want to replace every occurrence of the text, use the Find Next and Replace buttons, instead of Replace All. Click Find Next to locate the first occurrence. If you want to leave this occurrence unchanged, click Find Next again to locate the next occurrence; otherwise, click Replace. Word makes the replacement and then searches for the next occurrence. Click Cancel to close the dialog box.

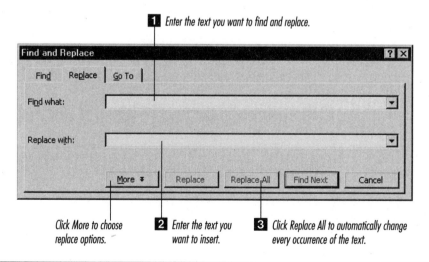

1 Enter the text you want to find and replace.

Click More to choose replace options.

2 Enter the text you want to insert.

3 Click Replace All to automatically change every occurrence of the text.

FIGURE 6-6   Find and Replace options

As you revise and refine a document, you may not be sure which version you want to use for final distribution. Rather than save each version as a separate file, you can actually save all the versions together. With the Version feature, Word keeps track of your changes each time you save the document, so you
can quickly open the file and choose which version to display, edit, and print.

When you are ready to save the first version of your document, choose File | Versions to see the dialog box in Figure 6-7. Click Save Now. In the dialog box that appears, type some comments describing the version, and then click OK to display the Save As dialog box. Enter a name for the document, select a location to store it, and then click OK.

You can now edit the document. To save another version, repeat the same procedure. Because the document already has a name, however, the Save As dialog box will not appear.

When you open the document, you'll see the last saved version. To open an earlier version, choose File | Versions to see the Versions In dialog box listing each of the saved versions. Click the version you want to open, and then click Open. Both versions now appear in their own document window.

To save a version in a separate file, open it, make its window active, and then click the Save button on the Standard toolbar.

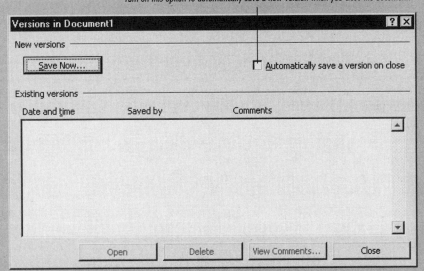

FIGURE 6-7   Tracking document versions

Finding and Replacing Formats and Special Characters

Sometimes you want to find information that you cannot type into the Find What box. For example, suppose you want to find a word, but only when it is in italic format, or where you have an extra blank line between paragraphs. Or perhaps you want to find and replace keystrokes such as TAB and ENTER. When you click More in the Find And Replace dialog box, you'll see command buttons labeled "Format" and "Special."

To find or insert a format, first enter the text you want to find or replace in the Find What or Replace With text box. Next, click More to expand the box, and then click the Format button to display the list shown here:

Selecting an item from the list will display the Word dialog box that controls that format, such as selecting Font to display the Find Font dialog box with a list of font options. Choose the format that you want to find or insert, and then select OK. The format will appear in the Replace dialog box, below the text it refers to.

T I P : Once you select a format, the No Formatting button is no longer dimmed. Click No Formatting to remove the formats from the dialog box.

Locating and inserting special characters and codes is even easier. To find a code, place the insertion point in the Find What text box, and then click the Special button to display a list of codes that you can search for. Click the item that you want to locate or insert. Word will insert a special code into the text box starting with a caret (^). For example, when you want to locate a paragraph mark (which is inserted when you press CTRL-ENTER), Word will insert "^p" into the text box.

To insert special codes, place the insertion point in the Replace With box, and then click the Special button to see a list of codes that you can insert.

The Find All Word Forms feature is so amazing that you must try it. Suppose you type the sentence *He was going to sing to the police, but if he sang he'd be in trouble.* Now to avoid using colloquialisms, you want to change "sing" to "speak" and "sang" to "spoke."

Select Edit | Replace. Type **sing** in the Find What text box. Press TAB, and then type **speak** in the Replace With text box. Click More to display the additional options and select Find All Word Forms.

Select Replace All. Word displays a warning that using Replace All with Find All Word Forms is not recommended. Go ahead—click OK, anyway. A message box appears reporting that two replacements have been made. Select OK to clear the message box, and then close the Replace dialog box. Your sentence now reads *He was going to speak to the police, but if he spoke he'd be in trouble.*

Using Bookmarks

Word lets you set *bookmarks* where you may want to return quickly. For example, suppose you often refer to a specific passage in a long document. If you set a bookmark at that passage, you can quickly move to it when you need to.

T I P : Word automatically sets some bookmarks for you. When you open a document, press SHIFT-F5 to return to your last editing position. In fact, Word actually sets bookmarks at your last four positions. Press SHIFT-F5 to move from position to position.

To set your own bookmark, place the insertion point where you want to set it—or select text at the position—and then choose Insert | Bookmark to see the dialog box shown here.

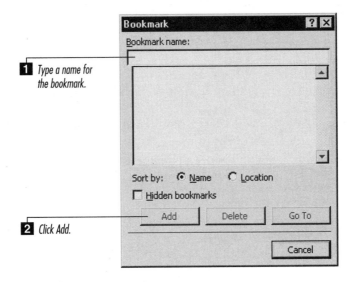

1 Type a name for the bookmark.

2 Click Add.

To move to a bookmark location, select Insert | Bookmark. Your bookmarks will be listed in the dialog box. Note that you can sort the bookmarks by their names or by their location in the document. Double-click on the name of the bookmark, or select it and then choose Go To. Word moves the insertion point to the bookmark position, scrolling the document if necessary. If any text was selected when you created the bookmark, the same text will be selected again.

 N O T E : To delete a bookmark, select its name in the Bookmark dialog box and select Delete.

Highlighting Text

Almost everyone has seen those highlighting pens with brightly colored transparent ink, such as yellow and pink. You use a highlighting pen to mark a section of text that you want to bring to someone's attention. Word comes with its own highlighting pen that lets you mark sections of text in color.

 T I P : The colors also print if you have a color printer. If your printer is not a color printer, Word replaces the colors with varying shades of gray—the lighter the color, the lighter the shade.

 The picture on the Highlight button on the Formatting toolbar (you may have to click More Buttons to display it) shows the highlighting pen with a small square indicating the current highlight color. If the square is white, then highlighting is turned off.

You can highlight text either before or after you select it. If you select the text first, just click the Highlight button to apply the color. To use a different color for selected text, pull down the Highlight list and click the color that you want to apply. The color you select from the list becomes the new default color, indicated in the square on the button.

You can also select text and apply a highlighting color at the same time. When no text is selected, click the Highlight button, or pull down the list and select another color. The mouse pointer will appear as an I-beam with the highlighter pen. Now select the text to apply the color to. To stop highlighting, click the Highlight button again.

To remove highlighting from text, select the text and then choose None from the drop-down list, or select None and then drag over the text. You can also remove highlighting by applying the same color.

TIP: To hide highlighting, clear the Highlight option in the View section of the Options dialog box.

- Turn off Overtype to make sure you don't delete text accidentally.
- After scrolling with the scroll bar, you have to click the mouse where you want to type.
- If you have fax software installed, fax your Word document by choosing File | Send To and then clicking on Fax Recipient.
- To edit an AutoText entry, insert the text into the document, edit it, and then save it again as an AutoText entry using the same abbreviation.
- Don't select dark highlight colors that make text difficult to read onscreen and when printed.
- If you click Replace All by mistake when replacing characters, click the Undo button before doing anything else.
- Save important documents at regular and frequent intervals.
- Use Match Case and Find Whole Words Only with Replace All to avoid unwanted results.
- Do not insert the date as a field in letters or other documents where you want the date to reflect when the document was created, printed, or sent.
- Turn off AutoFormat As You Type when creating documents planned for plain text e-mail.

Formatting Documents

No matter how well written your document, it should look good, too. There are thousands of combinations of formats that you can apply to make your documents look attractive.

Many of the most common formats used in documents are provided as buttons on the Formatting toolbar. Here's the Formatting toolbar moved to a separate line showing all its buttons:

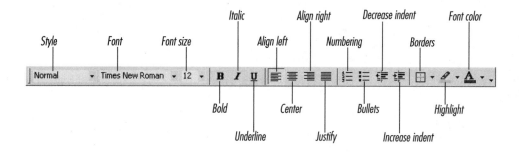

TIP: If you're going to do a lot of formatting, drag the Formatting toolbar below the Standard toolbar, so all its buttons are displayed and easily accessible.

To format new text, choose a format and then type your text. To format text that you've already typed, select the text first and then apply the format. To use a combination of the formats, click each button that you want to apply. You can click the buttons in any order.

TIP: You can format a single word by clicking anywhere in the word and then choosing the button you want from the toolbar—you do not have to select the word first.

Changing Fonts

Office comes with a number of fonts that can be printed in almost any size and any style, and in a variety of colors. To select the font, choose from the Font list in the Formatting toolbar. The fonts are listed in alphabetical order, with recently used fonts beginning the list, separated from the rest by a double line.

To select a font, click its name in the list.

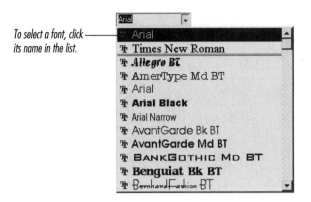

To select a font size, choose from the Size list, or type another size directly in the text box. Fonts are measured in *points.* There are 72 points in one inch, so a 12-point typeface measures 1/6 inch.

The character formatting options in the toolbar are only a sampling of Word's formats. To see all the character formats, select Format | Font. In the dialog box that appears, click the Font tab to display the options shown in Figure 7-1. Make your choices from the dialog box, watching the preview panel to see their effects, and then click OK to apply the formats to your text.

The Text Effects tab of the Font dialog box lets you create text that blinks, flashes, and even looks like little ants moving around the screen. The effects are interesting, but only useful when you look at your document onscreen.

 N O T E : The Character Spacing tab lets you stretch or condense your characters. Use it, for example, to make headlines fit in a certain space.

Selecting Styles

The Style list in the Formatting toolbar lets you quickly apply a combination of formats to selected text or to text you are about to type. (If the list doesn't

Click Default to make the settings the default font for all new documents.

| FIGURE 7-1 | Formatting options in the Font dialog box |

appear, it will after you choose your first style from it when you click More Buttons.) Just pull down the list and choose the style that you want to apply—each is illustrated in the list.

NOTE: You'll learn more about styles, and how to format an entire document at one time, in Chapter 11.

Aligning Text Between the Margins

Probably the first paragraph format you'll want to use is centering. To horizontally center a title, a line of text, or an entire paragraph as you type it, click the Center button on the Formatting toolbar. The insertion point moves to the center of the screen and, as you type, Word shifts characters to keep them centered between the margins. When you want to stop typing centered text, press ENTER to end the centered paragraph, and then click the Align Left button or press CTRL-L. To center text that you've typed, place the insertion point anywhere in the paragraph, and then click the Center button. To center several paragraphs, select them before centering.

Word provides three other formats for aligning text between the margins: Left, Right, and Justify.

- Click the Align Right button (use More Buttons to access it) to align text on the right margin (or press CTRL-R).
- Click the Justify button (use More Buttons to access it) to align every line of a paragraph except the last on both the left and right (or press CTRL-J).
- You can turn off both these formats by clicking on the Align Left button, or by pressing CTRL-L.

TIP: Remember, you can center and right-align text when typing by double-clicking at the center of the page or at the right margin.

Changing Line Spacing

Large sections of single-spaced text can be hard on the eyes and difficult to read. By adjusting the line spacing, you can give your document more impact. To set the line spacing, use these key combinations:

KEYSTROKE	FORMAT
CTRL-1	Single spacing
CTRL-5	1.5 line spacing
CTRL-2	Double spacing
CTRL-0 (zero)	Double spacing between paragraphs

Press the combination before you type to set the spacing for new text. To change line spacing, place the insertion point in the paragraph, or select multiple paragraphs, and then change the spacing.

Except for the CTRL-0 command, the keystrokes are not toggles. After typing double-spaced text, for example, return to single spacing by pressing CTRL-1.

Indenting Paragraphs

If you want to indent the first line of a paragraph, just press the TAB key. But you might want to indent every line of a paragraph from the left margin, or from both the right and left margins. You might also want to automatically indent the first line of every paragraph to save yourself the trouble of pressing TAB.

To indent every line of a paragraph from the left margin, click the Increase Indent button in the Formatting toolbar. Each time you do, Word moves the indentation to the next tab stop to the left. As with other formats, indentation will be carried to the next paragraph when you press ENTER.

To clear the indentation—that is, to move the paragraph back toward the left margin—click the Decrease Indent button.

You can also create indentations by using the ruler. To indent text from the right, drag the Right Indent marker, the small triangular object at the right end of the ruler, to the position at which you want to indent the text.

Right Indent marker

Right Indent

TIP: The numbers along the ruler indicate the distance from the left margin, not from the left edge of the page.

To indent text from the left, drag the appropriate indentation markers on the left section of the ruler:

First Line Indent marker indents just the first line of each paragraph.

Hanging Indent marker indents every line except the first.

Left Indent marker indents every line in the paragraph.

T I P : When you insert a tab at the beginning of an existing paragraph, Word moves the First Line Indent marker to the first tab stop position instead of actually inserting a tab code.

You can also indent the first line of every paragraph and create hanging indentations by using the Tab Type button to the left of the ruler. As you'll learn in Chapter 8, when you click the button, it cycles through the types of tab that will be set. In addition to tab types, it also cycles through these options:

First line indentations

Hanging indentation

Click the button to choose the type of indentation you want, and then click on the ruler where you want to set the indentation.

To create a hanging indentation with the keyboard, press CTRL-T. Each time you press CTRL-T, the hanging indentation will increase to the next tab stop. Cancel hanging indentation, or just reduce the distance, by pressing CTRL-SHIFT-T.

You can set text alignment, spacing, and other formats from the Paragraph dialog box, shown in Figure 7-2. To display the dialog box, select Format | Paragraph, and then click on the Indents And Spacing tab.

Duplicating Formats with Format Painter

 Once you go to the trouble of selecting a combination that you like for one section of text, you do not have to make the selections all over again for some other text. For example, if you choose a font, size, and style combination for a subtitle, you can use the Format Painter button (use More Buttons to access it) in the toolbar to quickly apply the same combination to another subtitle.

To copy a *character format*, place the insertion point in the text that uses that format and then click the Format Painter button. To copy *paragraph formats*, drag past the end of the paragraph so the selection includes what appears to be a blank space at the end of the paragraph, and then click the Format Painter button.

The mouse pointer appears as an I-beam and a small paintbrush. Select the text that you want to apply the format to, and then release the mouse button to apply the formats and turn off Format Painter.

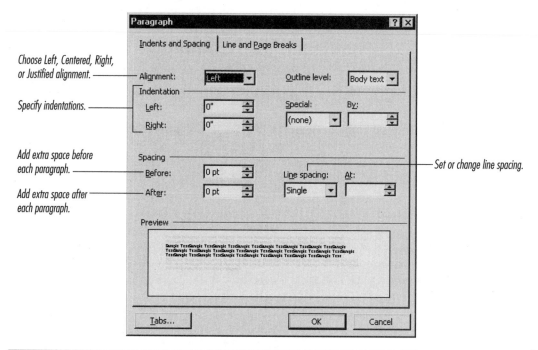

Choose Left, Centered, Right, or Justified alignment.

Specify indentations.

Add extra space before each paragraph.

Add extra space after each paragraph.

Set or change line spacing.

FIGURE 7-2 Use the Paragraph dialog box to format paragraphs

If you want to apply the same formats to more than one section of text, double-click the Format Painter button. After you select text and release the mouse button, the Format Painter function stays on, and the paintbrush will remain with the I-beam. Select any other sections of text to which you want to apply the same format. To turn off the Format Painter function, click the Format Painter button again or press ESC.

Hyphenating Text

Hyphenation divides some words between lines to avoid large blank spaces between words or at the right margin. You can have Word hyphenate automatically as you type, or you can have it hyphenate a selection of existing text. To turn on hyphenation, select Tools | Language and click Hyphenation to display the dialog box shown here.

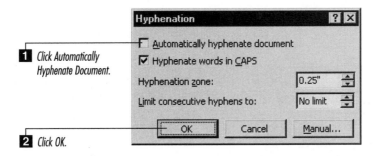

1 *Click Automatically Hyphenate Document.*

2 *Click OK.*

Now as you type, Word decides if a word can be hyphenated at the right margin and adds the hyphen for you.

Changing Margins

The top, bottom, left, and right margins determine how much text you can fit on a page. Word uses default left and right margins of 1.25 inches and top and bottom margins of 1 inch. You can change the margins with the ruler as well as with a dialog box.

To set an exact margin position, select File | Page Setup, and then choose the Margins tab. Enter your settings in the Top, Bottom, Left, and Right text boxes of the dialog box that appears, and then select OK.

To change margins by dragging along the ruler, you must be in either Print Layout or Print Preview view. In these views, you drag the *boundary markers,* the lines between the white and gray areas of the ruler, as shown in Figure 7-3. To see the top or bottom boundary markers, you have to scroll to see the top or bottom of the page. You'll know you're pointing to the marker if the mouse pointer is shaped like a two-headed arrow and the name of the margin appears in a screen tip. As you drag the mouse, a dotted line appears down or across the screen to help you judge the width of the margin.

T I P : If you want to be more exact, hold down ALT while you drag the mouse so Word displays the exact measurements in inches along the ruler.

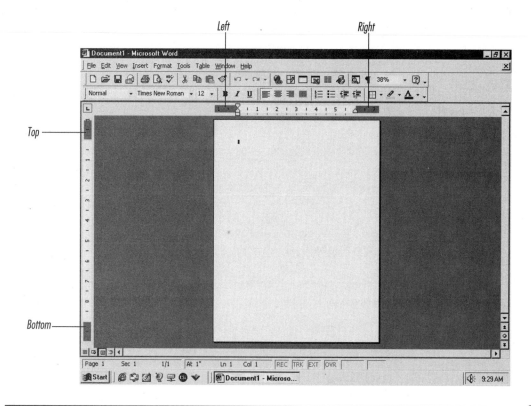

FIGURE 7-3 Use these boundary markers to change margins

If your document is not divided into sections, which you'll learn about later, changing margins affects the entire document, regardless of the position of the insertion point. For example, if you are on page 10 of a 50-page document, changing the margins affects all 50 pages.

NOTE: To see the rulers in Print Preview mode, click the View Ruler button in the Print Preview toolbar.

Pages destined to be bound—if only in a three-ring binder—present some additional formatting opportunities.

In most cases, the binding will take up some of the space on each page, such as space taken up by the punched holes for a ring binder. When you open a book, this space in the middle between the two pages is called the *gutter*. Half of the gutter is on the right side of even-numbered pages; the other half is on the left side of odd-numbered pages.

To compensate for this space, so that the text will still appear centered between the margins when readers open the book, set the width in the Gutter text box in the Margins tab of the Page Setup dialog box, and make sure the Gutter Position is set at Left.

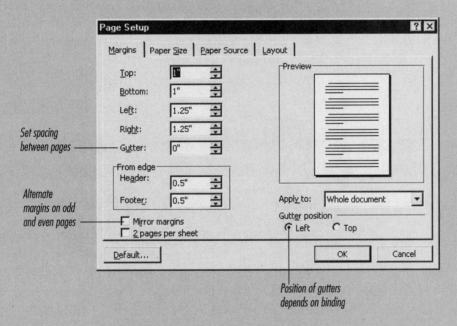

Set spacing between pages

Alternate margins on odd and even pages

Position of gutters depends on binding

To leave extra space on the outside of the pages, the margins on the right of odd-numbered pages and on the left of even-numbered pages must be expanded. The opposite is true if you want the extra space on the inside edges of the page. To format pages with extra inside or outside margins, turn on Mirror Margins in the Page Setup dialog box.

The Page Setup dialog box also includes the 2 Pages Per Sheet option. Use this feature to divide each printed sheet into two pages—each with its own headers, footers, and page numbers. You can cut the printed sheets in half.

Changing Page Size

Word's default page size is 8½ by 11 inches. To use a different page size, such as legal size, you click the Paper Size tab in the Page Setup dialog box and select from the options shown in Figure 7-4.

To use a size that is not already defined, select Custom Size from the Paper Size list, and then enter the dimensions in the Width and Height boxes. Changing the paper size does not change the default margins, so you may want to check the margins before selecting OK.

To change orientation, click either Portrait or Landscape in the Orientation section. The default setting is *portrait,* in which your lines of text print across the narrow dimension of the page. You can also select *landscape* orientation, in which your lines print across the longer dimension of the page. Landscape orientation is useful when you're printing wide tables and other documents that require long lines.

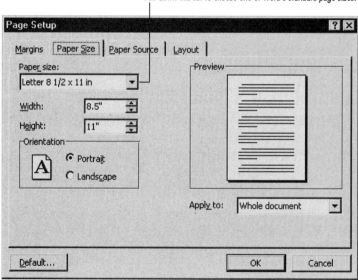

FIGURE 7-4   The Paper Size options

Paper Source

If your printer is equipped with more than one paper tray, you may use one for letterhead paper, another for plain paper or even envelopes. One tray will be used as the default. To use a tray other than the default, you must select it in the Paper Source tab of the Page Setup dialog box.

In the First Page list, select the source that you want to use for the first page of the document. In the Other Pages list, select the source you want for the second and subsequent pages. If you want every page to be from the same source, select the same options in both lists.

Using Sections

Now that you know how to format pages, you are ready to delve into Word's sections. *Sections* let you have more than one page format in the same document. Formats such as page size and top and bottom margins apply to an entire page. If you want to type a letter and an envelope in one document, for instance, you need to have two sections. One section will be formatted in the size of the letter; the other section will be formatted in the size of the envelope. Each section is on its own page. To combine single-column and double-column text on the same page, you'll need two sections as well. In this case, each column arrangement is in a different section but on the same page—the single-column text will be in one section, the double-column text, in another section.

The type of break determines how Word applies the formats of the section. Here are the options:

OPTION	EFFECT
Next Page	The section break is also a page break, and the section starts after the section break line. The option is also called *New Page*.
Continuous	The section break does not insert a page break, so you can combine multiple formats on one page, such as left and right margins.
Even Page	The section break is also a page break, and Word forces the next page to be even numbered.
Odd Page	The section break is also a page break, and Word forces the next page to be odd numbered.

N O T E : If you select a page setting that cannot exist on the same page as the previous section, Word will insert a page break for you and the format will continue on the next page.

To have Word insert the section breaks for you, place the insertion point where you want to change the format. Select File | Page Setup and select the tab (Margins, Paper Size, and so on) containing the option you want to change. Adjust the formats as desired, and then pull down the list labeled "Apply To" to see these options:

- **Whole Document**   Applies your changes to the entire document, without inserting a section break.
- **This Point Forward**   Inserts a section break and applies the format to all the text from the insertion point to the end of the document or to the next section break, whichever is first.
- **This Section**   Only appears if your document already contains sections and applies the format only to the current section.
- **Selected Text**   Only appears if you select text before displaying the Page Setup dialog box and inserts section breaks before and after the text.

The default section break when you choose This Point Forward will also insert a page break. If you want to combine formats on one page, click the Layout tab and choose Continuous from the Section Start list.

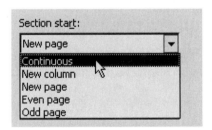

 T I P : As you scroll through a document that contains sections, the Sec indicator in the status bar will show you which section you are in.

Using the Break Dialog Box

Another way to create a section is to enter the section break yourself and then apply the formats to it. To insert a section break, select Insert | Break to display the Break dialog box.

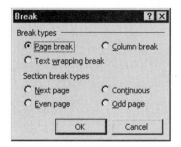

Select the type of break you want to insert, click OK, and then use the Page Setup dialog box to format your page, choosing This Section in the Apply To list.

 NOTE: To delete a section break, click on it and then press DEL. This also deletes the formats applied to the text above the section break line, and the text will become formatted according to the page setting of the text that is below the line.

Envelopes and Letters

One of the most common reasons to use two paper sizes in one document is to create a letter and its envelope. Rather than mess with sections and page sizes yourself, however, let Word handle it for you.

 TIP: To get help writing a letter, choose Tools | Letter Wizard; then choose options from the dialog box that appears.

Type your letter, including an inside address. Then select Tools | Envelopes And Labels, and click the Envelopes tab to display the options shown in Figure 7-5. Word copies the mailing address from the letter and displays it in the Delivery Address box. If the address is incorrect, click in the box and edit the address. To include your return address on the envelope, select the Return Address box and type your address.

TIP: If your letter contains more than one address, select the address you want to appear on the envelope before displaying the dialog box. Word will use the selected text for the mailing address.

Now click Add To Document. A dialog box appears asking if you want to save the return address as the default for other envelopes. Select No or Yes as it pleases you. Word inserts the envelope at the beginning of your document, separated from the letter with a section break.

NOTE: If you want to print the envelope without adding it to the document, click Print in the Envelopes tab.

Click here to select a name from your Windows address book.

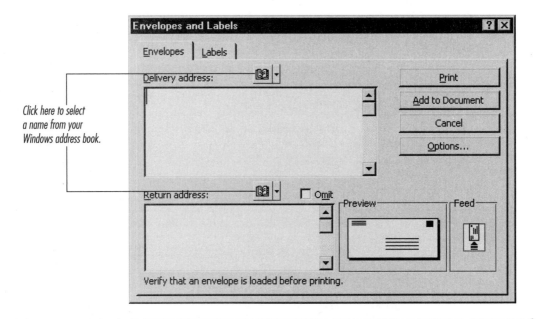

FIGURE 7-5 The Envelopes options in the Envelopes And Labels dialog box

Enhancing Envelopes

You have many options for customizing envelopes. One of the most common customizations is adding a barcode so the automatic sorting equipment at the post office reads the code to speed your letter's progress.

In the Envelopes And Labels dialog box, click the Options command button to display the Envelope Options dialog box. Click the Envelope Options tab to see the options shown in Figure 7-6.

To add the barcode, click Delivery Point Barcode. The POSTNET barcode using the ZIP code in the delivery address will appear just above the address in the Preview panel. If you choose to include a delivery point barcode, you will also see the FIM-A Courtesy Reply Mail option on the dialog box. The FIM-A code identifies the front side of the envelope for automated presorting equipment.

The other envelope options determine the size of the envelope, the font used to print the delivery and return addresses, and the position of the addresses. If you want to select another standard envelope size or set a custom size, pull down the Envelope Size list. If you want to print the address in another font, select the appropriate font button, and then choose a font from the dialog box that appears. To change the position of either address, enter the measurement in the appropriate From Left and From Top boxes.

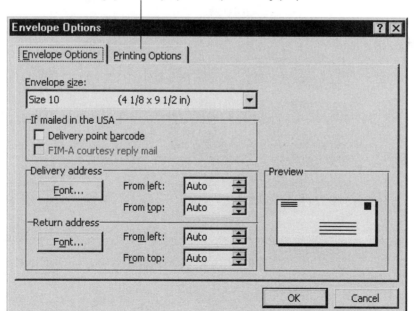

Use the Printing Options tab to specify how envelopes feed through your printer.

FIGURE 7-6 More envelope options

Creating Drop Capitals

A nice finishing touch for a professional-looking document is a *drop capital*. A drop capital is a large initial letter or letters that begin a paragraph, as illustrated here:

> Sliding Billy Watson was a vaudeville star and producer who gave W. C. Fields his first job and who started Fanny Brice in her career. He gained his name from his trademark slide across the stage, a precursor to Michael Jackson's now famous Moon Walk. As a comedian, Billy worked his way up from a bit player to the lead role, but he gained most fame as both actor and producer in many popular vaudeville and burlesque shows. One of his most popular shows was Girls From Happyland, which Billy wrote with lyricist Albert Bagley.
>
> Billy was born as Wolf Shapiro on October 12, 1876. His family moved from New York to Philadelphia, where Billy tried to settle down into a quiet family life. However, the call of the stage was too difficult for him to resist. He abandoned his wife and two children for the limelight and fame of vaudeville. In 1907, Billy married his second wife, Nellie Pfleger, who starred with him in many shows. However, life was to take some strange twists. Nellie was murdered in 1926 by a disgruntled employee of her club, the Three Hundred Club in Freeport, Long Island. Throughout the 1930s, Billy's first wife pursued him for failure to pay her $25 per week alimony. Billy was arrested a number of times, appeared in court in several states, and was even accused of bigamy.

To create a drop capital, select the letter or letters that you want to use, and then select Format | Drop Cap (you may have to expand the menu) to see this dialog box:

Select the position for the character.

Choose an alternate font, if desired.

Enter the number of lines high you want the character.

Set the distance of the letter from the text in the Distance From Text box.

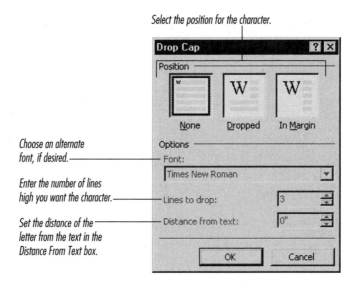

If you are in Normal view, a dialog box appears asking if you want to change to Page Layout view—select Yes to see the drop capital.

Adding Backgrounds, Borders, and Shading

To really call attention to text, consider surrounding it in borders or shading its background. You can add a background and border to the entire page, or just to selected paragraphs.

Formatting Pages

To add a color background to the entire document, choose Format | Background (you may have to expand the menu), and then choose a color from the palette that appears. For even more special effects, however, choose Fill Effects from the palette to display the dialog box shown in Figure 7-7 and then make your selection.

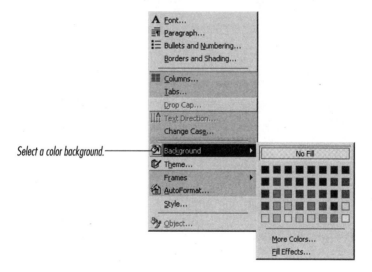

Select a color background.

Here's a summary of the pages of this dialog box.

- Gradients fill the background with colors. You can choose one color and have it range from light to dark, two colors, or from 24 preset color combinations.
- Textures are photograph-like backgrounds. Word gives you 24 to choose from, such as weave, stone, and denim.
- Patterns are geometric patterns of lines, dots, or boxes. Word gives you 48 choices, such as a checkerboard or brick pattern, and you can select foreground and background colors.
- Picture lets you choose any graphic file, even scanned pictures.

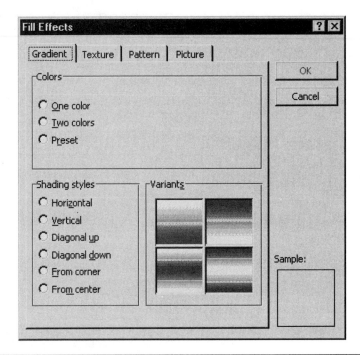

FIGURE 7-7 Adding borders and backgrounds to pages

To add a border around the entire page, select Format | Borders And Shading. Click the Page Border tab of the dialog box that appears to see the options shown in Figure 7-8. Use the presets to quickly remove all borders, surround text in a box, and create a shadow or 3-D box. Create a custom box using the steps shown in Figure 7-8.

The buttons in the Preview section let you choose where to insert a line. To change a line style, click the line in the Preview section and then choose the style.

Formatting Paragraphs

You can also add a background and borders to individual paragraphs. Use the Shading tab of the Borders And Shading dialog box to add shading or a pattern

1 Select the line style.

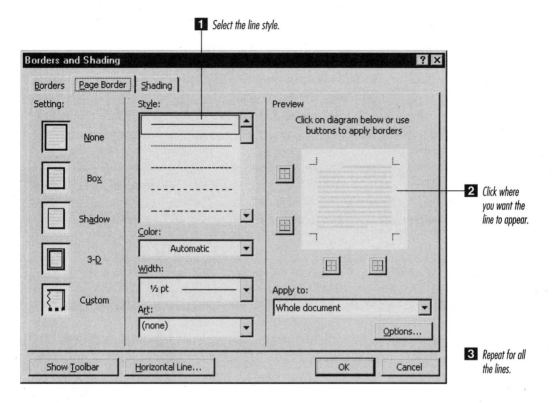

2 Click where you want the line to appear.

3 Repeat for all the lines.

FIGURE 7-8 Placing a border around the page

behind selected text. To add a border, use either the Borders tab of the dialog box, or pull down the list next to the Borders button on the Formatting toolbar (use More Buttons to access it) and choose from these options:

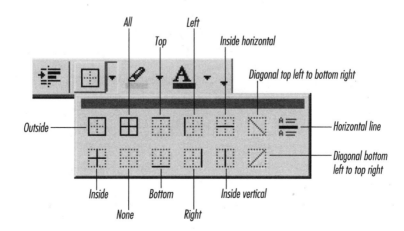

TIP: Clicking on the button, rather than pulling down the list, applies the line shown in the button icon.

When you enclose text in a box, Word extends the box from the left to the right margin, even if you've selected a short title centered on the page. Indent the paragraph on the left and right to make the box narrow enough to just surround the text.

If you only want to insert a horizontal line across the screen, the quickest way is to use AutoFormat As You Type. Type at least three hyphens or equal signs and then press ENTER. Word replaces the hyphens with a single line across the screen and the equal sign with a double line across the screen.

 TIP: For a different line across the screen, click the Horizontal Line button in the Borders And Shading dialog box, and then double-click on the line you want to add. To learn more about the window that displays these lines, see "Inserting ClipArt" in Chapter 10.

Printing Labels

Labels are easy to print in Word. Select Tools | Envelopes And Labels, click the Labels tab, and then click Options.

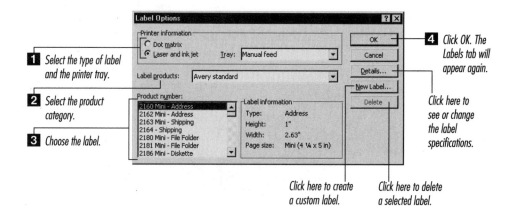

1 Select the type of label and the printer tray.

2 Select the product category.

3 Choose the label.

4 Click OK. The Labels tab will appear again.

Click here to see or change the label specifications.

Click here to create a custom label.

Click here to delete a selected label.

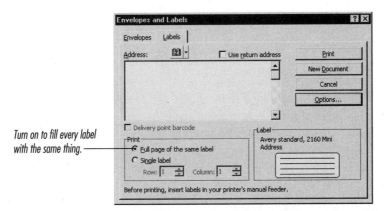

Turn on to fill every label with the same thing.

If you want text to appear on every label, enter it in the Address box. If you want to type different information in each label, leave the Address box blank. Click New Document to display labels as shown in Figure 7-9; then edit, format, and print the labels.

T I P : If you want the same text on each label without adding any other text or formats, enter it in the Address box and then click Print.

Use the Single Label option in the Envelopes And Labels dialog box to print one label on the page of labels. Turn on the option, designate the row and column of the label you want to print, and then enter the information in the Address box. Click Print to print the label.

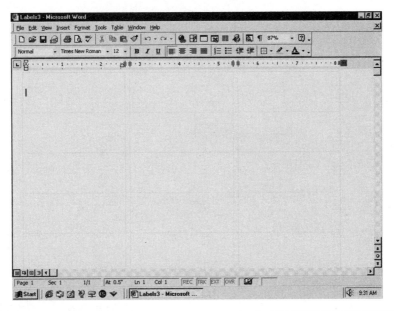

FIGURE 7-9 Labels in a document

- Avoid having too many fonts and sizes in a document—it makes text more difficult to read.
- Font animations look great onscreen, but affect how the text appears when printed.
- If you change line spacing frequently, add line spacing buttons to the Formatting toolbar by clicking on its More Buttons option, then clicking Add or Remove Buttons.
- If you have difficulty setting indentations and margins with the ruler, just use the Format Paragraph or Page Setup dialog boxes instead.
- Some older laser printers have difficulty printing pages dense with text, so test your printer ahead of time.
- Word warns you if you set your margins too close to the edges of the page—select Fix if you see this warning to use the minimum margins your printer allows.
- Make sure you don't choose a page size your printer cannot handle. Check your printer's documentation for a list of supported page sizes, or experiment with various sizes when you have time.
- The concept of sections may appear confusing, but it pays to learn about them to get the most from Word.
- Before feeding labels through your printer, make certain that they are attached solidly to their carrier sheet and avoid feeding partial sheets.
- Some envelopes are not designed for laser printers, and the flaps will stick when printed. Buy a good quality envelope or one designed for copiers and printers.

Working with Tabs, Tables, and Columns

Not all text is most effective in regular paragraph format. There are times when you'll need to enter columns of words or numbers in a document, or to create a table to best illustrate a point. You might even want to type in columns if you're producing a newsletter, annual report, or other publication. All these formats are easy to use with Word.

Setting Tabs

Some information just looks best in orderly columns across the screen. It's quick and easy to line up columns of names or numbers, for example, by just pressing the TAB key to reach the spot you want and then typing. While Word comes with tab stops set every half inch, you can set various types of tabs and change their position. Figure 8-1 shows some of the types of tabs you can set, and how text looks using them.

It is easiest to set tabs with the ruler. On the far left of the ruler is a button that represents the type of tab. Each time you click the button, the icon on it changes to illustrate the type of tab that you set:

| Left | Center | Right | Decimal | Bar |

TIP: As with other formats, setting, moving, and deleting tab stops affect only the paragraph in which the insertion point is placed, selected paragraphs, or new text starting at the position of the insertion point.

To set a tab, first select the type of tab, and then click on the ruler where you want to set the tab stop. Word deletes the default tab stops to the left of those you set.

Left	Center	Right	Decimal	Bar
Harvey	Sweig	Planner	11.00	50
Alan	Woodin	Entertainer	256.00	54
Ellen	Miller	Salesperson	5.70	46
Alan	Zakuto	Doctor	76.09	35
Adam	Chesin	Writer	4454.09	36

FIGURE 8-1 Types of tabs

To delete a tab stop, point to its marker in the ruler, and then drag the mouse down into the typing area. To move a tab stop to a different position, drag its indicator to a new position on the ruler.

Setting Tabs with the Dialog Box

For even more tab options, select Format | Tabs (you may have to expand the menu) to display the dialog box shown in Figure 8-2.

- To change the type of the tab, click it in the list and then click the alignment option.
- To delete a tab stop, click its position on the list box, and then click the Clear command button. To delete all your custom tabs, reinstating Word's defaults, click the Clear All command button.
- To set a series of evenly spaced tabs, such as every 0.75 inch along the ruler, enter the spacing in the Default Tab Stops box.

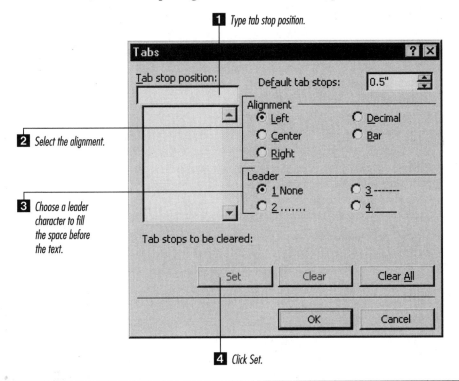

1 Type tab stop position.

2 Select the alignment.

3 Choose a leader character to fill the space before the text.

4 Click Set.

FIGURE 8-2 The Tabs dialog box

Typing Lists with Bullets and Numbers

Word has several built-in features that let you create numbered lists and bulleted lists. A *numbered* list inserts a number in front of each paragraph; a *bulleted* list inserts a bullet. The default bullet is a small circle, although you can change it to an arrow, diamond, asterisk, or any other character in any font. You can create lists as you type or by selecting existing text.

Using AutoFormat As You Type

The quickest way to create a list is to use AutoFormat As You Type. For a numbered list, type a number or letter, followed by a period (1., A., a., I., or i.). For a bulleted list, type an asterisk (*) or hyphen (-). Then press the SPACEBAR or TAB to insert space, type the first entry of the list, and press ENTER. Word inserts the next number in the sequence, or replaces the character with a bullet, and turns on hanging indentation. To stop the list, just press ENTER to insert a blank line after the last item.

N O T E : You can also start and stop a numbered list by clicking on the Numbering button on the Formatting toolbar, and, a bulleted list by clicking the Bullets button on the toolbar.

When you create a numbered list, you can type an outline. Enter a lower level for the outline by pressing TAB or by clicking on the Increase Indent button in the Formatting toolbar. Enter a higher level by pressing SHIFT-TAB or by clicking on the Decrease Indent button.

To select other list formats, to turn lists on or off, or to change the type of numbers or bullets, select Format | Bullets And Numbering to see the dialog box shown in Figure 8-3.

Click the Customize button to change these settings:

- The number format, style, starting number, and font
- The bullet character
- The alignment (Left, Center, or Right) of the number or bullet in the space before the first line of text
- The amount of indentation of the text from the number or bullet

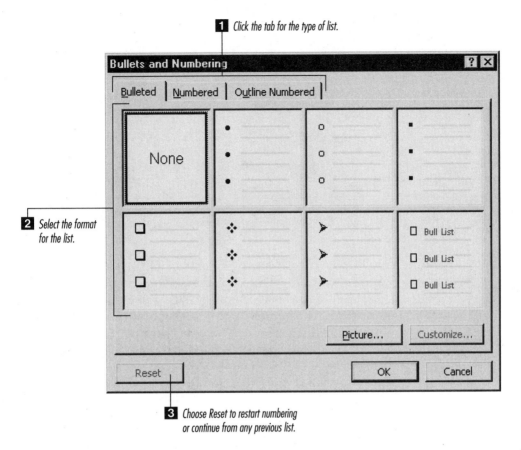

1 Click the tab for the type of list.

2 Select the format for the list.

3 Choose Reset to restart numbering or continue from any previous list.

FIGURE 8-3 The Bullets And Numbering dialog box

Creating Tables

Tab stops are great for creating lists on the fly, but when you really want to organize columns, nothing beats a table. Tables make it easier to read columns of numbers, and they help show relationships and trends that cannot easily be expressed in text. You can create a table by dragging the mouse or by selecting from a dialog box.

Building a Table

To create the table with the mouse, click the Insert Table button on the Standard toolbar. A miniature grid appears representing the rows and columns of a table.

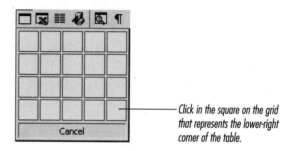

Click in the square on the grid that represents the lower-right corner of the table.

To create a table up to 16 rows and 10 columns, hold down the mouse button and drag down and to the right. As you drag, squares in the grid become selected and the number of rows and columns will be indicated at the bottom of the grid. Drag the mouse until you select the number of rows and columns that you want in the table, and then release the mouse button.

Word inserts a blank table extending from the left to the right margin, with equal columns. The gridlines indicate the size of each *cell*—the intersection of a row and column where you enter text—but they will not print. As with a spreadsheet program, the table's row and column numbers reference each of its cells; for example, the upper-left cell is A1. The ruler shows the width of the cells.

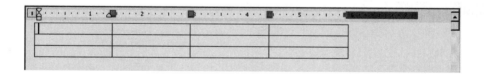

To enter text into a table, place the insertion point in a cell and type. You can place the insertion point by clicking in the cell or by pressing TAB, SHIFT-TAB, or the arrow keys. If you type more text than can fit in a cell, Word automatically wraps the text and increases the row height.

CAUTION: Do not press ENTER to move out of a cell. When you press ENTER, the height of the current cell will increase by one line. To delete the extra line, press BACKSPACE.

When you want to perform a function on a cell, row, or column, you have to select it first. Click in the cell you want to select, or any cell in the row or column; pull down the Table menu; point to Select; and choose what you want: Table, Row, Column, or Cell. To select a single cell, click three times in it. Or, point just inside the left margin of the cell so the pointer is shaped like an arrow and click once. Drag over cells to select more than one.

Other Ways to Create Tables

To create a table up to 31 columns and thousands of rows, select Table | Insert and click Table. In the Insert Table dialog box that appears, enter the number of columns and rows desired in the appropriate text boxes. Click OK to create the table—or to create a formatted table, click the AutoFormat button, and then in the AutoFormat dialog box that appears choose a table style. The Insert Table dialog box also lets you set the size of the columns or have columns adjust automatically as you enter text.

When you want to create a complex table layout, the easiest way may be to draw it. This is especially true when you are trying to duplicate a table that you have on paper or on a form. Select Table | Draw Table to switch to Page Layout view and to see the Tables And Borders toolbar. The mouse changes to a pencil. Drag the mouse in the document to draw a rectangle the size of the table. Continue using the mouse to draw connecting lines. Point to one border line and drag toward the other side. You don't have to draw all the way—just enough until you see a dotted straight line. Then release the mouse and Word completes the line for you.

Working with Tables

Word provides a number of special ways to work with tables. When the insertion point is in a table, you can use the Table menu, the shortcut menu that appears when you right-click on the table, or the Tables And Borders toolbar, shown here. If the toolbar is not displayed, right-click on any toolbar and choose Tables And Borders from the shortcut menu that appears. The Table menu, shortcut menu, and toolbar contain some features in common, but may offer different options as well. In this chapter, assume that a feature is in all three locations unless otherwise mentioned.

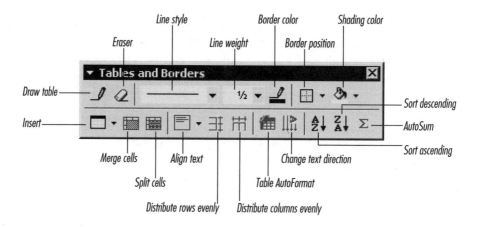

Table Position and Size

Word treats a table like a graphic object. In Print Layout view, you can move the table anywhere on the page and change its size by dragging. Move the mouse pointer anywhere in the table to see these two items:

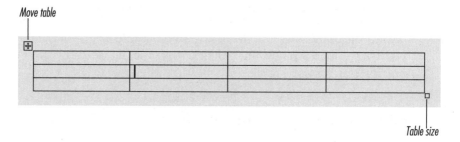

To change the position of the table, point to the Move Table box so the mouse appears as a four-headed arrow and then drag. You can move the table anywhere on the page. If the table is not as wide as the page, text flows around it on either side.

To change the size of the table, drag the Table Size handle at the lower-right corner. This changes the height of rows and width of columns, but not the size of text.

Formatting Text in Tables

Use the Formatting toolbar and the Format menu to format text in a table just as you can for any text. You can also adjust the alignment of text in a cell, and its *direction*. Right-click on a cell and choose Text Direction, for example, to place text vertically in the cell, in either direction, such as this:

TEXT DIRECTION	TEXT DIRECTION	TEXT DIRECTION	

To adjust the position of text within the cell, right-click on the cell and choose Cell Alignment to display these options:

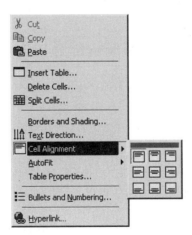

Splitting and Merging Cells

After you create a table, you may not want each cell to be the same size. Use the Split Cells command to divide one or more cells into columns or rows. Select the cell you want to split, and then choose the command from the Table menu, shortcut menu (only for a single cell), or the Tables And Borders toolbar.

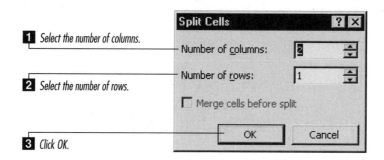

1 Select the number of columns.

2 Select the number of rows.

3 Click OK.

Use the Merge Cells command to combine two or more adjacent cells in a row into one. Select the cells that you want to combine and then choose Merge Cells. Any contents in the cells will also be combined. Merge Cells is useful when you want to use one column label for two existing columns of data. You can also merge cells by clicking on the Eraser button on the Table And Borders toolbar and dragging over the gridline you want to remove.

Changing Column Width

When you create a table with each column the same width and each row the same height, there may be a lot of wasted space. You can make a column narrower, for example, if it contains all short entries, or you can make it wider to display more text. You can also change the height of rows.

To automatically adjust columns for the amount of text they contain, choose Table | AutoFit and click AutoFit To Contents. Now as you enter text, columns expand to accommodate your entry. Choose AutoFit To Window to expand the table so it fits between the margins. To quickly make all columns the same size, choose Distribute Columns Evenly from the menu.

If you have a steady hand, you can adjust the width of columns with the mouse and the ruler. When you place the insertion point in a table, the horizontal ruler indicates each column width, and you'll see *column markers*—the gray boxes with cross-hatching—indicating the space between columns.

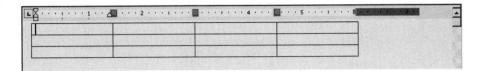

Drag the column marker to change column width.

Changing Gridlines and Shading

The gridlines that you see around the table add visual impact. You can customize the lines, and even add shading to highlight specific rows, columns, or cells.

Use the Border button on the Tables And Borders toolbar to remove or change border lines just as you learned to use it for paragraphs in Chapter 7. Select the cell that you want to apply the border to; then select an option from the Border button list, or click the button to accept the default shown on the button icon.

Inserting and Deleting Cells, Rows, and Columns

You may create a table, only to realize later that you did not make it the correct size. When this happens, you'll need to insert or delete rows or columns.

If you only need to insert an additional row at the end of the table, place the insertion point in the last cell of the last row and press TAB. Word inserts a blank row.

To insert rows, columns, or cells elsewhere, use the Table | Insert command:

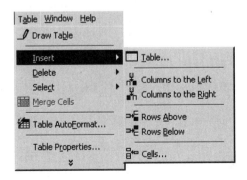

To insert a column into your table, for example, click in a column that you want to appear to the right of the new one, and then choose Columns To The Left from the menu.

If you choose to insert cells, you'll see this dialog box:

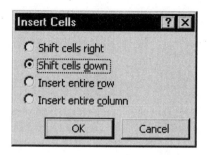

Choosing Insert Entire Row or Insert Entire Column will add a row or column, respectively. If you select Shift Cells Right, Word adds a cell just to that row. If you select Shift Cells Down, Word inserts a new row at the end of the table and shifts down only the cells in the current column.

Use the Table option to create a table within a table, such as this:

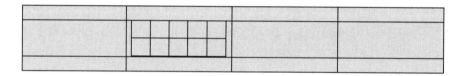

Delete the entire table, cells, rows, or columns in the same way, by using the Table | Delete command.

 TIP: To delete table lines but leave the text as tabbed columns, click anywhere in the table, point to Convert in the Table I, and choose Table To Text.

Special Table Formatting

There are several ways to make changes to the entire table at one time.

To format the entire table, place the insertion point anywhere in the table, and then select Table | Table AutoFormat. Word displays the dialog box shown in Figure 8-4.

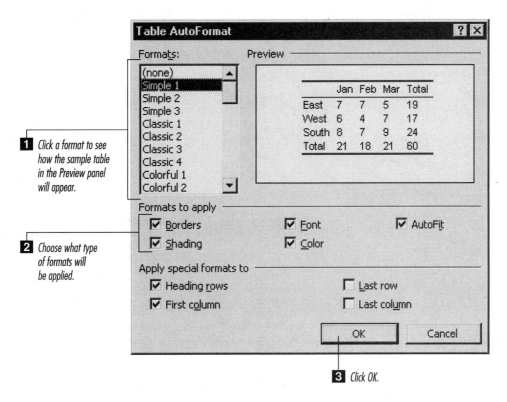

1 *Click a format to see how the sample table in the Preview panel will appear.*

2 *Choose what type of formats will be applied.*

3 *Click OK.*

FIGURE 8-4 The Table AutoFormat dialog box

By default, the command applies the borders, shading, and font of your selected format, and AutoFit will make the columns the proper width. If the format calls for it, heading rows containing column labels and the first entire column will be formatted differently than the other rows and columns. Customize the formats by selecting the appropriate check boxes. For example, deselecting Heading Rows will format the first row of the table like the remaining rows.

You can also choose Table | Table Properties to display a dialog box with four tabs:

- **Table** Lets you position the table between the right and left margins, and choose how text wraps around tables that do not fill the page.
- **Row** Sets the row height and creates *headers,* rows that are repeated on each page.
- **Column** Sets column width.
- **Cell** Adjusts cell width and the alignment of text within the cell.

Performing Calculations in Tables

A Word table has many of the same characteristics as a spreadsheet. Just as with a spreadsheet, you can perform calculations on the numbers in your table. You can display the sum of values in a row or column, compute averages, and insert formulas that reference cells and other values.

The quickest calculation you can make is to total the values in rows or columns. Place the insertion point in a blank cell below the column of numbers or to the right of a row of numbers, and then click AutoSum on the Table And Borders toolbar. If the toolbar is not displayed, select Table | Formula to display the dialog box shown here.

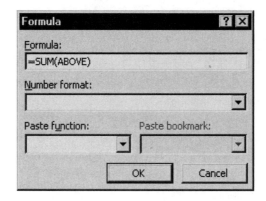

The formula =SUM(ABOVE) indicates that it will calculate the sum of the values above the current cell; =SUM(LEFT) means that Word will calculate and insert the total of the values in that row. You can also select a format in which to display the resulting value. When you select OK, Word will compute and display the value in the cell.

Create your own formulas using cell references, numeric values, and mathematical operators. For example, entering **=A10–A9** will calculate and display the difference between the values in cell A10 and cell A9. Note that all formulas must start with the equal sign.

In addition to formulas, you can also use *functions*. The default formula using the word "SUM" is an example of a function. It automatically includes all the values above or to the left of the cell. So the formula =SUM(LEFT) might perform the same math as =A1+B1+C1+D1+E1+F1, and so on. To choose another function, such as AVERAGE, select it from the Paste Function list.

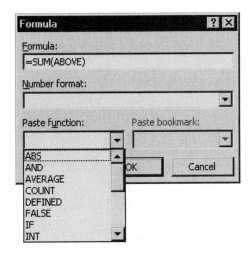

Word inserts the function in the Formula text box. Then you can edit the formula so it includes the cell references or values that you want to use in the calculation. For instance, you can compute an average on a range of cells using ABOVE, BELOW, LEFT, or RIGHT, as in =AVERAGE(ABOVE), or you can use specific cells, as in =AVERAGE(A1, A2, A3).

 TIP: If you change the value in a referenced cell, select the entire table and press F9 to recalculate values.

Creating Columns

Newsletters, annual reports, and other published documents may be formatted in columns, where text flows from one column to the next on the page, from left to right. Columns make a document look special, yet with Word they are easy to create. Once you tell Word the number of columns you want, Word will take care of the text flow for you. As you insert or delete text, Word will shift text from column to column, or from page to page, as necessary.

Using the Toolbar

Columns that you create with the toolbar affect the current section. So if your document is not divided into sections, all of it will be affected. To combine a single column and multiple columns on the same page, or in the same document, you have to insert a section break where you want the change in columns to occur.

By selecting text first, however, you can avoid having to create a section yourself. For example, suppose you want to type some single-column text to be followed by two columns, as shown in Figure 8-5. Type all the text of the document. Then select the text that you want to appear in two columns.

To create columns, pull down the Columns button on the Standard toolbar (you may have to use More Buttons to display it) to see an illustration of four columns and the word "Cancel":

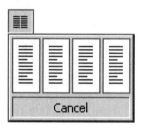

To create columns, click the column in the diagram that represents the number of columns you want. For example, to create two columns, click the second column from the left in the diagram.

The column layout will be created when you release the mouse button, and Word changes to Print Layout view if you are not already in it. The ruler will indicate the width of each column and the spacing between them, in much the same way it indicates the space between table columns.

If you want to insert the section break yourself, type the single column text, or if you've already typed it, place the insertion point after it. Then select Insert | Break, choose Continuous, and then click OK to insert a section break without a page break. You can now format the new section into multiple columns without affecting the single-column text on the page.

Typing Columns

If you created columns for a section of existing text, all the text in the section will flow from column to column and from page to page. You will only see the columns side-by-side in Print Layout view. In Normal view, the columns will appear below each other, separated by a column break line.

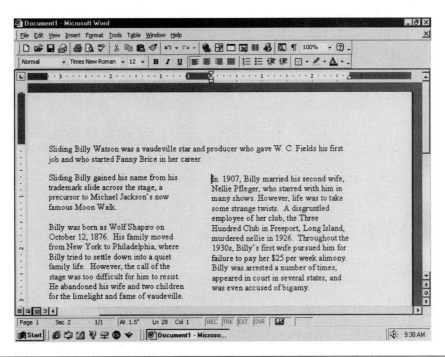

FIGURE 8-5 Single-column text followed by two columns requires two sections

Type, edit, and format your text in columns just as you would for any document. When you reach the bottom of one column, Word will begin the next column. If you want to start a new column before filling the current one, press CTRL-SHIFT-ENTER. Word will move the insertion point to the next column, starting a new page if you are on the rightmost column. If you press CTRL-SHIFT-ENTER when the insertion point is in existing text, the text following the insertion point will shift to the next column.

When you want to start typing in a different number of columns, such as to enter single-column text after two columns, insert another continuous section break, pull down the column button, and select the number of columns. Word will balance out the existing columns on the page above the section break.

Changing the Column Width

You change the width of columns, and the amount of space between them, by dragging the gray area in the ruler that indicates the space between columns.

When you point to the area, the mouse pointer will appear as a two-headed arrow. To create columns of unequal width, while retaining the same space between them, drag the gray area by the crosshatch pattern in the center:

To change the width of a column as well as the space between them, drag one of the lines on the left or right of the gray area, as shown here:

Dragging a line toward the crosshatch pattern will decrease the space between the columns while increasing the width of the column on that side. Dragging a line away from the crosshatch pattern will increase the space between columns while decreasing the width of the column. For example, drag the line on the left to widen the space between columns, making the column on the left narrower.

Using the Dialog Box

If you want to create more than six columns, create columns without manually inserting a section break, or specify an exact column width and spacing, then select Format | Columns to see the dialog box shown in Figure 8-6.

Select the number of columns and their spacing, and then select an option from the Apply To section. Choosing This Point Forward before you change column formatting will insert a continuous section break so you can combine column layouts within a document, even on one page. Select Whole Document to apply the style to the entire document. Choose This Section—if it is an option in the list—to apply the layout to the current section.

Select the Line Between check box to insert a vertical line between the columns.

Create two or three columns of equal width, or select the Equal Column Width check box and then enter a number into the Number Of Columns box.

To modify the width of the columns or the spacing between them, enter a measurement in the Width And Spacing section. When you select Equal Column Width, only the first column will be active; the others will be dimmed.

When you set the width of the first column, all the columns will change to the same size, and Word will calculate the spacing to fit the columns on the page. If you enter a measurement for the spacing, Word will adjust the width automatically.

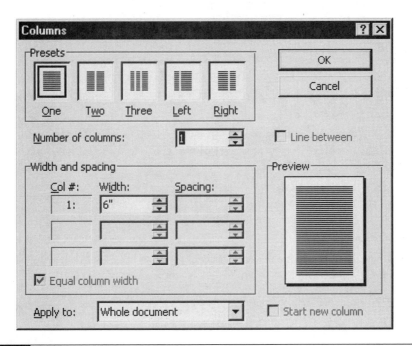

FIGURE 8-6 Columns dialog box

With equal-width columns, the gray area in the ruler does not have a crosshatch pattern. When you set Equal Width Columns, you can only drag the left or right side of the area to increase or decrease the gutter size. All of the columns in the section, however, will adjust so they are the same width. If you have three or more columns, as you increase or decrease one gutter, the others will change as well.

Uneven Columns

To create columns of different width, click the Left or the Right preset option in the Columns dialog box. Alternatively, you can deselect the Equal Column Width check box and enter a number in the Number Of Columns box and then enter dimensions in the Width And Spacing section. Changing the width of one column will affect the size of the columns to its right while maintaining the same spacing.

- Use the Bar tab type, in the Tabs dialog box, to draw a vertical line on the screen at the tab stop position. In the ruler, a small vertical line indicates a bar tab.
- To change a tab that affects several paragraphs, select the text first, and then change the tab position or type.
- Remember, you can set tabs in Print Layout view by double-clicking in blank areas—double-click in the center of the screen to insert a center tab, and at the right margin to insert a right tab.
- Choose Table | Hide Gridlines if you do not want table gridlines to appear onscreen and when printed.
- If you use the Tables And Borders button often, add it to the Standard toolbar. Click More Buttons in the toolbar, and then click the Tables And Borders button.
- If you've already typed information in columns separated by tabs or commas, you can automatically convert the text into a table. Select the text, choose Table | Insert, and click Table.
- Use the Insert Microsoft Excel Worksheet button on the Standard toolbar to insert a table that accesses Excel's formatting and mathematical features.
- When changing the column width of tables and text by dragging, hold down ALT while you drag to display column and spacing dimensions in the ruler.
- You can drag the border of a table or text column into the margin area and beyond the edge of the page, but it will not print. Use Print Preview to check the position of columns before printing.
- Insert a continuous section break after the text on the last page of columns to balance the columns on that page. Do not insert a column break after the last column, unless you want following text to start on a new page.

Working with Long Documents

Long documents are easy to create in Word; they just need some special handling. You may need headers, footers, or page numbers to identify pages, or footnotes to cite references in the text. Word even lets you outline and summarize a document with ease.

Working with Headers and Footers

Pages of a long document can easily get separated, out of order, or misplaced. *Headers* and *footers* help to identify the pages of your document, as well as the document itself. They can even create pleasing visual effects that grab and hold the reader's attention.

 N O T E : A header is text or graphics that prints at the top of every page. A footer is text or graphics that prints at the bottom of every page.

Adding a Header or Footer

To add either a header or footer (or both!), select View | Header And Footer. Word switches to Print Layout view and displays the header area in the top margin of the document and also displays the Header And Footer toolbar, as in Figure 9-1. The text of the document appears dimmed so you can see the spacing between the header or footer and the text.

Type the text that you want to appear in the header, using the toolbar buttons to insert other elements, such as the page number, date, or time. The Insert AutoText list in the toolbar lets you add other elements, such as "Created by" followed by your name, the document name, and "Page *X* of *Y*":

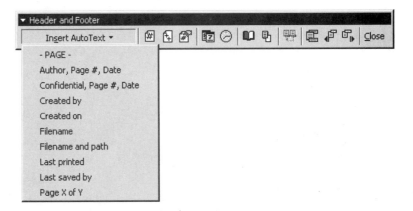

There is a center tab stop in the center of the header and footer area, and a right-aligned tab stop on the right edge. To number the pages in the center of the header, for example, press TAB to reach the center tab stop and then click the Insert Page Number button on the toolbar.

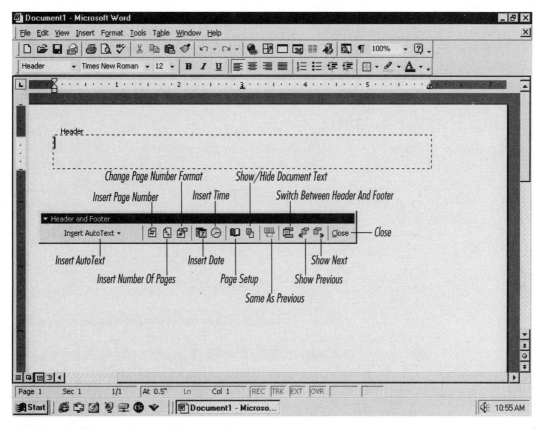

FIGURE 9-1 Word displays the header area and the Header And Footer toolbar in Print Layout view

To switch between the header and footer area, click the Switch Between Header And Footer button on the toolbar. Enter the text you want in the footer the same way. Click Close on the toolbar when you're ready to return to your document.

N O T E : Headers and footers appear dimmed onscreen in Print Layout view, but do not appear at all in Normal view.

If you have to change a header or footer, select View | Header And Footer, or click the header or footer area in Print Layout view. Word displays the Header And Footer toolbar and the header or footer area. Edit the header or footer, and then click Close.

Adding Page Numbers

When all you want is a page number at the top or bottom of a page, you don't have to use a header or footer. You can number every page of your document consecutively, or restart numbering in each section. You can also use Roman numerals for a table of contents and index.

To number pages, place the insertion point anywhere in the document, or in the section that you want to number. Select Insert | Page Numbers to display the following dialog box:

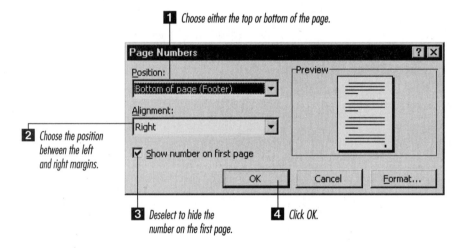

1 Choose either the top or bottom of the page.

2 Choose the position between the left and right margins.

3 Deselect to hide the number on the first page.

4 Click OK.

The Alignment options are Left, Center, Right, Inside, or Outside. The Inside and Outside options alternate the placement of numbers on the odd and even pages. Selecting Inside, for example, places even numbers on the right of the page and odd numbers on the left.

Use the Format button to change the number format, to number pages consecutively across sections, or to number each section separately.

Inserting Footnotes

Footnotes are not only found in academic reports and scholarly articles.
Documents of all types can benefit from notes—to cite the source of
information, to provide some extra insight or explanation, or to give
a personal aside.

To type a footnote, place the insertion point where you want the reference
number or mark to appear, and then select Insert | Footnote to display the
dialog box shown in Figure 9-2.

 NOTE: Endnotes are references that appear at the end of the document rather
than on the same page as the reference number. You insert an endnote in much the
same way as a footnote, except you select Endnote from the Footnote And Endnote
dialog box. By default, endnote references use lowercase Roman numerals.

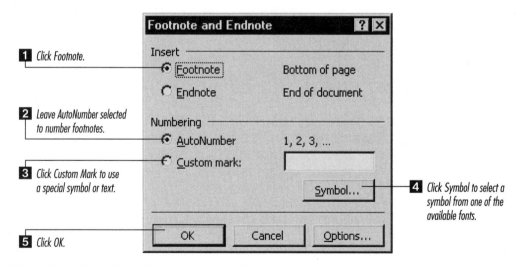

1 *Click Footnote.*

2 *Leave AutoNumber selected to number footnotes.*

3 *Click Custom Mark to use a special symbol or text.*

4 *Click Symbol to select a symbol from one of the available fonts.*

5 *Click OK.*

FIGURE 9-2   The Footnote And Endnote dialog box

Word inserts the reference number in the text. If you are in Normal view, Word displays the Note pane at the bottom of the screen, as shown in Figure 9-3. If you are in Print Layout view, Word moves to the bottom of the page and displays a separator line and reference number.

Type the text of the footnote. To return to the document leaving the Note pane displayed, press SHIFT-F5. To return to the document and hide the Note pane, click Close in the Notes toolbar.

Word numbers the notes consecutively. If you insert a new note in the text, or delete an existing note, Word automatically renumbers those following the insertion point. Word also automatically adjusts your text so footnotes appear on the same page as their reference numbers. You can insert or delete text—even insert and delete footnotes—and Word takes care of the rest.

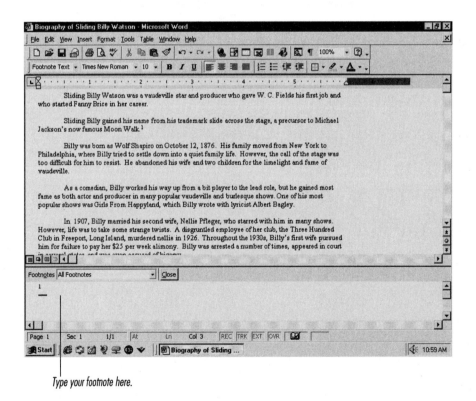

Type your footnote here.

FIGURE 9-3   The Note pane in Normal view

TIP: To quickly read the text of a footnote, just point to its reference number in the text.

To move or copy a footnote, just drag its reference number in the text, holding down CTRL while you drag and drop if you want to make a copy of the note. Word automatically renumbers the other notes accordingly. To delete a note, select its reference number and press DEL.

To edit a note, just click it. In Normal view the Note pane must be displayed—choose View | Footnotes if necessary. Change the text of the note as you would any other text in your document.

 TIP: If the footnotes do not appear in the Note pane, choose All Footnotes from the list box above the pane.

Inserting Comments

Sometimes you need to jot down a message, note, or reminder to yourself while you're working on a document. You might want to remind yourself to check a certain section of text or to leave a note to someone else who will be reading or editing the document onscreen. These types of notes are called *comments*.

Place the insertion point where you want to insert the comment, and then choose Insert | Comment to display a pane at the bottom of the screen, shown here. Word highlights the word to the left of the insertion point. Then it inserts a code in the text and in the Comments pane showing the initials of the default user and the number of the annotation—such as "[AN1]" to represent the first annotation of user AN.

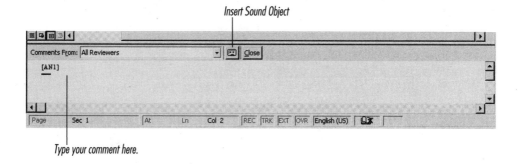

Insert Sound Object

Type your comment here.

Type the text of your comment, and then click Close in the Comment toolbar to remove the pane and to turn off the display of the comment codes.

TIP: If you press SHIFT-F5 after typing the comment, Word leaves the Comments pane on the screen along with the display of the annotation codes.

Displaying and Printing Comments

To read a comment, just point to the highlighted text. A box appears with the name of the person who made the comment and the comment itself. To review all the comments in the document, select View | Comments to open the Comments pane.

Comments do not normally print with your document, but you can print them in two ways. To print just the comments with page references, select File | Print, pull down the Print What list, and select Comments. To print the comments at the bottom of each document page, just like footnotes, select File | Print and click Options. In the dialog box that appears, click Comments in the Include With Document section, select OK, and then print the document.

Recording Voice Comments

If your computer is equipped with hardware for recording and playing sounds, you can record a comment instead of typing one. You, or anyone else, can later play the comment to hear your message. To record a comment, click the Insert Sound Object button in the Comment toolbar. Windows starts the sound recorder program installed on your system, such as this one:

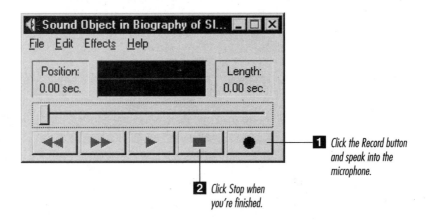

1 Click the Record button and speak into the microphone.

2 Click Stop when you're finished.

TIP: To use an existing WAV-formatted file as the annotation, select Insert File from the sound recorder's Edit menu.

When you close the application, the sound comment appears as an icon of a speaker.

 To listen to the recorded message, display the annotation pane and double-click the speaker icon.

Automatically Summarizing Your Document

A summary shows just the key sentences of a document. Rather than scan the document to copy key sentences for the summary, let Word create the summary for you automatically.

Start by selecting Tools | AutoSummarize. Word scans the document for key sentences and then displays the AutoSummarize dialog box shown in Figure 9-4. Choose the type of summary, the level of detail, and then click OK.

When you click OK, Word displays the summary of your choice. If you selected either to highlight the key points or to hide everything, Word displays the AutoSummarize toolbar:

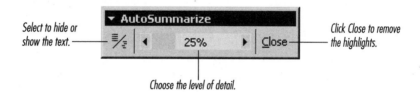

Select to hide or show the text.

Click Close to remove the highlights.

Choose the level of detail.

Using the Document Map

The Document Map shows each of the headings in your document by using the heading styles from the Style list in the Formatting toolbar. It is helpful when you need to see the document's organization, and to quickly move from heading to heading.

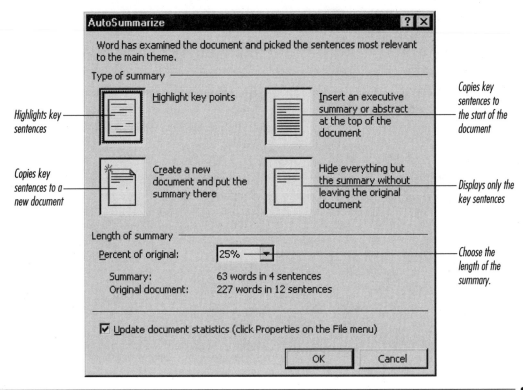

Highlights key sentences

Copies key sentences to a new document

Copies key sentences to the start of the document

Displays only the key sentences

Choose the length of the summary.

FIGURE 9-4　Creating an automatic summary

　To display this feature, click the Document Map button in the Standard toolbar, or choose View | Document Map. To close the Document Map, use either technique again.

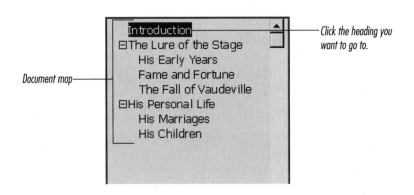

Document map

Click the heading you want to go to.

Creating Outlines

In Chapter 8 you learned how to create a numbered list. Outlining, however, goes far beyond simply numbering paragraphs—it lets you integrate your outline with the document itself. You can work with one document that serves both purposes.

Outlining is easy to understand if you picture a document as having two parts—headings and body text. *Headings* are titles and subtitles; *body text* is the text of paragraphs under headings.

If you already typed the document by using the heading styles, then just select View | Outline. In Outline view, headings and subheadings appear indented to reflect outline levels, and you'll see the Outline toolbar in place of the ruler (Figure 9-5).

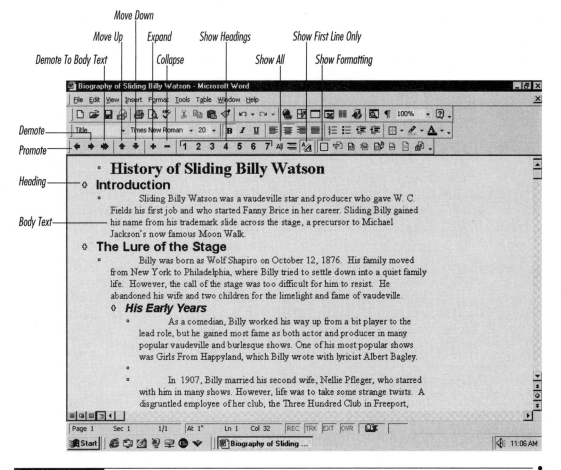

FIGURE 9-5 Outline view with the Outline toolbar

> **N O T E :** The remaining buttons on the toolbar are used to create master documents with subdocuments. The Master Document feature lets you create an outline in which outline families can be stored as separate documents on your disk, called *subdocuments*. You can edit the subdocuments within the master or in their own window, and save subdocuments independently from the master.

To create an outline as you type a new document, select View | Outline. Word displays the Outline toolbar and a symbol that indicates an outline heading level, and it applies the Heading 1 style.

Type a heading and then press ENTER. Word moves the insertion point to the next line and inserts the same level-indicator symbol with Heading 1 formatting.

- To type a heading at a lower level—indented further to the right—press TAB or click the Demote button in the Outline toolbar.
- To type a heading at a higher level—further to the left—click the Promote button in the Outline toolbar or press SHIFT-TAB.

You can insert and delete outline headings, and change levels—Word will automatically adjust the levels for you.

Adding Body Text

You use body text to incorporate the text of the document itself with the outline. Body text is any text that does not have an outline level applied. To add body text to a document, start a new line at any level, and then click the Demote To Body Text button in the Outline toolbar.

How the text appears when in Outline view depends on the Show Formatting button. When the button is pressed, your text will appear according to the applied styles and formats. When the button is not pressed, all the text appears in one font, size, and style, although the outline levels are still applied. Whether or not the button appears pressed, the text will appear formatted when you change to Normal or Page Layout view.

Moving Outline Families

The arrangement of outlines in families makes them easier to work with. An outline family consists of a heading and all the subheadings and text under it. To rearrange a document, you can move sections of the outline by dragging or by clicking on the Move Up and Move Down buttons in the Outline toolbar.

To move just the heading, without affecting its family, place the insertion point anywhere in the heading. To move an entire *family*—a heading and all subheadings and body text under it—point to the level indicator at the uppermost level of the family so the pointer will be shaped like a four-headed arrow and then click the mouse. Then click Move Up or Move Down as desired.

Collapsing and Expanding Outlines

One of the advantages of working with an outline is that it lets you visualize the organization of topics and subtopics. To view the document's overall organization, you can hide the body text and selected headings using a process called *collapsing*. For example, to visualize the order of just the major topics—those formatted with the Heading 1 style—you collapse the outline so just the first levels appear.

Expanding an outline is just the reverse—it displays the collapsed sections.

To collapse or expand a specific family, double-click the heading-level indicator or place the insertion point anywhere in the heading and use the Expand or Collapse button.

To expand or collapse the *entire outline* to one level, click one of the Show buttons on the Outline toolbar:

1 2 3 4 5 6 7 All

Click the numbered button for the lowest level that you want to display. Clicking on Show Heading 3, for example, displays just the level 1 through 3 headings. You'll see wavy lines below the level indicating that some headings or body text is not displayed.

Word only displays body text in Outline view when the entire outline is expanded, that is, when all levels are displayed. Click Show All now to display the entire outline—every level and all body text.

Creating Cross-References

A *cross-reference* refers the reader to the location of a heading, bookmark, footnote, endnote, equation, figure, or table. For example, you can refer the reader to a section titled "Computers" using the reference "Please see the section 'Computers' on page 23." Or if you make changes to a paragraph on page 20, you can insert a bookmark in that paragraph and use a cross-reference such as "Also see my additions on page 20."

To create a cross-reference, place the insertion point where you want the cross-reference to appear in the document. Type any text that you want to appear with the reference, such as "Please refer to," and then select Insert | Cross-reference to see a dialog box like the one shown in Figure 9-6.

Select the type of item you want to reference in the Reference Type list. For example, do you want to refer to a heading or figure? Word changes the contents of the Insert Reference To and the For Which Heading lists based on your choice. If you choose to reference a heading, for instance, all the headings appear on the For Which Heading list.

Next, select what you want to reference in the Insert Reference To list. You can choose, for example, to add the text of a heading or its page number in the cross-reference. Finally, select the specific item, such as the heading, in the For Which Heading list, click Insert, and then click Close.

Cross-references are fields. If editing changes the page numbers or text of a reference item, select the entire document and press F9 to update the references.

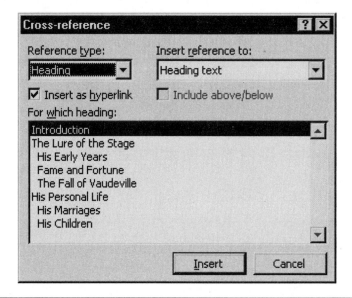

FIGURE 9-6   Inserting a cross-reference

Numbering Lines

Legal documents, such as contracts, pleadings, and depositions, often have line numbers down the left margin. Fortunately, and to the delight of many legal assistants and secretaries, Word can number lines automatically for you.

When you want to number lines, select File | Page Setup and then click the Layout tab. Click the Line Numbers command button to display the dialog box you see here.

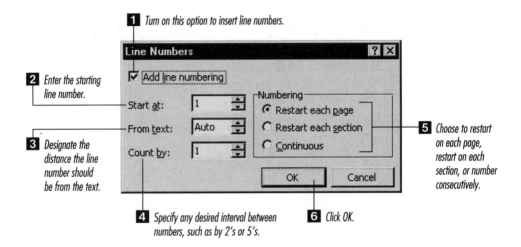

1 Turn on this option to insert line numbers.

2 Enter the starting line number.

3 Designate the distance the line number should be from the text.

4 Specify any desired interval between numbers, such as by 2's or 5's.

5 Choose to restart on each page, restart on each section, or number consecutively.

6 Click OK.

The line numbers appear in Page Layout view and in Print Preview, but you cannot edit them. The only way to change numbering is to select options from the Page Setup dialog box.

- If your document is divided into sections, use the Same As Previous button in the Header And Footer toolbar to continue headers and footers from the previous section.
- Use the Layout tab of the Page Setup dialog box to choose different headers and footers for the first document page, or for odd and even pages.
- If your document is divided into sections, you can choose to number pages consecutively, or to restart at the beginning of a section. Choose Insert | Page Numbers, and then click Format to select options.
- Click Options in the Footnote And Endnote dialog box to control where your notes appear. You can choose to place notes at the bottom of the page or at the end of the document, the number format and starting number, or to number consecutively or to restart at each page or section.
- Change the initials that appear with comments on the User Information tab of the Options dialog box—choose Tools | Options to open the box.
- To insert a recorded sound clip into the document rather than as a comment, choose Insert | Object, choose Create New, scroll the Object Type list, and double-click Wave Sound.
- To delete a comment, drag over its notation in the document and press DEL.
- If you are working with other persons on a document, right-click any toolbar and choose Reviewing to display a toolbar for adding, editing, and working with comments and revisions.
- Word does not automatically number outlines. To number the outline levels, select the outline, choose Format | Bullets And Numbering, and then click one of the heading formats in the bottom row of the dialog box.
- Page numbers, cross-references, line numbers, dates that can be updated, and many other items that you insert are field codes. Before printing any document, play it safe and update the fields. Press CTRL-A to select the entire document and then press F9.

Working with Graphics

B A S I C S

- Inserting ClipArt
- Working with Graphics
- Creating Text Boxes
- Special Effects with WordArt
- Creating and Editing Drawings

B E Y O N D

- Linking Text Boxes
- Shadow and 3-D Effects
- Using AutoShapes
- Editing ClipArt Graphics
- Creating Charts and Graphs

While lists and tables add visual impact to a document, nothing does it better than pictures. You can enhance documents with pictures from the Office CD, pictures from other applications (even WordPerfect!), and pictures that you scan or create yourself. You can also enhance documents by applying special effects to text.

Inserting ClipArt

Office comes with a wide variety of eye-catching graphics called *ClipArt*. To insert a ClipArt graphic, place the insertion point where you want the graphic to appear. Choose Insert | Picture, and click Clip Art to display the window shown in Figure 10-1.

Click a category to display choices. Then click the graphic you want, in order to display these options:

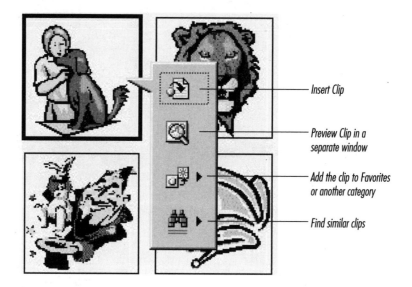

When you choose Insert Clip, the graphic appears in your document. You can then close the ClipArt window.

 N O T E : Use the other Clip Gallery pages to insert sounds and videos. An inserted sound appears as a speaker icon—double-click the icon to play the sound. When you insert a video, you'll see the first scene—double-click to play the video.

You can also insert a graphic that you have on your disk, such as one downloaded from the Internet. To do so, choose Insert | Picture, and then click

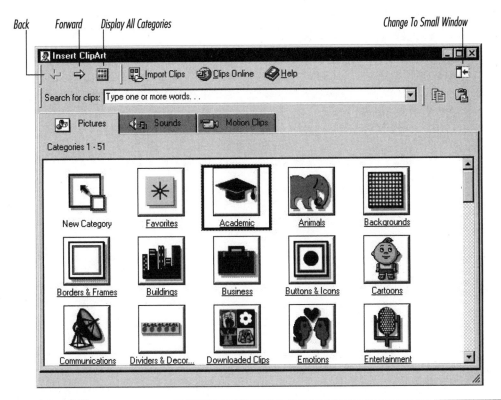

Back   Forward   Display All Categories   Change To Small Window

FIGURE 10-1   Adding ClipArt to a document

From File. You'll see the Insert Picture dialog box where you navigate to and select the picture you want to insert. Select the graphic you want to use, and then pull down the Insert list to choose from these options:

- **Insert**   This inserts the graphic so it is saved in the same file as the document.
- **Link To File**   This saves a link to the graphic with the document, not the graphic itself. This reduces the document's file size and lets you use graphics that might later change. When you open the document, Word automatically displays the most recent version of the graphic.
- **Insert And Link**   This inserts the graphic and saves a link to it.

Working with Pictures

Once you insert a graphic into your document, you can customize it in a number of ways. To work with a picture, click it so that small boxes (handles) surround it. You use the handles to change the graphic's size, and the Picture toolbar also appears:

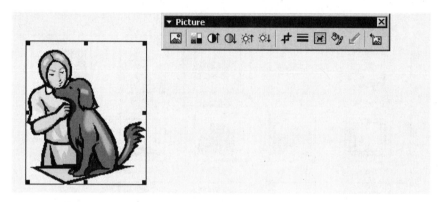

N O T E : You may or may not see a border around the picture as well. Refer to "Customizing Pictures" later in this chapter. The Picture toolbar will not appear when you insert certain basic shapes from categories such as Banners and Miscellaneous.

To delete a picture from your document, select it and then press DEL, or select Edit | Clear. To deselect the picture, click away from it.

To change the size of a picture, point to one of the handles so the mouse pointer changes to a two-headed arrow and then drag—a dotted box will show the size of the picture.

- Drag the handle on the left or right side to change just the width.
- Drag the handle on the top or bottom to change just the height of the box.
- Drag a corner handle to change the height and width of the box while maintaining the original proportions.

You can also move a picture by dragging or by using the Cut, Copy, and Paste commands to copy or move it. If the selected graphic appears with a border around it, you can only drag the picture within text. If there is no borderline, you can drag the picture anywhere on the page, even in the margin area. This is determined by the Text Wrapping option that you'll learn about later in this chapter.

Customizing Pictures

You can customize the look of a graphic in a variety of ways, by using either the Picture toolbar or the Format Picture dialog box. (If the Picture toolbar does not appear, right-click a graphic and choose Show Picture Toolbar from the shortcut menu.) Table 10-1 shows the functions of the toolbar buttons.

The Image Control button offers four options. Choose *Grayscale* to replace the colors in the graphic with shades of gray, *Black & White* to remove all colors and shades of gray, *Watermark* to dim the entire graphic, and *Automatic* to restore the colors to the original.

The Crop button lets you hide portions of a graphic, such as cutting out an ex-boyfriend. Click the Crop button to change the mouse pointer to the shape on the button, and then drag one of the handles. As you drag, a dashed line indicates where the cropping will occur; when you release the mouse, that portion of the picture will not be visible. The cropped part of the image is not deleted from the graphic—it's just hidden. You can later use the Crop button to drag the handle back to its original position to redisplay the hidden portion of the image.

Text Wrapping

Text wrapping refers to the way text flows around a graphic. The default setting for a graphic is *Top And Bottom*—that is, text will not appear on either side, only above and below it. Click the Text Wrapping button on the Picture toolbar to select other wrap methods. The Square and Tight options let text flow on all four sides of the graphic, with Tight letting text more closely follow the graphic's contour. The Behind Text and In Front Of Text options let the graphic overlap with text. Choose Behind Text if you want to see the text over the graphic; choose In Front Of Text when you want the graphic to cover the overlapped text. Figure 10-2 illustrates some of the text wrapping effects.

> **TIP:** Use the Edit Wrap Points option to customize the way text wraps around the graphic.

If a borderline surrounds the selected graphic, then it is treated as text. This is called the *in line with text* setting, and it means you can only move the graphic within text. Once you select a wrapping option, however, the graphic is *floating*. You can now drag the graphic anywhere on the page, even in the margin areas and blank space following the last text.

> **NOTE:** The Edit Wrap Points option in the Wrap menu lets you customize how text wraps around the graphic.

BUTTON	BUTTON NAME	FUNCTION
	Insert Picture From File	Displays the Insert Picture dialog box to insert another graphic.
	Image Control	Sets the overall look of the picture.
	More Contrast	Increases the picture's contrast with each click.
	Less Contrast	Decreases the picture's contrast.
	More Brightness	Makes the picture lighter.
	Less Brightness	Makes the picture darker.
	Crop	Hides or redisplays sections of the graphic.
	Line Style	Sets the type of border around the picture.
	Text Wrapping	Determines how text flows around or through the graphic.
	Format Picture	Displays a dialog box for setting the properties of the graphic.
	Set Transparent Color	Enables you to designate a selected color as transparent so the background shows through. Click this button and then click the color to make it transparent.
	Reset Picture	Returns the graphic to its original appearance.

TABLE 10-1 Function Buttons of the Picture Toolbar

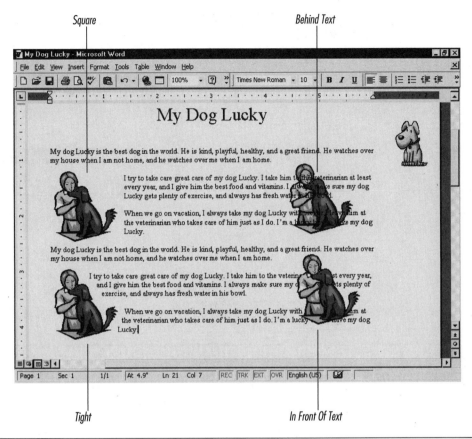

FIGURE 10-2 Text wrapping

Other Formatting Options For even more graphic formatting options, choose Format | Picture, and then choose options from the dialog box that appears. You can also right-click a graphic and choose from the shortcut menu. The options shown depend on whether the graphic is floating or in line with the text.

When the picture is floating, for example, you can choose the Order and Grouping options. The Order option affects how overlapping graphics appear, while Grouping lets you combine several graphics into one, or separate a graphic into its individual elements. By grouping graphics, you can then move and customize them all at the same time. Both shortcut menus include the Format Picture command to open the Format Picture dialog box.

Creating Text Boxes

A *text box* lets you create a graphic-type box that only contains text. Select Insert | Text Box, and then drag the mouse to form a rectangle the size of the box you want. Word displays the insertion point within a box with handles, and the Text Box toolbar. Type and format the text that you want to appear, and then click outside the box.

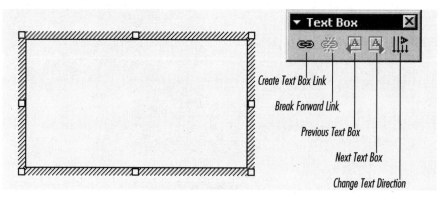

 N O T E : If the Text Box toolbar does not appear, right-click any other toolbar and choose Text Box from the shortcut menu.

You move, copy, and format the box in much the same way as a graphic. Use the Text Box toolbar to create links between boxes—when one box fills up, the overflow text automatically appears in the other. To produce linked boxes: create the boxes, click in the first box in the chain (where you want to start typing), and then click the Create Text Box Link button so the mouse pointer changes shape and looks like this:

Point to the text box where you want text to flow—the mouse pointer should look like this—and then click:

Now just type in the first box. If it becomes full, click outside of it and you'll see the extra text appear in the linked box.

To change the format of a text box, such as the color and type of borderline around it, select the box, right-click its border, and then choose Format Text Box from the shortcut menu.

Special Effects Using Microsoft WordArt

With Microsoft WordArt you create special graphic effects for logos, headings, or just eye-catching graphics. To start WordArt, choose Insert | Picture and click WordArt. You'll see the preset WordArt options shown here.

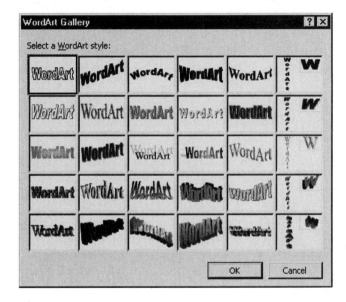

Select the design that you want to use, and then click OK to display the Edit WordArt Text dialog box, as shown in Figure 10-3.

When you click OK, Word displays the graphic, selected and surrounded by handles, along with the WordArt toolbar, as shown here.

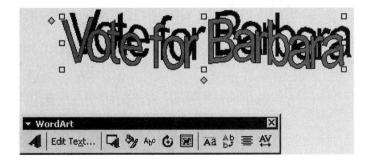

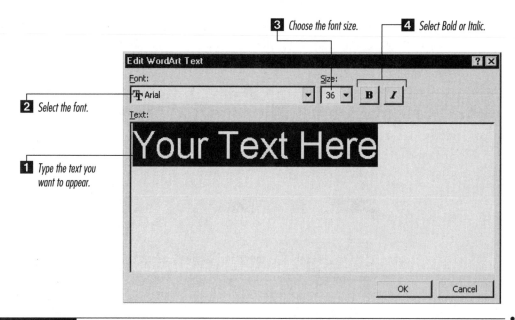

3 *Choose the font size.*

4 *Select Bold or Italic.*

2 *Select the font.*

1 *Type the text you want to appear.*

FIGURE 10-3 Creating a WordArt graphic

Change the size and position of the graphic by dragging, use the toolbar to customize it, or click elsewhere to deselect it. You'll notice that WordArt graphics include an extra diamond-shaped handle. When you point to the handle, the mouse pointer becomes shaped like an arrowhead, and dragging the handle adjusts the shape of the graphic, as shown here:

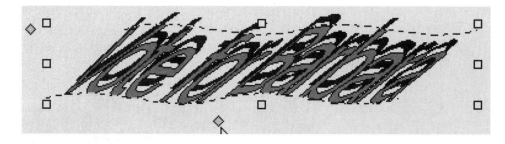

NOTE: To later redisplay the WordArt toolbar, just click the WordArt image, or double-click the WordArt itself to display the Edit WordArt Text dialog box.

You use the WordArt toolbar to customize the WordArt graphic, as shown in Table 10-2.

The WordArt Shape button, for example, displays the following:

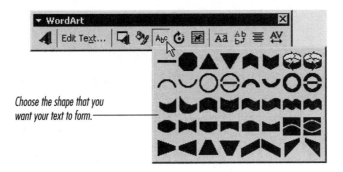

Choose the shape that you want your text to form.

Creating and Editing Drawings

While you can create a drawing in the Paint accessory and then paste or insert it in your document, you can also draw directly on the Word screen. Word includes a set of drawing tools for creating freehand and geometric objects, and for editing ClipArt and other graphics that you insert into your document. To create a drawing, click the Drawing button in the Standard toolbar to change to Print Layout view and to display the Drawing toolbar, shown here:

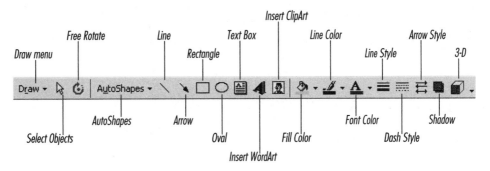

Use the Line, Arrow, Rectangle, Oval, and Text Box tools to create basic objects and shapes. As a general rule, click the tool and then drag to create the object in the document:

- Drag without holding down any key to draw freehand.
- Hold down the SHIFT key while dragging to draw a straight line or arrow, a square, or a circle.
- Hold down the CTRL key while dragging to create the object around a center point.

BUTTON	BUTTON NAME	FUNCTION
	Insert WordArt	Creates another WordArt graphic
Edit Text...	Edit Text	Lets you edit the WordArt text
	WordArt Gallery	Lets you change the graphic to another of the preset combinations
	Format WordArt	Displays a dialog box for changing the colors and lines, size, protection, and properties of the graphic, much like the options in the Format Picture dialog box
Abc	WordArt Shape	Lets you select another shape for the text
	Free Rotate	Replaces the square handles around the graphic with four round ones that you drag to rotate the graphic
Aa	Same Letter Heights	Makes all the letters the same size, regardless of their case
Ab	Vertical Text	Positions the text vertically down the page
	Alignment	Lets you adjust the alignment of multiple lines
AV	Character Spacing	Lets you adjust the spacing between characters

TABLE 10-2   WordArt Buttons

After you draw, the object appears selected with handles. You can then change the size and position by dragging, and apply colors and other formats available on the Drawing toolbar.

As you draw an object, you may notice that its size jumps in small increments rather than flows freely with the mouse. If this occurs, Word is set to *snap to grid*. This means that the ends of all lines must correspond to the intersecting points of an invisible grid pattern set by default every 0.13". For example, you may try to end an arrow at a certain spot, only to see it jump slightly to the right or to the left to align with the nearest grid line. You can turn on and off snap to grid, and customize the grid pattern, by choosing Draw | Grid on the Drawing toolbar and selecting options from the dialog box that appears.

TIP: Hold down the ALT key while you draw an object to toggle the current snap to grid setting.

Once you create an object, you can use the Drawing toolbar to set the line type and color, or to add a background color or fill effect. Use the Draw menu on the toolbar to align multiple objects in relation to each other, and to flip and rotate objects.

For example, the Draw | Rotate Or Flip option lets you rotate an object by dragging it, or rotate it counterclockwise or clockwise in 90-degree increments. You can also flip an object from left to right or from top to bottom. In addition, you can *distribute* objects horizontally or vertically. Distributing spaces objects evenly between the first and last object in the group.

Using AutoShapes

AutoShapes might just be one of the most fun things about using Word. With AutoShapes, you drag to create a variety of decorative and complex shapes, such as stars, banners, flowchart symbols, and decorative arrows.

To create an AutoShape, click the AutoShapes button on the Drawing toolbar to see a list of categories, each with a submenu of shapes that you can draw. You can also select Insert | Picture and click AutoShapes to see a toolbar with buttons for each of the categories:

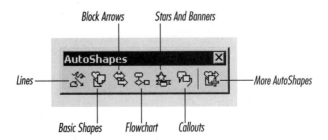

Choose the shape you want to draw from the submenu, or click the category button on the toolbar and choose from the list that appears.

The Lines category, for example, lets you draw lines and arrows, arcs and curves, and even freehand doodles. The shapes in the Block Arrows category are shown here.

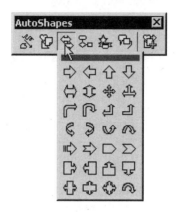

For most of the AutoShapes, just select the object you want, and then drag to create it in the size and position desired. With most of the shapes, you can also select the object and then click in the document to insert it in a default size.

To customize an AutoShape, double-click it to display the Format AutoShape dialog box. The options in the dialog box are similar to those in the Format Picture dialog box, although the options depend on the type of object you have selected.

The three most notable exceptions to the drag-and-draw rule of AutoShapes are the Freeform and Curve tools in the Line category, and all the Callouts.

With the Freeform tool, you can create an object composed of any number of connected lines. To just doodle, select the Freeform tool and then drag the mouse with the mouse button held down. To draw a shape consisting of line segments, however, follow these steps:

1. Select the Freeform tool from the Line submenu.
2. Click in the document where you want the first line to begin.
3. *Release* the mouse button, drag to where you want the line to stop, and then click the mouse.
4. Repeat step 3 to draw all the other line segments.
5. Double-click to stop drawing.

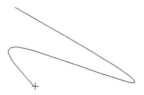

The Curve tool in the Line category works similarly. However, after you click the mouse to end the line segment, release the button and drag to form the curve. Double-click to end the drawing, or click once and draw another curved line segment.

 N O T E : When selected, most AutoShapes, except for simple lines, rectangles, and ovals, have one or more diamond-shaped yellow handles, just like the handle on a WordArt graphic. You use the diamond-shaped handles to change the shape of the graphic.

Callouts are the other exception to the rule. A *callout* is a text box with a pointer to something else in the document, as shown here:

After drawing the callout, you can drag the box to change its position, or the end of the pointer to change where it is pointing.

Adding Text to AutoShapes

You can add text to any AutoShape and create text boxes. To insert text in an object, right-click it and choose Add Text from the shortcut menu. Word displays the Text Box toolbar, just in case you want to link the shape to another, and places the insertion point within the shape for you to add and format text. The text stays within the boundaries of the object.

You can also create a separate text box object. Click the Text Box button in the Drawing toolbar, and then either click or drag on the worksheet to add the box.

More AutoShapes

The More AutoShapes button displays a window similar to ClipArt but with black-and-white graphics. Some of the graphics are more advanced than other

AutoShapes, such as a CD player, several pictures of computers, and some office furniture.

Add a graphic from this window just as you learned how to do for ClipArt. In fact, selecting one of these AutoShapes in a document displays the Picture toolbar. So work with these graphics as you would ClipArt. Some of the choices in the More AutoShapes dialog box are considered ClipArt rather than AutoShapes, so graphic commands that apply only to AutoShapes can not be used with these items.

Creating Shadows and 3-D Effects

The last two buttons on the Drawing toolbar offer high-impact ways to customize drawing shapes and clipart. Use the Shadow button to add depth to a graphic, and the 3-D button to create three-dimensional objects.

To create a shadow, select a graphic (one that you've drawn or inserted as ClipArt), and then click the Shadow button to choose from these options:

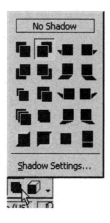

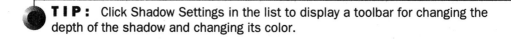

TIP: Click Shadow Settings in the list to display a toolbar for changing the depth of the shadow and changing its color.

To turn a two-dimensional object into a 3-D one, select it, click the 3-D button in the Drawing toolbar, and choose from these options:

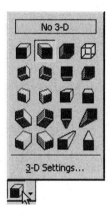

T I P : Click 3-D Settings in the list to display a toolbar for customizing the 3-D effect.

Editing ClipArt

You can use the Fill Color, Shadow, and 3-D Effects buttons on the Drawing toolbar to customize AutoShapes and inserted clipart, as well as to customize graphics you create with the drawing tools. Add a color to a clipart background, for example, by using the Fill Color list.

For even more ways to customize a ClipArt graphic, right-click it and choose Edit Picture from the shortcut menu. Word opens the graphic in a special window that includes the Drawing toolbar. In this window, you can select and change the individual parts that make up the graphic, as shown in Figure 10-4. In the figure, for example, the main section of the dog was selected and a new color applied.

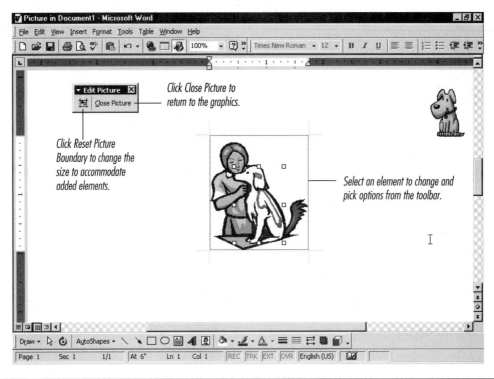

FIGURE 10-4 Edit a graphic to change its individual parts

After you click Close, you can quickly display the editing window again by double-clicking on the graphic.

Creating Charts and Graphs

In Chapter 8, you learned how to display text and numbers in a table. Sometimes, however, numbers can have even more impact when presented as a chart or graph, as shown in Figure 10-5. Word lets you easily insert two- and three-dimensional charts into a document. You can enter the information for the chart directly in the Graph application, or you can use information already entered into a Word table.

To create a chart from a Word table, select the cells of the table containing the information you want to chart. Otherwise, just place the insertion point on the page where you want the chart to appear. Then choose Insert | Picture and click Chart. As you can see in Figure 10-6, Word displays a datasheet containing the information you selected, or just some generic sample data, along with a chart of the data.

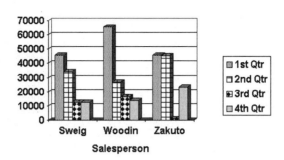

FIGURE 10-5 Charts and graphs can add impact to your document

Use the Standard toolbar to change the look of the chart.

Use the Formatting toolbar to change the format of text and numbers.

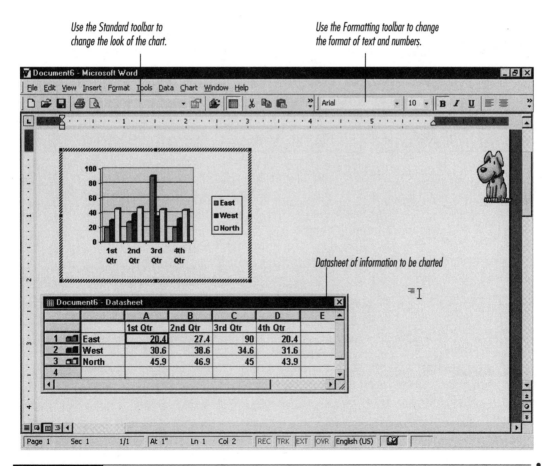

Datasheet of information to be charted

FIGURE 10-6 Creating a chart in Word

The File, Edit, Window, and Help menu items contain the same options as those in a document window. Table 10-3 shows the new functions available in the other menus. Table 10-4 shows the functions of the new buttons in the Standard toolbar, and Table 10-5 shows the new buttons in the Formatting toolbar.

You edit or enter the information that you want to chart in the datasheet. To delete all the sample information from the table, click the box in the top left corner to select the entire datasheet, and then press DEL. The datasheet is just like a spreadsheet, but you enter the row headings in the column to the left of column A, and enter column headings in the row above row 1. Use the other rows and columns for the numeric values that you want to graph. As you enter data into the datasheet, Word creates the graph in the background.

To display the graph in the foreground, click the View Datasheet button. Then select options from the menu bar or toolbar to format the chart as you want it to appear in the document. When you're done, click outside the chart to return to the document. The chart appears as a graphic object, so you can add a border, insert a frame, and change its size and position. To edit the graph itself, double-click it to return to the Graph application.

MENU ITEM	FUNCTIONS
View	Switch between the datasheet and graph, select toolbars, and zoom the display
Insert	Add cells, titles, data labels, a legend, axis labels, gridlines, and trend lines
Format	Format the appearance of text and chart elements, and the order of elements
Tools	Select default colors and graph type, allow drag and drop of cells, and move the insertion point to a new cell when you press ENTER
Data	Display data series from row or column information, and include or exclude specific rows or columns
Chart	Change the chart type and chart options, create trend lines, and format the 3-D appearance

TABLE 10-3 Menu options for graphs

TOOLBAR BUTTON	FUNCTION
	Select the part of the chart to format
	Format the selected part
	Import information from a spreadsheet program to chart
	Toggle between the datasheet and the graph
	Create data series from rows
	Create data series from columns
	Display a table with the charted data and the chart
	Select the chart type
	Display category axis gridlines
	Display value axis gridlines
	Toggle the legend
	Choose a color for graph objects

TABLE 10-4 Microsoft Graph Toolbar Buttons

TOOLBAR BUTTON	FUNCTION
$	Display numbers in dollar amounts
%	Format numbers as percentages
,	Add commas to separate thousands
+.0 .00	Increase the number of decimal places
.00 +.0	Decrease the number of decimal places
	Angle text downward
	Angle text upward

TABLE 10-5   The Formatting Toolbar

Experiment with the menu bar and toolbar in the Graph application on your own to learn more about creating graphs. You can select or change the type of graph by selecting an option from the Chart Type list. To add titles, a legend, gridlines, a data table, or data labels, choose Chart Options from the Chart menu or shortcut menu. To quickly choose formatting options for a specific part of the chart, such as the legend, bar in a bar chart, or an axis, double-click the part to see a dialog box of options.

- For convenient access to a graphic, choose Import Clips to copy it from your disk to the ClipArt Gallery, or choose Clips Online to download additional graphics from the Microsoft web site.
- Right-click a graphic in the ClipArt gallery, and choose Clip Properties to display detailed information about it, change the categories in which it is listed, and add or remove keywords that identify it.
- Choose Insert Picture | From Scanner Or Camera to scan a graphic into the document or to retrieve a picture from a digital camera.
- To create a watermark effect, choose Watermark from the Image Control list and Behind Text in the Wrapping list of the Picture toolbar.
- To move an object a small amount, try nudging it instead of dragging. Click the border around the object to select it, and then press an arrow key to move the graphic in the direction of the arrow.
- Once you customize an AutoShape, you can make the settings the default for new shapes by right-clicking on its border and choosing Set AutoShape Defaults from the shortcut menu.
- If a Drawing toolbar button is dimmed or an option in its menu is dimmed, then the feature cannot be applied to the selected graphic.
- Three-dimensional charts can have quite a visual impact. Use the Chart | 3-D View command to fine-tune the chart by changing the elevation and rotation of the dimensions and the height of the walls.
- Word gives you two ways to chart information from an Excel worksheet in your document. Create the worksheet by using the Insert Microsoft Excel Worksheet button in the toolbar and then creating the chart, or start a default chart and import the worksheet data by using the Edit | Import File command.
- Use the Drawing toolbar to add special effects and other elements to a completed chart.

Formatting Shortcuts

11

If there is one theme that applies generally to Word, it is ease of use. In this chapter, you'll learn several powerful features that exemplify this theme. Wizards and templates, for example, help you create completely formatted documents with a few clicks of the mouse. Styles give you consistent formatting and make it easy to change how your document appears.

Word Magic with Wizards

A *wizard* is a series of dialog boxes that takes you step-by-step through inserting text and formatting a document. Word comes with wizards for newsletters, resumes, memos, letters, faxes, agendas, legal pleadings, calendars, and tables.

To start a wizard, select New from the File menu to display the New dialog box, and then click the tab for the category of document you want to create. Icons that have little magic wands indicate the wizards.

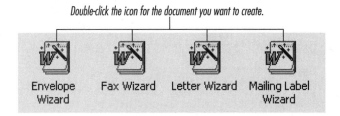

Double-click the icon for the document you want to create.

Envelope Wizard   Fax Wizard   Letter Wizard   Mailing Label Wizard

TIP: Have your Office CD handy when you use wizards. Then those wizards that have not been installed, can be installed from the CD when you first need them.

In a series of dialog boxes, you select options or enter text to appear in the completed document, as shown here. In this case, the steps to be followed by the wizard are listed on the left.

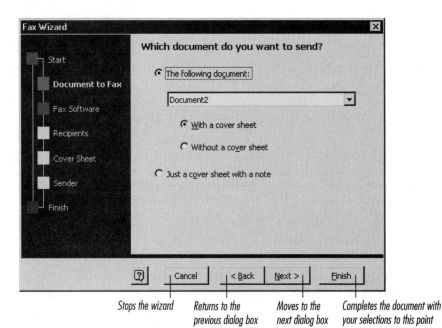

Stops the wizard   *Returns to the previous dialog box*   *Moves to the next dialog box*   *Completes the document with your selections to this point*

Figure 11-1, for example, shows a completed wizard for a fax cover sheet. You can now complete the fax as needed, clicking on the prompts to enter your information. Click the Send Fax Now button when you're ready to send the fax using your fax modem.

TIP: If you do not have information to enter at a prompt, click the prompt and press DEL. If you do not delete the prompt, it will print with the document.

Edit or delete the sample text as necessary.

Click the prompt to enter your information.

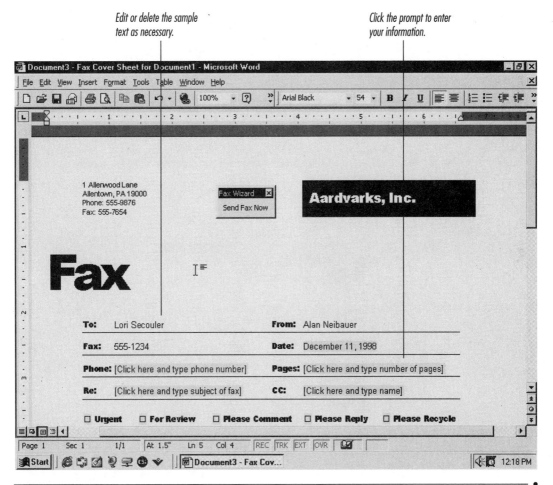

FIGURE 11-1 The completed fax, reduced to 75 percent to show the heading information

When you want to write a letter, consider the Letter Wizard. Instead of displaying a series of dialog boxes, this wizard has just one, but with four pages of options. Choose Letter Wizard from the Tools menu to see the dialog box in Figure 11-2. Enter the appropriate information in the dialog box, and then click OK to display the completed letter.

N O T E : If you start this wizard from the New dialog box, you'll be asked if you want to create one letter or use a mailing list. You'll learn about mailing lists in Chapter 12.

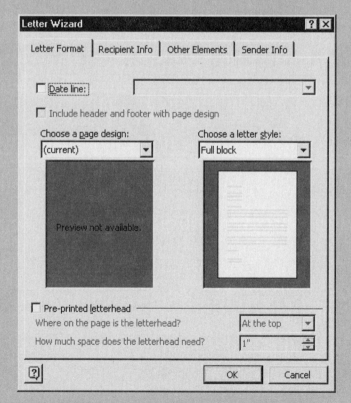

FIGURE 11-2 Using the Letter Wizard

Word Templates

A *template* is just like a document that wizards create, except that no dialog boxes appear. You start a new document by using the template and then customize it for your needs. Most templates have prompts that show you where to enter your information, and some templates have extensive details on how to use the styles and formats that are available. When you save the document, the original template remains unchanged so you can use it again.

 NOTE: When you start Word, it automatically uses a *Normal* template that contains all the default Word values.

Word comes with a number of templates that help you create common types of documents. For example, suppose you want to write a purchase order. Instead of worrying about the format and style, you start a new document based on the Purchase Order template. Then you need only enter name and address information and the details of the order itself.

To use a template, select New from the File menu, and then click the tab for the type of document you want to create. Templates use the icon shown here.

Double-click the template you want to use, and then wait until Word displays the document on the screen. As with wizard documents, the template may contain illustrative text and prompts in square brackets.

You'll note that the title bar shows a generic name—Document1, Document2, and so on. This indicates that you have not really *opened* the template, but are just using it as a basis for your own document. Any changes that you make to the text or formats will not affect the template itself, just the current document.

Creating Your Own Templates

Templates are so useful that you may want to create your own. For example, suppose you frequently write legal documents. Each time you start such a document, you change the page size to legal, type your letterhead, add a line down the left margin of the page, and turn on line numbering. Instead of doing this for every new legal document you type, create a template with these formats. Then just use the template when you need to type a legal document.

To create a new template, follow these steps:

1. Select New from the File menu.
2. In the New dialog box, click the Template option button to tell Word that you are creating a template rather than a document.
3. Next choose Blank Document on the General page to start with a blank document, or choose one of the existing templates to use it as the basis of your own template.
4. Click OK to see a document window labeled "Template1."
5. Change any of the page layout options, and add and format any text that you want to appear on every copy of the template. For example, to change the paper size, select Page Setup from the File menu, and then click the Paper Size tab. Pull down the Paper Size list and select Legal 8½ x 14 In. To add line numbers, click the Layout tab and then the Line Numbers command button. In the dialog box that appears, click Add Line Numbering.
6. Once the template is complete, choose Save from the File menu, type a name for the template, and click Save. Word saves new templates in the TEMPLATES folder with the extension DOT. Close the document window.

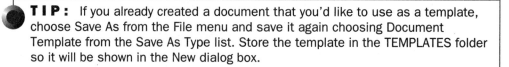

T I P : If you already created a document that you'd like to use as a template, choose Save As from the File menu and save it again choosing Document Template from the Save As Type list. Store the template in the TEMPLATES folder so it will be shown in the New dialog box.

Using Your Templates

When you want to type a document using the template, choose New from the File menu and click the General tab if that page is not already displayed. Double-click the icon named for your template.

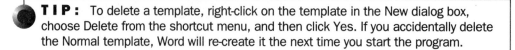

T I P : To delete a template, right-click on the template in the New dialog box, choose Delete from the shortcut menu, and then click Yes. If you accidentally delete the Normal template, Word will re-create it the next time you start the program.

Modifying Templates

You can modify a template, even those supplied with Word, by opening the template into a document window. To modify a template, select Open from the File menu. Use the Look In list to select the TEMPLATES folder or the other location where you may have saved your own templates. Pull down the Files Of Type list and select Document Templates. Double-click the template you want to edit.

TIP: By default, Word lists only documents with the DOC extension in the Open dialog box. So when you change to the template folder, you will not see your templates listed. Choosing Document Templates from the Files Of Type list will display files with the DOT extension.

With the template opened in a document window, modify the text or formats so the template is the way you want it for new documents. Then click the Save button or select Save from the File menu.

Formatting with Style

Templates and wizards streamline your formatting because they are based on *styles*. Styles let you apply even the most complex combinations of formats easily and consistently any number of times. A style is just a collection of formats that you can apply to text. You can store many different styles—collections of formats—and then apply them to text whenever you want.

There are two general types of styles: character and paragraph. A *character* style can only contain font formats—such as the typeface, size, style, effect, and color of characters—and language options. A *paragraph* style can contain any font or paragraph format that you can apply to text, including line spacing, text flow options, borders, and text alignment. You can apply both a character and paragraph style to the same text.

Using Word's Styles

The Normal template has about 75 styles defined for you—styles for all Word's built-in features, such as footnotes, tables of contents, and indexes. You can take advantage of these built-in styles to format your own documents.

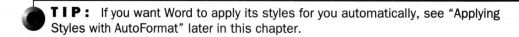

TIP: If you want Word to apply its styles for you automatically, see "Applying Styles with AutoFormat" later in this chapter.

You can see what style is applied to the text at the location of the insertion point by looking in the Style box—the first text box in the Formatting toolbar. The word "Normal" means that you are using the Normal style, with the default font, line spacing, and text alignment that Word automatically applies to new documents. You can apply another style to text by selecting it from the pull-down list.

The list displays only a basic set of the styles in the Normal template. As you apply or create other styles, however, they will be added to the list. To display all the styles, hold down SHIFT while you pull down the list. The list will now contain a scroll bar so you can see all the built-in styles. The box to the right of each style indicates its type, alignment, and font size.

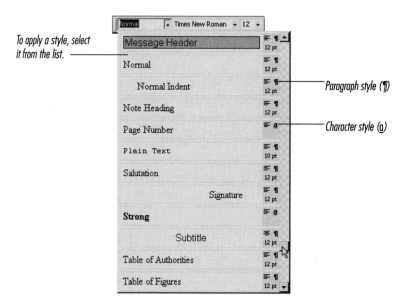

To apply a style, select it from the list.

Paragraph style (¶)

Character style (a)

- To apply a paragraph style to a single paragraph, or a character style to one word, place the insertion point anywhere in the paragraph or word.
- To apply a style to more than a paragraph or word, select the text first, and then choose the style.
- To apply a style to new text, choose the style from the list, and then type your text.

Some styles remain in effect when you press ENTER, so subsequent text will appear in the same format. Other styles end when you press ENTER, so subsequent text is in the Normal style. This is useful for formats that you only want to apply to one paragraph, such as headings or titles.

Applying Styles with the Style Dialog Box

You can also apply styles through the Style dialog box. Select Style from the Format menu to display the dialog box, and then look in the List section. If the setting is Styles In Use, then the dialog box only displays the styles currently applied to the document. Pull down the list and select All Styles. You will now see a list of the styles in the Normal template, as shown in Figure 11-3. When you select a style from the list, Word illustrates its formats in the Paragraph Preview and Character Preview panels, and lists the formats in the Description box. Choose the style you want to use, and then click the Apply button.

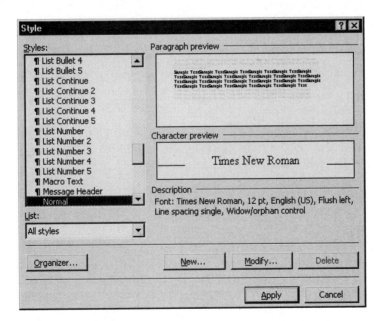

FIGURE 11-3 Applying Styles with the Style dialog box

Creating Your Own Styles

You may decide that you want to use combinations of formats other than those provided in Word's built-in styles. You can create your own styles—even add them to the Normal template or to another template. The easiest way to create a style is *by example*. Format text using the options that you want to save in a style. Place the insertion point in the text, and then click the Style box in the toolbar. Type the name you want to give to the style and press ENTER.

N O T E : Styles by example are always paragraph styles. To create a character style, use the New Style dialog box, as explained in the next section.

Word records the paragraph formats of the text in the style. If you also want to record character formats with the style, select a word in the paragraph with the formats you want to save.

N O T E : A style that you create by example can only be used in the active document. To use the style with all new documents, it must be added to the template, as explained in "Creating Styles with the New Style Dialog Box" or in "Modifying Styles with the Dialog Box."

Creating Styles with the New Style Dialog Box

To create character styles and more sophisticated paragraph styles, use the New Style dialog box. Choose Style from the Format menu, and then select New to see the dialog box shown in Figure 11-4.

If there already is a style that contains similar formats, choose it in the Based On list. This will save you from reselecting those formats.

Next, pull down the Style For Following Paragraph list, and select the style to take effect when you press ENTER after typing text in your new style. The default is to use the same style so the formats are carried down to the next paragraph. If you want the style to affect only one paragraph at a time, select Normal in the Style For Following Paragraph list.

N O T E : You cannot select a Style For Following *Paragraph* for character styles.

1 Enter the style name.

2 Choose the style type.

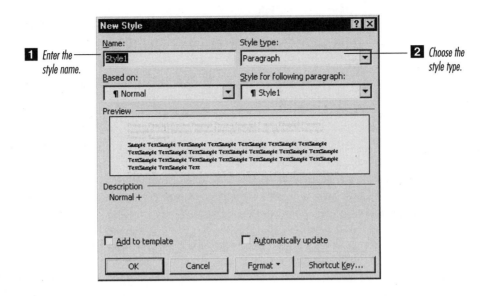

FIGURE 11-4   Creating a new style

Now you have to choose the formats that you want to apply to the style. Click the Format button to see the options shown here.

Choose an option from the list to display the appropriate dialog box.

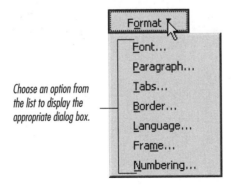

N O T E :   All the formats except Font and Language will be dimmed for character styles.

For example, if you select Paragraph, Word displays the Paragraph dialog box. Choose formatting options from the dialog box and then click OK. Repeat the procedure for each type of format that you want to apply.

 TIP: If you create a style by example and want to add it to the template, select the style in the Style dialog box, click Modify, and then select the Add To Template check box. You'll learn more about modifying styles soon.

Finally, click OK to accept the new style and to return to the New Style dialog box. Before choosing OK to save the style, however, consider these two options in the New Style dialog box:

- **Add To Template**   Unless you save your new style in a template, it is only available for use with the current document. Turn on this option if you want to use the style with every document that uses the current template.
- **Automatically Update**   You'll soon learn how to change a style. If you turn on this option, however, Word will automatically modify a style if you change the format of text to which the style was applied.

Modifying Styles

You can modify a style, even those in the Normal template, to change the formats that it applies. When you change a style, all text formatted by the style in the current document changes automatically to reflect the new formats. For example, suppose you use the Heading 1 style to format a series of headings in Arial, 14 points, bold. If you change the style to Times New Roman, 18 points, all the headings will immediately be changed to that style.

You can modify a style by example or by using the Style dialog box.

Modifying a Style by Example

To change a style by example, select text that is already formatted using the style. Then use the toolbar or dialog boxes to format the text as you want to modify the style. Next, pull down the Style list in the toolbar, and select the same style already applied to the text.

Word displays the Modify Style dialog box shown here.

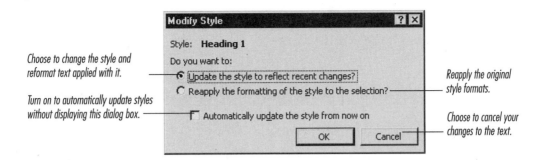

Choose to change the style and reformat text applied with it.

Turn on to automatically update styles without displaying this dialog box.

Reapply the original style formats.

Choose to cancel your changes to the text.

Modifying Styles with the Dialog Box

You can also modify a style by using the Style dialog box. This way you can change the based-on style and the style for the following paragraph, and you can add the style to the template. To change the style, place the insertion point in text formatted with the style, and select Style from the Format menu. Click the Modify button to display the Modify Style dialog box, which has the same options as the New Style dialog box. Make your changes and then click Close.

Formatting Pages and Text Automatically

Sometimes it is easier to concentrate on writing the text of the document if you leave formatting for later. You can always go through the completed document to apply styles, but it may be easier to have Word apply styles for you. In fact, you can have Word insert backgrounds and even add styles.

You can use the Theme command from the Format menu to format your document at once. However, themes work best when the document already uses styles, such as the Title and Heading styles. So before picking a theme, let Word apply styles for you.

 N O T E : If you have already applied heading styles yourself, or have no headings in the document, jump ahead to "Using Themes."

Applying Styles with AutoFormat

When you type your document, you may be too busy to worry about selecting styles to format titles and headings. Rather than going through your document again just to format it, let Word do that for you.

Choose AutoFormat from the Format menu (you may have to expand the menu) to see this dialog box:

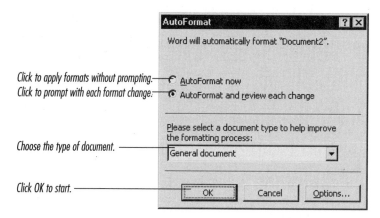

Click to apply formats without prompting.
Click to prompt with each format change.

Choose the type of document.

Click OK to start.

When you choose to apply the formats without prompting, Word scans your document, formatting text with styles and adjusting the layout. Word distinguishes titles, subtitles, and headings based on their current format and using a set of rules that may seem somewhat contrived. For text to be converted into a *title,* for example, it must be centered at the beginning of the document, it must start with an uppercase letter, and it must not wrap at the end of the line. A blank line or a subtitle—another line of text meeting the same criteria as the title—must follow it. A *heading* is text that starts with an uppercase letter and ends with a carriage return, without wrapping at the end of the line. *Subheadings* are headings that are indented.

Reviewing AutoFormat Changes

If you choose to review the format changes, Word performs the AutoFormat and then displays this dialog box.

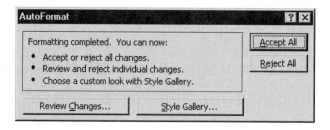

If you opt to review the changes, Word highlights the first text that was changed and displays this dialog box:

If the Reject button is dimmed in the dialog box, press ENTER or click the Find button.

N O T E : Word also displays revision marks on the document. Click the Hide Marks button in the Review AutoFormat Changes dialog box to remove the marks from display. Revision marks *indicate where changes have been made.*

Choose Reject to undo the change to the text, and then click one of the Find buttons to move forward or backward through the document, stopping at the next or previous change. To accept a change, just click one of the Find buttons. If you change your mind about the last item you rejected, click Undo.

T I P : Click Find Next After Reject to have Word automatically move to the next change in the document when you click Reject.

When you have finished reviewing the changes, close the Review AutoFormat Changes dialog box. Word displays the AutoFormat dialog box again. Select Accept All to accept those changes that you did not reject, or choose Reject All to remove all the changes from the document.

Using Themes

Once your document is formatted by use of styles, you can take advantage of collections of styles that will apply different formats to the elements in your document.

Word has two general ways to do this. The most graphic and eye-catching method is to select a *theme*. Themes include backgrounds, graphic lines, and vivid colors. You also apply less-graphic formats by using the Style Gallery. The Style Gallery replaces the styles already applied with a set of other styles.

To select a theme, choose Theme from the Format menu to see the dialog box shown in Figure 11-5. Choose the theme you want to apply and then click OK.

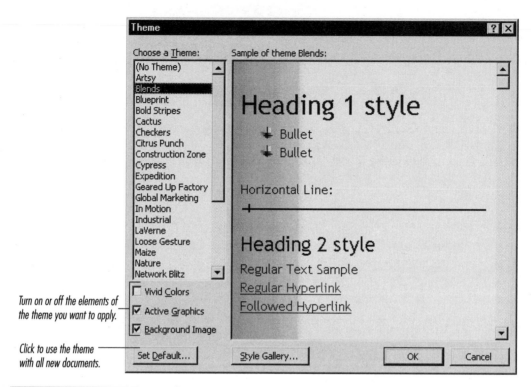

Turn on or off the elements of the theme you want to apply.

Click to use the theme with all new documents.

FIGURE 11-5 Selecting a theme

Using the Style Gallery

If you are printing your document with a monochrome printer, or just don't need the high-fashion look of themes, then choose from the Style Gallery. Click the Style Gallery button in the Theme dialog box to display the dialog box shown in Figure 11-6.

The list of templates on the left of the dialog box represents the collections of styles. To see how a template will affect your document, click the template in the list and then select the Document option in the Preview section. Your document will appear in the Preview Of panel. You can also select Example to see a sample document that uses most of the styles, or you can select Style

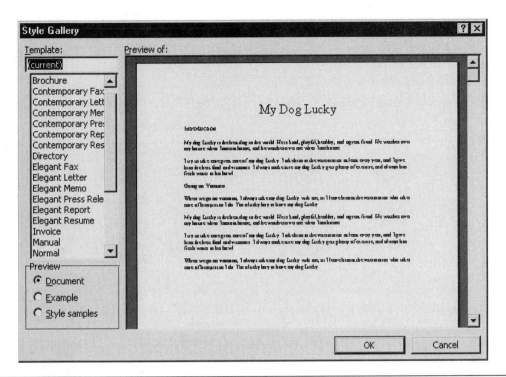

FIGURE 11-6 Selecting from the Style Gallery

Samples to see the name of each style in its format. Select OK from the dialog box to apply the formats to your document.

Attaching a Template

Now that you know about templates, you may have existing documents that you'd like to format using one of Word's templates or one of your own. It's not too late. To apply the styles of a template to an existing document, you *attach* the template.

Attaching a template makes its styles as well as its AutoText entries, macros, and other custom features available to the active document. To attach a template to the open document, select Templates And Add-ins from the Tools menu to see the Templates And Add-ins dialog box.

Select Attach to see the Attach Template dialog box. This box is just like the Open dialog box, except by default it lists template documents in the TEMPLATES folder. Use the dialog box to select the template you want to attach, and then select OK to return to the Templates And Add-ins dialog box.

 N O T E : Attaching a template does not insert any text from that template into the current document. For example, attaching the Fax template will not display the text that appears if you start a new document using that template.

To automatically apply the styles to existing text, click the Automatically Update Document Styles check box and then choose OK. Word will reformat any text using a style with the same name as a style in the attached template. For example, it will reformat paragraphs using the Heading 1 style with the formats of the Heading 1 style in the template.

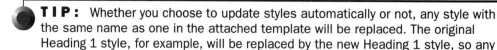 **T I P :** Whether you choose to update styles automatically or not, any style with the same name as one in the attached template will be replaced. The original Heading 1 style, for example, will be replaced by the new Heading 1 style, so any text to which you now apply the style will use the new formats.

Using Global Templates

If you want to use AutoText and macros from another template, but not that template's styles or any standard text, then make the template *global*. To create a global template, choose Templates And Add-ins from the Tools menu to display the Templates And Add-ins dialog box, and then select Add. You'll see the Add Template dialog box, which is the same as the Attach Template dialog box but with a different title. Select the template that you want to make global, and then click OK to return to the Templates And Add-ins dialog box. The name of the template will appear in the Global Templates And Add-ins list with a selected check box. The check mark indicates that any macros and AutoText entries of the template will be available for use in the document. You can add more than one global template.

The next time you start Word, the global templates will still be listed in the Templates And Add-ins dialog box, but the check box will not be selected. Select the check box if you want to make the template's resources available.

TIP: When you no longer want to use a global template, select its name in the Global Templates And Add-ins list and then click Remove. To temporarily make the resources unavailable, uncheck the check box.

- Word saves your wizard dialog box selections so the next time you run the wizard, it will have those same settings. To use them all, just click Finish in the first Wizard box.

- If you accidentally make unwanted changes to the normal template, search for and delete the file NORMAL.DOT on your hard disk. Word will re-create a new normal template the next time it starts.

- If Microsoft Outlook is set as your default e-mail program for Internet Explorer, you can create an e-mail by clicking on the E-Mail button on the Standard toolbar or by selecting E-Mail Message from the General tab of the New dialog box.

- Use the Web Page Wizard from the Web Pages tab of the New dialog box to create a professional looking web page.

- If you installed Office over a previous edition, your old templates are not lost. Click the Office 97 Templates tab of the New dialog box to access them.

- Be careful saving your templates. Make sure to save them in the same folder where Word stores its own templates, so you can access them from the New dialog box.

- Some themes are highly decorative and may not appear well when printed on a monochrome printer. If you select a colorful theme, print a test page of your document.

- Unless you only plan to use a new style in the current document, turn on the Add To Template option in the New Style dialog box. Do not turn on Update Automatically unless you plan to be very careful. With this option turned on, you can accidentally affect text throughout the document by changing the format of text to which the style was applied.

- Heading styles are used by a score of Word features, such as tables of contents, indexes, and the Style Gallery. It pays to use these styles if you're creating a long document.

- Remember, you can always use the Undo button if you apply an incorrect format or style, or choose Undo AutoFormat from the Edit menu if you change your mind about applying automatic formats.

Streamlining Repetitive Work

12

When you find yourself doing the same thing over and over again, do you say to yourself, "There's just got to be a better way?" Well, there is. In fact, Word has two powerful features just to cut down on repetitive routine chores. Using Mail Merge, you can create form letters, envelopes, labels, and even price lists and catalogs. With the Macros feature, you can quickly repeat any operation or series of tasks regardless of how many steps are involved.

Creating Form Letters

A *form letter* is a document that you send to more than one person. You just need to change some of the text, even if it's only the address and salutation, to customize it for each recipient. To create a form letter, you need a mailing list and a form document. In Word, the mailing list is called a *data source,* and the form document is called the *main document.*

The data source can contain information about products, clients, and any other type of information that you might want to use for form documents. A data source for letters, for example, may contain the recipients' first and last names, address, city, state, and ZIP code. Each of these items in the data source is called a *field.*

You link the main document with the data source so it can access the name and address information. Every place in the document where you want an item from the mailing list, you insert a code giving the name of the field that you want inserted. So instead of actually typing the recipient's name, for example, you insert a *field code* for the last name and first name. When you merge these two parts, Word inserts the information from the mailing list into the appropriate locations in each letter.

Creating a Mailing List

Mail Merge Helper helps you design the data source to avoid errors during the merge process. Start by selecting Mail Merge from the Tools menu to display the dialog box shown in Figure 12-1, and then click Create to see the four types of main documents that you can create—Form Letters, Mailing Labels, Envelopes, and Catalog.

Click Form Letters to see these options.

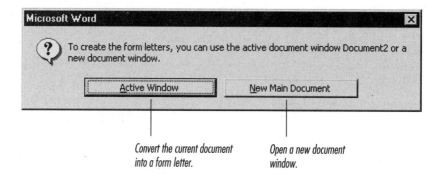

Convert the current document into a form letter.

Open a new document window.

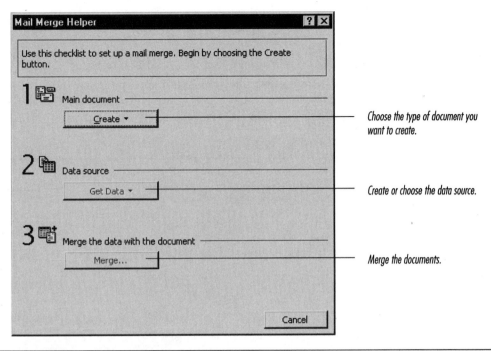

Choose the type of document you want to create.

Create or choose the data source.

Merge the documents.

FIGURE 12-1   Mail Merge Helper

Click New Main Document to open a new document window and to redisplay Mail Merge Helper. You have just created a blank form letter. Before entering information into the form letter, however, create the data source that will be linked with it.

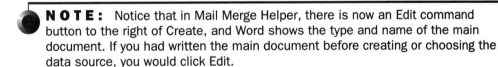

NOTE: Notice that in Mail Merge Helper, there is now an Edit command button to the right of Create, and Word shows the type and name of the main document. If you had written the main document before creating or choosing the data source, you would click Edit.

Click Get Data to display these options:

- **Create Data Source** Lets you create a new data source.
- **Open Data Source** Lets you choose an existing data source.
- **Use Address Book** Lets you use information from the Outlook address book, a personal address book, or Microsoft Schedule+.

- **Header Options** Lets you link an existing data source with a separate list of field names.

Click Create Data Source to see the dialog box shown in Figure 12-2.

To remove a field from the list, click the field name in the Field Names In Header Row list, and then click Remove Field Name. To add a field to the list, type it in the Field Name box, and then click the Add Field Name button.

 N O T E : Field names cannot include spaces. If the Add New Field button is dimmed, then the field name is invalid.

When you are done working with the fields, click OK to see the Save As dialog box. Type a name for the data source, such as **Mailing List**, and then click Save. A dialog box appears with the options Edit Data Source and Edit Main Document.

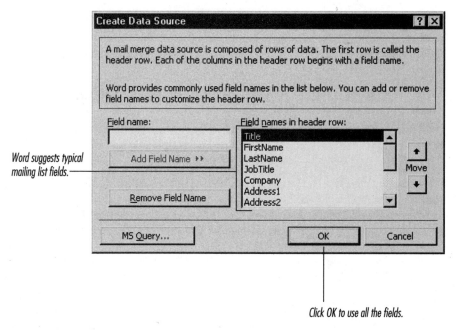

Word suggests typical mailing list fields.

Click OK to use all the fields.

FIGURE 12-2 Word suggests fields for a mailing list

Click Edit Data Source to display the Data Form dialog box, shown in Figure 12-3. (If you wanted to type the main document now and complete the data source later, you would choose Edit Main Document.) The Data Form box makes it easy to enter information into the data source, as well as to edit and find records. The insertion point will be in the text box for the first field.

Type information for the field and then press ENTER to move the insertion point to the next field. Fill in the rest of the fields, pressing ENTER after each. If you don't have any information for a field, such as a second address line, just leave it blank. By default, Word will not print a blank line for the field that contained no information. When you press ENTER after typing the entry for the last field, Word adds the information to the data source, clears all the text boxes, and places the insertion point in the first text box to start another record.

When you're done entering information, click OK. Word clears the Data Form box from the screen and displays a blank main document window. The window is the same as any document, except that it includes the Mail Merge toolbar shown here.

FIGURE 12-3 Enter and edit records in the Data Form dialog box

Writing the Form Letter

You write, format, and edit a main document using the same techniques you use in any Word document. However, when you come to a place where you want Word to insert information from the data source, you enter a field code.

Click the Insert Merge Field toolbar button to display a list of field names in the data source:

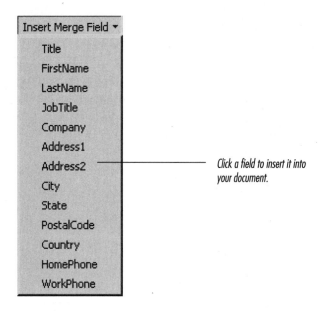

Click a field to insert it into your document.

Merge fields appear surrounded by chevrons (« »). Continue entering fields, text, and punctuation as needed to create the letter. You can use the fields in any order in the main document, and you can use a field more than once—or not at all. A completed form letter is shown in Figure 12-4.

TIP: If a field appears in curly brackets, such as {MERGEFIELD name}, then the display of merge fields is turned on. Although you can still complete and merge the letters this way, turn off the option by pressing ALT-F9. Showing the fields in brackets makes it more difficult to read your letter and to judge its spacing on the screen.

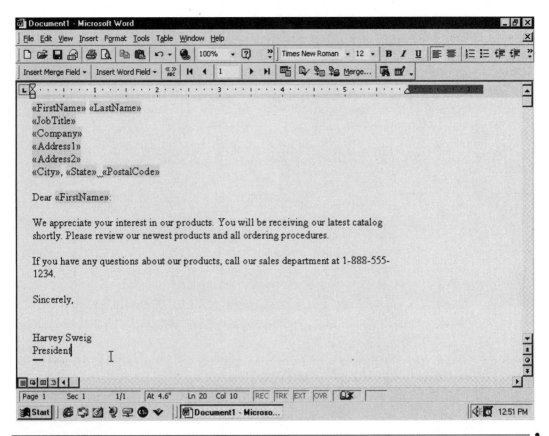

FIGURE 12-4 The completed sample form letter

Viewing Records

To see how the form letter will appear with the information from the data source, click the View Merge Data button. Word replaces the field codes with the actual information from the first record in the data source.

Use the buttons shown here to change the record, or to indicate which record is being displayed.

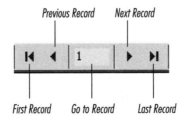

If you are looking for specific information, click the Find Record button on the Mail Merge toolbar. In the dialog box that appears, enter the information you are looking for and the field where Word can find it, and then click OK. Word will display that record onscreen in the form document.

Before you merge, you should also check for errors. An error will occur, for example, if you use a field code for a field that does not exist. This may occur if you edit the field code after you insert it, or if you enter the codes manually. Click the Check For Errors button in the Mail Merge toolbar to select from these choices:

Merging Form Documents

With the main document and data source complete, you can merge them at any time. Whenever you open the main document, it automatically appears with the Mail Merge toolbar and will be linked with the data source.

Open the main document, and then click either of these buttons:

- **Merge To New Document**   Word performs the merge, creating one large document containing all the form letters, each of the letters separated by a page break.
- **Merge To Printer**   Word merges the main document with the data source records, printing a completed letter as each record is merged.

Controlling Your Merge

When you click Merge To Printer or Merge To New Document, Word merges all the records in the database. You can customize the merge process by clicking on the Merge button to display the dialog box shown in Figure 12-5.

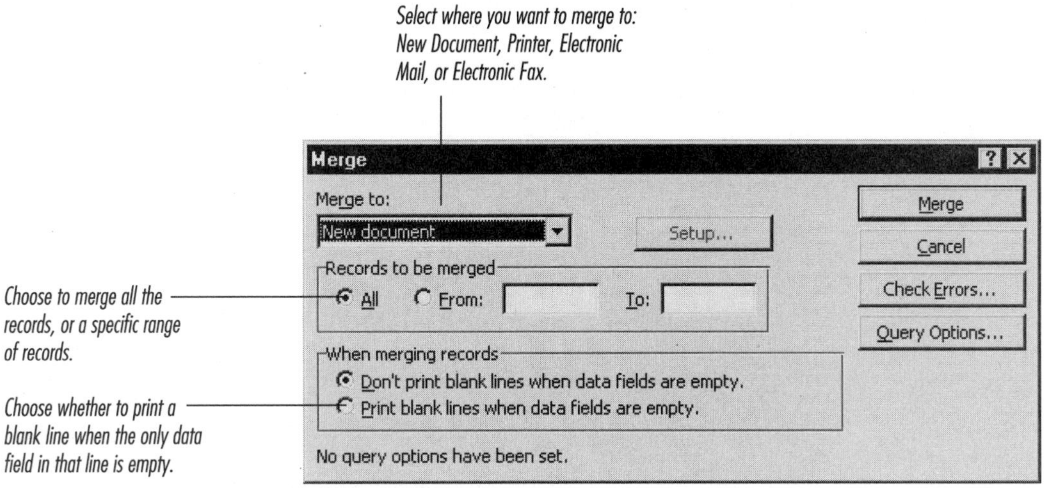

Select where you want to merge to:
New Document, Printer, Electronic
Mail, or Electronic Fax.

Merge [?][X]

Merge to:
[New document ▼]   [Setup...]   [Merge]

┌Records to be merged──────────────   [Cancel]
  ⊙ All   ○ From: [   ]   To: [   ]   [Check Errors...]

┌When merging records──────────────────   [Query Options...]
  ⊙ Don't print blank lines when data fields are empty.
  ○ Print blank lines when data fields are empty.

No query options have been set.

Choose to merge all the
records, or a specific range
of records.

Choose whether to print a
blank line when the only data
field in that line is empty.

FIGURE 12-5 Control the merge with the Merge dialog box

 TIP: You can also display the Merge dialog box by choosing Merge from Mail Merge Helper.

Printing Envelopes for Form Letters

You can use Mail Merge Helper to print a series of envelopes for everyone on your mailing list. To print envelopes, start Mail Merge Helper, click Create and choose Envelopes, and then select New Main Document. To use the same data source as you used for the letters, click Get Data, choose Open Data Source, and then select the data source filename in the dialog box that appears. Next, choose Setup Main Document to display the Envelope Options dialog box—the same box you learned about in Chapter 7. Once you select the options, including envelope size, select OK to display the Envelope Address dialog box, shown in Figure 12-6.

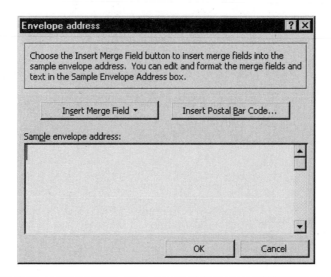

FIGURE 12-6 The main document window for envelopes

This dialog box serves as the main document for envelopes. Use the Insert Merge Field button to insert the merge codes for the address, just as you did when creating the inside address for the letter. If you want to include a bar code, click Insert Postal Bar Code to display the options shown here.

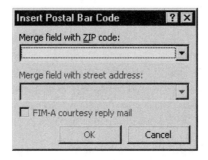

Pull down the Merge Field With ZIP Code list, and select the name of the field containing the ZIP code. Then pull down the Merge Field With Street

Address list, and select the field with the address. Select OK twice to return to Mail Merge Helper, and then complete the merge.

Merging to Labels

You can merge data onto mailing labels as easily as onto envelopes. Follow the same procedure as you did with envelopes, but choose Mailing Labels from the Create list. When you choose to set up the main document, you'll see the Label Options dialog box, shown in Figure 12-7.

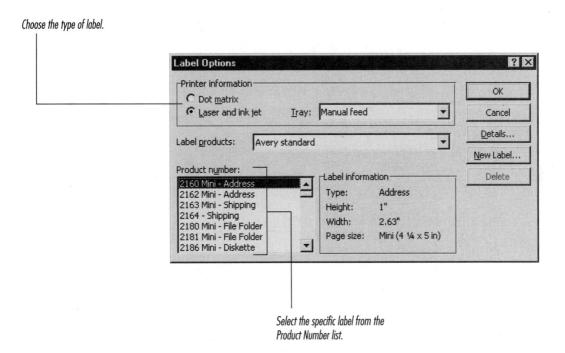

Choose the type of label.

Select the specific label from the Product Number list.

FIGURE 12-7 The Label Options dialog box for mailing lists

If you are using a label that is not listed in the dialog box, select one that is similar, and then click the Details button to see the dialog box shown in Figure 12-8.

Select OK from the Label Options dialog box to see the Create Labels dialog box, with the same options as Create Envelopes. Enter the field codes just as you did for envelopes, and select postal code fields.

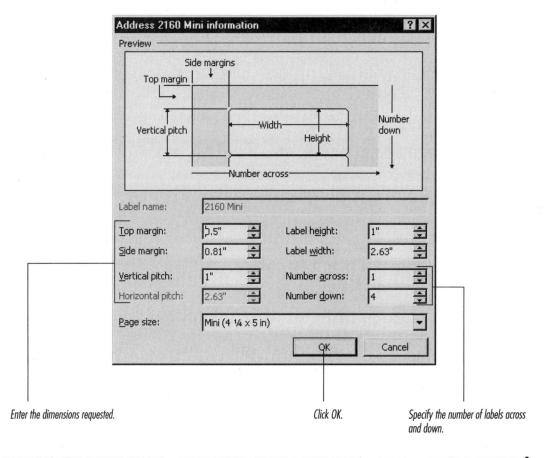

Enter the dimensions requested.

Click OK.

Specify the number of labels across and down.

FIGURE 12-8 Create a custom label if yours is not already defined

Do you need to produce mailing lists, price lists, sales catalogs, or other documents that list a series of items on each page? Let Word help you.

When you merge to letters or envelopes, each one prints on a separate sheet. But by using the Catalog option in Mail Merge Helper, you can merge your data into a list. With this option Word does not insert a page break between each record. Instead, it prints one after the other, adding a page break only after each page becomes full. Here's an example of a merged document using the Catalog feature:

Stock and Price List

Item	Stock#	Price	Category
Sweig Scanner 101	FSTR101	129.50	Hardware
Woodin CD-R/RW	WDN76652	352.35	Hardware
Jimmy's Flight Simulator	JM716Wa	54.75	Software
All-In-One-Office	SH612v4	412.00	Software
All About Office	665-39834-98	19.95	Book
Disk 3.5"	FD3500	.54	Supply
Disk 5.25	FD525	.25	Supply
Toner HP111	HP67254a	65.00	Supply

To create this type of list, start with a main merge document and enter and lay out the field codes for how you want each record to appear, something like this:

«ProductName»	«ProductID»	«Price»	«Type»

Press ENTER one, two, or more times, after the final line so the merged document has blank spaces between records. Then complete the merge to a new document—you cannot merge a catalog directly to the printer.

When the merged documents appear onscreen, add any page titles, column headings, or other text you want to dress up the catalog, and then print it.

Working with Mailing Lists and Data Sources

Chances are that your data source will not remain constant. When you need to add, delete, or edit records in the data source, display the main document, and then click the Edit Data Source button in the Mail Merge toolbar to display the Data Form box.

 TIP: You can also display the Data Form box by selecting Edit from the Data Source section of Mail Merge Helper.

Use these options in the Data Form box:

- **Add New** Saves the record being displayed and is used to start a new record.
- **Delete** Removes the displayed record from the data source.
- **Restore** Cancels the changes you made to the displayed record.
- **Find** Locates a specific record.
- **View Source** Displays the data source as a Word table.

When you select the View Source command, Word displays the data source as a table, along with the Database toolbar:

ProductName	ProductID	Price	Type
Sweig Scanner 101	FSTR101	129.50	Hardware
Woodin CD-R/RW	WDN76652	352.35	Hardware
Jimmy's Flight Simulator	JM716Wa	54.75	Software
All-In-One-Office	SH612v4	412.00	Software
All About Office	665-39834-98	19.95	Book
Disk 3.5"	FD3500	.54	Supply
Disk 5.25	FD525	.25	Supply
Toner HP111	HP67254a	65.00	Supply

The Database toolbar buttons are described in the following table.

BUTTON	NAME	FUNCTION
	Data Form	Display the Data Form dialog box
	Manage Fields	Add, remove, and rename fields
	Add New Record	Insert a new row at the end of the table
	Delete Record	Delete the record in which the insertion point is placed
	Sort Ascending	Sort the rows of the table in ascending order, using the column in which the insertion point is located
	Sort Descending	Sort the rows in descending order
	Insert Database	Insert records from another data source
	Update Fields	Update any selected Word fields in the data source
	Find Record	Locate a record
	Mail Merge Main Document	Display the main document

Working with Fields

When you want to change the actual fields in the data source, click the Manage Fields button in the Database toolbar to display these options:

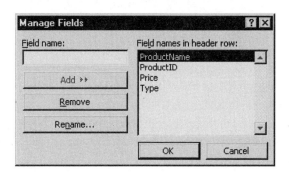

To insert a new field into the data source, type the name in the Field Name text box, and then select Add. To delete a field, select it in the list box, click Remove, and then select Yes from the confirmation dialog box. To change a field's name, select it in the list box, click Rename, type the new name in the box that appears, and then select OK.

Linking a Main Document with Another Source

When you create a form letter, you have the option of editing it even before you create or select a data source. You can select the data source at a later time, or change the source if you merge it with records from another data source.

 REMEMBER: The new data source you select must include the field names used in the main document.

To select a data source, open the main document and click the Mail Merge Helper button, or select Mail Merge from the Tools menu. Click Get Data, and then select either Create Data Source to create a new data source for the document, or Open Data Source to merge the document with an existing data source file.

Selecting Merge Records

If you want to merge a specific record from the data source, you can display the main document, click the View Data button in the Mail Merge toolbar, and then use the other buttons to display the record you want on the screen. You can also select a specific record, or a range of records, in the Merge dialog box.

When you want to merge records based on the contents—such as all clients in California—use the Query Options command to create a filter. A *filter* tells Word to use only the records that meet certain conditions for the merge operation, ignoring those that do not meet the conditions. The records not used during the merge remain in the data source—they are just ignored, not deleted.

To create a filter, display the Mail Merge dialog box and click Query Options. Click the Filter Records tab in the Query Options dialog box to display the options shown in Figure 12-9.

FIGURE 12-9 Use the Filter Records options to select records for your merge

You use the six rows of text boxes to specify up to six conditions that a record must meet to be used for the merge. There are three steps to setting a condition:

1. Select a field.
2. Select a comparison operator.
3. Enter a value.

In the first row of the dialog box, pull down the Field list and select a field that you want to use as a condition. Then choose an operator from the Comparison list, shown here:

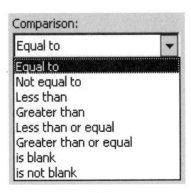

Finally, enter a value to compare with in the Compare To box. For example, to send letters to California clients, select State as the Field, choose Equal To as the Comparison, and type **CA** in the Compare To box.

Use the remaining rows of boxes to specify additional conditions. For each condition, pull down the And/Or box and select either an AND or an OR operation. An *AND* operation will select records that meet both of the conditions; an *OR* operation selects those meeting one, the other, or both. So suppose you want to send letters to all clients in California who owe over $1,000. This is an AND operation because the records must meet both conditions—they must be in California and owe over $1,000. But suppose you want to send letters to clients in California and Oregon. This is an OR condition because the client must meet at least one of the conditions.

When you've completed the conditions, select OK and perform the merge. To erase all the conditions, choose Clear All.

 REMEMBER: Word saves your conditions with the main document. If you later want to merge all the records, you must display the Query Options dialog box and choose Clear All.

Creating a Macro

A *macro* is a stored collection of keystrokes and mouse actions that performs a task. For instance, suppose you regularly create a shadow box around text by using the Borders And Shading dialog box. Each time you create the box, you must display the dialog box, click the Shadow preset, and then choose the line and shading options. If you store that series of actions in a macro, you can repeat all of them by running the macro, rather than performing the individual steps. You can even assign the macro to a button on the toolbar, to a shortcut key combination, or to one of Word's menus. When you want to create the shadow box, just click the toolbar button, press the key combination, or select the option from the menu.

You create a macro by recording the keystrokes and mouse selections as you perform the task. To create a macro that prints the current page, for example, you actually print a page of a document, recording the actions that you perform. You can then run the macro later to print whatever page the insertion point is located on.

Start by double-clicking on the dimmed characters "REC" in the status bar, or select Macro from the Tools menu, and then select Record New Macro. You'll see the dialog box shown in Figure 12-10. Type a Macro Name—it must

Name your macro.

Create a key combination to run the macro.

Click OK to start recording.

Add your macro to a toolbar.

Select where the macro is saved.

Enter a description of the macro.

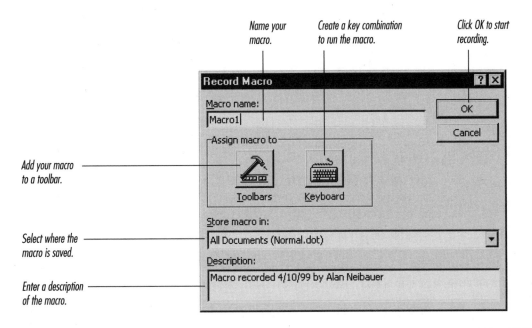

FIGURE 12-10 Word's dialog box to record macros

start with a letter and cannot contain punctuation marks or spaces—in the Record Macro dialog box.

The setting in the Store Macro In box determines which template the macro will be stored in. When set at All Documents (Normal.dot), the macro will be available for use with every document. If you are using another template, you can store the macro there by choosing that template in the Store Macro In list. Choose the name of the current document to make the macro only available in the document.

 N O T E : If you type an invalid macro name, the OK button will be dimmed.

When you click OK, the Macro toolbar appears, and the mouse pointer includes an icon of a cassette tape when it is in the text area, as shown here.

When you're recording a macro, select text and move the insertion point by use of the keyboard—you can use the mouse only to select menus and dialog box options. Perform the steps that you want to record, and then click the Stop button in the Macro toolbar. You can also stop recording by double-clicking on the REC indicator in the status bar or by selecting Macro from the Tools menu and then choosing Stop Recording.

Running a Macro

Whenever you want to perform the recorded function, you run the macro. If you've saved the macro in the Normal template, you can run it when any document is on the screen, not just the document that was displayed when you recorded the macro.

Select Macro from the Tools menu, and click Macro to display the dialog box shown in Figure 12-11. If the Macros In list is set at All Active Templates And Documents, you'll see all the macros available in the Normal template, and any attached or global templates. Double-click the macro name, or select it and click Run. Word runs the macro, repeating its commands.

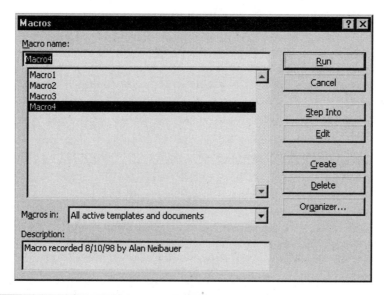

FIGURE 12-11 Run and delete macros in this dialog box

- While this chapter illustrates mail merge by use of a mailing list, you can merge any type of information.

- If you selected the wrong main document type, such as Form Letters when you really wanted Catalog, it is not too late to change. With the main document open, choose Mail Merge from the Tools menu, and then select the new type of document from the Create list. Finally, click Change Document Type from the box that appears.

- Want to incorporate graphics in a catalog or other merge document? Use the View Source command to display the data source table, and then insert graphics in one of the unused table columns. Don't have an unused column? Choose Insert from the Table menu and add a new column.

- You can merge form letters and their envelopes at the same time. Create the main document for the letter, choose Envelopes And Labels from the Tools menu, and click Add To Document. In the envelope section that Word inserts, add the field codes for the mailing address. When you merge the document, each envelope will precede its corresponding letter.

- If you use Microsoft Outlook, you can merge information from the Outlook or Personal address book. In Mail Merge Helper, choose Use Address Book from the Get Data list, and then choose the source of the information. Create a distribution list in Outlook's Contacts folder to merge documents with a subset of the contact listings.

- Deleting a field from the Manage Fields dialog box also deletes all the information for that field in the data source. Use this option with caution.

- Use the Sort buttons in the Database toolbar, or the Sort command from the Table menu, to sort records in ascending or descending order before you merge them. Sort an address list by the ZIP code field, for example, to prepare for bulk mailing.

- Choose Security from the Tools Macro menu to select a security level. It is possible, but not probable, that some downloaded Word macros may contain a computer virus. The Security option lets you specify that only macros from trusted sources be run, that you be warned about potential viruses, or that every macro is run without warning.

- Use the Pause button in the Macro toolbar to temporarily stop recording so you can perform a task that you do not want as part of the macro. Click the Pause button again to continue recording.

- In the Macros dialog box, you can choose to modify a recorded macro by selecting it and clicking on the Edit button. This opens the Visual Basic Editor that requires specialized knowledge of this programming language.

Working with Excel

Introducing Excel Worksheets

13

With Excel, you can create financial documents and business forms, plot charts and maps, and work with information in databases. But Excel's ability to solve real-world problems stands out. For example, how would your profits change if you gave employees a raise? Excel can automatically recalculate values when you change even a single number, so you can see the effects of that change every place it affects.

Introducing Excel

Start Excel just as you learned in Chapter 2, to see the screen shown in Figure 13-1. Excel contains most of the common elements that you'll see in typical Office programs. Below the formatting toolbar, however, is the *Formula bar,* where you enter and edit information, and the *Name box,* which tells you where you are working in Excel.

The word "Ready" on the left on the status bar means that Excel is ready to accept your commands. As you work with Excel, you'll see other modes displayed in the status bar, such as "Enter" when you are typing information, or "Edit" when you are changing information.

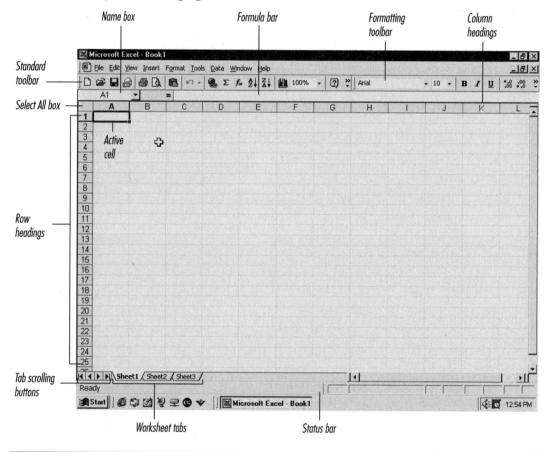

FIGURE 13-1 The Excel window

An Excel file is called a *workbook,* and it consists of one or more pages, called *worksheets.* Each new workbook contains three worksheets, but you can add and delete sheets as needed. The first workbook you open during an Excel session is called Book1, the second Book2, and so on, but you give the workbook a more meaningful name when you save it.

A worksheet is organized into lettered columns and numbered rows. Worksheets have 256 columns, numbered A through Z, then AA through AZ, BA through BZ, and so on, up to column IV. There are 65,536 rows. The intersection of a row and a column is called a *cell,* and you refer to a cell by its column letter and row number—called its *address* or its *reference.* So the address of the cell in the upper-left corner of the worksheet is A1 (the column letter always comes first) because it is in column A and row 1. The cell to its right is B1, and the cell below that is B2.

Entering Information

To create a worksheet, you move from cell to cell to enter or edit information. The cell that is ready to be filled or formatted is called the *active cell.* Its address appears in the Name box, the cell is surrounded by a dark rectangle, and its row number and column letter appear in boldface. Using the mouse, click in the cell that you want to make active. Use the scroll bars if necessary to bring the cell into view, or use the Go To command from the Edit menu to move to a specific cell.

Whatever you type also appears in the Formula bar, along with two additional buttons:

Click this Cancel button or press ESC if you change your mind and want to leave the cell unchanged.   Click this Enter button or press ENTER or any other cursor movement key, to accept your changes to the cell.

As you type in a cell, you can use the BACKSPACE key to erase characters, but you can't use the arrow keys to move the insertion point. Pressing an arrow key accepts your entry and moves to another cell.

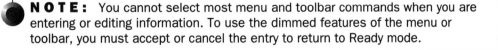

N O T E : You cannot select most menu and toolbar commands when you are entering or editing information. To use the dimmed features of the menu or toolbar, you must accept or cancel the entry to return to Ready mode.

A cell can contain text, numbers, formulas, or dates and times. It is important to distinguish between these, and to know how to enter them.

Typing Text

Text is any information that contains nonnumeric characters, other than a date or formula, and it appears on the left side of the cell. If you enter more information than can fit in the cell, Excel runs the overflow into adjacent blank cells. If an adjacent cell is not empty, however, Excel displays only as many characters as fit. The complete entry is still stored in the worksheet, and it appears in the Formula bar when the cell is active.

When you start typing text, Excel automatically displays an entry already in the column that begins with those characters. Press ENTER to accept the suggested entry or just continue typing.

	A	B	C	D
1				
2				
3				
4		Sales		
5		Rentals		
6		Leases		
7		Total Income		
8		Salaries		
9		Supplies		
10		Rental		
11		Total Income		
12				
13				

Typing Numbers

To enter a number into a cell, start with a number, an equal sign, plus sign, or minus sign. When you accept the entry, the number appears on the right of the cell, and Excel removes any zeros that come at the end of a number following the decimal point. If you enter **12.10**, for example, Excel displays "12.1."

If you type a whole number up to 11 places, Excel widens the column to display it without running long numbers into adjacent cells. If the number contains decimal places or is larger than 11 places, Excel may display the number rounded, show it in scientific notation (such as 6.24E+09), or even display a series of "#" signs. You'll have to reduce the font size, widen the column, or change the format to display the value.

Entering Dates and Times

To enter a date, just type it using either a slash or a hyphen between the month, day, and year. When you accept the entry, Excel moves the date to the right of the cell and changes hyphens to slashes. Dates always appear in the format *mm/dd/yyyy* in the Formula bar.

 TIP: To enter today's date in the active cell, press CTRL-; (semicolon). To enter the current time, press CTRL-SHIFT-: (colon).

To enter the time, separate the hours, minutes, and seconds (which are optional) with colons as in 11:16:45. Follow the time with "A" or "AM," or with "P" or "PM." If you do not indicate AM or PM, Excel assumes AM. You can also type times in 24-hour format, but times are shown in 12-hour format in the Formula bar.

 NOTE: Internally, Excel stores dates and times as serial numbers so it can perform math operations on them. Days are numbered starting with 1 for January 1, 1990. Decimal numbers starting with 0.000 for midnight to 0.99999 for one second to midnight the next day represent times.

Entering Formulas

A formula is a mathematical operation that uses any combination of cell references and actual values. You can use a formula to simply perform math, such as entering 106*3 to display the result of the calculation, but the most important use of formulas is to reference other cells.

You should start every formula with a plus or equal sign. For example, the formula to subtract whatever is in cell A1 from what is in cell A2 is =A2-A1. When you accept the entry, Excel calculates and displays the result in the cell. If you later change the value in either cell A1 or A2, Excel recalculates and displays the new result.

You can also start a formula by clicking on the equal sign in the Formula bar to display the Formula palette:

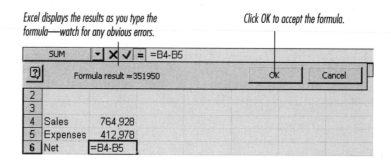

Excel displays the results as you type the formula—watch for any obvious errors.

Click OK to accept the formula.

Excel reports some types of errors when you try to accept the formula. In some cases, it may suggest a correction. If so, click Yes in the message box to accept its suggestion, or No to fix it yourself.

You can also create formulas by using dates. If cells F10 and H23 contain dates, for instance, calculate the number of days between them by using the formula =H23-F10. Excel displays the result in the format *mm/dd/yy*, showing the number of months (mm), days (dd), and years (yy) between the dates.

Precedence of Operators

Excel, and almost every similar program, does not perform math in the exact order of operators from left to right. Instead, it scans the entire formula, giving precedence to certain operators over others. So when you're typing formulas, remember "My Dear Aunt Sally." This little memory helper stands for Multiplication-Division-Addition-Subtraction, because Excel performs multiplication and division first (in whatever order they are in) and then addition and subtraction.

The most common example of this is computing an average. If you enter the formula =100+100+100/3, Excel displays the result as 233.3333 because it first divides 100 by 3 and then adds 100 twice. To perform the calculation correctly, use parentheses to force Excel to follow a different order, such as =(100+100+100)/3.

You can use more than one level of parentheses, but you must have a closing parenthesis for every opening parenthesis. To help you as you enter a formula, each opening parenthesis appears in a different color. When you type a closing parenthesis, it appears in a matching color—so make sure you have a closing parenthesis in each of the colors of the opening ones.

Clicking Referenced Cells

Rather than trying to remember the address of a cell that you want to enter into a formula, you can insert it by clicking. When you reach the place in the formula where the address belongs, just click the cell you want to insert. Excel inserts the address of the cell into the formula and surrounds the cell in a *moving border*—dashed lines moving clockwise around the cell. For example, suppose you want to enter the formula =G12*A1. Here's how you'd do it:

1. Select the cell where you want to put the formula, and then type = (the equal sign).
2. Click cell G12. Excel inserts the address G12 into the Formula bar and displays the moving border around the cell.
3. Type * (the symbol for multiplication).
4. Click in cell A1 to insert its address into the formula.
5. Press ENTER.

Typing Cell References

In dialog boxes and when creating some formulas, you need to designate a range of cell addresses rather than a single cell. If the cells are all in one row or column, just type the two end cells in the format A1:A5.

If the cells are in more than one row and column, use the two cells in opposite corners. For example, the range A1:B5 includes the ten cells shown here:

If the cells are not contiguous, separate the addresses with commas, as in A1,B4,C7, or in combination, as in A1:A5,C15.

Selecting Cells

You'll have to select cells to perform an action on more than one cell at a time, such as to apply a format, or to enter their addresses into formulas and dialog boxes.

To select a group of cells, point to a cell at one end of the group so the mouse pointer appears like a white plus sign and then drag to the other end. As you drag, the cells become highlighted, and the number of rows and columns being selected appears in the Name box. Release the mouse when the cells you want are selected, or drag back while holding down the mouse button if you've selected too many. The first cell you selected will stay white, which means that it is the active cell.

You can also select entire rows and columns:

- To select an entire row, click its row number.
- To select an entire column, click its column letter.
- To select the entire sheet, click the Select All button—the empty shaded cell to the left of column A.

TIP: Drag down row headers with the white plus sign pointer to select adjacent rows, or drag across column headers with the white plus sign pointer to select adjacent columns.

Selecting Cells in Dialog Boxes

Many dialog boxes can perform a function on a range of cells. Sometimes you can select the cells before displaying the dialog box, and the reference will appear automatically. In most cases, you can insert the range of cells by selecting them after the dialog box is open. Look for the Collapse Dialog button next to a text box where you would otherwise enter a range of cells:

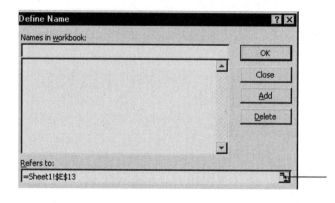

Click this Collapse Dialog button to collapse the dialog box, showing just the text box and the Expand Dialog button.

Drag over the cells you want to insert into the box, and then click this Expand Dialog button to return the dialog box to its full size.

You can also collapse and expand the dialog box automatically if you can see the start of the range in the background of the box. Click in the text box associated with the button, and then click the first cell of the range and start to drag. Excel automatically collapses the dialog box. When you release the mouse, the dialog box expands automatically.

Saving, Opening, and Printing Workbooks

Excel uses the same general Office techniques for working with files:

- Click the Save button to save your workbook with the XLS extension.
- Click the Print button to print your worksheet. When the worksheet reappears, you'll see lines indicating the page breaks.
- Click the workbook's Close button or choose Close from the File menu to close the workbook without exiting Excel. If you have not saved the workbook since you last changed it, a dialog box will appear giving you the chance to do so.
- Click the New button to start a new workbook, or choose New from the File menu to start a workbook using a template.
- Click the Open button to open a workbook, or select it from the Recently Used File list at the bottom of the File menu.

Changing Column Width

You can widen columns to display long entries, or reduce the width of a column that has short entries where space is being wasted. To quickly make a column as wide as its widest entry, double-click the line to the right of its column letter.

You can also change column width by dragging. Point to the line to the right of the column letter so the mouse pointer appears as a two-headed arrow. Then hold down the left mouse button and drag. As you drag, a box appears showing the width of the column, so drag until the column is the size you want.

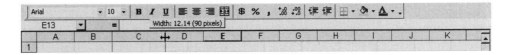

To adjust the height of rows by dragging, point to the line under the row letter so the mouse appears like a double-headed arrow and then drag.

You may have trouble setting a precise column width by dragging. If so, click in any cell in the column, choose Column from the Format menu, and click Width. In the dialog box that appears, enter the width in number of characters and then click OK. To change row height, choose Row from the Format menu, click Height, and then enter the desired height in points.

The AutoFit option on the Format Row submenu sets the row height for the largest entry. The AutoFit Selection option from the Format Column submenu adjusts the column to the current cell entry—wider entries in the column will not fully appear.

Editing Your Work

If you click a cell and start typing, anything already in the cell is deleted. (If you do this by mistake, press ESC or click the Cancel button in the toolbar before moving off the cell.) This is fine if you want to replace the entire contents, but what if you just want to correct a small typo or change a number? Instead of retyping the entire entry, you can just make any required changes to it.

You can edit a cell either in the cell itself or in the Formula bar. To edit the entry in the cell, double-click the cell, or make it active and press F2. To edit it in the Formula bar, make the cell active, and then click the Formula bar. Click the Enter button in the Formula bar or press ENTER to accept your changes. Press ESC or click the Cancel button to restore the cell's contents.

You edit formulas just as you do text and numbers. If a cell address is incorrect, switch into Edit mode and retype the address, or drag over the incorrect address and click the cell you want to insert. In Edit mode, by the way, Excel surrounds all the referenced cells in colored frames and displays their addresses in the formula in matching colors. This feature, called *Range Finder,* helps you keep track of the cells being referenced in the formula.

Erasing Information from Cells

There are two ways to get rid of information—clearing and deleting—and they are quite different. *Clearing* erases what's in a cell, row, or column. *Deleting* actually removes the cell from the worksheet, moving other cells up or over to take the place of the deleted cells. Don't delete cells if you don't want to change the position of other cells.

 N O T E : You'll learn about deleting cells later in this chapter.

The quickest way to clear a cell is to select it and press DEL. This erases what you see in the cell but not any formats that you've applied to it. To delete everything from the cell, select Clear from the Edit menu and choose All. To just remove the formats, leaving the contents, choose Formats from the Clear submenu.

Having AutoFill Complete Entries

In many cases, you'll need to enter a series of sequential entries, such as incrementing numbers (1, 2, 3…), or the days of the week, months of the year, and so on. Rather than type each of the values yourself, you can start the series and have Excel complete it for you by using *AutoFill*. The trick is to drag the Fill handle, the little black box in the lower-right corner of the selected cell:

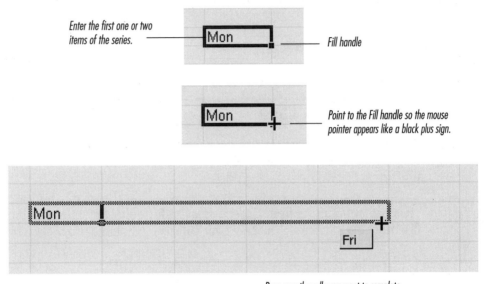

Enter the first one or two items of the series. — Fill handle

Point to the Fill handle so the mouse pointer appears like a black plus sign.

Drag over the cells you want to complete.

For example, if you type **Mon** in cell C4, and then drag its Fill handle across to cell G4, Excel inserts Tue, Wed, Thu, and Fri, completing the weekdays. As you drag the mouse, a ScreenTip appears showing what will be inserted into the cell under the mouse cursor. Other AutoFill series that Excel can complete are shown in Table 13-1.

NOTE: If Excel does not recognize the series, it copies the entry into each of the cells.

1st, 2nd, 3rd, 4th, 5th,...
Qtr 1, Qtr 2, Qtr 3, Qtr4, Qtr 1,...
Jan, Feb, Mar...
January, February, March...
Mon, Tue, Wed, Thu...
Monday, Tuesday, Wednesday...
Day 1, Day 2, Day 3...
Week 1, Week 2, Week 3...
Jan 98, Feb 98, Mar 98, Apr 98...
101 Days, 102 Days, 103 Days...
10/23/98, 10/24/98...

TABLE 13-1   Series that Excel can complete

Totaling Numbers with AutoSum

Because calculating the total of the values in a row or column is such a typical task, Excel gives you a one-click solution, the *AutoSum* button on the Standard toolbar.

To use AutoSum, select the cell where you want the total to appear, and then click the AutoSum button. Excel displays a formula containing the Sum function and surrounds the cells that will be totaled in a moving border:

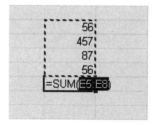

If the moving border is not around the cells you want to total, drag over the cells now. Finally, click the Enter toolbar button to insert the total.

You can also use AutoSum to add the values in a row. However, if the cells above where you want to add the total contain numbers, Excel inserts the column total instead. In this case, select the cells in the row along with the blank cell to their right, and then click the AutoSum button.

Selecting cells, by the way, is a good way to use AutoSum for totaling more than one row or column, as shown in Figure 13-2. Select cells as shown in the figure, and then click AutoSum to add row or column totals, or both.

Displaying Calculations

When you are just interested in seeing a calculation, such as the total or average of a series of values, you don't actually have to perform the math. When you select a series of cells, Excel automatically displays their total in the status bar like this:

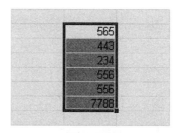

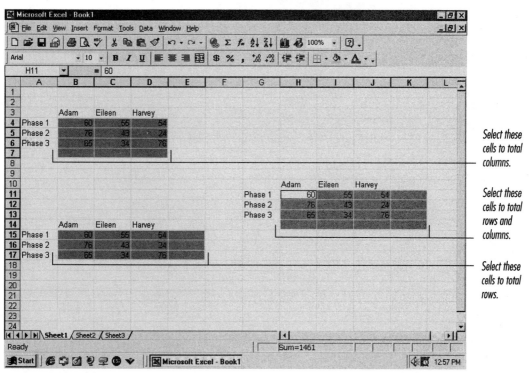

FIGURE 13-2 Selecting cells for AutoSum

Sometimes you may have a series that doesn't increment in some even number. Let's say that you want to meet with your vice president every two days starting on March 3, but skipping weekends, until May. So if you meet on a Friday, you don't want to meet again until the following Tuesday. This series really isn't every two days. To display these dates across a row, enter the starting date (3/3) in the first cell and then click the Enter button to keep the cell active. Next, choose Fill from the Edit menu, and click Series to see this dialog box.

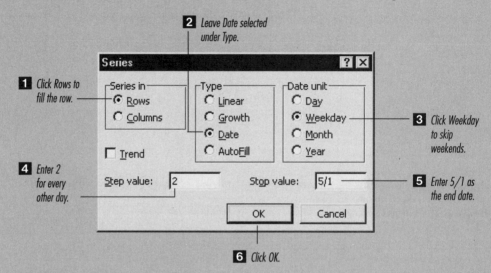

1 Click Rows to fill the row.

2 Leave Date selected under Type.

3 Click Weekday to skip weekends.

4 Enter 2 for every other day.

5 Enter 5/1 as the end date.

6 Click OK.

There are also some series that just don't follow a pattern. For example, let's say that your company has sales offices in seven states, and that you often create a worksheet with the state abbreviations as row headings. You can create your own AutoFill list to enter the series by typing the first state abbreviation and then dragging its fill handle. Here's how:

1. Type the series (or just find it in an existing worksheet).
2. Select the series.
3. Choose Options from the Tools menu.
4. Click the Custom Lists tab.

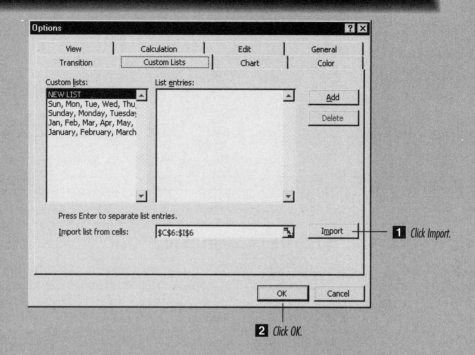

1 Click Import.

2 Click OK.

The range of selected cells is shown here.

Now when you need to add the series to a worksheet, just type the first abbreviation in the series and drag its fill handle.

To change the calculation displayed, leave the cells selected and right-click the status bar to choose from these options:

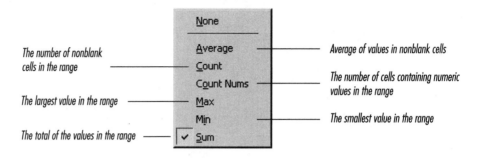

The number of nonblank cells in the range — Count

The largest value in the range — Max

The total of the values in the range — Sum

None

Average — Average of values in nonblank cells

Count Nums — The number of cells containing numeric values in the range

Min — The smallest value in the range

Moving and Copying Information

Sometimes you insert information in the wrong location, or you want to add the same entry to selected cells in the worksheet. Excel lets you move and copy information in much the same way as you can for any Office document—by using drag or drop, or the Cut, Copy, and Paste commands.

Using Drag and Drop

To drag and drop, point to the border around the selected cell or group of cells so the mouse pointer appears like an arrow, and then drag. As you drag, an outline of the selected cell or cells moves with the mouse cursor, and a ScreenTip reports the location where the cells will be dropped. Release the mouse button when you're at the correct location. (Hold down CTRL as you release the mouse button to copy the cells.)

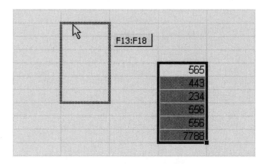

To move or copy entire rows, select the rows, point to the top or bottom border around the rows so the mouse appears as an arrow, and then drag and

drop. To move or copy entire columns, select the columns, point to the left or right border around the columns so the mouse appears as an arrow, and then drag and drop.

Using the Clipboard

In Chapter 2, you learned how to use the Clipboard to move or copy information, and to store up to 12 different entries. The Clipboard works the same in Excel, except when you cut or copy a cell, it appears in the moving border. You can then paste the cell by using any of these techniques:

- Press the ENTER key.
- Click the Paste button in the Standard toolbar.
- Choose Paste from the Edit menu.
- Right-click and choose Paste from the shortcut menu.

If you use any technique other than pressing ENTER to paste the cells, the moving border stays around the cells and you can paste the same information repeatedly. Just press ESC to remove the border when you are done pasting the cells.

When you copy cells into the Clipboard, you can also paste information into cells using the Paste Special command from the Edit menu to display this dialog box:

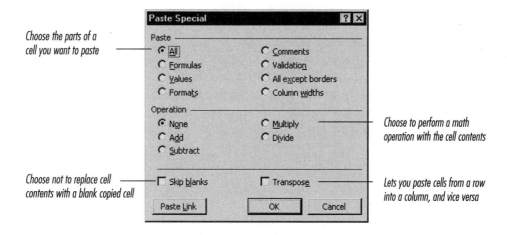

Choose the parts of a cell you want to paste

Choose to perform a math operation with the cell contents

Choose not to replace cell contents with a blank copied cell

Lets you paste cells from a row into a column, and vice versa

Moving and Copying Formulas

Because formulas contain cell references, Excel applies some special rules when they are moved or copied.

- When you *move* a formula, it is inserted so it still references the same cells it did in its original position. The formula moved is unchanged.
- When you *copy* a formula, Excel inserts it using a *relative reference*. This means that the cell addresses are adjusted to refer to the corresponding cells in the new location.

Think of a relative reference as a generic group of cells. While the original formula in the following illustration, for example, contains a list of five cell addresses, it really means "total the five cells above my location." When you copy the formula, it still means the same thing—generically—so it now totals the five cells above its new location.

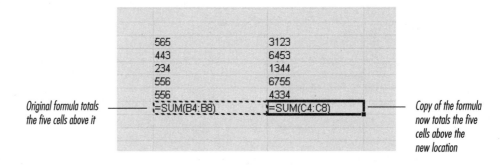

Original formula totals the five cells above it

Copy of the formula now totals the five cells above the new location

TIP: If you want to move the displayed *value* of a formula to a new location, *not* the formula itself, drag it with the right mouse button and choose Copy Here As Values Only.

This makes it easy to copy formulas. Remember, when you use the Fill handle on something other than a series, Excel copies the value into the cells. When Excel copies a formula, it changes it using a relative reference, so the Fill handle is a quick way to enter a formula once, then duplicate it in a series of cells as shown here:

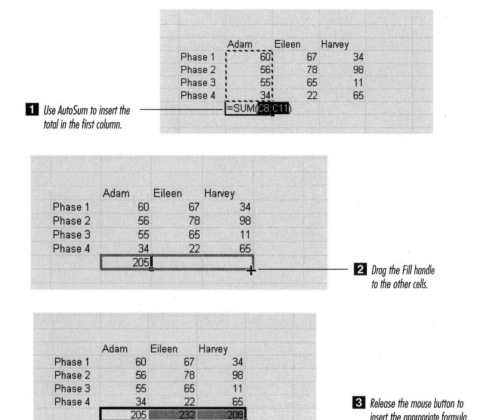

1 Use AutoSum to insert the total in the first column.

2 Drag the Fill handle to the other cells.

3 Release the mouse button to insert the appropriate formula into each cell.

TIP: Remember, you can use the Fill handle to copy formulas across rows or up or down through columns.

Inserting and Deleting Cells

Inserting and deleting cells, rows, and columns actually changes the position of other cells. When you delete a row, for example, the rows following it move up and are renumbered. When you delete a column, the columns to its right shift over and are relettered. Inserting works in the reverse. When you insert a row, the ones below it move down and are renumbered.

To insert a new row or column, right-click the row or column header and choose Insert from the shortcut menu. To insert several rows or columns at one time, select the number of rows or columns you want to insert first, and then right-click and choose Insert.

To delete a row or column, right-click its header and choose Delete from the shortcut menu. Select several rows or columns to delete them at the same time.

You can also insert or delete specific cells. Let's look at how to delete cells first. Select the cells you want to delete; then right-click and choose Delete from the shortcut menu to see these options:

Choose the effect you want. ———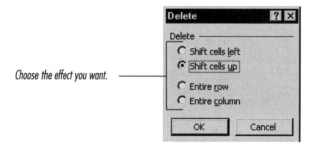

The Shift Cells options delete just the selected cells, moving existing cells up or to the left. If you choose Shift Cells Up, for example, the cells below the deleted one will move up in their columns. Excel doesn't shift up the entire row below the inserted cells, just the number of cells that you are deleting. If you choose Shift Cells Left, the cells to the right of the deleted ones will move toward the left in their rows.

When you insert cells, you can choose the opposite effects. You can choose to Shift Cells Down, for example, so it moves just the number of cells that you are inserting.

Rather than insert blank cells, you can also insert cells that you cut or copy from another location. To move a cell and insert it in another location, drag it with the SHIFT key held down. When you release the mouse, the cell will be moved to the new location, shifting existing cells down the column. Hold down SHIFT and CTRL to copy and insert a cell when you release the mouse.

- As a general rule, use cell references in formulas whenever possible so Excel will recalculate its result if referenced cells change.
- To print a specific group of cells, select the cells first, and then choose Print from the File menu. Click the Selection option in the Print What section of the dialog box that appears, and then click Print.
- To copy a cell by dragging without holding down the CTRL key, drag it with the right mouse button, and then choose Copy Here in the shortcut menu that appears when you release the button. From this same shortcut menu, you can also move cells, copy just the formats applied to the cell, copy the value of a formula, create a link, or insert the cell.
- After you insert or delete cells, rows, or columns, check your cell references in formulas to make sure they are still valid.
- Don't worry about the Year 2000 problem. If you do not type a year with a date, Excel adds the current year for you. If you only enter the last two digits for the year, Excel adds the first two. For example, Excel inserts "20" if you type **00** through **29** for the year (displaying 10/22/23 as 10/22/2023) and inserts "19" if you type **30** through **99** for the year.
- You can copy a text entry from a cell already in the column by using Pick From List. Right-click a cell and choose Pick From List from the shortcut menu to see a list of text entries in contiguous cells, and then click the entry you want to insert.
- Be careful when you're inserting or deleting cells. When you delete cells, not an entire row or column, some values may move away from the row or column labels that describe them. Check your work carefully to make sure values are aligned with their labels.
- To copy the contents of a cell to cells below it, select the cell and the ones that you want to fill, and then press CTRL-D. To copy the contents of a cell to those on the right, select the cells and press CTRL-R.
- When the values in a series you want to insert are not consecutive, enter the first two or three of the series. For example, to insert alternating dates down a column, enter the first date in one row and the second date in the next row. Select both entries and then drag the Fill handle of the second to complete the series.
- Use the Spelling command described in Chapter 2 to check your worksheet for spelling and typographical errors.

Formatting and Printing Worksheets

Your worksheets should be easy and pleasant to read—formatted to enhance the material, not distract from it.

You can format cells before or after you enter contents into them. You can also format text as you enter or edit it. Once you apply a format to a cell, the format is not removed when you clear the cell's contents. The format will automatically be applied to the next information you enter into the cell. To remove the format, you must choose Edit | Clear | Formats, or Edit | Clear | All.

Formatting the Entire Worksheet

To save time, you can apply a ready-made design to a selected group of cells or to the entire worksheet. Start by selecting the group of cells that you want to format, and then choose Format | AutoFormat to display this dialog box:

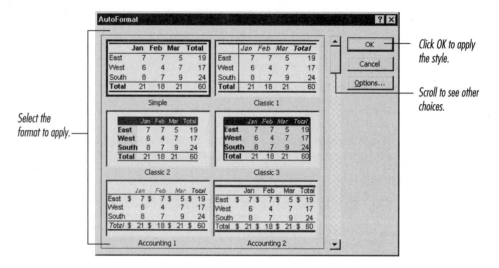

Select the format to apply.

Click OK to apply the style.

Scroll to see other choices.

Most AutoFormat styles apply a combination of fonts and colors, text alignments, and border styles. If you don't want to apply all the formats of the style, click Options in the AutoFormat box to display these choices:

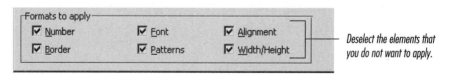

Deselect the elements that you do not want to apply.

Applying Formats to Text

Formatting the contents of cells is very much like formatting text in a Word document—you can change its font, size, style, color, and alignment. While you can format the individual characters in a *text* entry, all the characters in a *number* or *date* must use the same format.

You can stay in Ready mode if you want to apply a format to all the characters in a cell. For example, to boldface a single cell, just click the cell to make it active and then click the Bold button in the Formatting toolbar. To boldface all the text in a row or column, select the row or column first. If you want to apply formats to individual characters, you must do so while entering or editing information in the cell, not in Ready mode.

 N O T E : Formats only appear in the cell, not in the Formula bar.

Use of the Formatting toolbar, shown on its own line in Figure 14-1, is the quickest way to format cells. In fact, use the Font, Font Size, Bold, Italic, Underline, and Font Color buttons just as you learned in Word.

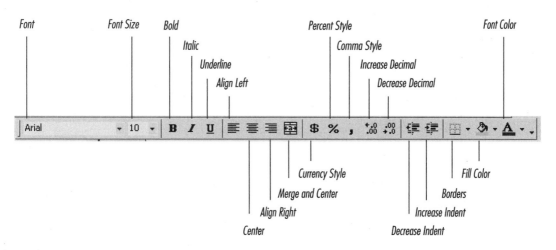

FIGURE 14-1 Excel's Formatting toolbar

As an alternative to the toolbar, you can apply any number of formats at one time with the Format Cells dialog box. To display the dialog box, choose Format | Cells, or right-click the cell you want to format and choose Format Cells from the shortcut menu. Make your choices from the box, and then click OK to apply them.

 TIP: Turn on the Normal Font check box in the Format Cells dialog box to restore the text to the default format.

Aligning Text in Cells

While text to the left and numbers to the right is Excel's default alignment, you can place text in other positions, as shown in Figure 14-2. The quickest way to

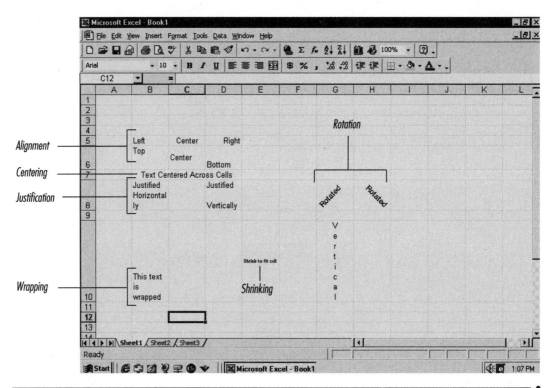

FIGURE 14-2 Positions for text in cells

change alignment is to select the cells you want to format, and then click one of these buttons on the Formatting toolbar:

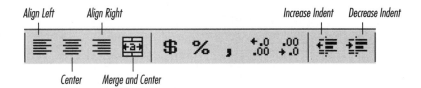

If you want to center a title across the entire page, use the Merge And Center button.

For example, suppose you want to center a title across the page. Here's how:

1. Type the text in the leftmost cell in the group of cells where it will be centered.
2. Select the cell containing the text and the cells you want it to be centered between.
3. Click the Merge And Center button.

Excel merges all the selected cells into one large cell and centers the text within it. To center text between columns A and H of a worksheet, for example, enter it in column A, drag over the cells in columns A to H of that row, and then click Merge And Center.

More Alignment Options

You can align text horizontally and vertically, indent text, and rotate text, using the Alignment tab of the Format Cells dialog box.

From the Vertical list on the page, for example, choose to place text in the top, center, or bottom of the cell. When you're using the default font and row height, you won't notice much difference, if any, in vertical alignments. These options are most useful when you increase the row height or use small fonts.

To create a special effect, you can rotate text in cells by using the Orientation section of the Alignment tab:

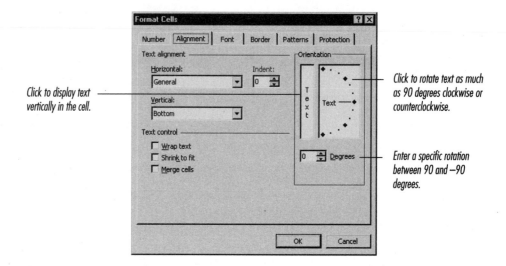

Click to display text
vertically in the cell.

Click to rotate text as much
as 90 degrees clockwise or
counterclockwise.

Enter a specific rotation
between 90 and –90
degrees.

Formatting Numbers

You can apply all the formats already discussed to numbers as well as text. With numbers, however, you can also select the numeric format, and the quickest way is to select from these buttons in the Formatting toolbar:

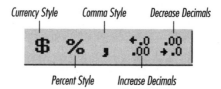

Currency Style   Comma Style   Decrease Decimals

Percent Style   Increase Decimals

The Currency style displays numbers with dollar signs, commas separating thousands, and two decimal places. The Comma style is just like Currency but without the dollar sign. The Percent format displays numbers with a percent sign. The Increase Decimal and Decrease Decimal buttons insert or delete another decimal position with each click.

 N O T E: Decreasing decimals will round off the value displayed in the cell, but not in the Formula bar.

While all the styles can be applied to numbers already in a cell or to a value you are about to type, the Percent style works differently. Applying the Percent style to an existing value converts it to its percentage equivalent. A cell that contains .05 will display 5%, and a cell that contains 5 will display 500%. Once you apply the percent style, however, you can enter a percentage as a nondecimal number—typing 7 will display 7%.

Using the Format Cells Dialog Box

When you want to format dates, create custom formats, or see more choices than you have on the Formatting toolbar, display the Number tab of the Format Cells dialog box.

When you select a general format in the Category list, Excel displays additional options to the right. For example, suppose you're preparing a worksheet as part of a bid for work in London. You don't want to display currency amounts as dollars, but as British pounds. If you choose Currency in the Category list, you can choose to use the pound symbol rather than the dollar. If you're an accountant, you'll find the options in this box handy because you can select how you want negative values displayed and the number of decimal places.

Some of the more interesting category choices are as follows:

- **Fraction**   Displays decimal values as fractions in your choice of formats.
- **Special**   Lets you choose such formats as Zip Code, Zip Code + Four, Phone Number, and Social Security Number. If you were to choose Phone Number and enter **2225551234**, Excel would display it as (222) 555-1234.
- **Custom**   Lets you create your own format.

Adding Lines and Colors

The gridlines that you see on the Excel screen make it easy to visualize rows and columns, but they do not print with your worksheet. This can make it difficult to read a printed worksheet. By adding printable gridlines to a worksheet, you not only make it easier to read, but you can create some eye-catching effects. You also can fill cells with colors and patterns for a professional looking presentation.

The quickest way to add lines and fill colors is to use the Borders and Fill Color buttons on the Formatting toolbar.

Click the button to apply the color shown.

Click the button to apply the border shown. — *Pull down the list to select a color.*

Pull down the list to select a border position.

For example, the border options are shown here:

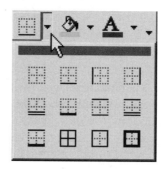

Your choice is applied to the selected cell or group of cells and becomes the new default option shown on the face of the button. When you select more than one contiguous cell, the border is applied to the group, not to individual cells in the group. So, for example, if you select six consecutive cells in one column and choose the bottom border option, the border will only appear under the last cell in the group. To add borders around every cell in a group, choose the All Borders option.

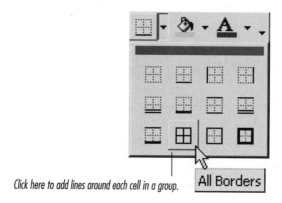

Click here to add lines around each cell in a group.　All Borders

NOTE: If you select noncontiguous cells, the border is applied to each.

The Border tab of the Format Cells dialog box, shown in Figure 14-3, offers additional features.

On the Patterns tab of the dialog box, you can choose from 56 colors, choose none at all, or choose a pattern. With patterns you can choose a foreground color and a background color. The *foreground* color takes the place of the black lines or dots in the pattern; the *background* color takes the place of the white between the lines or dots.

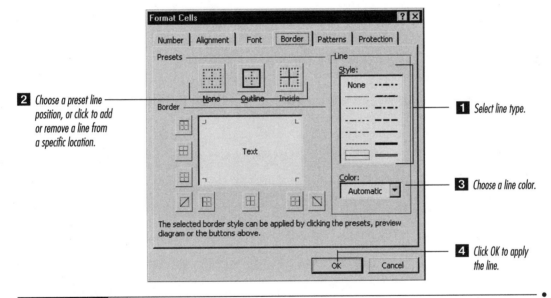

2 *Choose a preset line position, or click to add or remove a line from a specific location.*

1 *Select line type.*

3 *Choose a line color.*

4 *Click OK to apply the line.*

FIGURE 14-3 Border tab

Printing Worksheets

Now that you've learned how to format your worksheet, let's take a closer look at printing it. When you click the Print button on the Standard toolbar, Excel prints your worksheet using all the default formats. It knows how much to print by the contents, printing a rectangular area starting with cell A1 and including every cell with any content.

You can also choose to print specific pages, worksheets, or a range of cells. So if you want to print a hardcopy reference of a certain range of cells, you don't have to print the entire workbook. Most of the options in the Print dialog box (displayed by choosing File | Print) are generic to Office, as you learned in Chapter 2. But there are some differences, as shown in Figure 14-4.

Setting a Print Area

In some cases you'll want to print just a selected group of cells. To save the trouble of selecting them each time, you designate them as the *print area*.

1. Select the cells you want to print.
2. Choose File | Print Area | Set Print Area.

Excel displays a dashed line surrounding the cells, indicating the print area. Now when you click Print, only those cells will be printed, and if you choose Print Preview, only those cells will appear. When you want to again print the entire worksheet, choose File | Print Area | Clear Print Area.

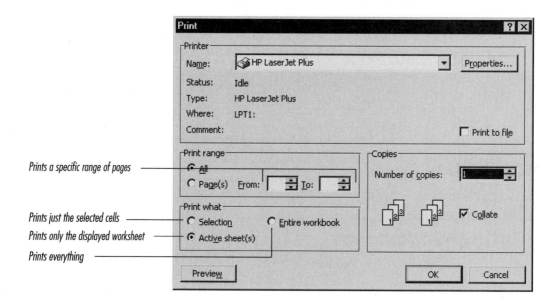

FIGURE 14-4 Print dialog box

TIP: You can only have one print area at a time—setting a new one replaces the other.

Dividing Your Worksheet into Pages

When you print a large worksheet, Excel divides it into pages for you. After you print or preview a worksheet, you'll see dashed lines on the screen showing where each page ends and begins. If you do not like how Excel divides the worksheet into pages, you can add your own page breaks.

 NOTE: As with Word, page breaks inserted by Excel are soft breaks, and they change as you insert and delete rows and columns. Your own breaks are hard breaks that do not move unless you change them.

You can insert vertical and horizontal page breaks. A *vertical* page break divides columns across pages; a *horizontal* page break divides rows across pages.

- To insert a horizontal page break, select the cell in column A where you want the new page to begin; then choose Insert | Page Break. Excel inserts a page break line above, so the row starts a new page.
- To insert a vertical page break, select a cell in row 1 where you want the new page to begin, and then choose Insert | Page Break. Excel inserts a page break line just to the left, so the column starts a new page.
- To insert both a horizontal and vertical page break, select the cell that you want to start the new page, other than in row 1 or column 2, and then choose Insert | Page Break.

 TIP: To remove a hard page break, select a cell in the top row (horizontal) or first column (vertical) of the page and choose Insert | Remove Page Break.

To visually change page breaks, choose View | Page Break Preview. Then click OK in the help message that appears to see page break lines and page numbers, as shown in Figure 14-5. The solid dark lines show the printable portion of the worksheet; the dashed lines are soft page breaks inserted by

Worksheet areas that will
be printed appear white.

Nonprinting
areas are gray.

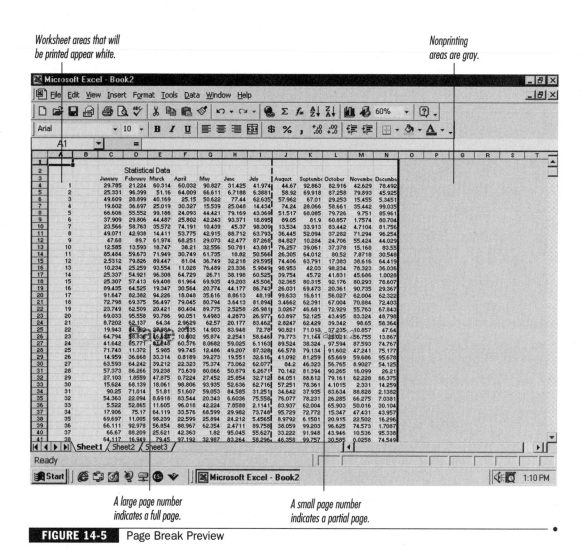

A large page number
indicates a full page.

A small page number
indicates a partial page.

FIGURE 14-5 Page Break Preview

Excel. To change a page break, just drag the break line. After you move a line, however, it becomes solid, indicating that it is now a hard page break.

To enter information into the gray area, just click and type as you would in Normal view. Excel automatically extends the printing area to encompass that cell.

To exit Page Break Preview, choose View | Normal.

Setting the Page Layout

Before printing your work, you should make sure the page layout is appropriate. The page layout determines the page size, margins, and orientation, as well as page titles, headers, and footers.

To set the page layout, choose File | Page Setup and then use the Page tab of the dialog box to change the size and orientation of the printed page, the print quality, and the print scale, as shown in Figure 14-6.

The Scaling setting lets you reduce the size of the printout to fit into a smaller area (values less than 100), or enlarge it to fit in more sheets (values over 100). To fill a specific number of pages, click Fit To and enter the numbers in the two text boxes for that option.

Use the Margins tab of the Page Setup dialog box to change the margins around the page, and the distance between headers and footers to the edge of

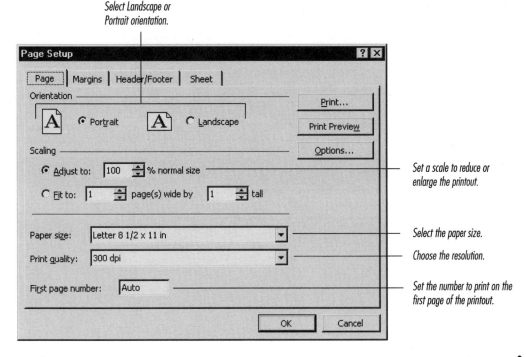

FIGURE 14-6   Changing the page size and orientation

the page. You can also choose to center the worksheet on the page vertically, horizontally, or both. Choose both vertical and horizontal centering when you have a small worksheet that fits entirely on one page.

Adding Headers and Footers

Headers and footers serve the same purpose in Excel as they do in Word—they help identify the worksheet and keep pages in order. You can only see headers and footers in Print Preview, but you create them in the Header/Footer tab of the Page Setup dialog box, shown in Figure 14-7.

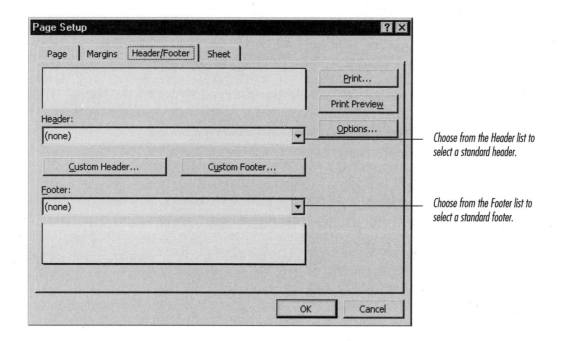

Choose from the Header list to select a standard header.

Choose from the Footer list to select a standard footer.

FIGURE 14-7 Inserting headers and footers

TIP: To quickly open the Header/Footer page of the dialog box, choose View I Header And Footer.

The standard headers and footers contain combinations of items including the page number, workbook name, worksheet number, your name, and the date. The sample panel will display how your selected header and footer will appear, as shown here:

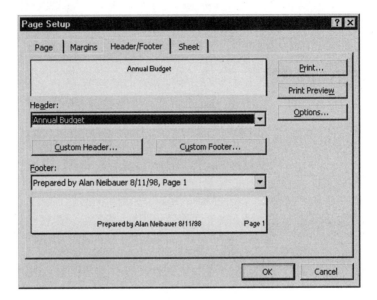

Customizing Headers and Footers

While the standard headers and footers offer a variety of formats, you may want to add your own text. Choose a standard header or footer that contains some of the elements that you want, or select None in the Header or Footer list to start from scratch. Then click either Custom Header or Custom Footer to display a dialog box like this:

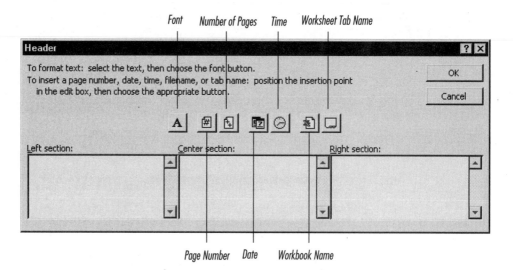

You can customize a header or footer by adding or editing the text in their three sections: Left, Center, and Right. Enter any text that you want to appear, or click the buttons on the toolbar to add an element, such as the date or name of the workbook.

Setting Sheet Options

Finally, the Sheet tab of the dialog box, shown in Figure 14-8, determines the order pages will be printed, and what gets printed on each page.

- **Print Area**   Lets you set or change the print area.
- **Print Titles**   Prints the rows or columns that appear on every page.
- **Gridlines**   Prints the normally nonprinting lines.
- **Black And White**   Prints all text, lines, and graphics in black.
- **Draft Quality**   Prints a quick copy without graphics and custom borders.
- **Row And Column Headings**   Prints the row numbers and column letters.
- **Comments**   Lets you skip printing comments that may appear onscreen or print them in a group at the end of the worksheet.
- **Page Order**   Determines how the pages are numbered.

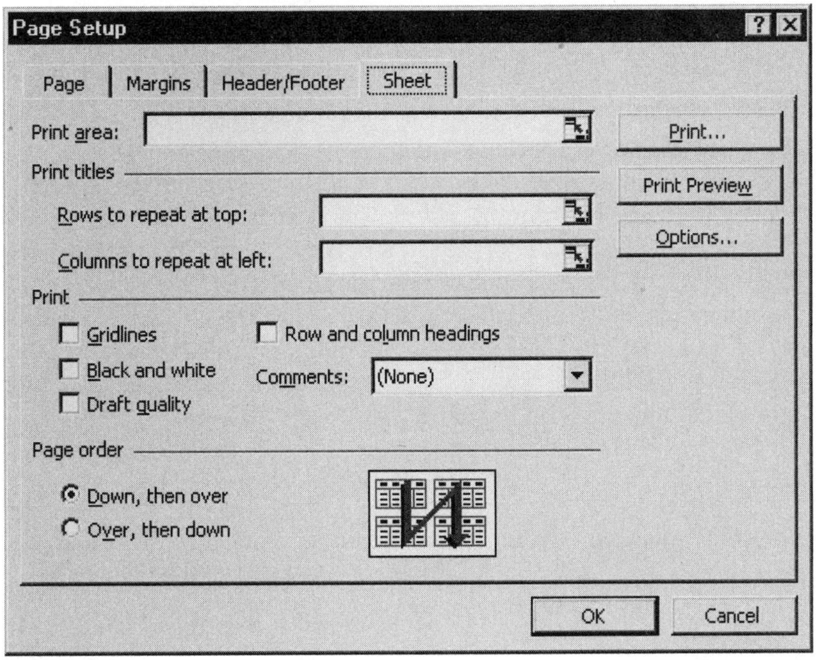

FIGURE 14-8 Sheet options

Turn on Gridlines, for example, if you did not insert your own borderlines but want lines printed to help identify rows and columns. You can also turn on Row And Column Headings to see the row numbers and column letters on the printout. This will help you later identify cells that need changing or must be referred to.

Use the Print Titles options to repeat row or column headings on each page. For example, suppose your budget worksheet spans several pages. Your income and expense categories that you listed down column A will not appear on other pages, so readers will have difficulty identifying the information. To repeat a column on every page, follow these steps:

1. Click in the Columns To Repeat At Left text box.
2. Click its Collapse Dialog button.

3. Drag over the column headers for the columns you want to repeat.

4. Click the Expand Dialog button.

Use a similar technique to repeat rows on each page.

Use the Page Order options to determine the order that pages are numbered. In the default setting, called *Down, Then Over,* Excel fills the first printed page with as many rows and columns as will fit. The next page prints more rows of the same columns, and so on, until all the rows have been printed. It then starts over from the top, printing more columns. This means that readers see all the rows of your worksheet as they turn pages, before they see all the columns. Click *Over, Then Down* to print additional columns on the second and subsequent pages, and then to start over with more rows. Using Over, Then Down, readers see all the columns as they turn pages, before they see all the rows.

- Make sure you can see onscreen what you want to print. If a column is not wide enough to display its contents onscreen, for example, it will not be wide enough when printed.

- When you choose a font larger than the default, Excel automatically increases the row height to accommodate the larger font but it does not widen columns. Check your worksheet carefully.

- You can apply a numeric style by typing the value using its format. Entering **$5.00** in an empty cell applies the currency format, for example, so trailing zeros are not deleted. If you type a value followed by a percent sign, the cell will be formatted in Percent style.

- Decreasing the number of decimal places and applying some formats will display some values rounded. Rounding may make some calculations appear incorrect, although the actual values are still maintained in the worksheet. To avoid confusion, widen columns, increase decimals, or change the format so the results appear correct.

- To return the worksheets to the default automatic page breaks, right-click the worksheet and select Reset All Page Breaks from the shortcut menu.

- To display a graphic or photograph behind the entire worksheet, choose Format | Sheet | Background. In the dialog box that appears, choose the graphic file you want to use and then click Insert. The graphic will be tiled (repeated) behind the entire worksheet.

- Large fonts, wide columns, and some other formats reduce the number of cells that print on each sheet of paper. You have to balance formatting with the convenience of seeing more data on each page.

- You can enter and edit information into a worksheet in either Normal or Page Break view.

- Format | Conditional Formatting lets you apply a format based on the contents of the cell.

- You can change the look of numeric formats by choosing Format | Style. In the dialog box that appears, choose the style you want to modify, and then change its number format, alignment, font, borders, pattern, and protection level. Select the item you want to change, and then click the Modify button.

Working with Workbooks

15

As your Excel skills grow, your worksheets will become more sophisticated and larger. You'll find yourself scrolling more to find information, and referring to various parts of the worksheet. By using more than one worksheet, and even multiple workbooks, you can create projects for even the largest business or most important task.

Working in Panes

It is easy to scroll back and forth to see rows and columns when you're working with a small worksheet. With a larger worksheet, however, you can spend too much time looking for things by scrolling. The solution is to divide the worksheet into *panes* so you can see different sections of the worksheet at one time. So, for example, you can work with column A in one pane and column Z in the other, scroll each independently, and even drag and drop information between the two.

To create panes, you use the *split boxes,* the small rectangles at the top of the vertical scroll bar (just above the up arrow) and to the right of the horizontal scroll bar (just to the right of the right arrow).

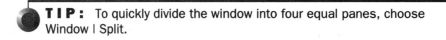

TIP: To quickly divide the window into four equal panes, choose Window | Split.

To see two different sets of rows, split the worksheet into two horizontal panes. Double-click the split box above the vertical scroll bar to quickly divide the window into two equal panes, or drag the split box down, as shown here:

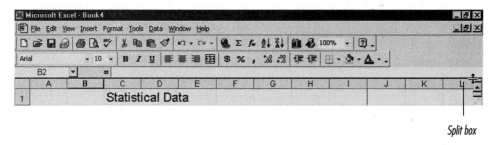

Split box

As shown in Figure 15-1, each pane has its own scroll bars, but the two panes are *synchronized* in the direction of the split. This means that with horizontal panes, you scroll each pane up and down independently to display different rows in each. When you scroll left or right, however, the columns in the panes move together, so you're always looking at different rows of the same columns.

To move from one pane to another, click the desired pane with the mouse or press the F6 key. To remove the pane, drag the split box or bar up or down all the way off the window or choose Window | Remove Split.

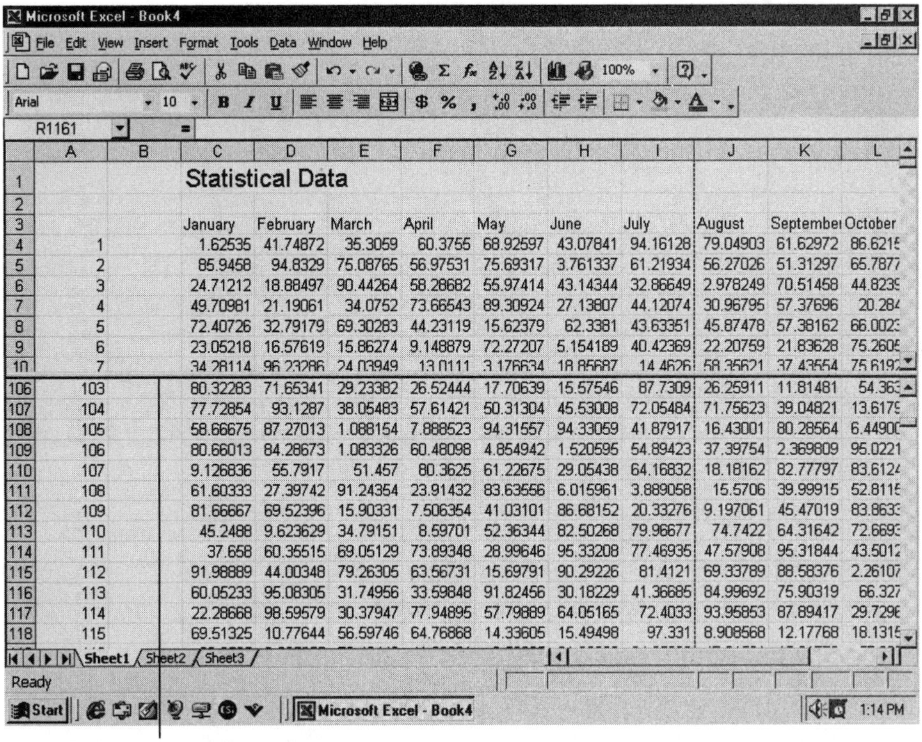

To change the size of the panes, drag the split box or the split line across the window.

FIGURE 15-1 Creating horizontal panes to see different sets of rows

When you want to display different columns of the same rows, create vertical panes. Double-click or drag the split box to the right of the horizontal bar. Vertical windows are synchronized so you can display different columns of the same rows.

TIP: When you need to move or copy information between panes, just select the cells you want to move or copy, and then drag them from one pane to another. Remember, hold down CTRL when you release the mouse to copy rather than move the cells.

Locking Titles in View

Most worksheets have both column labels that describe the information in each column and row labels that describe the information in each row. As you scroll the worksheet, these titles may scroll out of view, making it difficult to tell what the values refer to. To keep these titles onscreen as you scroll, you *freeze* rows or columns so they will not scroll.

Here's how it works. When you choose Window | Freeze Panes, whatever is above and to the left of the active cell becomes fixed. So if you want to keep the first three rows onscreen at all times, start in cell A4. To keep the first three rows and two columns on the screen, start in cell C4. When you choose Freeze Panes, Excel inserts solid black lines indicating the rows and columns that will not scroll, as shown in Figure 15-2. Choose Window | Unfreeze Panes to remove the titles so all rows and columns scroll.

Scrolling rows will not scroll the frozen rows;
scrolling columns will not scroll the frozen columns.

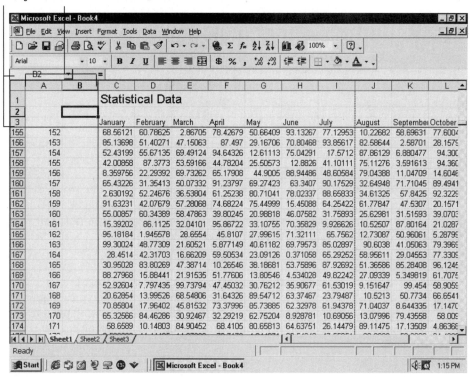

| FIGURE 15-2 | Creating horizontal panes to see different sets of rows

N O T E : You do not have to divide the window into panes to freeze titles into view.

Working with Multiple Worksheets

Would you fill out one page of a notebook, then store the notebook on a shelf and buy another? Pretty silly. But that's what it's like when people use only one worksheet in an Excel workbook. It's OK to do if you're creating worksheets that have nothing to do with each other. But when worksheets are somehow related—for the same project or client, for instance—create them in separate sheets of the *same* workbook. You can then open all the sheets by opening the workbook, and can even move information between them or share information by referencing cells in formulas.

To open another worksheet in the same workbook, just click the sheet tab above the status bar. Since the default is only three worksheets, it is easy to move between them. If you have more sheets than you can see tabs for, use the tab scrolling buttons to move between them:

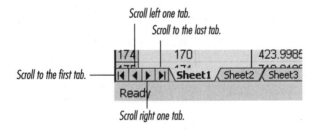

Clicking on a tab scrolling button, however, only scrolls other tabs into view, not their sheets. So after scrolling the tabs to see the one for the sheet you want to open, you still have to click its tab to see the sheet.

 **T I P :** Hold down SHIFT when you click a tab scrolling button to scroll an entire set of tabs into view, or right-click a tab for a shortcut menu of sheets you can open.

You can also go to a specific worksheet by right-clicking on any of the scrolling buttons to display a shortcut menu of tab names. Click the name of the tab you want to open.

To refer to a cell on another sheet, however, you must include its sheet name with the address in the format *Sheetname!Address*. So to refer to cell B3 on the sheet named Budget, use Budget!B3 as the reference.

Inserting and Deleting Worksheets

When you need more than the three worksheets Excel gives you by default, you can add your own. First click the tab for the sheet that you want to follow the new one. To insert a sheet between 2 and 3, for instance, click the Sheet 3 tab. Then, choose Insert | Worksheet.

To insert several sheets, select the same number of tabs that you want to insert. To add two new sheets, for example, select two existing tabs. Click the first tab, and then hold down the SHIFT key while you click other tabs. To select all the sheets, right-click any tab and choose Select All Sheets from the shortcut menu.

When you no longer want a worksheet and all its contents, click its tab and then choose Edit | Delete Sheet. You'll see a warning that the sheet will be permanently deleted, so click OK to remove the sheet, or click Cancel to retain it.

Renaming Worksheets

The default names on the worksheet tabs—Sheet1, Sheet2, and so on—don't do much to identify what's on the sheet. To make a tab more meaningful, change its name to reflect its contents. Seeing tabs like the ones shown here, for example, makes it much easier to find information that you're looking for:

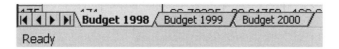

To change the worksheet name, double-click the tab to select it and highlight the sheet name. Then just type a new name.

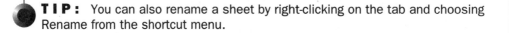

TIP: You can also rename a sheet by right-clicking on the tab and choosing Rename from the shortcut menu.

Rearranging Worksheets

Since you cannot automatically insert a new sheet at the end of the existing tabs, you may want to move your new sheet to the end yourself. You may also want to move sheets to arrange them in some special order.

Point to the tab of the sheet you want to move, and then hold down the mouse button to see the sheet icon and a small down arrow at the left side of the sheet tab:

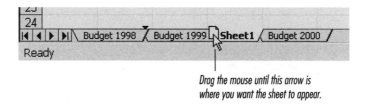

Drag the mouse until this arrow is where you want the sheet to appear.

For example, to move the sheet to the end of the workbook, drag the mouse so the down arrow follows the last tab.

To copy the sheet rather than move it, hold down the CTRL key when you release the mouse.

Hiding and Displaying Worksheets

Sometimes when you're working with a large workbook, you may use a sheet to store references for formulas, or just to store notes. If you want to make sure that you don't accidentally change the information on that sheet, or want to keep it from prying eyes, hide the sheet.

To hide a worksheet, click its tab and then choose Format | Sheet | Hide. While the sheet's tab will no longer appear, you can still reference its cells in formulas.

To later display the sheet, choose Format | Sheet | Unhide. In the dialog box that appears, click the sheet you want to display and click OK.

Grouping Worksheets

When you are using more than one worksheet, you don't always have to work with them individually. You can add information to cells and format cells in more than one sheet at a time. So let's say that you need to enter the same title, row, and column headings on more than one sheet. Rather than work with one sheet at a time, you can *group* sheets together and work with them all at once.

To group sheets, just select all their tabs. Click the first tab in the group, and then hold down SHIFT or CTRL while you click the others. Excel inserts the notation "(Group)" to the right of the workbook name in the title bar. Now any action that you take will be repeated on all the sheets—entering and formatting data, clearing cells, inserting and deleting, completing a series with AutoFill, or performing math with AutoSum.

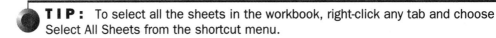

T I P : To select all the sheets in the workbook, right-click any tab and choose Select All Sheets from the shortcut menu.

If you already entered information into a worksheet, you can copy its contents to other sheets in the group by using these steps:

1. Display the sheet containing the information you want to copy.
2. Select the cells that you want to copy.
3. Hold down SHIFT or CTRL and select the other sheets.
4. Choose Edit | Fill | Across Worksheets to display this dialog box:

5. Choose the option for what you want to copy (see previous illustration).
6. Click OK.

To ungroup sheets, click a tab of a sheet outside of the group, or right-click and select Ungroup Sheets from the shortcut menu.

Using 3-D Ranges

If the worksheets in your workbook are related, you may need to perform math on cells in more than one sheet. For example, suppose you keep a worksheet with commission information for each salesperson. Each sheet contains a cell with the salesperson's total commissions for the year. When you want to display the total sales commissions your company paid, you use a 3-D range for a grand total of the individual worksheet totals.

A *3-D range* is simply a cell or group of cells in more than one worksheet. To type a 3-D range, use the format =SUM(*Sheetname:Sheetname!Celladdress*). For example, suppose your worksheets are named for salespersons like this:

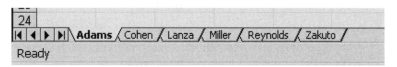

Each sheet contains the salesperson's total in cell H24. The range Adams:Zakuto!H24 represents that cell on each sheet and can be used in a formula such as =SUM(Adams:Zakuto!H24).

To point to a range of cells, use these steps:

1. When you reach the position where you want the cell reference, click the tab for the first sheet in the group.
2. Hold down SHIFT and click the other tabs in the group.
3. Select the cell or cells to include in the formulas.
4. Click the Enter button in the Formula bar.

Using Multiple Windows

In Chapter 2 you learned how to take advantage of windows to work with more than one document at a time. Excel is no different than any other Office program in its use of windows. With Excel, however, you can use windows to display more than one worksheet from the same workbook, or to display sheets from different workbooks.

To display windows containing different sheets from the same workbook, choose Window | New Window to open another window with the current sheet. Then choose Window | Arrange to see this dialog box:

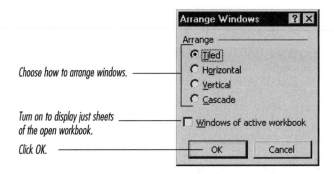

Choose how to arrange windows. ——————

Turn on to display just sheets ——————
of the open workbook.

Click OK. ——————

Both windows now display the same worksheet, and each has a set of worksheet tabs. In either window, click the tab for the other sheet you want to display.

To display windows with different workbooks, open both and then choose Window | Arrange. Choose how you want the windows displayed, but turn off the Windows Of Active Workbook option.

When you have more than one workbook open at the same time, the Save button or File | Save saves only the active workbook.

If you want to be able to open all the workbooks in the same screen arrangement later, choose File | Save Workspace; then in the dialog box that appears give the workspace a name and click Save. To reopen all the worksheets, select the workspace name from the File Open dialog box.

NOTE: Workspaces are saved with the XLW extension and are listed along with workbook files in the Open dialog box.

Moving Information Between Windows

You can move or copy information between windows as easily as within the same worksheet. If the two sheets are displayed, just select and drag the cells, or use the Cut, Copy, and Paste commands.

To drag information from one worksheet to another in the same workbook, you don't even have to display multiple windows. Here's how:

1. Select the cells that you want to move or copy.

2. Hold down ALT and drag to the tab of the sheet where you want to place the cells, but keep the mouse button down. When you point to the tab, Excel opens that sheet.

3. Continue dragging to the location where you want to place the cells.

Creating Hyperlinks

In Chapter 3, you learned how to create a hyperlink to connect to another workbook and to a site on the Internet. Excel lets you also use a hyperlink to move to another location in the current workbook.

Select the cell that you want to move to, and then click the Copy button on the Standard toolbar. Then click the cell where you want to place the hyperlink, and choose Edit | Paste As Hyperlink. If the cell already contains information, it will be formatted as a link—underlined and in blue. Otherwise, type the text you want to use for the link. Finally, click the Enter button on the Formula bar.

When you click the link, Excel moves to the linked site.

Linking Cells

One other type of link you can create in Excel is a data link. A *data link* connects two cells so they will always contain the same information. For example, suppose you create a worksheet called Rates that contain your standard discount rates. You want to use one of the rates in another worksheet that contains a customer invoice. By linking cells in the two workbooks, you ensure that the invoice automatically contains the most recent discount. If you make a change to the discount rate in the Rates workbook, the change is automatically reflected when you next open or print the invoice.

To link cells in one workbook to another, use this procedure:

1. Open both workbooks.

2. Select the cell that you want duplicated in the other worksheet. Using the example, you'd select the appropriate discount cell in the Rates workbook.

3. Click the Copy button on the Standard toolbar.

4. Open the other workbook and click the cell where you want to place the link, such as the Invoice workbook.

5. Choose Edit | Paste Special | Paste Link.

You see the *value* from the linked cell where you pasted it, but in the Formula bar you'll see a *reference* to it.

When you open a workbook that contains data links, you'll see a message like this one:

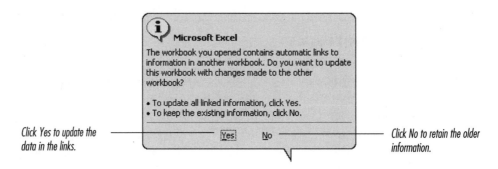

Click Yes to update the data in the links.

Click No to retain the older information.

 T I P : If you already have the workbook open when another user on the network changes the linked information, the cell will not be updated. Choose Edit | Links, and then in the dialog box that appears choose the link you want to update and click Update Now.

Protecting Your Work

There's probably nothing so frustrating (at least in Excel) as carefully creating a worksheet only to find that you or some other user accidentally changed it. It is all too easy to mistakenly type a value in a cell containing a formula, or to delete a cell that is referenced in another sheet or workbook.

You can protect your work from being changed in three ways:

- Lock cells from being edited.
- Password-protect a worksheet from being opened.
- Protect a worksheet from changes to its structure.

Locking Cells

By default, all worksheet cells have locking turned on. To implement locking, however, you have to turn on worksheet protection—choose Tools | Protection | Protect Sheet to see the following dialog box.

If you work on a computer network or share your computer with others, then your workbooks are available for anyone to see and change. If you don't want your workbooks in the public domain, designate a password that must be entered to open or modify the workbook. Choose File | Save As, pull down the Tools menu in the Save As dialog box, and click General Options:

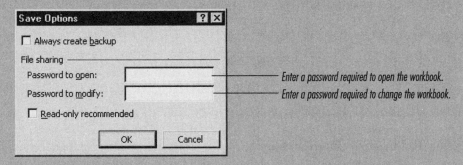

Enter a password required to open the workbook.
Enter a password required to change the workbook.

When you click OK, Excel displays a confirmation box for each password that you entered. In each box, type each password again and then click OK and continue saving the workbook.

You can also create a *read-only* workbook that can be changed or modified but not saved with the same name. To suggest that readers open it as read-only, turn on the Read-Only Recommended check box in the Save Options box, and then continue saving the workbook. Excel displays this dialog box when the workbook is later opened:

Click Yes to open the workbook as read-only.

Click No to open the workbook normally.

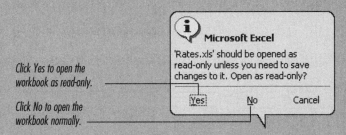

1 Leave all the check boxes selected for maximum protection.

2 Enter an optional password to later remove protection.

3 Click OK.

Excel now displays a message if you try to enter or edit information in a locked cell. To change a cell, you must turn off protection. Select Tools | Protection | Unprotect Sheet. If you designated a password when you protected the sheet, you'll have to enter it to unprotect the sheet.

If you only want to protect certain cells, not all of them, you must turn off locking for the cells you want to be able to change. When the sheet is unprotected, select the cells that you do not want to lock, and then choose Format | Cells and click the Protection tab.

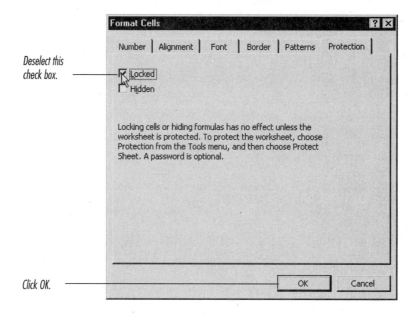

Deselect this check box.

Click OK.

Now you can turn on worksheet protection to lock just the cells that have locking still turned on.

N O T E : Turn on the Hidden check box to keep formulas in selected cells from being displayed onscreen.

Protecting Your Workbook's Structure

There is one big "gotcha" when it comes to locking cells. While you can't change information in a locked cell, you can still delete the entire worksheet. So to really be sure you can't lose your information, you'll also need to protect the structure of your workbook.

Select Tools | Protection | Protect Workbook to see these options:

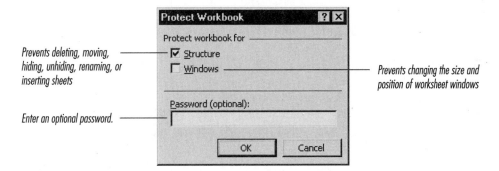

Prevents deleting, moving, hiding, unhiding, renaming, or inserting sheets

Prevents changing the size and position of worksheet windows

Enter an optional password.

To turn off worksheet protection, choose Tools | Protection | Unprotect Workbook.

- To designate a workbook so it automatically opens as read-only, you have to change its attributes. Right-click the file in Windows Explorer, and choose Properties from the shortcut menu. Turn on the Read-Only check box and then click OK.

- When you're printing a worksheet, use the Print Titles feature described in Chapter 14 to display certain rows and columns on each page.

- Remember, every open document appears as a separate item in the Windows taskbar. When you're working with more than one workbook, bring the one you want to the foreground by clicking on its name in the taskbar.

- If you are going to use a password to protect your work, select one that is easy to remember and use. Some people use the word "PASSWORD" for a low level of protection that is certainly easy to remember.

- To quickly open a workbook as read-only from the File Open dialog box, select the workbook in the dialog box, pull down the list on the Open button, and choose Open Read-Only.

- To share your workbook over a network, choose Protect And Share Workbook from the Tools Protection menu, and turn on the box labeled "Sharing With Track Changes." Use the Tools | Share Workbook to allow users to share the workbook at one time and to specify how changes are recorded, tracked, and updated. Check with your network administrator for more information about sharing over a network.

- The Tools | Protect Sheet only protects the current worksheet. Repeat the procedure with other sheets to protect them as well. As an alternative, group sheets and then protect them all at one time.

- No protection method is foolproof. If you really want to make sure no one can use or delete your worksheet, save it on a floppy disk that you take with you.

- When you're working with larger worksheets, locking rows and columns so they do not scroll out of view can be an invaluable time-saver. Don't underestimate the problems of creating a worksheet where row or column labels cannot be seen.

- Instead of typing the full address of a cell in another worksheet into the formula, you can also point to it. When you reach the position where you want the cell reference, click the tab for the worksheet where it is located and then select the cell.

Functions and Formulas

You use formulas and functions to take advantage of the recalculation and the "What if?" capabilities of Excel. In fact, you should use formulas whenever possible, especially when you need to perform a mathematical operation on the values in other cells. The few extra seconds or minutes it takes to enter a formula can save you countless hours manually recalculating and checking your work.

In Chapter 13, you learned how to enter formulas, and you saw how the AutoSum button quickly totals a row or column of numbers. In this chapter, you'll learn some ways to make your formulas even better.

Using Absolute References

When you copy a formula, Excel copies it using a relative reference, adjusting the cell address for its new position. This feature of Excel is usually desirable, but not in every situation. There are times when you do not want a cell reference changed when you move a formula. Take a look at Figure 16-1.

The formula shown in cell E5, =D5*B5, calculates the sales tax on a product by multiplying the sales amount in cell D5 by the tax rate in cell B5. In generic

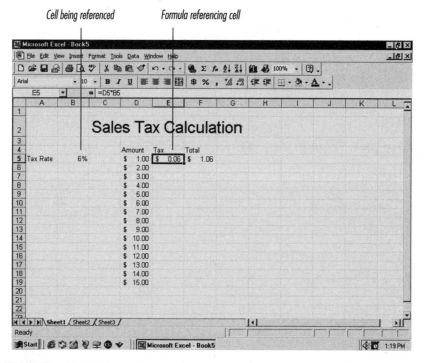

FIGURE 16-1   Worksheet needing absolute references

terms it means "multiply the value in the cell to the left times the value three cells to the left." Now suppose you saved time by copying the formula down the column to calculate the sales tax on the other products. You might save time, but you would have made a big mistake. Just look at how the formula would be in the cells:

This formula now incorrectly references. . .

. . .this cell ─────

. . .instead of this cell. ─────

			Amount	Tax		Total
3						
4			Amount	Tax		Total
5	Tax Rate	0.06	1	=D5*B5		=D5+E5
6			2	=D6*B6		
7			3	=D7*B7		
8			4	=D8*B8		
9			5	=D9*B9		
10			6	=D10*B10		
11			7	=D11*B11		
12			8	=D12*B12		
13			9	=D13*B13		
14			10	=D14*B14		
15			11	=D15*B15		
16			12	=D16*B16		
17			13	=D17*B17		
18			14	=D18*B18		
19			15	=D19*B19		
20						
21						

Each time Excel inserts the formula, it keeps the same general meaning. The amount is still "in the cell to the left," but the tax rate is no longer "three cells to the left." Now no copy of the formula references the cell containing the tax rate.

In situations where you do not want a reference changed, you have to enter it as an *absolute address*. This tells Excel not to adjust the address when the formula is copied. To enter an absolute address, just put a dollar sign ($) in front of each part of the address that you want to stay the same. In this case, the formula in the cell would have been written as =D5*B5. When you copy the formula down the column, Excel would leave the address exactly as it was and only change which product it was being multiplied by. So each product "in the cell to the left" would be multiplied times cell B5.

Referencing Cells by Name

Two of the most difficult problems in creating formulas are making sure you get the correct cell address, and later remembering what the formula does. You can click a cell to add it to a formula, but that often means scrolling back and forth. And what if you forget what the formula =G4*G12 means in a worksheet?

Instead of using cell addresses in a formula, you can use cell names. Our mystery formula, for instance, would be more meaningful written as =TotalSale*TaxRate, and you could write the formula without even knowing the actual address of the cells.

There are two ways to use names for cells. You can use the labels that you've entered as row and column headings, or you can give cells their own names.

Using Cell Labels

Since most worksheets will have row and column labels that identify information, Excel lets you use these labels to identify cells in formulas. Take a look at this worksheet as an example:

	A	B	C	D	E	F	G	H
1								
2								
3								
4								
5			Mon	Tue	Wed	Thu	Fri	
6		Supplies	2981	3167	1433	2091	1276	
7		Magazines	58	53	78	90	43	
8		Books	235	634	154	73	314	
9		Software	15745	18600	9076	10144	8955	
10		Hardware	32568	18900	21668	16595	123776	
11		Gross Sales	51587	41354	32409	28993	134364	
12		Returns	896	57	73	115	264	
13		Net Sales						
14								
15								

This cell represents Monday's gross sales.

Rather than refer to the cell that represents the gross sales amount for Monday as C11, you can call it either Mon Gross Sales or Gross Sales Mon. Cell names are the combination of the column and row labels, in either order. So, to calculate the Net Sales in cell C13, you could use the formula =Mon Gross Sales-Mon Returns.

Now for a shortcut: If you use the formula in the same column as the information you're referring to, you can skip the column heading. So you can actually type the formula as =Gross Sales-Returns. Excel uses the appropriate cells in that column automatically.

 C A U T I O N : You cannot refer to labels on another worksheet, even if you use the sheet name in the reference.

What about calculating the total of sales for cell C11? Nobody would claim that typing the formula =Mon Hardware+Mon Software+Mon Supplies+Mon Books+Mon Magazines would be a shortcut. Don't despair. To total the values in cells C6 through C10, just use the formula =SUM(Mon). Excel takes this to mean "total the values under the label Mon."

When you use the Fill handle to copy formulas with labels, Excel inserts the relative label into the cells being filled. If you copy the formula =SUM(Mon) across row 11, it will be inserted as =SUM(Tue), =SUM(Wed), =SUM(Thu), and =SUM(Fri).

Inserting Labels by Clicking

Labels make it easy to create and identify formulas, but they can require a lot of typing. You can always click a cell when creating a formula to insert its address, but clicking does not automatically insert the cell's label names.

To insert names by clicking, you have to first assign the row and column labels to the cells by creating a *label range*. You can then click a cell to add its labels into a formula.

To define a label range, use these steps:

1. Select the cells containing the row labels.
2. Choose Insert | Name | Label.

The range of the selected cells appears here.

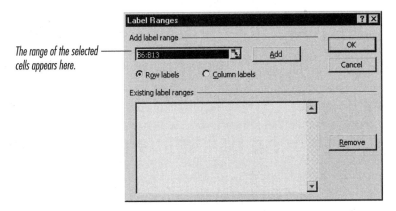

3. Click Add.
4. Click OK.

Now repeat the same procedure by selecting the cells containing the column labels. When you're creating a formula and you click a cell in an intersection of the row and column labels, Excel enters the labels rather than the address. So, for example, cell C8 appears referenced as Mon Books.

Giving Names to Cells and Ranges

Not every cell in a worksheet may be identified by row and column labels. In addition, you can only refer to a cell by its label in the same worksheet that contains the label. To use a cell name in any circumstance, you can assign a name rather than use an existing label. The defined name can then be used anywhere you would use an address.

CAUTION: A name that you assign to a cell is treated as an absolute address in a formula. It will not change relatively if you copy the formula.

Click the cell that you want to name, and then click in the Name box at the left of the Formula bar. Type the name you want to give the cell (a single word, no spaces are allowed), and then press ENTER.

You can now use the name wherever you would use the address. If you forget the name, choose Insert | Name | Paste to see a list of the names in the workbook:

Click the name you want to add and then click OK.

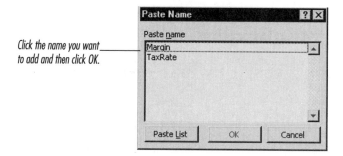

TIP: Click Paste List in the Paste Name dialog box to insert a list of cell addresses and names into the worksheet for reference.

Creating Cell Names from Labels

If you have labels but want the advantage of using them in another worksheet, you can have Excel assign them as cell names so you do not have to name them yourself. This is particularly useful when you only have row labels, without a column label, or vice versa, as shown here:

	A	B	C	D	E
1					
2					
3					
4					
5					
6					
7			Adams	876	
8			Sweig	6544	
9			Woodin	876	
10			Zakuto	8721	
11					
12					
13					

In this case, each of the values in column D is identified by a label in column C. To use the labels as names, select the cells and their labels (in this case cells C7 to D10), and then choose Insert | Name | Create Name to see the Create Names dialog box.

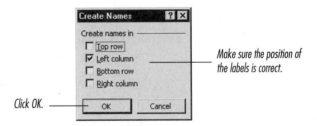

Click OK.

Make sure the position of the labels is correct.

The labels are to the left of the values, so Excel selected the Left Column check box. When you click OK, each of the cells in column D is named using the label just to its left, so cell D7 is named Adams, and so on.

N O T E : When you're defining names, Excel will replace spaces with underline characters.

You can use this same technique to name an entire range of cells, giving it a single name. Select all the cells and their labels, as shown here:

	A	B	C	D	E	F	G	H
1								
2								
3								
4								
5								
6				Qtr 1	Qtr 2	Qtr 3	Qtr 4	
7			Adams	876	556	238	655	
8			Sweig	6544	2357	8675	6665	
9			Woodin	876	567	4332	3345	
10			Zakuto	8721	456	7654	5445	
11								
12								
13								
14								

When you then open the Create Names dialog box, both the Left Column and Top Row check boxes are selected, so click OK. The column labels are now names for the range of cells in each column, and the row labels are names for the cells in each row. So the name Qtr_1 represents cells D7 to D10, and the name Woodin represents cells D9 to G9. Use =SUM(Woodin) in cell H9, for example, to total the cells in row 9.

Functions

A function is a built-in mathematical shortcut. You can use a function to perform in one statement what might otherwise take a very complex formula or even a series of formulas to accomplish. For example, suppose you need to calculate the average of the month's daily temperatures. Without a function, you'd need to count how many days you have listed (let's suppose 30), and enter a formula such as =(A1+A2+A3+A4+A5 ... and so on)/30. That's quite a lot of typing. If you now insert another day into the worksheet, you'd have to edit the formula, adding the other cell and increasing the count to 31.

The alternative is to use the built-in function for calculating an average, =Average. To average the values in cells A1 through A30, all you enter is =Average(A1:A30). The function calculates and displays the average of the values specified in that range. If you later add a row of information within the range, Excel automatically adjusts the range reference to include the additional values.

You can also use a function to perform a calculation that you would not know how to do using a formula. As an example, suppose you're looking for a home and want to calculate your monthly mortgage payments. Unless you're an accountant, you probably won't even know where to begin to write a formula to perform the calculation. Fortunately, Excel has a built-in function for this called PMT. Entering the function =PMT(.075/12, 30*12, 86000), for instance, would return the monthly mortgage payment for a loan of $86,000 for 30 years, at 7.5 percent annual interest. Just substitute your own values, or cell references to the values, in place of the numbers.

NOTE: The result of the PMT function, by the way, will appear as a negative number. For a positive result, precede the principal amount with a minus sign, as in –56000.

You don't have to know how the function works, just its syntax—its name and how to enter the information that it needs to calculate its results. Functions use the syntax of =*NAME(arguments)*. *NAME* is simply the name of the function. The *arguments,* in parentheses, are the cell references, values, or other instructions that the function needs to do its work. Commas separate multiple arguments. You don't even have to memorize the syntax, because Excel will take you step-by-step through the function.

Pasting a Function

Once you start using functions, you'll learn the names and syntax of those you use regularly. You can then enter the function by typing its name and arguments into the cell. If you do not know what function you need, or its arguments, you can consult a list, make a choice, and paste it into a cell.

TIP: To choose a recently used function, pull down the list next to the Name Box and click the function name.

Click in the cell where you want to insert the function, and then click the Paste Function button in the Standard toolbar. Excel inserts the = sign into the Formula bar and opens the Paste Function dialog box, shown in Figure 16-2.

Choose the category of the function in this list.

Then double-click the function to insert it.

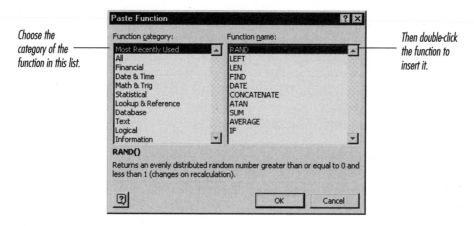

FIGURE 16-2 The Paste Function dialog box

 TIP: Select All in the Function Category list to display all the functions in alphabetical order.

When you insert a function, Excel opens the Formula palette, shown in Figure 16-3. The arguments shown in bold are required—you must enter them to use the function. The other arguments are optional and can be used if needed.

Collapse Dialog button to select cells for arguments

Text box for each argument

Description of function

Description of argument

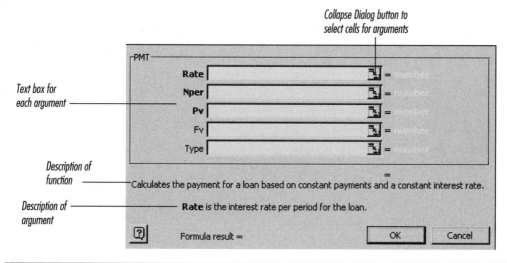

FIGURE 16-3 Formula palette

For each of the required arguments, enter the values or cell references that are appropriate. You can also click an argument's Collapse Dialog button to select cells rather than typing cell addresses.

As you complete the arguments, they appear in the Formula bar, and the value of the argument appears next to its text box:

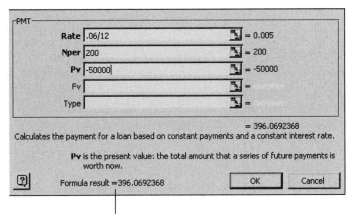

As you work, check the result for any obvious errors.

When all the required arguments are complete, Excel displays the results below the argument list and at the Formula Result prompt at the bottom of the palette. Check the result for any obvious errors. When you think the function is complete, click OK to insert it into the cell.

A Function Primer

Some functions, such as Sum and Average, are relatively easy to use. Others are quite complex, even if they require only one or two arguments. For example, consider the CHIINV function that calculates the inverse of a one-tailed probability of the chi-squared distribution. While it only requires two arguments, you'd need some statistical background to understand it fully and use it effectively.

Excel organizes its functions into nine categories:

- *Financial* functions   Perform financial calculations and operations.
- *Date and time* functions   Calculate dates, times, and days.
- *Math and trigonometry* Functions   Perform simple and complex mathematical calculations.
- *Statistical* functions   Perform statistical operations.

- *Lookup and reference* functions Help you find values in a range of cells.
- *Database* functions Let you analyze information in a group of cells.
- *Text* functions Perform operations in characters rather than numbers.
- *Logical* functions Determine if a condition is true or false.
- *Information* functions Tell you about the type of data in a cell.

In this chapter, we'll give a few samples of the functions available.

Financial Functions

These functions deal with arguments such as the present and future value of a loan or investment, the number of payments or periods, the periodic payment, and the interest rate. In addition to the PMT function described earlier, here are a few functions in this category:

- ACCRINT calculates the accrued interest for a security that pays periodic interest.
- DOLLARDE converts the dollar price of an investment expressed as a fraction into a decimal number. DOLLARFR does just the opposite.
- IPMT calculates the interest payment for a specified investment with constant payments and a constant interest rate.
- YIELDMAT returns the annual yield of a security that pays interest at maturity.

Date and Time Functions

Use these functions to perform calculations on dates and times. Typical arguments are a date or time, either formatted or as a serial number. Here are some date and time functions:

- TODAY( ), without any argument, represents the current date.
- DATE represents the serial number of a date, using the syntax DATE(*year,month,day*). Use DATEVALUE to get the serial number of a date using the syntax DATEVALUE("11/16/45").
- TIME returns the serial number of a time with the syntax TIME(*hour,minute,second*). Use TIMEVALUE for the serial number of the time using the format TIMEVALUE("1:16 AM").

Math and Trigonometry Functions

These functions perform mathematical calculations, including the now familiar =SUM( ) to calculate the total of a range of cells. The arguments are typically a range of cells, or one or more cells of values. Here are some samples:

- ABS returns the absolute value of a number.
- COS returns the cosine of the given angle.
- EXP raises a number to a given power.
- INT rounds a number down to the nearest whole number.
- LOG calculates the logarithm of a number to the base you specify. Use LOG10 to calculate the base-10 logarithm.
- SQRT calculates the square root of a number.
- RAND( ) returns a random decimal between 0 and 1. Use RANDBETWEEN to generate a random number between two values. For example, use the syntax RANDBETWEEN(1,50) to get a random number between 1 and 50.

Statistical Functions

Use these functions to perform statistical operations, such as calculating the average, standard deviation, and variance. Some of the less-complicated functions in this category include the following:

- AVERAGE calculates the mathematical average (the arithmetic mean) of a set of values.
- MAX returns the largest value in a range of values.
- MEDIAN returns the value in the middle of a set of values.
- MIN returns the smallest value in a range of values.
- RANK returns the position of a value in a set of values.

Lookup and Reference Functions

Use these functions to locate a value in a set of cells. These are highly specialized functions that typically use a range of cells, and a row or column within the range as arguments. The Index function is a good example. The function returns a value from a group of cells, using the syntax =INDEX(*Range, Row, Col*).

This category also includes the Address function. This function displays text that represents the absolute address of a cell. The syntax is =ADDRESS(*row number, column number*). For example, the function =ADDRESS(4, 1) displays the text A4, the fourth row and the first column in the worksheet.

Database Functions

These functions locate information in a range of cells that meet specific conditions. The arguments are generally the range of cells (called the *database* or *list*), the column name where the data is located (called the *field*), and the conditions the contents must meet to be selected (called the *criteria*). The criteria refer to a special set of cells containing values or formulas. Many are statistical functions but start with the letter D and use the three arguments, as in these examples:

- DAVERAGE returns the average of the values in a column that meet the conditions.
- DCOUNT returns the number of values in a column that meet the conditions.
- DMAX returns the largest number that meets the conditions.
- DMIN returns the smallest number that meets the conditions.
- DSUM returns the total of the values that meet the conditions.

Text Functions

Use these functions to manipulate text. Arguments are generally a text string to act upon, and the positions or place of characters within the string.

- CONCATENATE combines two strings into one.
- FIND locates the character position of one string within another.
- LEFT returns a number of characters from the left side of a string, as in =LEFT(C3,3) to display the first three characters of the text in cell C3.
- LEN returns the number of characters in a string.
- LOWER changes all uppercase letters in the string to lowercase. Use UPPER to do the opposite.
- MID returns the number of characters that you specify from a string, starting at a position that you specify.
- RIGHT returns a number of characters from the right side of the string.
- TRIM deletes blank spaces from a string, except one space between each word.

Text functions let you pull apart pieces of text and put pieces of text together. For example, an e-mail address is composed of two main parts, the recipient's user name and his or her e-mail server site. If you wanted to separate the two parts, you would use text functions as shown in the following worksheet. (All the functions, by the way, could be combined in one cell; we've done it this way to make it easier to understand.)

	A	B	C	D	E	F	G
1							
2	Complete E-Mail Address			alann@worldnet.att.net			
3							
4							
5							
6							
7		Position of @ character			6		
8		Length of the address			22		
9		User name			alann		
10		Mail server			worldnet.att.net		
11							
12							
13							
14							
15							
16							

The formulas that perform the calculations are shown in the following table.

CELL	FORMULA	PURPOSE
E7	=FIND("@",D2)	Locates the position of the @ character
E8	=LEN(D2)	Returns the length of the address
E9	=LEFT(D2,E7-1)	Returns the name from the start of the address
E10	=RIGHT(D2,E8-E7)	Returns the e-mail site from the end of the address

You can also use text functions to combine pieces of text with the Concatenate function. Just add the cells containing the text you want to combine as the function's argument. If cell A12 contains a person's first name, and cell A13 contains his or her last name, display the full name like this: =CONCATENATE(A12," ",A13). The purpose of the blank space between two quotation marks is to add a space between the two words. Without it, the two names would not have run together.

Logical Functions

Logical functions determine whether a condition is true or false. The arguments are usually one or more conditions that can be tested, returning the value True or False. For example, the function =OR(C3>9, D10<7) will return True if either the value in cell C3 is greater than 9 or the value in cell D10 is less than 7. It returns False if neither condition is met. The other logical functions are AND, FALSE, IF, NOT, and TRUE.

The most complex function in this category is IF. The function returns one value that you specify when the condition is true, or another value you specify when the condition is false. The structure is =IF(*condition, value-if-true, value-if-false*). For example, look at this portion of a worksheet:

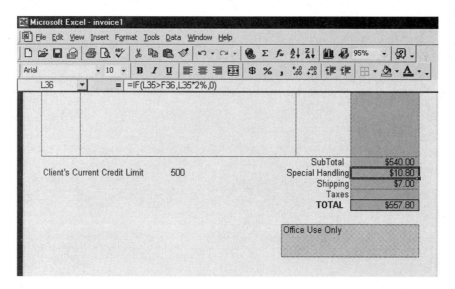

The formula in cell L36 is =IF(L35>F36,L35*2%,0). This means that if the subtotal of the order (L35) is more than the credit limit (F36), we'd want to add a 2 percent handling charge (L35*2%). Otherwise, no extra charge would be provided.

Information Functions

Use these functions when you want to know something about the contents of a cell other than its value or text. Functions in this category, for example, let you know if a cell is blank, contains an error, or is a number or text. For instance, the function =ISBLANK(A1) returns True if cell A1 is blank and False if the cell is not blank.

These functions can get complicated, so check out the help system for more information.

- Two cells cannot have the same name. Use cell names that clearly represent the contents or purpose of the cell.
- After creating cell names or assigning labels, display the Paste Name dialog box to confirm that the names were actually applied.
- If you name cells after you've used them in formulas, let Excel convert cell references to names for you. Select the cells containing the formulas, and then choose Insert | Name | Apply. Then click OK in the dialog box that appears.
- To quickly move to a named cell, pull down the list next to the Name box and click the cell's name.
- To make a reference absolute, type it and press the F4 key to cycle through the various references. For example, for cell B7, cycle through B7, B$7, $B7, and then back to B7, and select the desired reference.
- There is another category of functions, Engineering, that you must install separately with the Analysis ToolPak and then enable using Tools | Add-Ins.
- For help with a function in the Formula palette, click the Help button to launch the Microsoft Assistant. Select Help With This Feature in the first assistant, and then choose Help On Selected Function for detailed information.
- To edit a function, select the cell and click the Paste Function button to open the Formula palette. You can now change the value of references in an argument, check that you have the proper function or arguments, or get help with the function.
- The notation #NAME? in a cell usually means that you used an incorrect function name or argument.
- If you name many cells in a worksheet, it pays to get a printed record of their names and addresses. Click a cell in a blank worksheet, and then choose Insert | Name | Paste. In the Paste Name dialog box, click Paste List to get a complete record of cell names. Make sure you start by selecting a cell with enough empty cells around it so the pasted name list does not delete actual worksheet information.

Working with Excel Graphics

17

&

When you want your data to have maximum impact, try presenting the information as a graph or map. It is easier to see trends and interpret numbers presented graphically than as rows and columns in a worksheet. Graphic and maps are easy to create in Excel from information you've already entered.

Adding Pictures and Drawings

We'll get this out of the way quickly. Excel uses all the same techniques for using clipart and creating drawings as does Microsoft Word. If you've read Chapter 10, then you know all about using clipart and graphics from files, creating drawings, designing effects with WordArt, and using AutoShapes in Excel. If you did not read that chapter, then go back and do it now.

Creating Charts and Graphs

Creating a graph in Excel is similar to doing so in Word, but there are enough differences that you should review the techniques. This is especially true since an Excel worksheet typically contains more types of information than a table in Word. To get started, look at the Excel chart shown in Figure 17-1. This chart

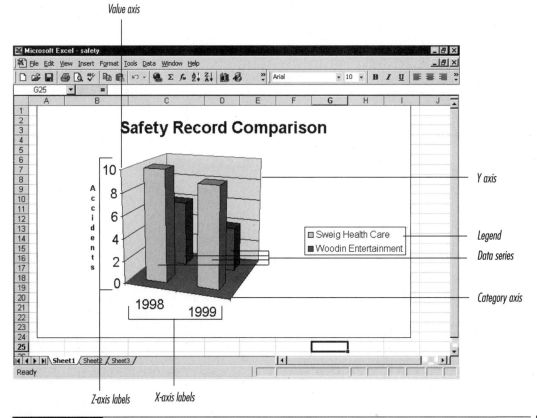

FIGURE 17-1   Three-dimensional Excel chart

uses three-dimensional columns to show the safety record of two companies over a two-year period.

A chart must have at least one *data series*—a set of numbers representing the values of something you are measuring or reporting. This graph has two. The first, represented by the lighter color bars, shows the accidents for one company. The second series, in the darker bars, shows the accidents for the other company.

You can place a chart either within a worksheet (called an *embedded* chart) or on a separate page called a *chart sheet*. You can print an embedded chart on the same sheet as the data that it represents. Chart sheets don't contain any worksheet cells of their own and must be printed separately from the worksheet. You create both types of chart using the Chart Wizard, and then select chart placement at the very end of the wizard.

Using Chart Wizard

To create a chart, start by selecting the cells that contain the information you want to chart. Include the row and column labels so Excel can use the row labels to identify the series on the legend, and the column labels for the X axis.

TIP: You can quickly create a chart in a separate chart sheet by selecting the cells and pressing F11. No Chart Wizard dialog boxes will appear.

Next, click the Chart Wizard button on the Standard toolbar to display the first Chart Wizard dialog box, shown in Figure 17-2. When you click a choice in the Chart Type list, Excel displays variations of the type in the Chart Sub-Type list. The Custom Types tab offers more graphically oriented charts that do not have subtypes.

1 Select the Standard Types or Custom Types tab.

2 Choose the overall chart type.

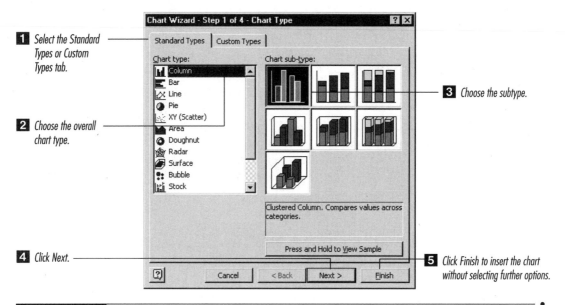

3 Choose the subtype.

4 Click Next.

5 Click Finish to insert the chart without selecting further options.

FIGURE 17-2 Chart Wizard

> **TIP:** Hold down the mouse on the Press And Hold To View Sample button to see how your chart will appear.

The second Chart Wizard box contains two pages.

On the *Data Range* tab, you can change the range of cells being charted, and choose to use the rows or columns for the series. The chart in Figure 17-1, for example, is charted by column, showing the column labels in the legend. If you selected to chart by rows, the years would be in the legend and the company names would be along the X axis. Your choice depends on how you want to illustrate your data.

On the Series tab of the dialog box, shown in Figure 17-3, you can add or remove series, and change the cells that represent their values and labels.

The next Chart Wizard dialog box lets you add titles and choose a variety of charting options. The pages of the dialog box depend on the type of chart, but all the pages are described in Table 17-1.

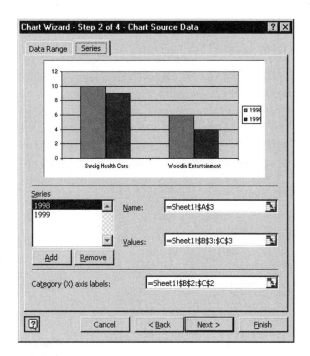

FIGURE 17-3 Series tab of the Chart Wizard

TAB	OPTIONS
Titles	Add a chart title, and titles for the X axis and Y axis. The number of options depends on the chart type.
Axes	Choose to use a timescale along the X axis, and hide or display the axis labels.
Gridlines	Hide or display horizontal and vertical gridlines.
Legend	Hide or display the legend, and choose a legend position.
Data Labels	Include numeric values, text labels, or percentages (with pie charts) with each series.
Data Table	Include the data being charted as a table under the chart, and color-code the table to match the legend.

TABLE 17-1 Setting Chart Options in Chart Wizard

In the last Chart Wizard dialog box, you choose either to insert the chart as an embedded object in a worksheet, or to create the chart on a separate chart sheet. If you choose to add the chart to a worksheet, you can also select which sheet to add it to. You do not have to insert the chart in the same sheet containing the data used to plot it.

If you choose to add the chart as an object to a worksheet, Excel displays the chart selected and surrounded by handles, along with the Chart toolbar, as shown in Figure 17-4. The cells used for the chart are also surrounded by colored borders to indicate their use for labels and series. The Chart toolbar is explained in Table 17-2.

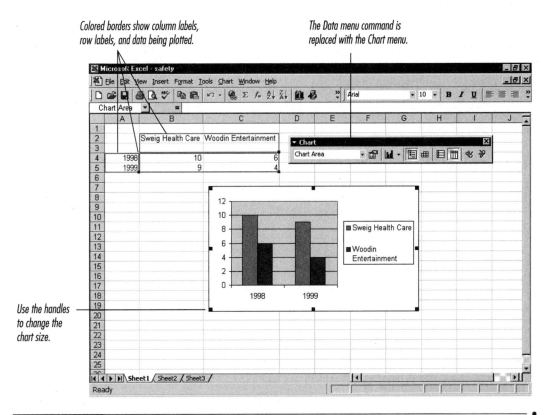

Colored borders show column labels, row labels, and data being plotted.

The Data menu command is replaced with the Chart menu.

Use the handles to change the chart size.

FIGURE 17-4 An embedded chart on a worksheet

BUTTON	NAME	PURPOSE
Chart Area ▾	Chart Objects	Selects an area of a chart to customize
	Format Chart Area	Displays options to format the selected area
	Chart Type	Changes the chart type and dimensions
	Legend	Hides or displays the legend
	Data Table	Displays a table of charted data under the chart
	By Row	Uses worksheet rows for the series
	By Column	Uses worksheet columns for the series
	Angle Text Downward	Tilts selected text downward
	Angle Text Upward	Tilts selected text upward

TABLE 17-2 Excel's Chart Toolbar

If you click outside of the chart, it will no longer be selected and the Chart toolbar disappears. Click the border around the chart to select it again. Whether or not the chart is selected, however, it is linked to the cells you used to create it. If you change any of the values or labels in the cells, Excel adjusts the chart automatically. To delete the chart from the worksheet, click it so the entire chart is selected, and then press the DEL key.

Use the handles to change the chart size, just as you learned for graphics. To move a chart, point just within its border and drag. Enlarge the chart if you can't see all the chart labels on an axis.

Creating a Chart Sheet

When you use Chart Wizard or the F11 key to place a chart on a separate sheet, Excel opens a new sheet containing the chart and the Chart toolbar. The sheet tabs will be labeled "Chart1," "Chart2," and so on, depending on the number of chart sheets in the workbook. You can customize the chart using the same methods you'll learn here for an embedded chart, although you cannot move the chart on the sheet.

To delete a chart sheet, right-click in its sheet tab and select Delete from the shortcut menu.

Working with Charts

After you create the chart, you can change its type, add titles, and customize it in a variety of ways. The first four items in the Chart menu, for example, present the same options as the four Chart Wizard dialog boxes. So you can use the Chart menu to change any of the settings you selected or skipped in Chart Wizard.

You customize charts using the Chart toolbar, the Format and Chart commands on the menu bar, and the shortcut menu that appears when you right-click the chart. Many tasks that you want to perform on a chart are available in all three places. For example, you can display a dialog box to format an area of the chart using either of these methods:

- Right-click the area and choose Format from the shortcut menu.
- Click the Format button on the toolbar.
- Choose Format | Selected.
- Double-click the area you want to format.

To avoid redundancy, in most cases I'll show you what I feel is the best way to perform a task, not all the places where the task can be accessed. You'll quickly discover these on your own.

 TIP: Use the Chart Options command from the Chart menu or shortcut menu to add titles, a legend, gridlines, a data table, or data labels. Use the Chart toolbar to add a legend, data table, and gridlines.

You can make changes to the entire chart, or to specific elements within it. It all depends on what part of the chart you select. There are two ways to select sections of the chart:

- Pull down the Chart Objects list in the Chart toolbar, and choose the object that you want to change.
- Point to the element with the mouse, making sure the ScreenTip that appears shows the element's name, and then click.

Handles will either surround the part that you select or appear in the middle. In the example shown in the following illustration, the Sweig Health Care series is selected as indicated by the handles in the center of the columns:

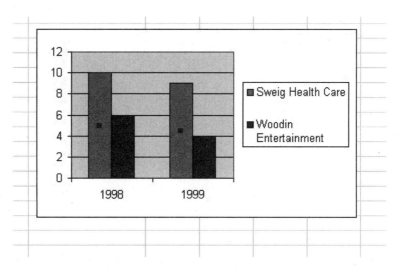

Changing the color of the series (by double-clicking on it to open a dialog box) will affect both columns. If you then click just one of the columns, only it will be selected, as shown here:

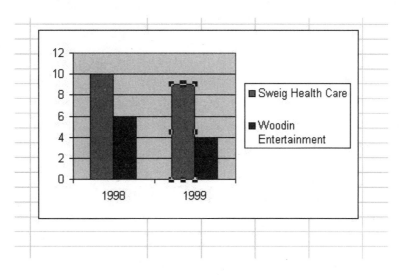

Now changing the color only affects that bar.

TIP: Before taking any actions on a chart, make sure that the proper part is selected.

Changing the Chart Type

To change the chart type, make sure that the entire chart is selected, and then use any of these options:

- Pull down the Chart Type list in the Chart toolbar.
- Right-click the chart area and choose Chart Type from the shortcut menu.
- Choose Chart | Chart Type.

When you use the shortcut menu or Chart menu, Excel opens a dialog box with the same options as in the first Chart Wizard. Use either the Standard Types or Custom Types tabs to select a chart type and subtype.

Pulling down the Chart Type list in the Chart toolbar displays these choices:

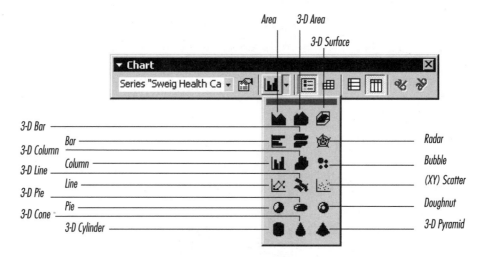

Point to an option to see a ScreenTip with its name, and click the type of chart you want to create.

Changing Chart Parts

You can customize a specific part of the chart, rather than the entire chart itself. For example, you may want to change the way one series is plotted, or change the text of the title or subtitle. Select the part of the chart, and then choose options from any of these sources:

- The Format or Chart menu
- The Chart toolbar
- The shortcut menu that appears when you right-click

For example, if you change the chart type when you have just a series selected, only that series will change. You can use that technique to combine types, as shown in the following illustration, which shows a combination line and bar chart:

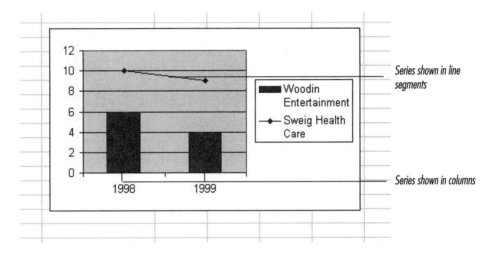

Series shown in line segments

Series shown in columns

N O T E: Some combinations of chart types are not allowed because their designs conflict.

Most customization options are displayed in a Format dialog box. Double-click the part of the chart you want to format to open the dialog box. The tabs and options in the dialog box depend on the part of the chart. Double-clicking on a series bar, for example, opens the Format Data Series dialog box shown in Figure 17-5.

This dialog box contains options for varying patterns, axis, Y error bars, data labels, series order, and formatting. Most of the dialog boxes have the Patterns tab in common, although some options vary. Use the Patterns tab to change the

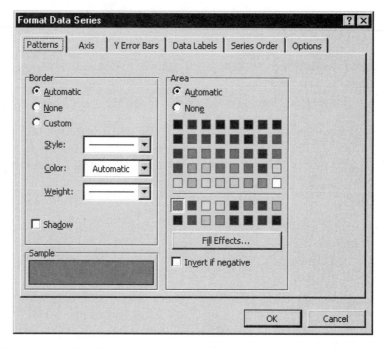

FIGURE 17-5 Formatting a chart element

border around the part, modify the fill color, add a shadow, and change the fill effects. For chart elements that contain text such as a title or legend, the Format dialog box contains the Font tab. Use it to change the font, font size, color, and effect of the text. The Format dialog box for titles contains an Alignment box for changing the position of text, while the dialog box for a legend contains a Placement tab for positioning the legend.

 N O T E : Click Fill Effects to add a pattern, gradient, texture, or photograph to the background, much like using the Format | Background command in Word.

When you're formatting a series, such as when you double-click a series column or line, you'll find an Options tab for fine-tuning its placement, such as overlapping columns and bars, and changing the distance between columns and bars, as shown here:

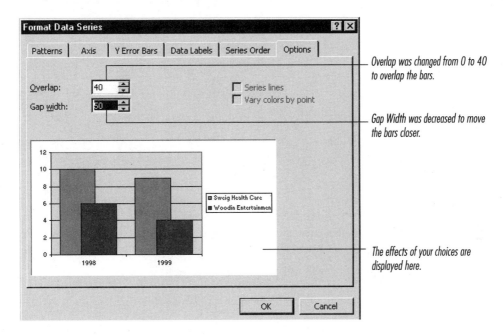

Overlap was changed from 0 to 40 to overlap the bars.

Gap Width was decreased to move the bars closer.

The effects of your choices are displayed here.

Customizing an Axis

There may be times when you want to format or customize a chart axis. The Format Axis dialog box has tabs to set the pattern, scale, font, format of numbers, and the orientation and rotation of text. The text and markings along the X axis and Y axis are important because they show the reader what your chart is all about. Sometimes, however, Excel doesn't automatically format the axis the way you want it. The default font may be too large to display all the labels, or the format or scale of the Y axis may need to be adjusted.

The scale, for example, determines the numbers at the bottom and top of the Y axis, as well as those in between. In this instance, the values being charted range from –60 to 89, but the scale shows values from –80 to 100 in increments of 20, called the *major unit* and marked with horizontal gridlines.

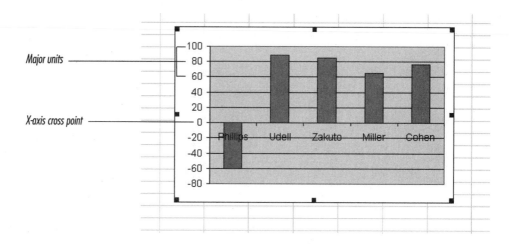

Major units ———————

X-axis cross point ———————

If you enlarge the chart, Excel may automatically change the major units and display gridlines at increments of 10, but you can change the major unit yourself using the Scale tab of the Format dialog box, shown in Figure 17-6. Use the Scale

FIGURE 17-6 Adjusting the scale

tab of the dialog box to adjust the low and high values along the axis, and the interval for major and minor units. You can also set the point along the Y axis where the X axis appears, called the *X-axis cross point*. You would change this, for example, if you did not want the X axis at the zero position.

Minor units are small lines called *tick marks* that appear along the Y axis to indicate values between the major units. You may, for example, have major unit gridlines in increments of 20 with minor units every 10 units. Once you select the interval for the units, you choose which to show on the chart and their placement in the Patterns tab of the Format Axis dialog box. In this example, the minor tick marks are set to cross the Y-axis line, but you could choose to have them on the inside or outside of the axis line:

Minor units

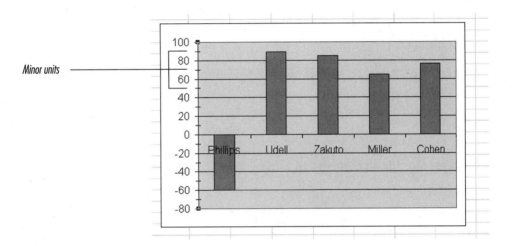

Formatting Three Dimensions

Three-dimensional charts can have a real impact because they add another axis indicating depth. You use all the formatting techniques already discussed to customize a three-dimensional chart. But you can also fine-tune the dimensions by choosing Chart | 3-D View to open the dialog box shown in Figure 17-7. In this dialog box, you change the rotation, elevation, and perspective.

To change a setting, either click the buttons for each, or type settings in the appropriate text boxes. For example, to rotate the chart so it appears as if you are looking at it from the right side, either click the Rotate Clockwise button or

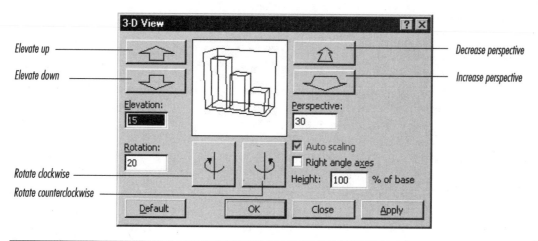

FIGURE 17-7   Working with 3-D charts

increase the setting in the Rotation text box. Rotating the chart to a setting of 70 would result in this:

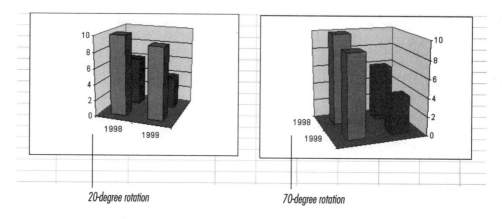

Here's a recap of the effects that can be set in this dialog box:

- **Elevation**   This adjusts the view from top to bottom, such as looking down at the top of the chart or looking up at it.
- **Rotation**   This adjusts the view of the chart as if you were walking around it, such as walking around a house to the left or right side.
- **Perspective**   This is the depth of the chart. Increase the perspective, for example, to make the back wall of the chart appear farther way.

- **Auto Scaling** This lets Excel scale the chart so it is closer in size to the two-dimensional version. You can only turn off this option if you select Right Angle Axes.
- **Right Angle Axes** This places the axes at right angles to each other, regardless of the rotation and elevation settings.
- **Height** This is the ratio of the height of the chart wall to the X axis. Setting the height at 50, for example, makes the chart half as high as it is wide.

Mapping Excel Data

When your data is organized by geographic areas, such as states or countries, you can chart it on a map. The map will use colors and patterns to represent the values, and they are quite useful in revealing trends. The map in Figure 17-8, for example, shows U.S. membership in Watson's Gyms by state. By studying the map, you can see where the sales need improvement.

N O T E : Excel creates the ranges of values shown in the map legend, although sometimes this results in a single value, as shown in Figure 17-8.

Creating a Map

Before creating a map, make sure you've used the names of states (either abbreviated or spelled out) or countries as the row labels. Then select the cells that you want to map.

If the Map button is in your toolbar, click that button. Move the mouse into the worksheet area to display a cross-hairs pointer. Then drag where you want the map to appear. Otherwise, follow these steps to start your map:

1. Choose Insert | Object.
2. Click the Create New tab if it is not already displayed.
3. Scroll the Object Type list and click Microsoft Map.
4. Click OK.

N O T E : Even though Excel only charts one series in a map by default, select all the series you may want to map. You can insert them later using the Map Control, which you will learn about shortly.

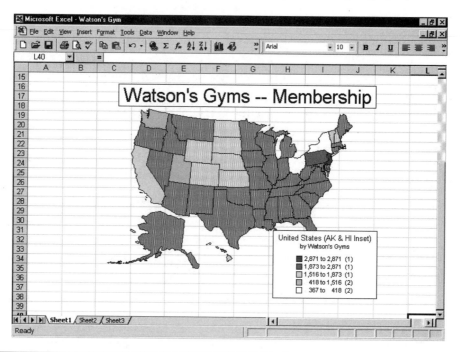

FIGURE 17-8   Using Excel to map worksheet data

Excel will start the map application, matching your information with its database of geographic locations. If it finds alternate maps, it will display a dialog box asking you to select the one to use, as shown here:

Excel then displays the map with your data, the Microsoft Map Control, and the Map toolbar, as shown in Figure 17-9. The legend divides the values from the plotted column into ranges and shows the number of states in each range.

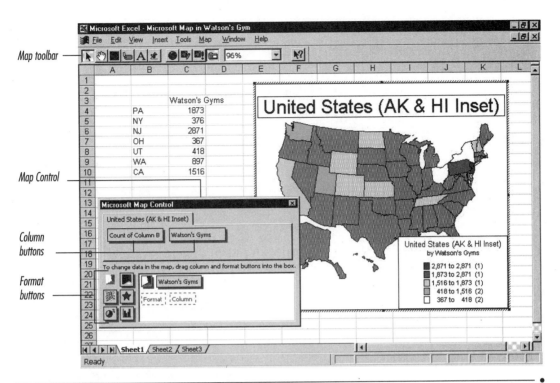

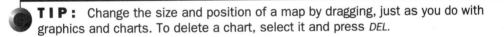

FIGURE 17-9 Microsoft Map Control

TIP: Change the size and position of a map by dragging, just as you do with graphics and charts. To delete a chart, select it and press *DEL*.

The Map Control and Map toolbar disappear if you click outside the map to deselect it. Click the map to select it for sizing or moving, or double-click the map to display the Map toolbar and Map Control for editing.

Editing a Map

You use the Map toolbar, the Map Control, and the menu bar to edit and change the map. The functions of the Map toolbar are shown in Table 17-3. Use the *View* menu to add a subtitle, the *Insert* menu to add other geographical data to the map or to import data from Microsoft Access, the *Tools* menu to set

BUTTON	NAME	FUNCTION
	Select Objects	Selects a map element, such as the title or legend, for moving or editing
	Grabber	Lets you drag the map within its box to change its position
	Center Map	Centers the map within the box at the position where you click
	Map Labels	Adds feature and cell labels
	Add Text	Inserts text within the map
	Custom Pin Map	Inserts a graphic symbol with text
	Display Entire	Displays the entire continent or world
	Redraw Map	Redraws the map to correct any graphic problems
	Map Refresh	Updates the map to any changes in plotted cells
	Show/Hide Microsoft Map Control	Turns on and off the Map Control
96%	Zoom	Enlarges the map within its box

TABLE 17-3

mapping options, and the *Map* menu to add features and save your edited map as a template for other maps. To subtitle the map, for example, select View | Subtitle to display a text box below the map title. Click in the box to edit and format the text.

You might, for example, want to add the state names to a map of the United States, or country names to a European map. To add names and some other features, such as the names of the Great Lakes, click the Map Labels button in the Map toolbar to see this dialog box:

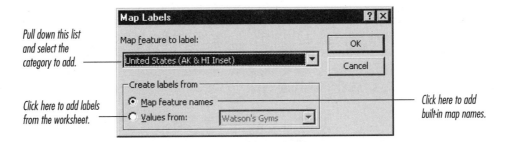

Pull down this list and select the category to add.

Click here to add labels from the worksheet.

Click here to add built-in map names.

After you click OK to close the dialog box, point to the item you want to label to see its name, as shown here. Position the name where you want it to appear and then click.

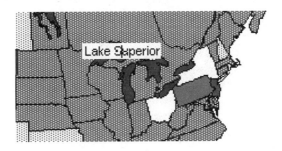

You can also add to maps geographic features, such as major highways, capitals, and oceans. To see what features Microsoft Map suggests, select Map | Features to see a dialog box such as this:

Turn on check boxes for items to add.

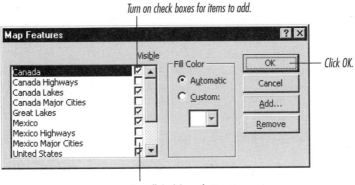

Click OK.

Turn off check boxes for items to remove.

Use the Fill Color options in the Map Features dialog box to change the color of the item selected in the list. Choose Automatic to use the default colors, or click Custom and select a color from the pull-down list.

To add other features to the map, click the Add button in the Map Features dialog box to see these choices:

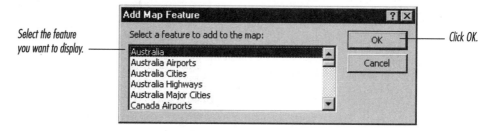

Select the feature you want to display. ——

Click OK.

 N O T E : You can also display the Add Map Feature dialog box by choosing Map I Add Feature.

If you add a feature outside of the geographic area displayed on the map, click the Display Entire button on the Map toolbar after you close the Map Features dialog box. You may then have to click the Redraw Map button to display all the features you've inserted.

Using the Map Control

To change the format of the map, use the format buttons on the left side of the Microsoft Map Control. To add or remove data from the map, use the column buttons at the top. The box next to the format buttons shows the columns and their format. For example, in the Map Control shown here, the number of active members is plotted using the Value Shading format. "Value Shading" means that Excel displays ranges of values using colors or shades of gray in the geographic areas.

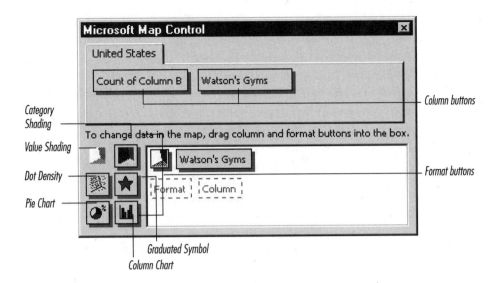

To change the format, drag the format button of your choice onto the format button for the column shown in the box. For example, Dot Density displays each geographic area in a density corresponding to its value. To use dot density for the format of the map, drag the Dot Density button over the Value Shading button that's next to Watson's Gym. The map will change to the Dot Density format.

To add or remove a series from the map, you drag its column buttons on or off of the large box. For example, suppose you also included a column labeled Inactive Members in the range of cells to be mapped. There would be an Inactive Members button on the top area of the Map Control. To also plot the inactive members on this map, you would drag its column button from the top of the Map Control onto the gray box labeled "Column." You could then drag a format button to select its format.

NOTE: To delete a series, drag its column button off of the large box.

- When you print or preview the worksheet, Excel also prints or previews any charts on the same sheet. To print or preview just the chart itself, select the chart first. If the chart doesn't show all its labels, print the chart by itself in landscape orientation.

- You must install Microsoft Map from the Office CD—it will not automatically be installed the first time you use it.

- You can insert charts and maps that you create with Excel into your Word documents. Create the chart or map, select and copy it, and then paste it into the Word document.

- Make sure your charts are easy to read onscreen and when printed. Some charts, especially three-dimensional ones, look great but make it difficult to analyze the information being presented. After creating a chart, try applying other types to see which most clearly presents the information.

- You can use the Drawing toolbar to add elements, such as arrows and text boxes, to charts and maps.

- Create a chart in its own sheet, using either F11 or Chart Wizard, when you want to print it on a separate page. Embed the chart on the worksheet when you want to print it and its associated worksheet data at the same time.

- If you cannot see all the axis labels on a chart, enlarge the chart size or reduce the font used for the labels. Right-click the labels and choose Format Axis from the shortcut menu. Click the Font tab of the dialog box that appears, and choose a small font or font size.

- In Chapter 19 you will learn how to assign a macro so that clicking on a chart or map repeats the steps recorded in the macro.

- Use the Center Map button on the Map toolbar to select what portion of the map is centered in its box. Click the button and then click the portion of the map you want in the center. Excel does not turn off this feature automatically, so click the button again when you are satisfied with the map's position.

- There's only so much information that you can include in a chart—if you want to make it readable. Three or four series are usually the maximum, and you can't fit many items along the X axis. If you have a lot if information, divide it into several charts.

Working with Lists and Databases

18

A database is a place where you store information, an electronic version of a box of 3×5 index cards, or even a filing cabinet full of folders and papers. While you might have Microsoft Access to work with databases, you can use Excel's statistical capabilities to analyze information in ways not possible in Access. In Excel you store information in a list, as a series of rows and columns. Each row holds a record, which is a collection of information about one object in the database, such as a client, inventory item, or sales record.

The columns represent the *fields,* each piece of information that makes up a record, as shown in Figure 18-1. The fields for a client record, for example, can include first and last names, address, and phone number. The fields for an inventory record might include the item name and stock number, quantity on hand, and price.

Excel has one other element in a database, the *criteria range.* This lets you find information quickly based on its content and allows you to create a subset of your database so you see only the information that you are interested in. A *criteria range* is a section of the worksheet that contains the names of the fields you want to use to locate information. It also contains the *criteria,* the text you are looking for or logical operators specifying information.

Sorting a Database

Sometimes it helps to look at the information in your database in an order other than you typed it. For example, suppose you use the database to record information about your clients, as shown in Figure 18-1. Sometimes you'll want to view the database sorted by client name. Other times it may be convenient to list them by their ZIP code to prepare a mailing. Sorting not only puts records in order, but it also groups them. If you sort the database shown in Figure 18-1 by the client's business category, for instance, all those in the same category will be listed together.

To quickly sort the database, select all of the cells in the database except for the heading row, and then click either of these buttons in the Standard toolbar:

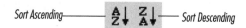

NOTE: You can try sorting the database by clicking in any of its cells and then one of the sort buttons. If the headings are sorted along with the other rows, however, click Undo and then use the Sort dialog box to perform the sort.

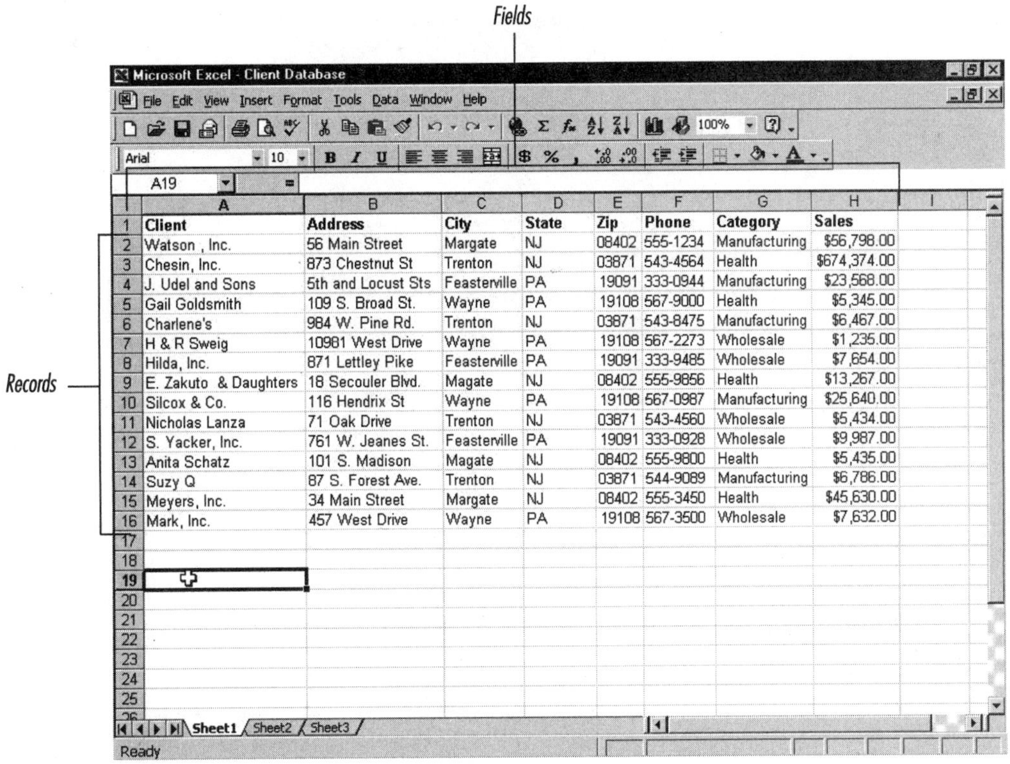

Fields

	A	B	C	D	E	F	G	H
1	Client	Address	City	State	Zip	Phone	Category	Sales
2	Watson , Inc.	56 Main Street	Margate	NJ	08402	555-1234	Manufacturing	$56,798.00
3	Chesin, Inc.	873 Chestnut St	Trenton	NJ	03871	543-4564	Health	$674,374.00
4	J. Udel and Sons	5th and Locust Sts	Feasterville	PA	19091	333-0944	Manufacturing	$23,568.00
5	Gail Goldsmith	109 S. Broad St.	Wayne	PA	19108	567-9000	Health	$5,345.00
6	Charlene's	984 W. Pine Rd.	Trenton	NJ	03871	543-8475	Manufacturing	$6,467.00
7	H & R Sweig	10981 West Drive	Wayne	PA	19108	567-2273	Wholesale	$1,235.00
8	Hilda, Inc.	871 Lettley Pike	Feasterville	PA	19091	333-9485	Wholesale	$7,654.00
9	E. Zakuto & Daughters	18 Secouler Blvd.	Magate	NJ	08402	555-9856	Health	$13,267.00
10	Silcox & Co.	116 Hendrix St	Wayne	PA	19108	567-0987	Manufacturing	$25,640.00
11	Nicholas Lanza	71 Oak Drive	Trenton	NJ	03871	543-4560	Wholesale	$5,434.00
12	S. Yacker, Inc.	761 W. Jeanes St.	Feasterville	PA	19091	333-0928	Wholesale	$9,987.00
13	Anita Schatz	101 S. Madison	Magate	NJ	08402	555-9800	Health	$5,435.00
14	Suzy Q	87 S. Forest Ave.	Trenton	NJ	03871	544-9089	Manufacturing	$6,786.00
15	Meyers, Inc.	34 Main Street	Margate	NJ	08402	555-3450	Health	$45,630.00
16	Mark, Inc.	457 West Drive	Wayne	PA	19108	567-3500	Wholesale	$7,632.00

Records

FIGURE 18-1   Database in Excel

The sort buttons on the toolbar only let you sort on one column. So looking again at Figure 18-1, if you sort your database by the client's business category and then by their sales, the categories will no longer be in category order. To sort on up to three columns, choose Data | Sort to see the dialog box shown in Figure 18-2.

1 *Pick a field to sort by and a sort order.*

2 *Pick up to two more fields and their order.*

3 *Make sure this option is turned on so the field names in the header row aren't sorted.*

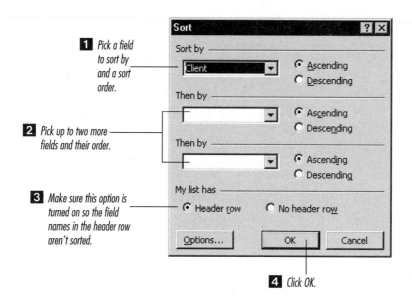

4 *Click OK.*

FIGURE 18-2 Sorting on up to three fields

 TIP: If you're sorting a worksheet that does not have column names, turn on the No Header Row option.

Filtering a Database

When you are interested in seeing just selected information, not every record in the database, apply a filter. A *filter* temporarily hides the rows that you're not interested in seeing. So, if you just want to see clients in one business area, using Figure 18-1 again as an example, you would create a filter that does just that. There are two ways to filter a database: AutoFilter and the Advanced Filter command. AutoFilter lets you choose criteria by selecting an existing value from a drop-down list. The Advanced Filter command lets you set up a criteria range containing a sample of the information you want to display.

Using AutoFilter

To quickly filter your database, make any cell within it active, and choose Data | Filter | AutoFilter. Excel adds drop-down arrows to each of the field names:

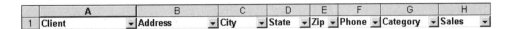

Clicking on the down arrow displays a menu of options and a list of each of the values in the columns:

To display records that match a value, just click the value in the list. When you select a value from the list, the arrow on the list button changes color to remind you that the display is being filtered.

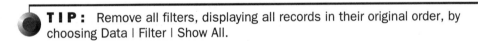

T I P : Remove all filters, displaying all records in their original order, by choosing Data | Filter | Show All.

If you select values from more than one of the drop-down lists, Excel only displays records matching all of the criteria. Use two lists, for example, to select records meeting two criteria, three lists for records meeting three criteria, and so on. When you use two lists, for example, you are specifying that the records must match the value in both lists (one *And* the other) to be selected.

To remove the filter from a column, pull down the list and choose (All). This removes the filter from the selected column, but not from others. So to display all the records in your database, you must choose (All) from every filtered column.

The Top 10 and Custom options give you greater control over selecting records, helping you analyze the information as well as limit the records displayed. The Top 10 option actually lets you select any number of records at the top or bottom in terms of value or percentage, such as the clients with the five highest sales, the top 20 percent, or the two lowest. Selecting (Top 10) displays the Top 10 AutoFilter dialog box:

 N O T E : You can only use the Top 10 option with a column containing numeric values.

From the first list, select whether you want to find records from the top or bottom. Use the second list to specify the number of values you want to locate, such as the top 10 or bottom 5. From the last list select whether you want to locate items by their value (the Items option) or by percent.

The Custom option lets you select records on up to two criteria, using these *logic operators:*

equals
does not equal
is greater than
is greater than or equal to
is less than
is less than or equal to
begins with
does not begin with
ends with
does not end with
contains
does not contain

You can choose an operator and value for each criterion, and select to perform an And or Or operation. Choose (Custom) from the drop-down menu of the column you want to filter, to display a dialog box like this one:

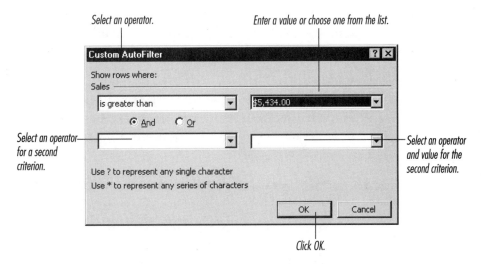

Select an operator.

Enter a value or choose one from the list.

Select an operator for a second criterion.

Select an operator and value for the second criterion.

Click OK.

For example, here's a custom filter that looks for clients whose name begins with the letter "C" or "W":

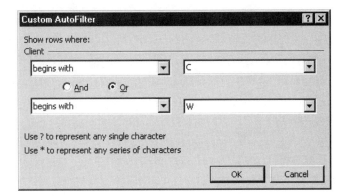

Using a Criteria Range

Excel lets you search for information in the database using a method called query by example. This means that you type the information you are looking for, as well as any logical conditions, and Excel searches the database for you.

You have to start by creating a *criteria table* of at least two rows anywhere in the workbook. The first row of the criteria table must contain the names of the fields that you want to search in the database.

You use the other rows in the criteria table to enter the information that you want to search for. For example, Figure 18-3 shows a criteria table to find a record in a database that has Trenton in the City column, and Health in the Category column. Searching for values in more than one column of a row is treated as an And operation. This means that a record must match all the information in the criteria table row. So, for example, the same search will not locate the record for any other client in the Health category.

To create an Or operation, enter search information in more than one row. The following criteria table will locate records for Chesin, Inc., as well as

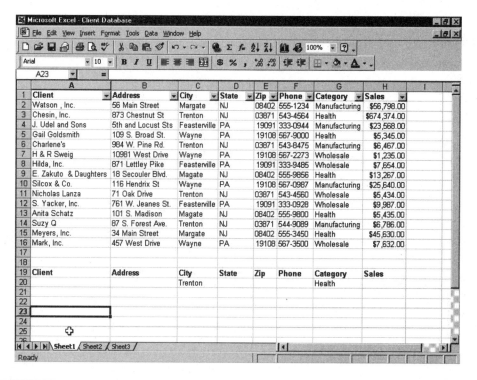

FIGURE 18-3 Criteria table using two fields

records for everyone in the Wholesale category, matching one row or the other in the criteria table:

19	Client	Address	City	State	Zip	Phone	Category	Sales
20	Chesin, Inc.							
21							Wholesale	

To activate the filter, follow these steps:

1. Click in any cell in the database.
2. Choose Data | Filter | Advanced Filter to see the Advanced Filter dialog box.

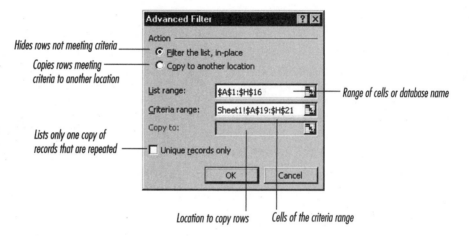

Hides rows not meeting criteria

Copies rows meeting criteria to another location

Lists only one copy of records that are repeated

Range of cells or database name

Location to copy rows   Cells of the criteria range

3. Make sure the List Range text box shows the range of cells of the database. If not, just enter the range of the cells or the name you assign to the range.
4. Click in the Criteria Range box.
5. Click the Collapse Dialog button for the Criteria Range box.
6. Drag over the cells in the criteria range, including its column headings.
7. Click the Expand Dialog button.
8. Click OK. Excel uses the criteria in the range to filter the rows.

T I P : If you later change the criteria but they are still within the same range of cells, you do not have to reselect the criteria range in the Advanced Filter dialog box. If you have to select a new range, first delete any text in the Criteria Range box.

 N O T E : When you select or change a criteria range, Excel automatically defines a name for it—"Criteria."

Remember, to remove the filter, choose Data | Filter | Show All.

In some cases, you want to do more than just see a selected range of your information. You may want to use that information to create a separate worksheet, or compare it with the original database. That's when you use the Copy To Another Location option in the Advanced Filter dialog box. Choosing that option lets you make a copy of the records that meet the criteria, leaving the original database untouched. When you select that option, the Copy To text box becomes active. Type the address of the cell that is in the upper-left corner of the range where you want to place the copied cells.

Filtering with Logic

Searching for specific values is useful, but it has limitations. For example, chances are you're not interested in clients who owe you an exact amount, but rather, a range, such as over $1,000. By using logical operations in the criteria table, you can design searches that pinpoint the information you are looking for.

To locate records that fall within a certain range, enter a logical condition in the form of a formula as the search criteria. The condition > 10000 in the Sales column, for instance, would locate records with a value greater than $10,000 in that field, like this:

	Client	Address	City	State	Zip	Phone	Category	Sales
19								
20								>10000

You can use any of the usual operators:

=	Equal to
<>	Not equal to
>=	Greater than or equal to
>	Greater than
<=	Less than or equal to
<	Less than

Using a Data Form

Creating a database is easy, and so is adding information to it. If you have more fields than you can see on the screen, however, you'll have to scroll the window to reach some. Instead of working with your database as a worksheet, you can use a *form*. The form lets you find, insert, and delete records just as if you were using a database program.

To use a form, click in any cell in the database, and then choose Data | Form. A form appears showing the first record (row) of the database, such as the one in Figure 18-4. The information accessible in the form is the same as in the worksheet. Adding, deleting, or changing a record on the form makes the same changes to the database itself. The form is just another way of working with the same information.

To move among records, click the Find Prev or Find Next button, or use the scroll bar next to the field names. To edit a record, navigate until its information appears in the field boxes, and then make your changes. To add a new row to the database, click the New button. The field boxes will empty so you can enter new information. When you move to a new record or close the form, your change is copied onto the database in the worksheet.

Use the Criteria button to apply a filter. Click the button to display empty field boxes. Enter the criteria in the boxes just as you would in a criteria range. The entries become a sample of what to display. Click Find Prev or Find Next, and then display the records that match the criteria.

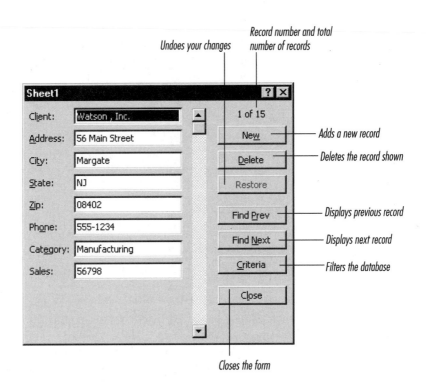

Record number and total number of records

Undoes your changes

Adds a new record

Deletes the record shown

Displays previous record

Displays next record

Filters the database

Closes the form

FIGURE 18-4 Using a data form

Calculating Subtotals

The database functions are powerful, but they can be rather complex to work with. When dealing with a database, you are more likely interested in summarizing the information, displaying subtotals based on certain groupings. For example, the worksheet shown in Figure 18-5 shows subtotals of sales in each business category, with a grand total at the end. The database was first sorted by category, so with each change in the category, Excel was able to calculate and display the subtotals. You can use Excel to produce a variety of calculations for each group, such as their subtotals, averages, the minimum or maximum values, the number of items in each group, and their product.

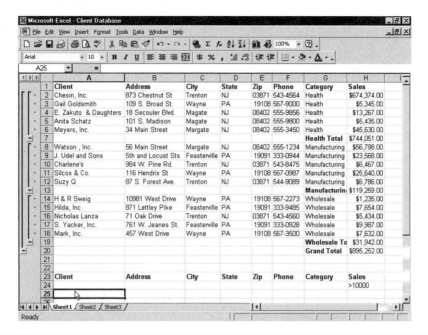

FIGURE 18-5 Worksheet with subtotals

To organize your information that way, take these steps:

1. Sort the database by the field you want to group by.
2. Click in any cell in the database, and then choose Data | Subtotals.

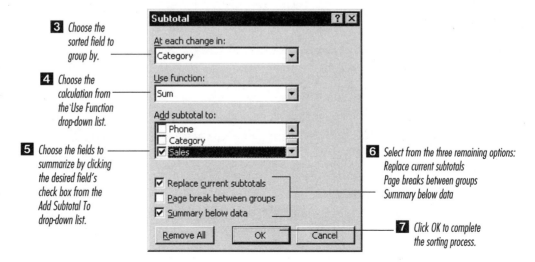

As shown in Figure 18-5, you'll see the area to the left of the worksheet has marks that show subtotals organized like an outline. As with an outline in Word, you can collapse and expand the outline to see various levels. You collapse the outline to see just the summary information, and you expand the outline when you want again to look at the details.

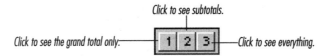

The numbers 1, 2, and 3 above the outline represent three levels of details. Click 1, for example, to see just the grand total of sales. Click 2 to see the subtotals and grand totals, and click 3 to see everything. The boxes and lines below the numbers graphically illustrate the levels, and show which ones are expanded or collapsed.

 N O T E : To remove the outline, choose Data I Subtotals I Remove All.

Adding Your Own Subtotals

The Subtotals command adds the subtotals and grand totals for you, but you can always do it yourself. Use of the AutoSum button on the Standard toolbar makes it easy. First sort your database so it is organized by the fields you want, and then add a blank row after each group:

	A	B	C	D	E	F	G	H
1	Client	Address	City	State	Zip	Phone	Category	Sales
2	Chesin, Inc.	873 Chestnut St	Trenton	NJ	03871	543-4564	Health	$674,374.00
3	Gail Goldsmith	109 S. Broad St.	Wayne	PA	19108	567-9000	Health	$5,345.00
4	E. Zakuto & Daughters	18 Secouler Blvd.	Magate	NJ	08402	555-9856	Health	$13,267.00
5	Anita Schatz	101 S. Madison	Magate	NJ	08402	555-9800	Health	$5,435.00
6	Meyers, Inc.	34 Main Street	Margate	NJ	08402	555-3450	Health	$45,630.00
7								
8	Watson , Inc.	56 Main Street	Margate	NJ	08402	555-1234	Manufacturing	$56,798.00
9	J. Udel and Sons	5th and Locust Sts	Feasterville	PA	19091	333-0944	Manufacturing	$23,568.00
10	Charlene's	984 W. Pine Rd.	Trenton	NJ	03871	543-8475	Manufacturing	$6,467.00
11	Silcox & Co.	116 Hendrix St	Wayne	PA	19108	567-0987	Manufacturing	$25,640.00
12	Suzy Q	87 S. Forest Ave.	Trenton	NJ	03871	544-9089	Manufacturing	$6,786.00
13								
14	H & R Sweig	10981 West Drive	Wayne	PA	19108	567-2273	Wholesale	$1,235.00
15	Hilda, Inc.	871 Lettley Pike	Feasterville	PA	19091	333-9485	Wholesale	$7,654.00
16	Nicholas Lanza	71 Oak Drive	Trenton	NJ	03871	543-4560	Wholesale	$5,434.00
17	S. Yacker, Inc.	761 W. Jeanes St.	Feasterville	PA	19091	333-0928	Wholesale	$9,987.00
18	Mark, Inc.	457 West Drive	Wayne	PA	19108	567-3500	Wholesale	$7,632.00
19								

Select the cell in the blank row under the first group, and then click AutoSum. Excel selects just the cells above, so click the Enter button. Next, select the cell in the blank row under the next group and click AutoSum. This time, Excel selects the cells up to the previous AutoSum, so when you click Enter, you'll get the other subtotal.

Continue adding subtotals in the same way, then to calculate the grand total, click in the cell under the last subtotal and then on AutoSum. Excel now selects just the subtotals above the cell holding the grand total.

Creating a Pivot Table

A *pivot table* lets you analyze information based on two or more variables. In addition to this capability, a pivot table lets you quickly change the way the information is organized and displayed. With pivot tables, you work interactively with the data to find the most suitable organization for the information.

For example, the pivot table shown in the following illustration compares the sales from four regions in three different years. The information for the pivot table was taken from a list in an Excel worksheet. The values across the top of the pivot table were taken from the Year column, and the values down the left of the pivot table, from the Region column. The data, analyzed according to the fields Year and Region, was summarized by another column in the table, the Sales column.

3	Sum of Sales	Year			
4	Region	1998	1999	2000	Grand Total
5	East	43546	12345	4322	60213
6	North	45446	12324	43456	101226
7	South	38733	4321	36900	79954
8	West	54433	23123	32234	109790
9	Grand Total	182158	52113	116912	351183

Excel helps you create pivot tables and pivot charts by dragging field names to different locations. A *pivot table* shows information in rows and columns, like a worksheet. A *pivot chart* displays the information in chart form. Here's how:

1. Click in any cell in the database.
2. Choose Data | PivotTable And PivotChart Report to start the Pivot Table Wizard. The first Wizard asks if you want to create the chart from Excel cells, an external file, multiple consolidation pages, or another pivot table or chart.

3. Click Next to accept the defaults and to see the PivotTable And PivotChart Wizard - Step 2 Of 3 dialog box, as shown:

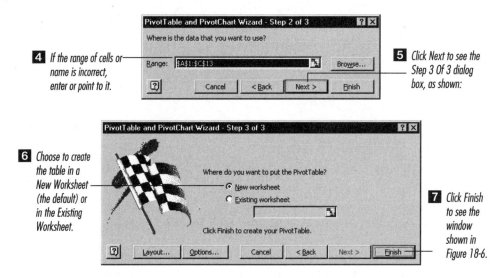

4 If the range of cells or name is incorrect, enter or point to it.

5 Click Next to see the Step 3 Of 3 dialog box, as shown:

6 Choose to create the table in a New Worksheet (the default) or in the Existing Worksheet.

7 Click Finish to see the window shown in Figure 18-6.

The Pivot Table toolbar shows the column headings of the table. You have to drag the headings to the Column, Row, Data, or Page area drop zone.

8. Drag the fields you want to use to the appropriate areas. In our example, we dragged Region to the area marked "Drop Row Fields Here," Year to the area marked "Drop Column Fields Here," and Sales to the area marked "Drop Data Items Here."

When three areas have fields, the pivot table appears with the areas surrounded by lines as shown here:

	Drop Page Fields Here			
2				
3	Sum of Sales	Year ▾		
4	Region ▾	1998	1999	2000	Grand Total
5	East	43546	12345	4322	60213
6	North	45446	12324	43456	101226
7	South	38733	4321	36900	79954
8	West	54433	23123	32234	109790
9	Grand Total	182158	52113	116912	351183

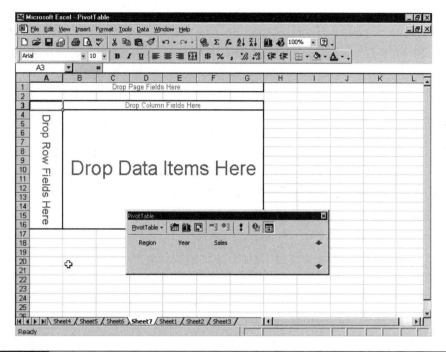

FIGURE 18-6 Creating a cross tab

The lines surrounding the pivot table, and any unused section, such as the Drop Page Fields Here area, disappear if you click outside the pivot table. Click in the pivot table to redisplay them.

The drop-down arrows next to the field names let you select which values are displayed. If you just want to view the statistics for the North region, for example, pull down the Region list to see these options:

Turn on only those check boxes for the fields you want to display.

		1998	1999	2000	Grand Total
3	Sum of Sales	Year ▾			
4	Region ▾	1998	1999	2000	Grand Total
5	☑ East		45	4322	60213
6	☑ North		24	43456	101226
7	☑ South		21	36900	79954
8	☑ West		23	32234	109790
9			13	116912	351183
10					
11					
12					
13					
14	OK	Cancel			

After examining the data in the table, you might want to review it in another way. To move a field from a row to a column, for instance, just drag its field button from one location to the other. Excel automatically adjusts the table. For example, the following illustration shows the same table after moving the Region field to the Drop Page Fields Here area. The down arrow on the Page field lets you quickly summarize all the field information for a specific value, such as one region.

1	Region	(All) ▾			
2					
3	Sum of Sales	Year ▾			
4		1998	1999	2000	Grand Total
5	Total	182158	52113	116912	351183

If you create a pivot chart, the Excel window appears as shown in Figure 18-7. Drag the fields into the areas marked Drop More Series Fields Here, Drop More Category Fields Here, Drop Data Items Here, and Drop Page Fields Here to create the chart.

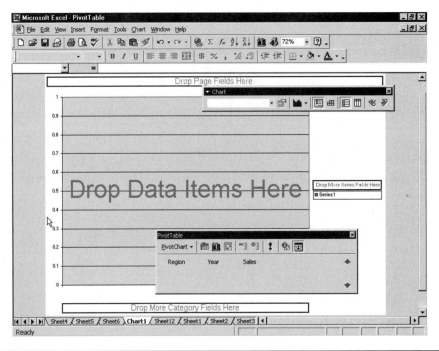

FIGURE 18-7 Creating a pivot chart

As with a pivot table, you can pull down lists in a pivot chart to select the fields to display on the chart. Figure 18-8, for example, shows a pivot chart using the same information represented by the Pivot table previously.

 TIP: To change the mathematical operation performed on the data field, choose Field Settings from the PivotTable list in the PivotTable toolbar.

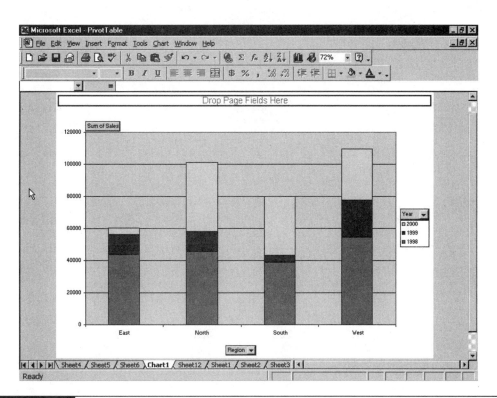

FIGURE 18-8 Pivot chart

- Give your database a name to make it easy to reference. Select the cells, and then choose Insert | Name | Define. Type **Database** as the name, click Add and then Close. Whenever you need to insert the database range, just use the name "Database."
- Define the field names as label names. Select the entire database, choose Insert | Name | Create. Make sure the Top Row option is selected and click OK.
- To change the way Excel sorts, click the Options button in the Sort dialog box. Use the First Key Sort Order list to sort items by days of the week, months of the year, school classes, or any custom AutoFill lists you may have created.
- You can use the wildcard characters "?" and "*" in filters. Use the "?" symbol to represent any single character and the "*" symbol to indicate any number of characters. If you want to find all clients whose names begin with the letter "N," for example, type **N*** in the Name column of the criteria row. The phrase **c*r** would locate all words that start with "c" and end with "r"—no matter how many characters were between them.
- As a shortcut to creating a criteria range as explained in "Using a Criteria Range" in this chapter, copy the field names from the first row of the database and paste them into the first row of the criteria table. This ensures that the field names in the criteria table exactly match those in the database.
- Database functions help you locate and analyze information in a database. Database functions have the same three arguments: Range is the range of cells that contains the database, Field is the column number (starting from number 1 in the range) where the data is located that you want to analyze, Criteria is the coordinates of the criteria table.
- You don't need to use database functions to perform math on a list. You can still use standard functions to calculate sums, averages, and other operations on rows and columns.
- Remember to remove all filters when you want to see all the information in the database.
- The Layout button in the final PivotTable And PivotChart Wizard lets you drag fields to drop areas before finishing the wizard. The Options button displays a dialog box for controlling the structure and look of the table, and how data is analyzed and displayed.
- The PivotTable toolbar gives you tools for working with pivot tables. Most of the options are advanced and require some in-depth knowledge about pivot tables.

Analyzing Information and Solving Problems

19

B A S I C S

- Using Goal Seek
- Recording and Playing Macros

B E Y O N D

- Creating Data Tables
- Using Solver
- Validating Input

All the techniques you've learned so far let you create worksheets and solve "What If" problems. Excel offers some special features, however, when you really have a difficult problem to solve. You'll learn how to use them in this chapter.

Using Goal Seek

In most cases, you use a formula or function to calculate and display results from the values you already know. Sometimes you have to work in reverse. You know the result you would like to achieve, but not the combination of arguments that will get those results. A mortgage payment function is a good example. If you know the loan rate, number of periods, and amount of principal, then you can calculate the amount of your monthly mortgage payment.

But suppose you already know how much you can afford to spend each month, and you'd like to determine how much of a dream home those monthly payments could obtain. You now have to work backward, a perfect use for Goal Seek.

To use Goal Seek, you need a formula that contains a reference to at least one cell. For example, look at the worksheet shown in Figure 19-1.

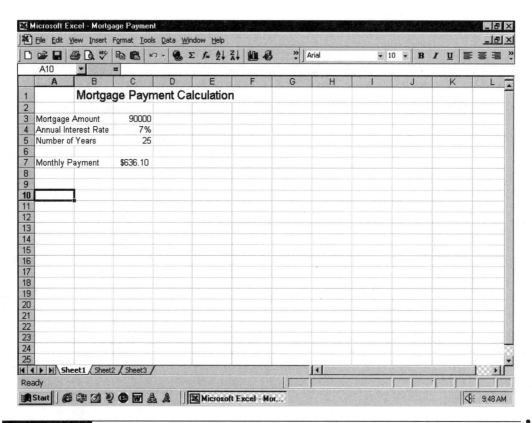

FIGURE 19-1   Setting up to use Goal Seek

The PMT function in cell C7 is =PMT(C4/12,C5*12,-C3). To automatically adjust the principal to find a mortgage payment of $1,000, follow these steps:

1. Click the cell containing the formula—in this case, cell C7.
2. Choose Tools | Goal Seek to display the dialog box shown here.

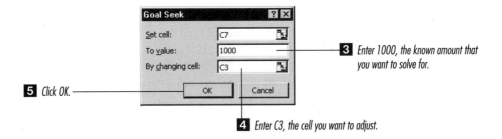

A dialog box appears with the solution.

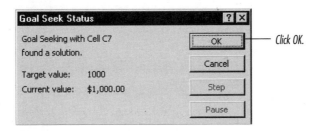

Creating Data Tables

Goal Seek varies one cell until it finds a specific solution to a formula. Sometimes, however, you want to vary a cell to see a number of possible solutions to a formula. Using the mortgage payment example, perhaps you'd like to see the monthly payments based on rates from 7 percent to 8 percent in one-tenth increments. Rather than change the rate ten times yourself, you create a data table that shows each of the results automatically. A *data table* is a series of rows and columns that shows the results of applying various values to the variables in a formula, such as the monthly mortgage payments for a range of mortgage rates or various loan periods. There are two types of data tables. A *one-variable* table displays the results of changing one cell in one or two formulas. A *two-variable* table shows the results of changing two variables in a single formula.

One-Variable Data Table

One-variable data tables are easy to create. First, you must have a formula that you're going to use. If the formula references more than one cell, you must have values in the cells that you are not going to change. In this case, we moved the PMT formula to cell F7. Cell C4 represents the interest rate that we'll vary, the principal and length of the mortgage remain constant.

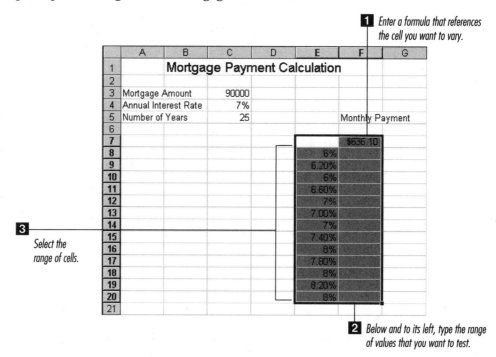

1 Enter a formula that references the cell you want to vary.

Mortgage Payment Calculation

	A	B	C	D	E	F	G
3	Mortgage Amount		90000				
4	Annual Interest Rate		7%				
5	Number of Years		25		Monthly Payment		
7						$636.10	
8					6%		
9					6.20%		
10					6%		
11					6.60%		
12					7%		
13					7.00%		
14					7%		
15					7.40%		
16					8%		
17					7.60%		
18					8%		
19					8.20%		
20					8%		

3 Select the range of cells.

2 Below and to its left, type the range of values that you want to test.

4. Choose Data | Table.

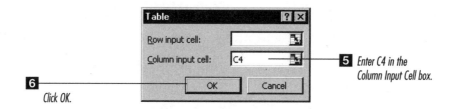

5 Enter C4 in the Column Input Cell box.

6 Click OK.

Excel fills in the blank cells by substituting the value in cell C4 with the values from the list, as shown in Figure 19-2.

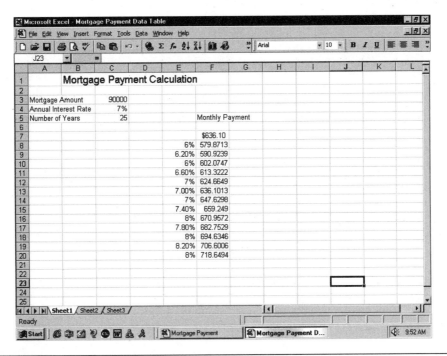

FIGURE 19-2 The result of creating a one-variable data table

Creating a Two-Variable Data Table

A two-variable data table works about the same, but you can vary two referenced cells. To create a two-variable table, construct a worksheet as shown in Figure 19-3.

Select the entire range of cells, and then choose Data | Table. In the Row Input Cell text box, enter the cell that is referenced by the values along the top row. In our example, it will be cell C5 that is referenced as the length of the loan. In the Column Input Cell text box, enter the cell that is referenced by the values down the column—in our case, cell C4. The completed data table will appear as shown in Figure 19-4.

Using Solver

Sometimes life is just not so simple. When you create a data table, for example, you simply substitute a range of values for a referenced cell. Although you can use up to two variables for a data table, you often have more variables to work with.

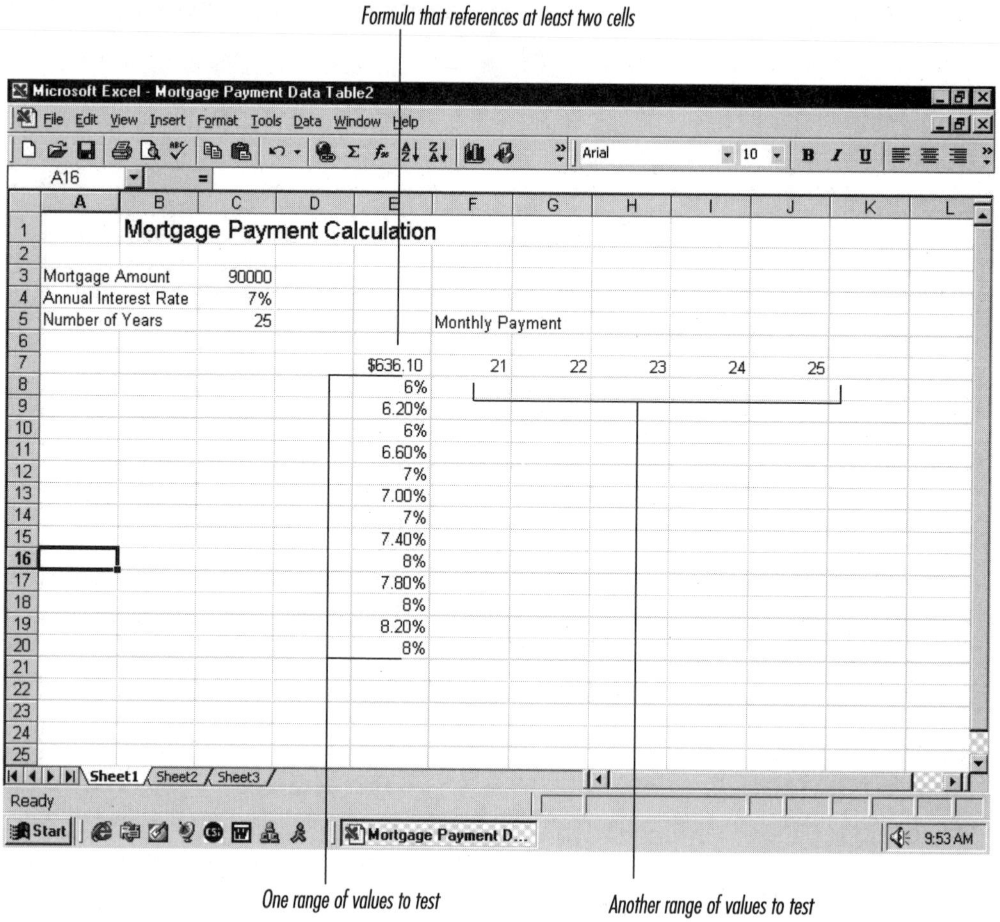

Formula that references at least two cells

FIGURE 19-3 Worksheet for two-variable data table

One range of values to test

Another range of values to test

There might also be constraints on the values that can be applied to calculate the formula. For example, let's consider again our friend the mortgage calculation problem. We know that a realistic mortgage rate might be between 6 and 8 percent, and that we need a loan for 20 to 30 years to minimize the size of our payments, and we'd like to not pay more than $1,000 per month. What is the maximum payment that follows these constraints?

With Solver, Excel can vary the changing cells—the cells containing the references in the formula—to find the values that represent a maximum or minimum solution, or a specific value.

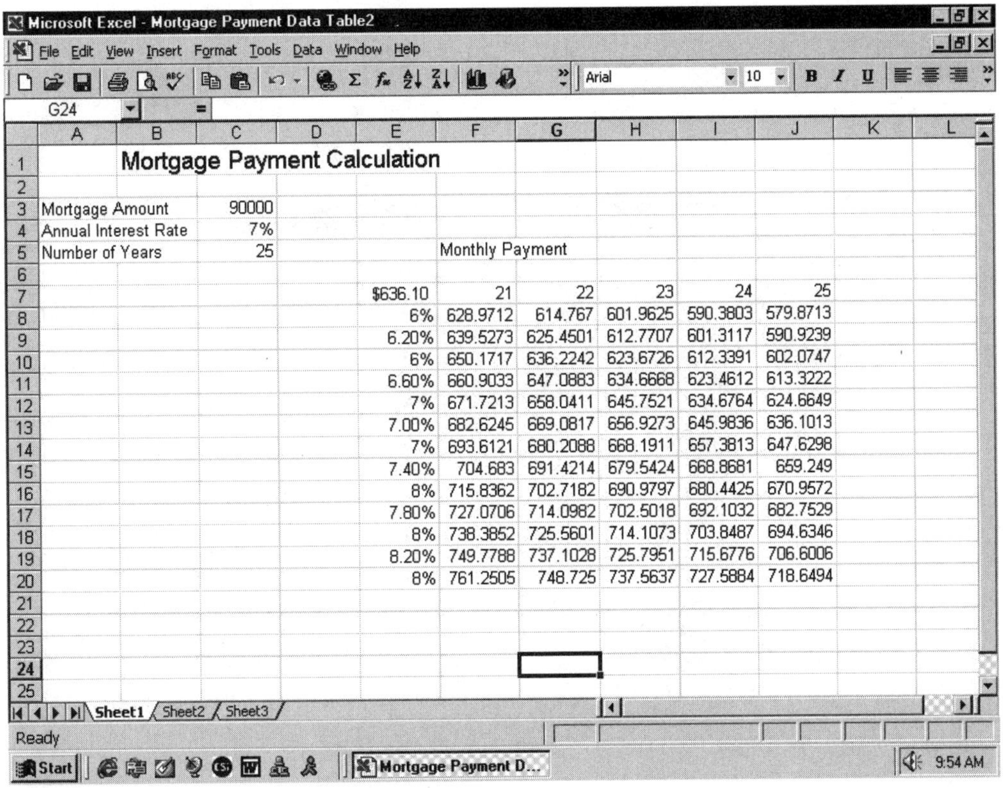

Microsoft Excel - Mortgage Payment Data Table2

	A	B	C	D	E	F	G	H	I	J	K	L
1		**Mortgage Payment Calculation**										
2												
3	Mortgage Amount		90000									
4	Annual Interest Rate		7%									
5	Number of Years		25			Monthly Payment						
6												
7					$636.10	21	22	23	24	25		
8					6%	628.9712	614.767	601.9625	590.3803	579.8713		
9					6.20%	639.5273	625.4501	612.7707	601.3117	590.9239		
10					6%	650.1717	636.2242	623.6726	612.3391	602.0747		
11					6.60%	660.9033	647.0883	634.6668	623.4612	613.3222		
12					7%	671.7213	658.0411	645.7521	634.6764	624.6649		
13					7.00%	682.6245	669.0817	656.9273	645.9836	636.1013		
14					7%	693.6121	680.2088	668.1911	657.3813	647.6298		
15					7.40%	704.683	691.4214	679.5424	668.8681	659.249		
16					8%	715.8362	702.7182	690.9797	680.4425	670.9572		
17					7.80%	727.0706	714.0982	702.5018	692.1032	682.7529		
18					8%	738.3852	725.5601	714.1073	703.8487	694.6346		
19					8.20%	749.7788	737.1028	725.7951	715.6776	706.6006		
20					8%	761.2505	748.725	737.5637	727.5884	718.6494		
21												
22												
23												
24												
25												

Sheet1 / Sheet2 / Sheet3

Ready

FIGURE 19-4 Completed two-variable data table

First, however, you have to make sure that Solver is installed and ready to use. Pull down the Tools menu, and look for the Solver option. If it is not on the Tools menu, follow these steps:

1. Select Tools | Add-Ins to see the Add-Ins dialog box.
2. Scroll the Add-Ins Available list in the dialog box until you see the option Solver Add-In.
3. Click the check box next to Solver Add-In and then click OK.

TIP: You may need your Excel or Office CD to install the Solver add-in the first time you use it.

Now that Solver is ready, let's start with the basic worksheet shown in Figure 19-5.

Notice that there are no values in the changing cells because we want Excel to calculate them for us.

1. Choose Tools | Solver to see the Solver Parameters dialog box:

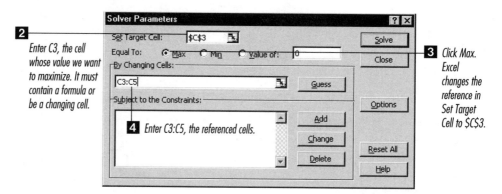

2 Enter C3, the cell whose value we want to maximize. It must contain a formula or be a changing cell.

3 Click Max. Excel changes the reference in Set Target Cell to C3.

4 Enter C3:C5, the referenced cells.

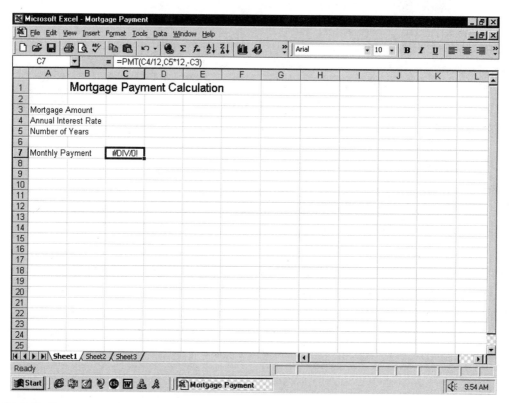

FIGURE 19-5 Worksheet for using Solver

You are now ready to enter the first constraint, that the rate in cell C4 must be 8 percent or less.

5. Click Add in the Solver Parameters dialog box to display the Add Constraint dialog box shown in the following illustration:

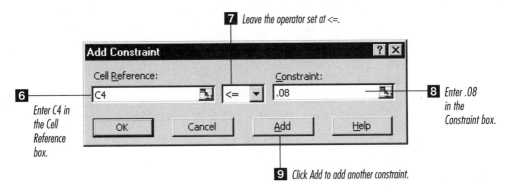

7 *Leave the operator set at <=.*

6 *Enter C4 in the Cell Reference box.*

8 *Enter .08 in the Constraint box.*

9 *Click Add to add another constraint.*

The second constraint is that the rate must be 6 percent or greater. Enter **C4** in the Cell Reference box, choose >= as the operator, and enter .06 in the Constraint box. With these two constraints, Excel will only test rates between 6 and 8 percent. Click Add.

Now finish entering the remainder of the constraints, clicking on OK after you enter the last constraint:

CONSTRAINT	CELL	OPERATOR	CONSTANT
Number of years less than or equal to 30	C5	<=	30
Number of years greater than or equal to 20	C5	>=	20
Mortgage payments no more than $1,000	C7	<=	1000

When you have finished entering the last constraint, click OK. The constraints will appear in your Solver Parameters dialog box, as shown in Figure 19-6. If the constraints that you entered do not correctly appear or contain a mistake, select the constraint that is incorrect and click Change. Use Delete if you want to remove a constraint. Now click Solve. Excel will calculate

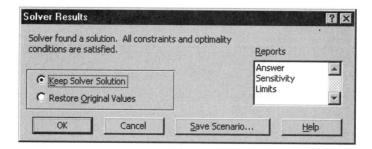

FIGURE 19-6   Constraints in Solver parameters

the maximum value for cell C7, using the constraints specified and will display the results as shown here.

If you do not want to change the worksheet to these values, select Restore Original Values. Click OK.

Validating Input

Once you design the layout and organization of your worksheet, you enter information into it. But even if all your formulas and math operations are correct, you may still type in the wrong information. For example, suppose you create a worksheet to use as an invoice. When you're ready to enter the sales tax percentage, however, you enter 17% instead of 7%. You'll have one angry customer on your hands. Excel gives you three ways to help you enter correct information. You can set validation rules, limit an entry to those in a list, and display custom input and error messages.

Creating Validation Rules

A *validation rule* specifies the range of information that you can enter into a cell. You can create a rule limiting the entry to a certain range of numbers, or even to make sure a cell isn't left blank.

1. Select the cell to which you want to apply a validation rule.
2. Choose Data | Validation and then click the Settings tab to display the Data Validation dialog box shown in Figure 19-7.
3. Choose an option in the Allow drop-down list to determine the type of entry that can be made into the cell. In this option window, you can select from the following validation options: Any Value, Whole Number, Decimal, List, Date, Time, Text Length, and Custom. Table 19-1 shows the other settings you can choose.

The setting Any Value means that you can enter anything in the cell. The other options in the dialog box depend on your selection from the Allow list.

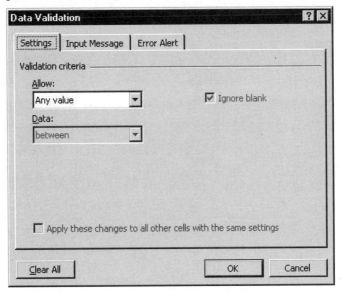

FIGURE 19-7 Validation settings

Each time you change a value, you can see the results throughout the worksheet. But once you change them again, the previous results are gone. What if you want to see the results of values that you entered before that, or even on another day?

A scenario is a set of values that you've used to generate results—a snapshot of the worksheet with one set of values. By saving a scenario, you can return to it when you want to see its effects. By saving a number of scenarios, you can quickly compare results to help make informed decisions.

For example, suppose you create a presentation for an important client. The worksheet contains a series of cost projections based on varying expenses. You can use scenarios to switch between the sets of data, so the client gets a feel for the pros and cons of each plan.

Create the worksheet using one series of values, and then choose Tools | Scenarios. Excel displays the Scenario Manager dialog box. Click Add to create the first scenario.

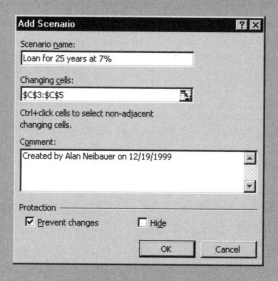

1. Type a name for the scenario, for example, "Loan for 25 years at 7%."
2. Enter the range of cells that change. Do not include a cell that contains a formula.
3. Click OK.

Optionally, lock or hide the scenario, and then turn on sheet protection by checking the Prevent Changes check box.

You'll see the Scenario Values dialog box showing the values in the cells. If any of the changing cells are empty, you can enter the value that you want to store with this first scenario, or you can change any of the values shown.

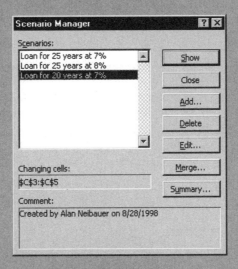

When the values for the scenario are correct, click Add to create another scenario.

When you click Add, the Add Scenario dialog box appears again. Enter the name for another scenario, and click OK to open the Scenario Values box. Now enter the values that you want to be represented by the scenario.

You can continue adding scenarios by repeating these steps. When you have entered the final scenario, click OK in the Scenario Values dialog box instead of Add. Excel now displays the Scenarios Manager dialog box listing each of your scenarios.

To see the effects of any scenario, click it in the list and then click Show. Click Add in Scenario Manager to add new scenarios, Edit to change an existing one, or Delete to remove a scenario. Your scenarios are saved along with the worksheet.

TIP: Click Summary to display a capsule of each scenario's changing cells and results.

As an example, if you were to choose Decimal to specify a range of decimal values, the dialog box options would appear as shown in the following illustration, including a box for both the minimum and maximum decimal values you would choose.

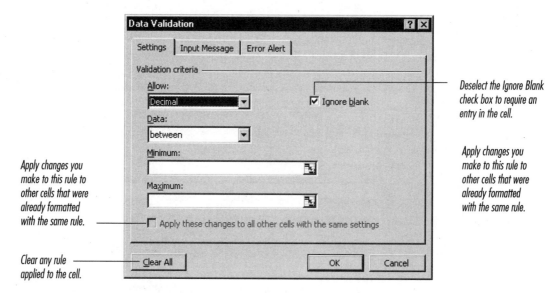

Deselect the Ignore Blank check box to require an entry in the cell.

Apply changes you make to this rule to other cells that were already formatted with the same rule.

Apply changes you make to this rule to other cells that were already formatted with the same rule.

Clear any rule applied to the cell.

1. Pull down the Data list and chose an operator. To specify a range of acceptable values, choose Between from the list. You can also choose options such as Not Between, Equal To, Not Equal To, Greater Than, Less Than, Greater Than Or Equal To, and Less Than Or Equal To. The remaining settings in the dialog box depend on your choice in the Allow box.

2. In the Minimum box, enter the smallest acceptable value.

3. In the Maximum box, enter the largest allowed value.

4. Click OK.

If you enter a value outside of the allowed range, or one that doesn't meet another rule that you establish, Excel displays a message that you've entered invalid information:

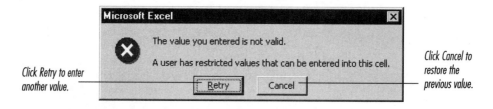

Click Retry to enter another value.

Click Cancel to restore the previous value.

Limiting Values to a List

From the Data Validation dialog box, you can choose the List option from the Allow drop-down list of options. You can then specify a range of cells containing entries that Excel would consider valid. You can also choose to limit the entry to an *in-cell drop-down*—a drop-down list that shows the possible entries. From the Data Validation dialog box, choose the List option from the Allow drop-down list box. Excel then displays the Source box. In the Source box, enter the range of cells containing valid entries. Make sure the option labeled "In-cell Dropdown" is selected. For example, in the worksheet shown in Figure 19-8, the Source box was set at B12:B22. When the user clicks on the cell containing the validation, a list appears with the possible choices from the range. The user can then either select an option from the list or type one of the choices in the box.

Customizing Error Messages

The generic error message that appears when you enter an invalid entry just tells you that you made a mistake. If you had no idea what the validation rule was, however, you'd have no clue about how to correct your error. By creating custom messages, you can warn users what type of values they have to enter, and then tell them what they did wrong if they do make an error.

It always pays to prevent errors if you can, so you should create an input message that appears onscreen when users select the cell, as shown in Figure 19-9:

SETTING	LIMITS ENTRIES TO
Whole number	Whole numbers
Decimal	Decimal numbers
List	Values in a list that you specify
Date	Valid dates
Time	Valid times
Text length	A number of characters that you specify
Custom	Those meeting a formula or calculation

TABLE 19-1   Validation Options

Cell containing a data validation rule

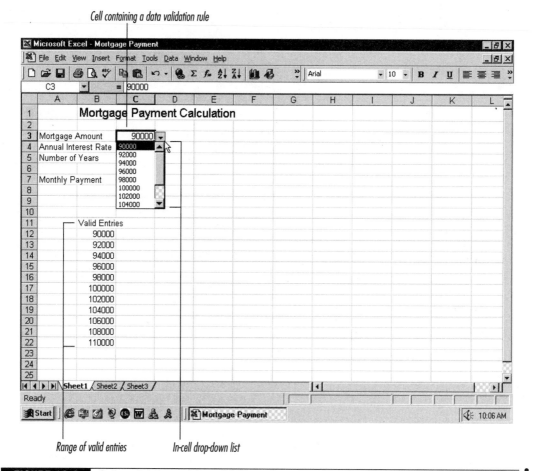

Range of valid entries

In-cell drop-down list

FIGURE 19-8 Cell containing a data validation rule

Enter this message on the Input Message tab of the Data Validation dialog box, shown in Figure 19-10.

Use the Error Alert tab of the dialog box to create a message telling users what they did wrong when they make a mistake. The options are the same as for the Input Message, but in addition to the title and message text, you can designate one of these styles from the Styles drop-down list of options:

- *Stop* will not allow users to continue until they make a valid entry.
- *Warning* reports that users made a mistake, but lets them choose to leave the incorrect value in the cell.

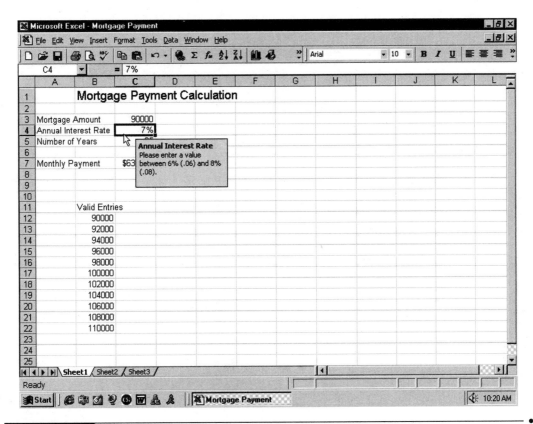

FIGURE 19-9 Input message to help the user enter information

 • *Information* reports that users made a mistake, but accepts the entries as they are.

Recording and Playing Macros

*Macro*s serve the same function in Excel as they do in Word and in any computer application. A *macro* lets you save a series of keystrokes and commands, and then replay the entire series at any time. Recording a macro in Excel, however, is a little different than in Word because of the nature of the program.

When you create a macro, you give it a name and select the location where it is stored. You can also assign it a shortcut key combination.

Leave this check box turned on to have Excel display the input message when the cell is selected.

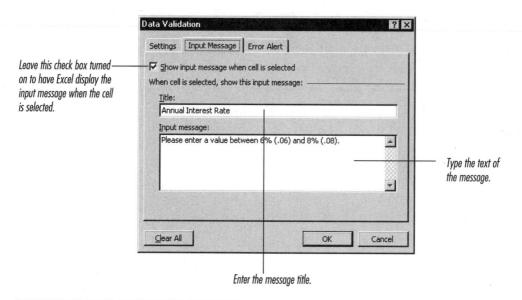

Type the text of the message.

Enter the message title.

FIGURE 19-10 Input Message tab

- Macro names can include letters, numbers, and the underline character, but must start with a letter. Excel will suggest the names Macro1, Macro2, and so on.
- The shortcut key combination is CTRL and a letter—either uppercase or lowercase. Hold down SHIFT when designating a letter to make it uppercase.
- You can store your macros in the workbook, another workbook, or something called the Personal Macro Workbook. Unless you save it in the Personal Macro Workbook, you can only run the macro when you open the workbook in which it is saved.

Recording a Macro

When you are ready to record a macro, choose Tools | Macro, and click Record New Macro.

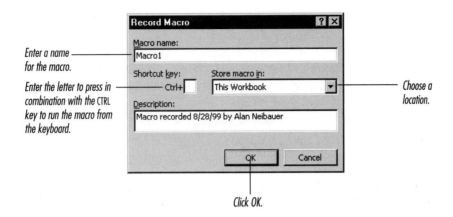

Enter a name for the macro.

Enter the letter to press in combination with the CTRL key to run the macro from the keyboard.

Choose a location.

Click OK.

N O T E : The letter you use with the CTRL key is case sensitive.

Excel displays the Macro toolbar:

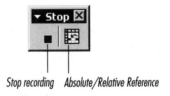

Stop recording   Absolute/Relative Reference

Now select the cells, enter and format information, and perform other Excel tasks that you want to repeat when you run the macro. When you're done, click Stop Recording in the Macro toolbar.

Relative and Absolute Addresses

By default, each time you start Excel, macros are set to be recorded by use of absolute references. *"Absolute reference"* means that if you click cell A1 when recording the macro, the macro will always select cell A1 when you run it. There's nothing wrong with that if that's what you want. But what if you want to record a macro that will insert a series of labels at a different location each time you run the macro?

To accomplish that, you must change to relative references. "Relative reference" means that the cell used when the macro runs is relative to the current active cell. You use the Absolute/Relative Reference button on the Macro toolbar to toggle between absolute and relative references. When the button appears pressed down, you are using relative references. Now each cell selection command you record will select a cell relative to whatever is the active cell at that time. So suppose you start recording when you're in cell A1, and your first action is to click in cell B2. When you run the macro, it will start by selecting the cell one column over and one row down from the current active cell.

Running a Macro

Running a macro couldn't be simpler. If you assigned a shortcut key combination to it, hold down CTRL and press the letter. If you assigned an uppercase letter, hold down CTRL and SHIFT and then press the letter.

You can also run a macro by selecting Tools | Macro | Macros to see the Macro dialog box. Double-click the macro you want to run, or select it and click Run.

Deleting Macros

To delete a macro, choose Tools | Macro | Macros to see the Macro dialog box. Choose the macro you want to delete, and then click the Delete button. Macros in the Personal Macro Workbook will start with the word "Personal."

Selecting a Macro Location

By default, Excel records your macro in the workbook itself. This means that you'll only be able to run the macro when the workbook is open. If you want to use the macro with every workbook, then you must record it in the Personal Macro Workbook. This is a special workbook automatically opened, but not displayed on the screen, when you start Excel.

When you record the macro, pull down the Store Macro In list and choose Personal Macro Workbook. That's all there is to it.

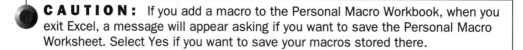

C A U T I O N : If you add a macro to the Personal Macro Workbook, when you exit Excel, a message will appear asking if you want to save the Personal Macro Worksheet. Select Yes if you want to save your macros stored there.

- You can customize the way Solver works by clicking on Options in the Solver Parameters dialog box. Most of the options, however, perform rather sophisticated operations, and they require an equally sophisticated understanding of data analysis.
- From Scenario Manager you can also delete scenarios and you can merge—copy them—from other worksheets.
- Using Excel's Analysis ToolPak, you can perform a wide variety of statistical tests. To make the ToolPak available, choose Tools | Add-Ins, turn on the Analysis ToolPak check box, and then click OK. Then to access the ToolPak, choose Tools | Data Analysis. Choose the test you want to perform and then click OK. Finally, a dialog box appears where you enter cells and values, and select options to perform the test.
- One great way to run a macro is by clicking on a graphic object. Draw a button or other shape on your worksheet, right-click it, and select Assign Macro from the shortcut menu. In the dialog box that appears, you can select to assign the graphic object an existing macro, or create and assign a new macro to it.
- The target cell in Solver must either contain a formula or be a changing cell.
- Always save a copy of your worksheet before using Goal Seek or Solver, since these can change the values in your cells.
- Each time you create a macro during the same Excel session, the Absolute/Relative Reference button will be set as you left it for the last macro. Check the setting to ensure it is how you want it.
- When Solver finds a solution, click Save Scenario in the Solve Results box to save it as a scenario. Use Scenario Manager to later show the results.
- In the Solver Results box, choose one or more options from the Reports list to create a worksheet with details of how Solver calculated the results.
- Validating entries helps ensure proper data. If you set limits to a cell entry, however, take the time to create custom input and error messages that make it clear what entries are valid.

Presenting with PowerPoint

Creating Presentations

20

PowerPoint is a remarkable program that lets you create anything from a simple cover page for a report to a complete multimedia slide presentation. You don't need a background in art or design, and you don't have to spend hours in front of your computer screen to create special effects.

Getting to Know PowerPoint

Let's review some basic concepts that will help you along the way. PowerPoint lets you create one or more slides. They are called *slides* even if you do not plan to convert them to photographic slides or show them on the screen.

PowerPoint comes with general slide layouts that offer combinations of titles and subtitles, text boxes, bulleted lists, boxes for clipart, and organization charts. The elements in the layouts are called *placeholders* because they represent the location of standard slide elements, such as titles, subtitles, graphics, and charts.

With PowerPoint you can work on your slides in five views. All the views, except Slide Show, divide the screen into two or more resizable panes.

- **Normal** Displays a large pane showing a single slide along with smaller panes displaying the outline of the entire presentation and any notes that you've associated with the slide.
- **Outline** Displays a large pane showing the organization of a presentation as a text outline, using titles, subtitles, and bullet lists as the outline levels. Smaller panes show the selected slide and the notes associated with the slide.
- **Slide** Displays a large pane with a single slide and a smaller pane with the outline. Notes are not displayed.
- **Slide Sorter** Displays thumbnail images of the slides for changing their order.
- **Slide Show** Displays the slides just as if you were showing them, including any animations and special effects.

 N O T E : In Normal, Outline, and Slide views you can add and edit slides. In Slide Sorter you can add or delete slides, but not change their contents.

There are three basic ways to create a presentation:

- The *AutoContent Wizard* lets you choose the general theme of your presentation. It then creates a complete slide show for you, including a background design and suggestions for the type of information to insert. Just fill in the information that you want to get across.
- *Design Templates* let you design your own presentation using either a basic background, or by selecting a presentation theme. If you select just a background design, you then create the individual slides. If you select a theme, it opens a sample slide show much like the one created by AutoContent Wizard.

- A *Blank Presentation* lets you design your presentation from scratch, although you can quickly add a background template.

PowerPoint offers many of the same features as Word and Excel. So, if you are familiar with one application, you'll feel at home here. In addition to the obvious common buttons in the toolbars, here are some of the similar features:

- Select Insert | Date And Time to insert the date as text or a code, or to select or create a date format.
- When you are editing a placeholder that contains text, choose to use the Spell check and AutoCorrect features from the Tools menu.
- Create hyperlinks and use the Web toolbar.
- Use the File menu to access file management options.
- Play and record macros by use of the Tools menu.
- Edit and format text.
- Use Tools | Customize to customize the toolbars and menus; use Tools | Options to adjust PowerPoint settings.

Starting a Presentation

Let's get right to it. To start a presentation, click Start in the taskbar, point to Programs, and click Microsoft PowerPoint to see the dialog box shown in Figure 20-1. In addition to the three basic options, you can choose to open one of your existing presentations.

Click Blank Presentation and then on OK to display the New Slide dialog box shown here:

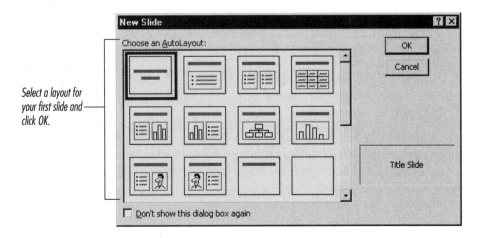

Select a layout for your first slide and click OK.

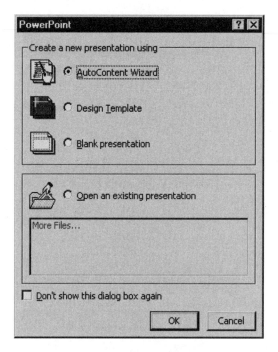

FIGURE 20-1 Choices when starting PowerPoint

You use this same box whether you are starting from scratch or adding slides at any time. You usually start with a title slide, the choice on the top left, but you can pick any type that you want. Click the layout of your choice and then click OK.

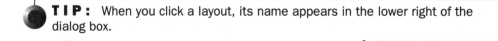

TIP: When you click a layout, its name appears in the lower right of the dialog box.

Figure 20-2 shows the title slide with its placeholders for a title and subtitle. Look at the PowerPoint window. Below the menu bar are the Standard and Formatting toolbars, shown moved to separate lines in the figure. In addition to the usual buttons you find in these toolbars in Office applications, the toolbars contain the buttons shown here:

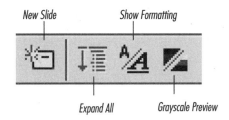

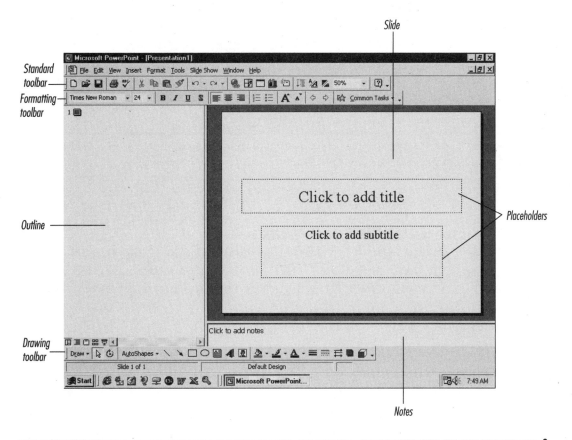

NOTE: The Formatting toolbar contains different buttons in Slide Sorter view.

FIGURE 20-2 PowerPoint window

The formatting toolbar contains these items:

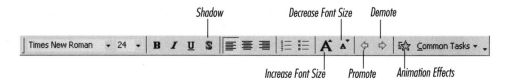

The Common Tasks list in the Formatting toolbar offers three choices: New Slide, Slide Layout, and Apply Design Template.

At the bottom of the screen is the same Drawing toolbar that you've seen in Word and Excel. It works exactly the same in PowerPoint. Above that are buttons to change the view:

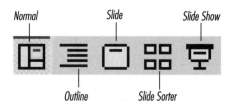

 N O T E : The status bar displays the current slide number, the total number of slides in the presentation, and the template or design being used.

Setting the Page Layout

One of the first choices you should make when creating a presentation is the overall size that is best suited for the type of presentation intended, such as using 35mm slides, an onscreen presentation, or printing on paper or overhead transparencies.

Choose File | Page Setup to display this dialog box:

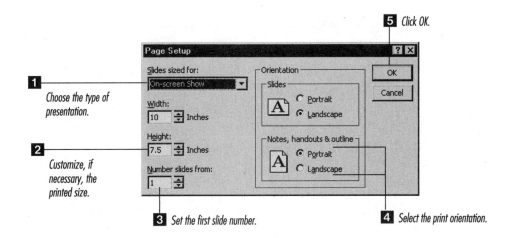

5 Click OK.

1 Choose the type of presentation.

2 Customize, if necessary, the printed size.

3 Set the first slide number.

4 Select the print orientation.

Selecting a Background Layout

Your next choice should be to select a slide background to set the overall look of the presentation. Choose Apply Design Template in the Common Tasks list or from the Format menu to see the dialog box in Figure 20-3.

You can change the background at any time using the same steps. Your choice will apply to all the slides in your presentation.

If you choose not to use a background design, you can add a background color, pattern, texture, or picture yourself. Choose Format | Background:

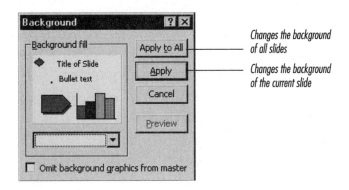

Changes the background of all slides

Changes the background of the current slide

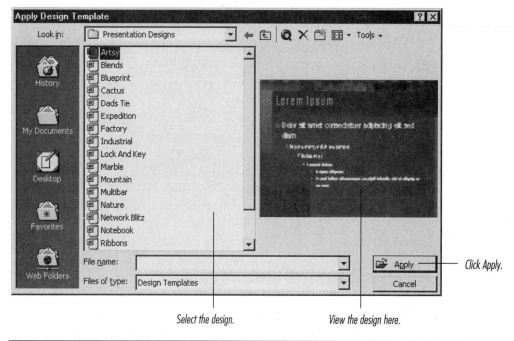

Select the design.   View the design here.

FIGURE 20-3   Choose a basic design for the presentation

Pull down the list in the Background Fill section and choose a solid color from those shown, choose More Colors to pick a custom color, or choose Fill Effects to add a gradient, texture, pattern, or a graphic from your disk to the background.

Working with Slides

You create slides by substituting text, graphics, and other elements for the built-in placeholders, or by adding your own elements.

A placeholder is similar to a graphic box in Word. Click the placeholder to display handles around it, and then drag the box by its border to change its position, or drag a handle to change its size. While a placeholder will not appear with the slide if you do not use it, you can delete unused placeholders to make it easier to select other objects that you add, without accidentally selecting the empty placeholder. To delete the placeholder, click its border and press DEL.

When you create a slide show, PowerPoint assigns the default layout of a master slide, which determines the font, alignment, bullet styles, and header and footer areas. Any graphic or text box on the master slide, for example, will automatically appear on all your slides. So, to add your company logo to all slides, for example, just add it to the Slide Master.

To add a logo or line of text to every slide in the show, you have to add it to the master slide. Choose View | Master | Slide Master. A Slide Master with a graphic added would appear as shown here:

It contains placeholders for all the slide elements. To add a graphic to every slide, insert it by use of the Insert | Picture command.

The text in the placeholders indicates the format applied to the text that you enter. To change the default format, just apply new formats to the sample text. Change to any other view to save your changes to the master.

Text Placeholders

Title and subtitle placeholders are designed for text. To change the text in these placeholders, just click it to display the insertion point. You can then enter, edit, and format text as you would any document. Use the Formatting toolbar, for example, to format the text, changing its font, size, style, alignment, and color. When you're done, click elsewhere in the slide.

NOTE: Use Format | Replace Fonts to automatically replace one font with another.

Creating Bullet Lists

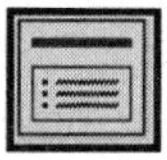

You can also create a slide using the bullet list placeholder. In the New Slide dialog box, these placeholders are indicated as shown here, and they come combined with title, subtitle, chart, graphic, and media clip placeholders. The placeholder itself appears, as shown here, in a slide, with some text already entered:

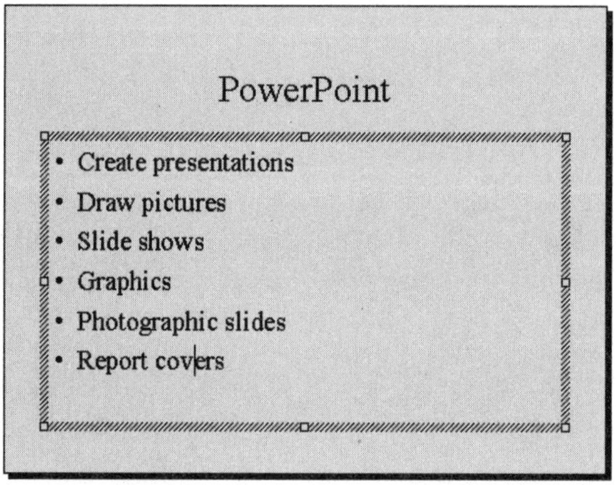

Here's how to use the placeholder:

1. Click in the placeholder to display the first bullet followed by the insertion point.

2. Type the text for the bullet.

3. Press ENTER to insert the next bullet in the series.

4. Continue entering items in the same way.

Bullet lists are similar to outlines. Press the TAB key or click the Demote button in the Formatting toolbar to indent the line and insert a second-level bullet; press SHIFT-TAB or click Promote in the Formatting toolbar to move back to a higher level.

If you need to edit a bullet list, just click it. To add a new bullet item at the end of the list, place the insertion point at the end of the last line and press ENTER. Use TAB or SHIFT-TAB to change the position of the item.

T I P : To insert an item within the list, place the insertion point at the start of a line, following the bullet, and press ENTER. Use this technique, for example, to insert a new item at the top of the list.

You can also create a bullet list manually, when it is not a placeholder on the slide, using these steps:

1. Select Insert | Text Box, and then click or drag to create a rectangle on the slide.

2. Click the Bullets button on the Formatting toolbar to display the first bullet, and then enter your items.

If you enter more information than can fit on one bullet list slide, PowerPoint will first resize the placeholder to accommodate the text. If you have more than six paragraphs, or continue entering information, a light bulb icon appears on the Office Assistant. Click the icon for the options to divide the slide into two slides, or create a slide for each paragraph.

Adding Graphics to Slides

Standard layouts in the New Slide dialog box let you insert a graphic from the ClipArt Gallery. When you select a slide layout with a clipart icon, the placeholder appears like this:

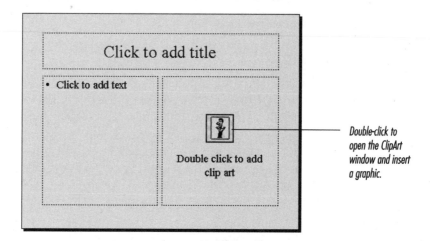

Double-click to
open the ClipArt
window and insert
a graphic.

You can also use the drawing tools to add other elements, and you can add graphics from your disk to any slide. Inserting graphics into a slide is similar to adding a graphic to a Word document or Excel worksheet.

- Use the Drawing toolbar to create and customize graphics and AutoShapes.
- Use Insert | Text Box to add a text box to a slide.
- Use Insert | Picture to add clipart, graphic files, WordArt, AutoShapes, organization charts, and scanned graphics.

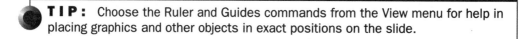

TIP: Choose the Ruler and Guides commands from the View menu for help in placing graphics and other objects in exact positions on the slide.

The graphic appears surrounded by handles, along with the Picture toolbar. The toolbar has the same buttons as the Picture toolbar you learned about in Chapter 10, but with one exception. The Recolor button replaces the Wrap Text button (used to wrap text around the graphic in Word). Use this to replace the existing colors in a graphic with colors of your choice, as shown in Figure 20-4.

Select the color you wish to replace.   Choose a replacement color.

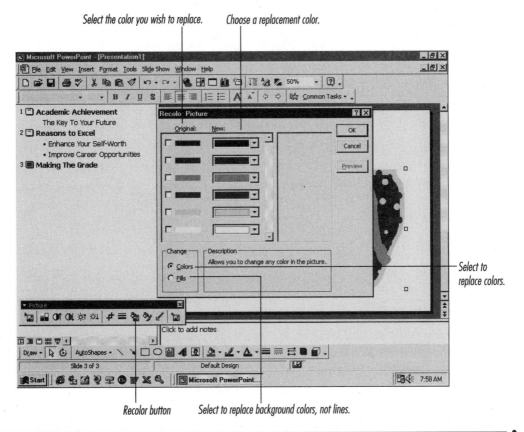

FIGURE 20-4   Use Recolor to change the colors in a graphic

For example, suppose you want to change each object that appears in red so it appears in a darker shade of red. Here's how to do it:

1. In the Original list, select the check box next to the bar shown in red.
2. In the New list, pull down the list next to the red bar.
3. Since dark red is not shown in the new sample colors, select More Colors from the list to see the following dialog box:

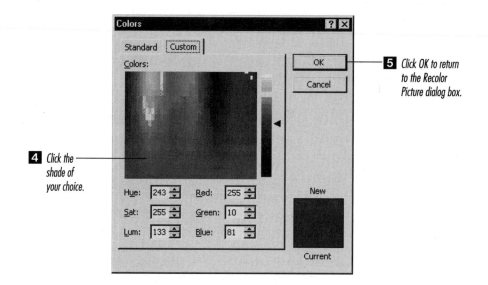

4 Click the shade of your choice.

5 Click OK to return to the Recolor Picture dialog box.

Adding Sounds and Movies

You can use similar techniques to add sounds and movies to a slide. Several slide layouts include a placeholder for a media clip, shown here. Double-click the placeholder to display the Clip Gallery with tabs for Sounds and Motion Clips. Select and insert a clip just as you would a graphic.

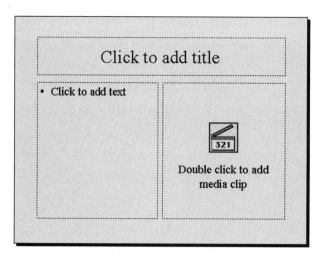

To add a media clip to any slide, choose Insert | Movies And Sounds. You can then choose to insert a movie or sound from the gallery or from a file on your disk, or to play an audio CD track or record your own sound:

A speaker icon represents sounds, while the first frame of a video indicates a video clip. When you're showing the slide show, you click the object to play it.

 N O T E : You'll learn other ways to control sounds and movies in Chapter 21.

Adding a Slide

To add another slide to the presentation, choose New Slide on the Common Tasks list or from the Insert menu to open the New Slide dialog box. Select the layout you want for the slide and then click OK. PowerPoint inserts new slides after the current slide. So, if you are working on the last slide of the presentation, the new slide will be inserted at the end. To insert a slide elsewhere, display the slide that you want to precede the new slide, and then add the slide. You can add a slide in any of PowerPoint's views. You can also change the order of slides in Outline and Slide Sorter views.

Use the scroll bar at the right of the screen to move from slide to slide in a presentation. The buttons below the scroll bar move to the first and last slide. To delete a slide, display or select it and choose Edit | Delete Slide.

Working with Tables

 Another way to add text to a slide is through a table. To add a slide with a table, choose a layout with a table in the New Slide dialog box.

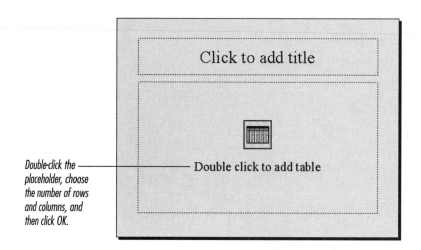

Double-click the placeholder, choose the number of rows and columns, and then click OK.

When you click OK to accept the number of rows and columns, you'll see the Tables And Borders toolbar along with the blank table, as shown in Figure 20-5. Create the table just as you learned in Word, and then click outside the table to insert it into the slide.

You can also add a table to any slide by using the Insert Table button in the Standard toolbar just like the Insert Table button in Word:

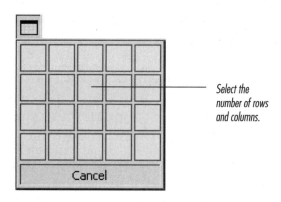

Select the number of rows and columns.

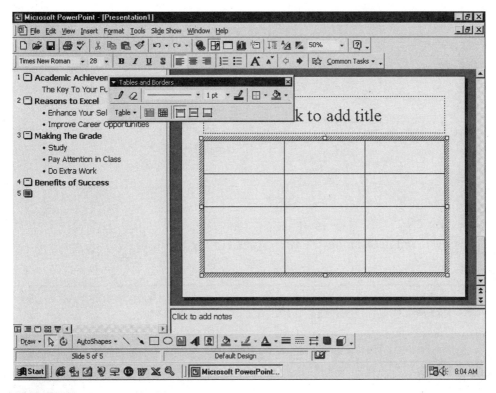

FIGURE 20-5 Creating a Word table in PowerPoint

Creating an Organization Chart

An *organization chart* shows the chain of command within an organization. The Organization Chart layout in the New Slide dialog box includes two placeholders:

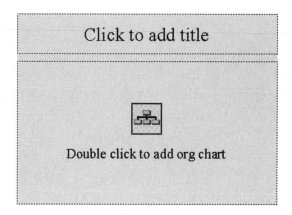

To create the chart, double-click its placeholder to begin the Microsoft Organization Chart application, shown in Figure 20-6.

TIP: You can add an organization chart placeholder to any slide. Select Insert | Picture | Organization Chart.

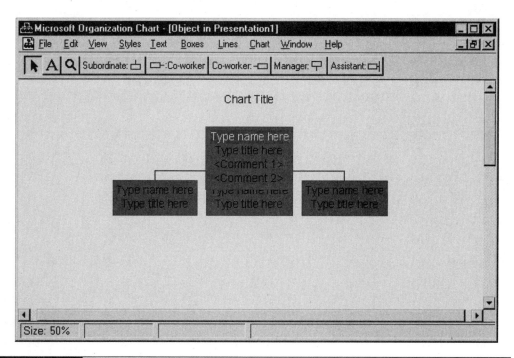

FIGURE 20-6 Creating an organization chart

To add text, such as names and titles, to the boxes of the chart, click the box and then edit the default text. When you click the box, it will expand to include two comment lines. Use the options in the Text menu to change the font, color, and alignment of your text.

The default organization chart includes a basic set of positions. You can add other positions as required by your organization's structure. Here are the positions that you can insert:

- An *assistant* position comes directly off another position, like the assistant position in the following example. The position is not on the chain of command.
- A *subordinate* is under another position in the chain of command.
- A *manager* is above another position.
- A *coworker* is a position of equal authority, neither above nor below the next box in the chain of command. You can insert coworkers with the connecting line to the left or right.

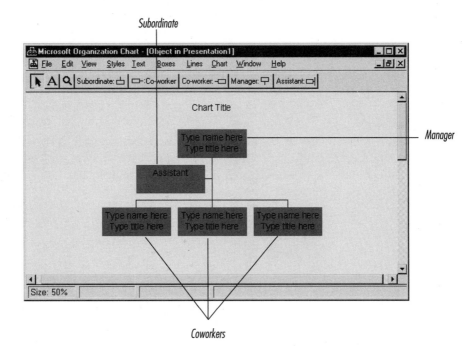

To add a position, use these steps:

1. Click the button for the position you want to add.

2. Click the existing position you want to add it to.

3. Click the new position to enter the name and title.

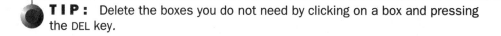

TIP: Delete the boxes you do not need by clicking on a box and pressing the DEL key.

You can also change the *style* of the chart—how positions are displayed in relation to each other. Select the boxes for the positions you want to format, using the SHIFT key to select multiple positions. Then pull down the Styles menu and choose from these options:

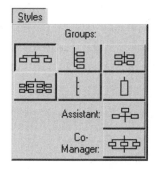

The Organization Chart program adds the lines connecting positions for you. While you can change the design of the chart by using the Styles menu, you may want to add additional lines yourself, perhaps showing informal connections or special positions. To draw lines on the chart, choose View | Show Draw Tools to see these tools:

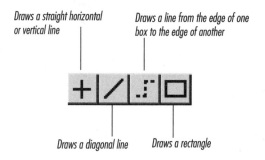

Draws a straight horizontal or vertical line

Draws a line from the edge of one box to the edge of another

Draws a diagonal line

Draws a rectangle

Click the tool for the type of object you want; then drag to create it. The line tools create lines that are lighter in color than those inserted by default. This is designed to show a less formal connection between positions.

To change the color, thickness, or style of any line, right-click it and choose options from the shortcut menu that appears. Use the Boxes menu to add color and shadows to boxes, and to change their border style.

When you're done designing the chart, select File | Exit And Return, and then click Yes to the message that appears. The organization chart appears on the slide surrounded by handles, so you can change its size and position as needed. To edit the chart, double-click it to start the Organization Chart program again.

Creating Charts and Graphs

 A number of standard layouts in the New Slide dialog box contain placeholders for charts. Double-click the placeholder to begin the chart application, which is much like adding a chart to a Word document, as explained in Chapter 10. In fact, you use almost the same techniques for working with charts—changing their type, customizing chart elements, adding legends, and so on.

TIP: To add a chart to any slide, choose Insert | Chart.

You'll see a chart with sample information, as shown in Figure 20-7.

1. Enter your own information into the chart.
2. Select options from the menu bar or toolbar.
3. Click outside the chart area.

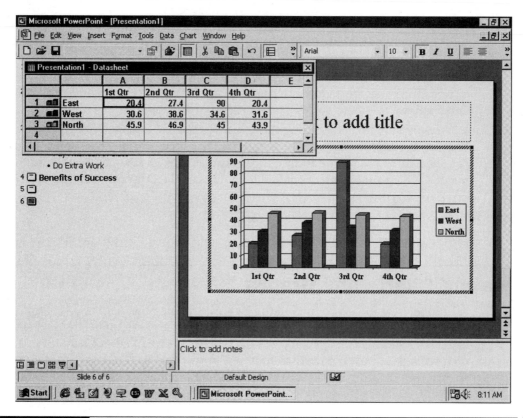

FIGURE 20-7 Creating a chart

Playing a Slide Show

To display a slide show of your work, with each slide displayed full screen, select the slide that you want to start with, and then click the Slide Show button above the status bar, or choose View | Slide Show. The first slide in your presentation will appear. To move from slide to slide, use these techniques:

- Click the left mouse button or press the SPACEBAR, RIGHT ARROW, or UP ARROW to display the next slide.
- Click the LEFT ARROW or DOWN ARROW key to display the previous slide.
- Press ESC to stop the slide show.

If you right-click a slide, you can also select options from this Shortcut menu:

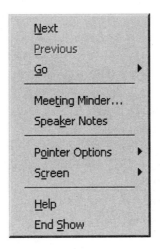

You'll learn all about playing slide shows in Chapter 21.

Saving a Slide Show

Before doing too much work on your slides, you should save them to your disk. PowerPoint uses the same file management dialog boxes as other Office applications. To save your slides, use these steps:

1. Click the Save button in the toolbar, or select File | Save.
2. In the Name box, type a name for your presentation.
3. Click OK. PowerPoint saves your work with the default extension PPT.

Starting a New Slide Show

When you are ready to start a new slide show after PowerPoint is started, you have several options. The quickest method is to click the New button on the Standard toolbar. This starts a new presentation and displays the New Slide dialog box.

To start a new presentation using AutoContent Wizard or a template, however, select File | New to see the dialog box shown in Figure 20-8.

Click this tab to choose graphic designs for a blank presentation.

Click this tab to choose a complete presentation without running AutoContent Wizard.

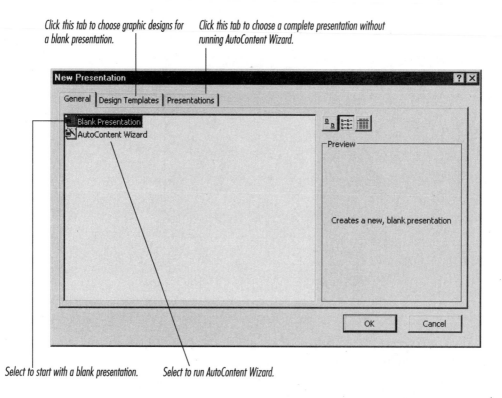

Select to start with a blank presentation.

Select to run AutoContent Wizard.

FIGURE 20-8   Starting a new presentation

Using the Slide Sorter

So far, we've been working with slides in Normal view, which lets you create and edit individual slides. For a general overview of your slides, change to Slide Sorter view by clicking on the Slide Sorter button or choosing View | Slide Sorter.

The Slide Sorter window, shown in Figure 20-9, displays thumbnail images of your slides. To change the order of a slide, just drag it to a new position. As you drag, a vertical bar will appear indicating the new position. Release the mouse when the position is correct.

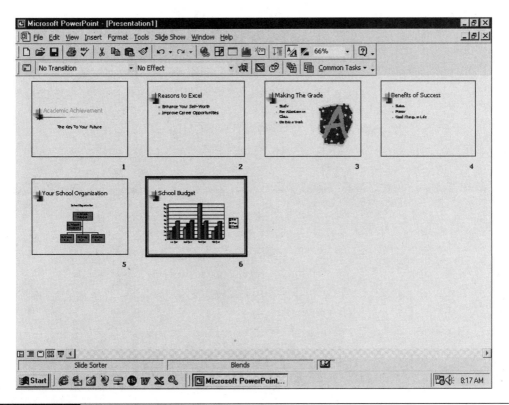

FIGURE 20-9 Slide Sorter view

Using the Slide Outline

While the Slide Sorter is useful for viewing your slides graphically, you cannot read much of the information on the slides. When you want to look at the overall contents of the presentation, use the Outline pane in Normal, Outline, or Slide view. In Normal or Slide view, you may have to widen the Outline pane to display the full contents.

The Outline pane shows the titles, subtitles, and other text from each slide in outline format that makes it easy to see the structure of your presentation without being distracted by graphics and backgrounds. To change the order of slides, for example, drag the slide icon up or down.

You can also use the Outline to add slides to the presentation, even to create an entire presentation of bullet lists, text, and titles by typing an outline. Changes to the outline are immediately reflected in the slide shown in the slide pane.

A typical Outline pane, in Outline view, is shown in Figure 20-10. The Slide icon marks each slide in the chart.

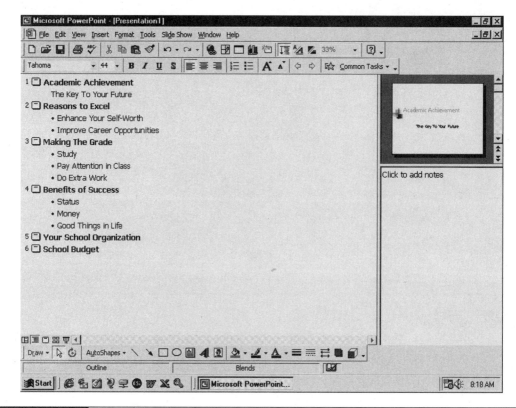

FIGURE 20-10 Slide Outline view

Headers, Footers, and Page Numbers

If you plan to print your presentation for distribution, as opposed to displaying it onscreen, you may want to add headers, footers, page numbers, or the date. You can add these to individual slides or to every slide in the presentation.

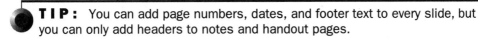

TIP: You can add page numbers, dates, and footer text to every slide, but you can only add headers to notes and handout pages.

To insert the date, page number, or footer to a particular slide, display it onscreen or select it first. Otherwise, it doesn't matter what slide is selected. Then choose View | Header And Footer to display the dialog box shown in Figure 20-11.

- To insert the date, turn on the Date And Time check box, and then choose to update the date automatically or enter a fixed date. The date will appear in the lower left of the slide.
- To number slides, turn on the Slide Number check box. The starting slide number is set in the Page Setup dialog box, and it appears on the lower right of the slide.
- To print a footer in the bottom center of the slide, turn on the Footer check box and enter the footer in the text box.

NOTE: The options on the Notes And Handouts tab are the same, but you can also add a header.

When you're done, click Apply To All to add the items to every slide, or click Apply to add them to just the current slide.

TIP: Turn on Don't Show On Title Slide to suppress the elements on title slides.

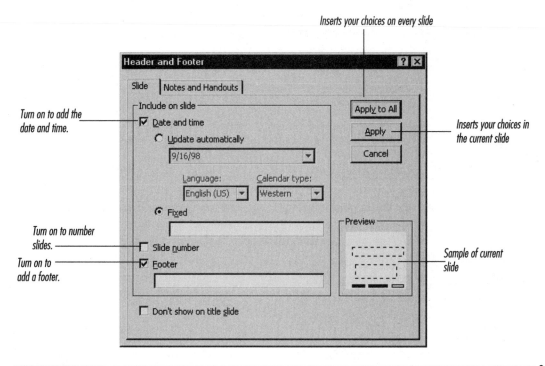

Inserts your choices on every slide

Turn on to add the date and time.

Turn on to number slides.

Turn on to add a footer.

Inserts your choices in the current slide

Sample of current slide

FIGURE 20-11 Adding a header or footer

Printing a Presentation

You need to print copies of your slides if you created them to be included in a report or as handouts. To print the entire presentation, just click the Print button in the Standard toolbar. To choose print options from the dialog box shown in Figure 20-12, choose File | Print.

The dialog box offers a number of options that should be familiar to you from working with other Office applications, such as the number of copies and collating choices, and the Print Range options to choose the number of slides to print. There are some new options that are only in PowerPoint.

Use the Print What list to print just the slides, handout sheets, multiple slides per page, your notes, or the slide outline. The check boxes below the list also determine what gets printed. The Grayscale option will be set by default if you don't have a color printer. Colors on the slides will be converted to shades of gray. Choose Pure Black And White if you want only those colors without any gray shades.

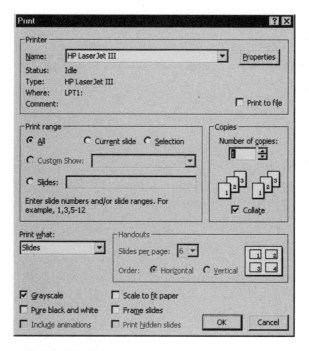

FIGURE 20-12 Printing a presentation

The Scale To Fit Paper option enlarges or reduces each slide to fill the page, and the Frame Slides option adds a border around each slide.

Printing Notes and Handouts

In addition to printing the slides, you can print handouts and speaker notes.

Handouts have several slides on each page. The audience can refer to them during your presentation, and take them home as a reference. To print handouts, select Handouts from the Print What list of the Print dialog box, and then choose options from the Handouts section of the dialog box. The options let you choose the number of slides to print on each page, and the order in which pages are printed—vertically or horizontally across the page.

It would be nice if you could memorize an entire presentation, but it is all too easy to lose track. Thus, you can print speaker notes—a thumbnail image of each slide along with your own script, reminders, or notes. Before printing speaker notes, however, you must create them. You enter notes in the Notes pane in Normal and Outline views, or by choosing View | Notes Page. In

Notes view, you'll see a thumbnail of one slide at a time with a large area for typing notes.

When you are ready to print the notes, choose Notes Pages from the Print What list of the Print dialog box.

- If you create a presentation using AutoContent Wizard but don't like the background, choose a new design using Format | Apply Design Template.
- If you want to restore the original placeholders on a slide, click Slide Layout in the Common Tasks list, click the layout, and then click the Reapply button. However, this procedure will also return anything you've moved or resized to its default settings, so use this option with caution.
- To change the layout of an existing slide, display the slide onscreen, click the Slide Layout button in the Common Tasks list, pick the new layout, and then click Apply.
- There are four master slides that you can modify to customize PowerPoint. In addition to the Slide Master, there is the Title Master, Handout Master, and Notes Master. Access them by choosing View | Master.
- Use Format | Bullets And Numbering to select a new bullet character or to choose a picture to use for the bullet.
- Each presentation starts with certain default values for text and line colors and the like, called the *color scheme*. To change the colors in the scheme, choose Format | Slide Color Scheme.
- To start with a blank slide and then add all your own elements, use the Blank Slide layout in the New Slide dialog box.
- Enlarging or reducing a table in a slide will not change the number of rows or columns, just the size of the text. To change the number of rows or columns, use the menu and toolbar commands as you learned in Word.
- Use Insert | Object to add Excel worksheets, Word documents, and other objects to a slide.
- To display each slide as large as possible, change to Slide view and drag the border between the slide and the outline to the left of the screen.

Creating and Showing Slide Shows

One of the most effective ways to display PowerPoint slides is as a slide show. If you use a large monitor or a video projection system, your slides become an instant multimedia presentation. You can add special effects (such as animation and transitions between slides), sound, and music. You can even add an Internet link to jump to a web page.

By publishing your entire presentation to the Internet, you make it accessible to the world. Web surfers can download your presentation to their own computer with a click of the mouse, and they can use a page frame to select slides from a table of contents.

In this chapter, you will learn how to create a slide show, adding effects and features that create professional presentations.

Slide Transitions

To display a slide show, you click the mouse or press a keyboard key to move from slide to slide. The next slide immediately replaces the previous one, just as if you had changed slides in a slide projector. By adding a *transition,* you create a special effect that takes place as one slide replaces the other. You can even add a sound, such as audience applause, a drum roll, or even the sound of a projector changing slides for that old-fashioned effect.

Here's how to add a transition and sound:

1. To add a transition to a specific slide, display the slide in Normal, Outline, or Slide view, or click the slide in Slide Sorter view. To add the same transition to every slide in the presentation, it doesn't matter which slide is displayed or selected.

2. Choose Slide Show | Slide Transition to see the dialog box in Figure 21-1. Pull down the list in the Effect section, and choose the transition you want. The graphic in the dialog box will animate to show you how it works.

 TIP: Choose No Transition in the Transition list to remove the effect from a slide.

3. For some transitions, you can then select the speed.

4. Pull down the list in the Sound section of the Slide Transition dialog box, and choose the sound you want played. Choose Other Sound from the end of the list to choose one you have on disk.

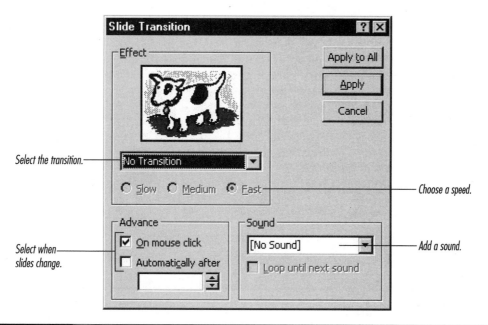

Select the transition.

Choose a speed.

Select when slides change.

Add a sound.

FIGURE 21-1 Adding a transition to a slide

5. Normally the sound plays just as the slide appears. Turn on the Loop Until Next Sound check box to play the sound continuously until another is played.

6. To use a transition for every slide in the show, click the Apply To All button; otherwise click Apply.

If you don't want every slide to have the same transition, it is easier to use the Formatting toolbar in Slide Sorter view. In that view, click the slide to which you want to assign a transition, and then select it from the transition list:

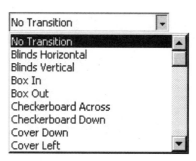

The transition will appear on the selected slide to show you its effect.

In Slide Sorter view, you'll see an icon to the left below the slide indicating that a transition has been applied to it. You'll also see the name of the transition on the Formatting toolbar when you select the slide.

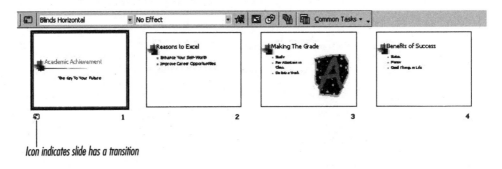

Icon indicates slide has a transition

Advancing Slides

The default slide show setting leaves a slide on the screen until you advance it manually. Rather than manually advancing slides, however, you can set a *time delay*—how long each slide appears in seconds. By using a time delay, you can leave your slide show playing while you do other things—walk about the room helping audience members, or just relax, off your feet.

There are two ways to set the timing. You can manually enter the number of seconds a slide should appear, or you can set it interactively while you rehearse the presentation.

Setting Timing

You determine the pace of your slides in the Advance section of the Slide Transition dialog box. Just follow these steps:

1. Display or select the slide that you want to time.
2. Choose Slide Show | Slide Transition to see this dialog box, which also shows steps 3 through 5.

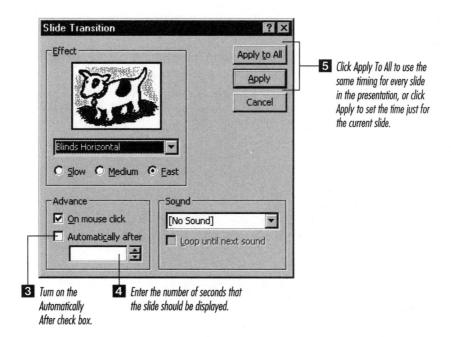

5 Click Apply To All to use the same timing for every slide in the presentation, or click Apply to set the time just for the current slide.

3 Turn on the Automatically After check box.

4 Enter the number of seconds that the slide should be displayed.

TIP: Also leave on the On Mouse Click box so you can advance a slide before its time is up, if desired.

If you find the amount of time isn't just right for a slide, display or select it again in any view, open the Slide Transition dialog box, and change the timing.

In Slide Sorter view, you'll see the number of seconds on the left below the slide indicating its timing.

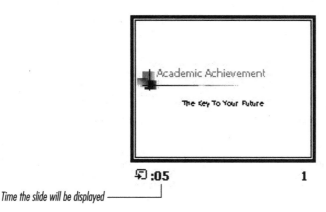

Time the slide will be displayed

Rehearsing Timings

Perhaps the best way to time your slides, however, is by basing the timing on your script. This ensures that the slide remains onscreen long enough for you to finish speaking. When your presentation is done and your notes are ready, select Slide Show | Rehearse Timings. The first slide appears onscreen with the Rehearsal box, shown here:

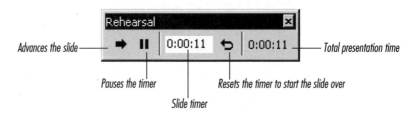

Advances the slide — **Rehearsal** [x] → ‖ | 0:00:11 | ↰ | 0:00:11 — Total presentation time

Pauses the timer — Resets the timer to start the slide over

Slide timer

Now rehearse your presentation just as you want to do it—reading your narration or giving the audience time to digest what the slide contains. Click the Advance Slide button to record the time for the slide and display the next. If you need to pause the timer while you review your notes, click the Pause button. Click Pause again to restart the timing.

When you're done, a dialog box appears reporting the total length of the presentation, asking if you want to record the timings. Click Yes. A box appears asking if you want to review the timing in Slide Sorter view, where you'll see the advance timing below each slide.

Finally, run the slide show, practicing your presentation again. If you need to change the timing of a slide, make a note of it, and then change the timing by using the Slide Transition dialog box.

NOTE: Switching to another application while rehearsing also pauses the timer.

Recording Your Narration

If you plan on showing your slide presentation several times, or creating a self-running automated presentation, then you may want to record your narration as part of the slide show. Your narration plays as each slide is displayed, so you don't have to read it yourself. You can record your narration while you rehearse the timings.

Select Record Narration from the Slide Show menu to see this dialog box:

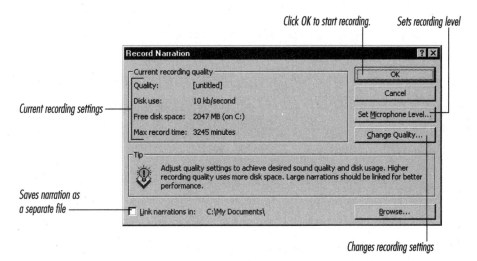

Click OK to start recording.

Sets recording level

Current recording settings

Saves narration as a separate file

Changes recording settings

By default, your narration will be saved as sound objects with each slide. You can also save the narration as a series of separate files, one for each slide. The files will be opened and played when you run the slide show. To save your narration in a separate file, turn on the Link Narrations In box, and use the Browse button to select the location for the stored files. Finally, click OK when you are ready to start recording.

PowerPoint now runs the slide show. As each slide appears, speak your narration into the microphone, advancing each slide when you are done. When you end the show, a box appears asking if you want to save the timings with the slide show. Click Yes.

 N O T E : To pause the narration, right-click the slide and choose Pause Narration from the shortcut menu. Choose Resume Narration from the shortcut menu when you are ready to continue.

Animating Slides

A slide transition determines how a slide appears on the screen. An *animation* determines how the objects on the slide appear. By combining transitions and animations, you can create some entertaining and unusual effects. As an example, you can have each item in a bullet list appear from outside the viewing area, flying into the screen. You can animate both the text on a slide and graphic objects.

Animating Text

To apply the same animation style to all the text in a slide, display Slide Sorter view, and then click the slide you want to animate. Pull down the Preset Animation list and choose an effect:

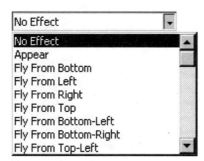

For some other animation styles, choose Slide Show | Preset Animation and choose from the submenu that appears.

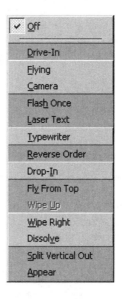

Your selection will affect all subtitles and each item in a bullet list in the slide, but not titles and other objects. The bullet list must have been created by use of a placeholder; the animation will not affect lists you create yourself by using Insert | Text Box. To automate an inserted text box list, see "Animating Objects" later in this chapter.

TIP: Choose Slide Show | Animation Preview to see the animation on the slide.

If you do not assign a delay to the slide but advance it manually, then you have to click to bring each animated object into view during the presentation. If you assigned an automatic advance time to the slide, the animated objects will appear within that time frame, equally distributed. For example, suppose you assigned a slide a 6-second delay. If you animate a bullet list with three items, the items will appear one after the other but within the 6-second period.

When you assign times by rehearsing, you'll have to click for each item during rehearsal. The total time for all the items is used for the slide's overall timing, with the time divided among all the items. For example, suppose you wait 6 seconds after the slide first appears to click to show the subtitle. You then wait another 6 seconds for the first bullet-list item. You then quickly display the remaining items in 2-second intervals, for a total of 18 seconds. When you play the slide, the 18 seconds will be divided roughly equally between all the objects, so the delay before the first two will be less than the rehearsed 6 seconds each.

To change the timing of individual objects, use the technique discussed next.

Animating Objects

In Slide Sorter view, the animation you select applies to all the subtitles and bullet list placeholders on the slide. In Normal, Outline, or Slide view, you can also assign a separate animation to each item in the slide, including the title, charts, graphics, and bullet lists that you inserted as text boxes. In fact, PowerPoint gives you three ways to do this—the Preset Animation list in the Slide Show menu, the Animation Effects toolbar, and the Custom Animation dialog box.

Selecting a Preset Animation

To choose from a list of built-in animation styles, display the slide in Normal, Outline, or Slide view, and then follow these steps:

1. Click to select the item you want to animate.
2. Choose Slide Show | Preset Animation, and then choose the effect from the list. Your selection will only affect the selected object.

Use this technique to apply a different animation to each of two bullet lists on the slide, to the title, or to a graphic object. Have a graphic of an arrow fly in from the edge of the screen, for example, or a chart slide up from the bottom of the screen.

All the items within a bullet list will appear with the same animation effect.

> **N O T E :** You can choose Random Effects from the Text Preset Animation list in Slide Sorter view to apply a different effect to each text item on the slide.

To see how the animation will look, choose Slide Show | Animation Preview to display a miniature of the slide on your screen. Click the miniature to see the animation.

Using the Animation Effects Toolbar

The Animation Effects toolbar offers a number of animation choices, but also lets you change the order in which elements appear. To display the toolbar, click the Animation Effects button in the Formatting toolbar to display these options:

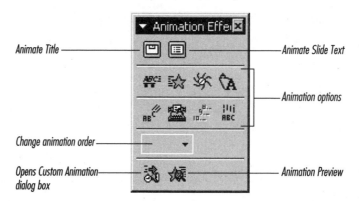

To animate an object on the slide, select the object and then click the desired animation effect. When you choose an effect for the title or slide text, PowerPoint pushes down the appropriate button on the toolbar. Click the button again if you want to turn off the animation.

You can also use the Animation Effects toolbar to change the order in which the animated objects appear. When you select an object, its order number appears in the list box. To change its order, pull down the list and choose another number. For example, suppose you animate the title, subtitle, and graphic object. If you want the title to appear last, select the title, pull down the list, and click the number 3.

Custom Animations

For even more control over animation, display the slide and choose Custom Animation from the Slide Show menu or on the Animation Effects toolbar. With this dialog box, shown in Figure 21-2, you can change the order in which objects appear, assign effects and sounds, animate the parts of a chart, and choose to have sounds and movies played separately or in the background while other animation occurs.

Turn on the check boxes for objects you want to animate, and then choose options from the Effects tab. Choose an animation style, an optional sound, and what occurs after the animation is complete. You can choose, for example, to have text change color or disappear when the next text or object appears

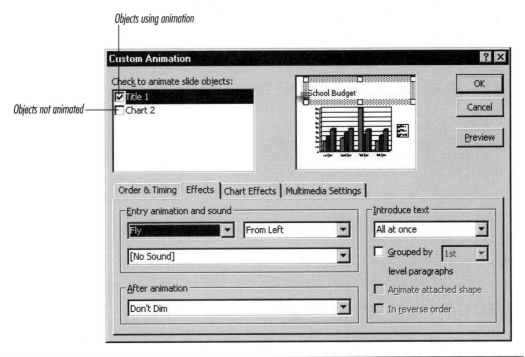

FIGURE 21-2 Customizing an animation

onscreen. In the Introduce Text section, choose to display text all at once, or a letter or word at a time. You can also group text by its levels to display outline families together, or in reserve order.

Use the Order & Timing tab of the dialog box to change the order in which objects appear and to set when they are animated. The items will appear onscreen in the same order as in the Animated Order list. To change the order, select an item and click the Up Arrow or Down Arrow button.

Animating Charts, Sounds, and Movies

For even more special effects, apply custom animations to charts, sounds, and movies. If you select a chart in the Custom Animation dialog box, you can animate it on the Chart Effects tab. You can choose to display each series or category separately, or even each element (such as a bar or pie slice) within each series or category. For each animated element, you can also select a sound.

Use the Multimedia Settings tab of the Custom Animation dialog box to control sounds and movies, even inserted tracks from an audio CD. You can choose to pause or continue the show while it is playing. For sounds, you can also choose to stop the sound when the slide is advanced, or continue for a specific number of slides.

If you are not narrating a slide show, for example, you may want to play music in the background as the presentation appears. To play a CD track in the background, follow these steps:

1. Select and display the slide where you want the sound to begin.
2. Use Insert | Sound And Movies to select the sound file or CD track, as discussed in Chapter 20, and then click the icon for the sound object.
3. Choose Slide Show | Custom Animation.
4. Click the Order & Timing tab, and turn on the check box for the sound object that you just inserted.
5. Click the Automatically option button, and leave the time set at 0 seconds.
6. Click the Multimedia Setting tab, and then follow the steps shown next.

12 *Click the More Options button.*

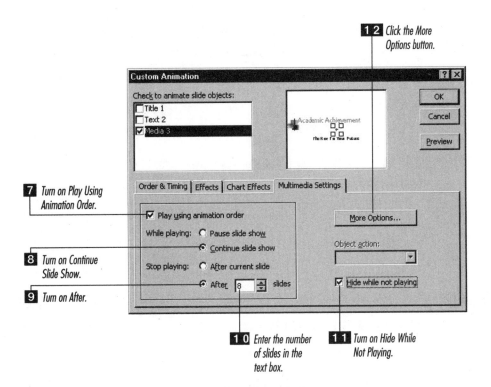

7 *Turn on Play Using Animation Order.*

8 *Turn on Continue Slide Show.*

9 *Turn on After.*

10 *Enter the number of slides in the text box.*

11 *Turn on Hide While Not Playing.*

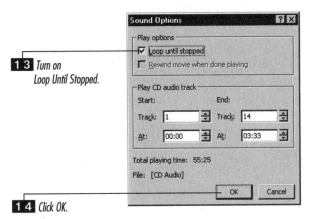

13 *Turn on Loop Until Stopped.*

14 *Click OK.*

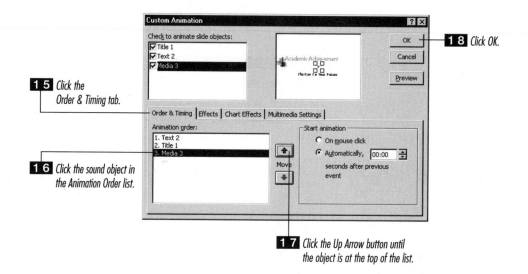

15 *Click the Order & Timing tab.*

16 *Click the sound object in the Animation Order list.*

17 *Click the Up Arrow button until the object is at the top of the list.*

18 *Click OK.*

Creating Action Buttons

An *action button* is an object on the slide that you click or point at to perform an action. Use an action button to play a sound file, launch your web browser and jump to a web site, open another application, or move to another slide in the show.

For example, suppose you have one or more slides in the show that you might not want to display, depending on the audience. You can add an action button to the slide before the ones you may want to skip. When you choose not to display the slides, just click the button to skip over them.

There are two general ways to initiate an action: a *mouse click* and a *mouse over*. With a mouse click, you must click the object to initiate the action. With a mouse over, you merely point to the object to perform the action.

You can add a set of predesigned buttons, and you can use any drawing object or graphics to perform an action.

To add a predesigned action button, select Slide Show | Action Buttons, choose from the options shown here, and then drag in the slide to draw a rectangle the size of the button.

To assign an action to text or to a graphic object in the slide, right-click it and choose Slide Show | Action Settings.

In both cases, PowerPoint opens the Action Settings dialog box shown in Figure 21-3.

The actions you can take are

- **Hyperlink To**   This jumps to another slide, another presentation, or to a web site. You can choose to go to the next or previous slide, first or last slide, the last viewed slide or a specific slide; end the show; jump to an Internet web site; or open another presentation.
- **Run Program**   This lets you start another program on your disk.
- **Run Macro**   This lets you run a macro that you recorded.
- **Object Action**   This lets you edit or open an embedded object that you inserted into the slide by using Insert | Object.
- **Play Sound**   This lets you play a sound file.

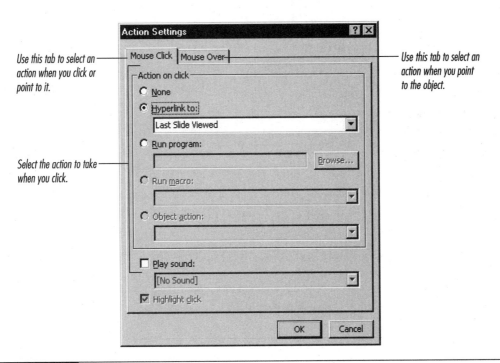

Use this tab to select an action when you click or point to it.

Select the action to take when you click.

Use this tab to select an action when you point to the object.

FIGURE 21-3   Designating an action

Playing a Slide Show

You can run your slide show in two ways—from within PowerPoint or directly from the Windows desktop.

- Run the slide show from PowerPoint when you are still working on it and may want to make changes as you go along.
- Run the show from Windows on machines that do not have PowerPoint installed, or when you don't want to start PowerPoint first.

In addition to the transition, animation, and sound effects that you've added to the slides, you can use the mouse as a pointing and highlighting tool. By dragging the mouse, you can draw directly on the screen, emphasizing major points.

Setting Up the Show

Before playing your slide show, you should determine some aspects of how it will appear. Do you want to control the slide show, for example, or have it repeat unattended, as part of a display? To set these options, choose Slide Show | Set Up Show to display the dialog box in Figure 21-4.

Choose options from the dialog box and then click OK. Use the Browsed At A Kiosk option, for example, to show the slides unattended. If there are slide timings, the show will run automatically, although viewers can advance slides manually, if desired. The show will repeat automatically within 5 minutes after each showing.

T I P : Use the Projector Wizard when you're ready to connect your computer to a data projector.

Playing a Show from PowerPoint

To play the show from within PowerPoint, open the presentation and then click the Slide Show button, or choose Slide Show | View Show.

While a show is playing, you can draw on the screen to add annotations, and navigate from slide to slide regardless of their order. You can also type notes and action items, even create tasks and schedule meetings in Outlook.

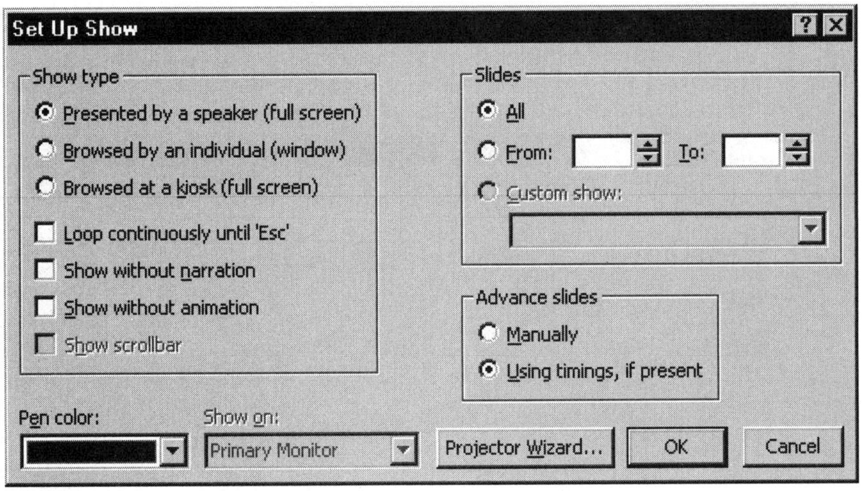

FIGURE 21-4 Setting up the slide show

To draw on the screen, right-click the mouse button, or move the mouse and click the icon in the lower-left corner to see the shortcut menu. Choose Pointer Options | Pen, and then draw on the screen by dragging the mouse. To change the drawing color, point to Pointer Options on the shortcut menu, point to Pen Color, and then select the new color to use. To stop drawing, right-click, point to Pointer Options, and then to Arrow in the submenu that appears.

N O T E : To erase your annotations, select Screen in the shortcut menu and click Erase Pen.

As you are giving a presentation, you may want to write notes or reminders to yourself. To write a reminder, select Speaker Notes from the shortcut menu. Type the note in the dialog box that appears, and then click Close to attach the text as a note to the slide.

If you are conducting a meeting, you can also type meeting minutes and assign tasks. Choose Meeting Minder from the shortcut menu to see this dialog box:

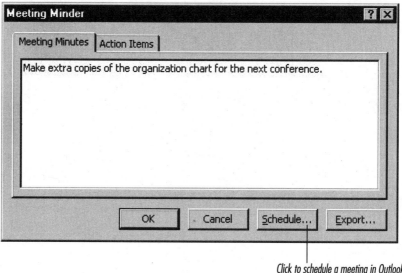

Click to schedule a meeting in Outlook.

TIP: You can also display the dialog box from within PowerPoint by choosing Tools | Meeting Minder.

Use the Meeting Minutes tab of the dialog box to enter text that is associated with the entire presentation, not with a specific slide. Use the Action Items tab of the dialog box to enter a brief description of a task, whom it is assigned to, and the due date. You can add multiple tasks, and edit or delete them from the same page.

Click Export to post the actions as tasks in Outlook, or to save the minutes and tasks as a Word document.

Running the Show from Windows

Once you perfect your slide show, why go through the trouble of starting PowerPoint just to show it? You can save the presentation in PowerPoint Show format, and then quickly run the show on any computer that has PowerPoint installed.

First, set up the show using either the Presented By A Speaker or the Browsed At A Kiosk options. Then choose File | Save As, pull down the Save As Type list, and choose PowerPoint Show. Enter a filename and choose the location, as usual, and then click Save. Store the show on the Windows desktop to access it quickly.

When you want to run the presentation, just double-click the file on the desktop or within Windows Explorer.

Taking the Show on the Road

If you plan to transport the show and show it on another computer, then be sure to copy it along with any associated files, such as linked sounds or graphics, and the same fonts that you used to created it. To run the show on a computer that does not have PowerPoint installed, you'll also need the PowerPoint Viewer, a special program that lets you display PowerPoint presentations. To get your show ready for the road, use the Pack And Go command. This command creates a single file with all the presentation elements and compresses the file.

Get your slide show ready, and then select File | Pack And Go. In a series of dialog boxes, you'll be walked through each of the steps of saving the presentation, including the disk to save the files, and whether to include linked files and fonts. When you finish with the dialog boxes, PowerPoint saves the presentation and its associated files, along with the viewer if you selected it, in a single file with the PPZ extension. It also creates a file called PNGSETUP.EXE. You'll need both these files to run the presentation on another computer.

When you want to prepare the presentation to run on another computer, run the program PNGSETUP. The program will prompt you for the location to store the presentation, then decompress all the files.

Using the PowerPoint Viewer

If you think you may need to show the presentation on a computer that does not have PowerPoint installed, then add the PowerPoint Viewer. You'll have the option to do so in one of the Pack And Go dialog boxes. The Viewer is a program that displays PowerPoint slide shows even when PowerPoint itself is not installed.

The Viewer, however, is not installed with a typical Office installation and is not set to be installed the first time you use it. So to use the Viewer, you need to install it from the Office CD. Insert the CD and choose Add Or Remove Features. Expand the listing for Microsoft PowerPoint for Windows, pull down the PPT Files Viewer list, and choose Run From My Computer. Finally, click Update Now.

The PowerPoint Viewer is a program called PPVIEW32. When you unpack a presentation that contains the viewer, it will be in the same directory as the presentation and its associated file. Double-click the viewer to run the presentation.

If you are on a network, you can show your presentation to other network users. Through PowerPoint, you store the presentation in a network drive and then send notices to your audience members via Microsoft Outlook. The notice announces the date and time you plan to show the presentation, so audience members can reserve time on their schedule.

To set up for a network broadcast, choose Slide Show 1 Online Broadcast, and then choose Set Up And Schedule from the submenu. In the box that appears, select the option button labeled "Set Up and Schedule a New Broadcast" and then click OK. PowerPoint displays the Schedule A New Broadcast dialog box shown here:

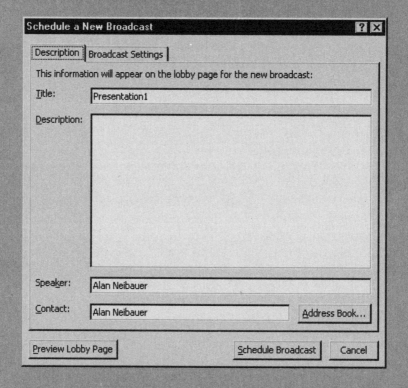

Click the Broadcast Settings tab and then click the Server Options button to see this dialog box:

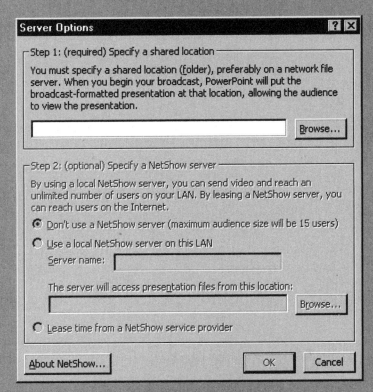

In the text box at the top of the box, enter the path of the shared location where the slide show files will be stored, and then click the Schedule Broadcast button. PowerPoint opens a Microsoft Outlook meeting planner window where you designate when you plan to show the presentation, who is invited to participate, and send e-mails to each participant.

When you are ready to show the presentation, select Slide Show | Online Broadcast | Begin Broadcast.

- Use Slide Show | Custom Shows to create one or more shows with the slides in a custom order.
- To some extent, the quality of your presentation will depend on your hardware. Watching a slide show on a small laptop monitor, or on a low-resolution desktop monitor, is not the best way to view your work. For greater impact, hook up your computer to a large-screen television or, better yet, to a projection device for even a larger screen.
- To apply the same animation to every title, apply it to the title in the Slide Master.
- No matter how well you plan your presentation, practice it completely, and several times, before showing it to an audience. This is particularly important if you prepared your show with Pack And Go and are showing it for the first time on hardware different than you used to create it.
- Use Slide Show | Hide Slide to prevent the displayed or selected slide from appearing in the slide show. Use the Slide Show | Hide Slide command again to reinsert the slide in the show.
- To make a copy of a slide, choose Insert | Duplicate Slide.
- Use Insert | Slides From Outline to create slides from a Word outline document.
- Use Insert | Slides From Files to copy slides from other presentations. In the dialog box that appears, use Browse to select the presentation, and then click Display to see thumbnails of its slides. Choose a slide and click Insert, or click Insert All to add all the slides to the open presentation.
- Choose View | Black And White to see how your presentation will appear if printed in black and white.
- Add a hyperlink to a slide by use of Insert | Hyperlink.

Managing Data with Access

Introducing Access **22**

B A S I C S

- Using the Database Wizard
- Working with Tables
- Access Forms and Reports
- Sorting Records
- Printing Forms, Reports, and Datasheets

B E Y O N D

- Customizing Tables
- Learning About Relationships
- Changing the Page Layout
- Customizing Access Startup

You can jump right into most programs and start working, learning as you go. Access is a little different. Before using Access, or any database management program for that matter, you should first understand a little about databases.

Anatomy of a Database

Information in a database is organized in a table. Visualize a table just as you would a table in Word or Excel, with information arranged in rows and columns. Each row contains a record and each column, a field. Each row, for example, would hold one person's address record, with columns for the person's first and last names, address, city, street, ZIP code, and telephone number.

In many tables, one or a combination of fields is designated as the *primary key*. When you enter records into a table, they will automatically be organized in the order of their key, although you can sort records to display them in other sequences.

You can spread information among several tables. If you store a lot of information about clients, for example, divide it into two tables, with one record per client in each. Both records contain the client's ID number, so you can match them up. We call this a *one-to-one relationship,* because for every record in one table there is just one record in the other table:

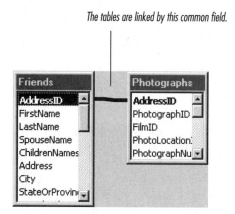

The tables are linked by this common field.

A company's database may have three tables, as shown here. The Clients table contains one record of general information for each client. Each record in the Orders table contains the client ID number, order number, and order date for one order. Each record in the Details table contains the product ID number and quantity ordered for one item in an order, as well as the order number, order detail ID number, and unit price.

These tables are linked by the ID field.

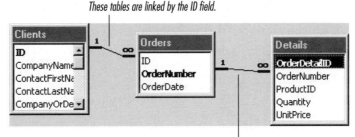

These tables are linked by the Order Number field.

Hopefully, clients order more than once, so you'll have one or more order records for each client. An order can be for more than one item, so you'll have one or more detail records for each order record. These relationships are called *one-to-many*. When you need to locate an order, you find the customer's ID in the Clients table, then locate the matching records in the Orders table. The ID number links those two tables. To see the items ordered, you use the Order Number from the Orders table to locate matching records in the Details table. The Order Number links those two tables.

 N O T E : A one-to-many relationship works in only one direction. For example, an order can only be from one client, so each order in the Orders table is connected to only one client record.

In addition to tables, an Access database contains other objects that you'll use to work with information:

- **Queries**   These let you access information in any combination, on the fly.
- **Forms**   These let you display, enter, and edit information in arrangements other than rows and columns, even from multiple tables.
- **Reports**   These let you print information from your database, even from related tables.
- **Pages**   These let you display, enter, and edit information from within your web browser and over the Internet.
- **Macros**   These are stored sequences of keystrokes and commands that play automatically when you initiate them.
- **Modules**   These use Visual Basic commands to automate tasks.

Starting Access

You run Access from the Start button and the Program menu on the Windows taskbar. Each time you start Access, you'll see the dialog box shown here:

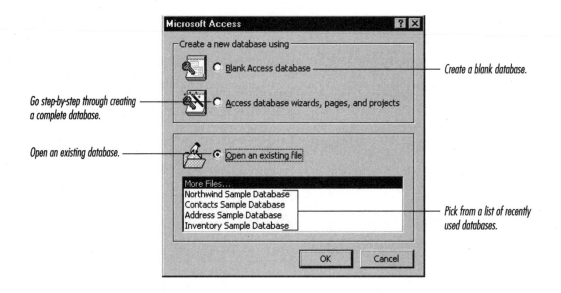

Create a blank database.

Go step-by-step through creating a complete database.

Open an existing database.

Pick from a list of recently used databases.

The Database Wizard

When you need to create a database, try the Database Wizard first—it can save you a lot of time. Click the Access Database Wizards, Pages, And Projects option button and then on OK. A dialog box appears with two tabs:

Create complete databases using wizards.

Use the General tab to start with a blank database, data page, or project.

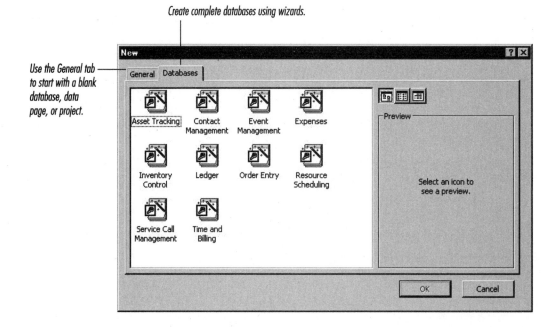

You could use the General tab to start a blank database, but you'd have to design the tables yourself. Instead, use these steps to create a database by using a wizard:

1. Click the Databases tab to see the types of databases you can create.
2. Double-click your choice.
3. In the dialog box that appears, enter a name for the database in the text box that appears, and then click Create.
4. A dialog box appears showing the type of information the database will store. Click Next.
5. You'll now see a list of tables that are included with the database and the fields that are in each, as in Figure 22-1. When you select a table on the left, its fields are listed on the right. A check mark next to a field means that it is included in the table. Fields in italics and unchecked are optional. Turn on a check box to include the field, turn it off to exclude it.
6. After choosing the fields you want for each of the tables, click Next.
7. You can now choose a design to use for forms. Choose the design that you like and then click Next.
8. The next wizard shows styles for reports. Choose the style you like and then click Next.

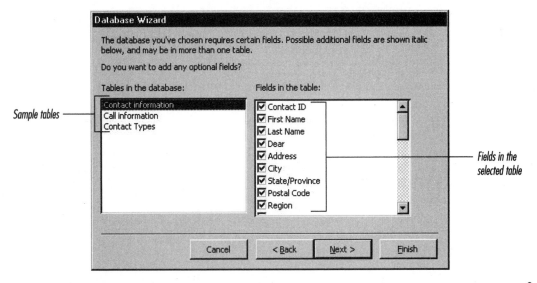

FIGURE 22-1 Wizard dialog box showing tables and fields

9. In the next dialog box, enter the title for the database and optionally choose a picture that you'd like to appear in all reports. Type the database title and then click Next.

10. In the final box choose "Yes, start the database" (selected by default) and then click Finish.

First, you'll see a blank Database window on the screen (you'll learn more about this later). Then the Database Wizard creates the tables, forms, reports, and other elements that make up the database and displays a Switchboard, as shown in Figure 22-2. In front of each Switchboard item is a button.

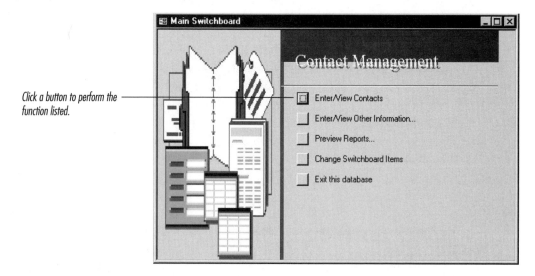

Click a button to perform the function listed.

FIGURE 22-2   Switchboard form

The Database Window

 Switchboards let you perform common functions. To access the entire database, click the Database Window button in the Standard toolbar to display the Database window, as shown in Figure 22-3.

Along the left of the window is a bar showing the types of objects in the database. Select the type of object to see a list of database contents. For example, to see a list of tables in the database, click Tables. To see a list of forms, click Forms.

You use the Groups section in the bar to create groups that store related items. The Favorites folder below Groups, for example, works the same as the

FIGURE 22-3 Database window

Internet Favorites folder. To add an item to Favorites, drag it from the Database window onto the Favorites icon. Access places a shortcut to the object in Favorites. To open any of your favorite items, click Favorites to display its contents, and then double-click the item you wish to open.

N O T E : To add a new group to the bar, right-click it and choose New Group from the shortcut menu. In the dialog box that appears, type the name of the group and then click OK. The shortcut menu also contains options to rename and delete your own groups.

At the top of the Database window are several buttons. The five buttons on the right let you delete a selected object and control the way objects are listed in the window, much like in a Save As or Open dialog box.

When you are looking at tables, forms, queries, and data pages, the three buttons on the left are

- **Open** This displays the table, form, query, or data page selected in the Database window.
- **Design** This lets you modify the table, form, report, query, or data page selected in the Database window.
- **New** This lets you create a new object.

Open is replaced by the Preview button when viewing Reports, and by Run when viewing the Macros and Modules.

In addition to the items in the database, the window also contains commands for creating new objects. When viewing tables, for example, you can choose among three ways to create a table—in Design view, by using a wizard, or by entering data.

Working with Tables

Open a table when you want to display and work with more than one record at a time. Click Tables to see the list of tables, and then double-click the table you want to open. You'll see a datasheet, a collection of rows and columns, as shown in Figure 22-4. The notation "(AutoNumber)" in the Call ID field means that in this table, Access automatically numbers the records as you enter them. You cannot type or change the value in that field.

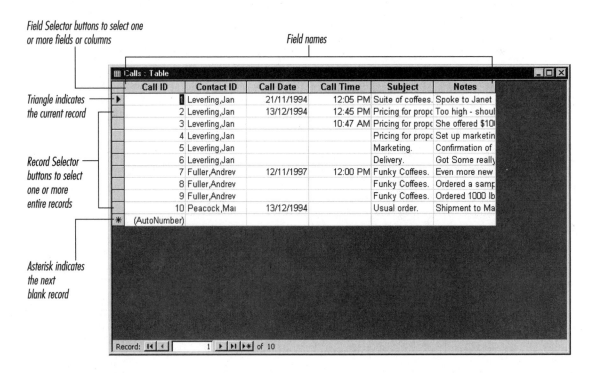

FIGURE 22-4 Table in Datasheet view

When your table has information in it, use the scroll bars and navigation buttons at the bottom of the datasheet to move from record to record:

Calls : Table					
Call ID	Contact ID	Call Date	Call Time	Subject	Notes
1	Leverling,Jan	21/11/1994	12:05 PM	Suite of coffees.	Spoke to Janet
2	Leverling,Jan	13/12/1994	12:45 PM	Pricing for propc	Too high - shoul
3	Leverling,Jan		10:47 AM	Pricing for propc	She offered $10l
4	Leverling,Jan			Pricing for propc	Set up marketin
5	Leverling,Jan			Marketing.	Confirmation of
6	Leverling,Jan			Delivery.	Got Some reall)
7	Fuller,Andrev	12/11/1997	12:00 PM	Funky Coffees.	Even more new
8	Fuller,Andrev			Funky Coffees.	Ordered a samp
9	Fuller,Andrev			Funky Coffees.	Ordered 1000 lb
10	Peacock,Mai	13/12/1994		Usual order.	Shipment to Ma
*	(AutoNumber)				

Record: |◄ ◄ [1] ► ►| ►* of 10

First Record   *Go to Record*   *New Record*

Previous Record   *Last Record*

Next Record

NOTE: The Previous Record button will be dimmed when there is no previous record, that is, when you're looking at the first one.

To enter information into the table, click in the column and start typing. You can also move from column to column using the TAB key, SHIFT-TAB combination, and the arrow keys.

Some fields created by the Database Wizard, and which you can create yourself, use an *input mask*. An input mask is a template that determines how information appears onscreen and the type of data that can be entered. The input mask for a telephone number looks like this:

(206) 555-1234

( )   -

Access will insert the parentheses and the hyphen for you—you do not have to type them yourself, so complete a phone number by typing **6096541248** to display (609) 654-1248.

When you start typing in the last blank row, Access begins a new blank row beneath it for the next record. Access automatically saves your information when you move to another record, or when you close the table, so you do not have to save your work manually.

 TIP: Press SHIFT-ENTER if you want to save the record before you leave it.

 To add a new record, move into the blank row. You can also click the New Record button in either the Navigation bar or the Standard toolbar.

If the table has a primary key, the records are automatically sorted according to the key value. If the key is not an AutoNumber field, you won't be able to leave a record if the key column is blank or a duplicate of some other record.

To delete a record, click any of its fields and then click the Delete Record button in the Standard toolbar. To delete several records, select them first. You can also select the row, or rows, and then press the DEL key on the keyboard.

 NOTE: Access does not "recycle" AutoNumber numbers. When you delete a record, its autonumber is gone and not reassigned.

If a table is related to another table, you'll see plus signs to indicate that there are related records. Click the plus sign to expand the record to see information from the related table. In the following example, clicking on a plus sign next to the Contact Type Buyer displays the contacts that have been classified as buyers:

ContactTypes : Table							
Contact Type I	**Contact Type**						
1	Buyer						
Contact ID	**CompanyID**	**First Name**	**Last Name**	**Dear**	**Title**	**Work Pl**	
1	4	Janet	Leverling	Janet	Vice President,	(206) 555-	
3	2	Margaret	Peacock	Margaret	Purchase Mana	(206) 555-	
4	1	Nancy	Davolio	Nancy	Technical Conta	(425) 555-	
(AutoNumber)	0						

When you are done working with the datasheet, click its Close button or choose File | Close.

Access Forms

Forms are a great way to work with a database. Not only can you use a form to enter, edit, and review information, but you can also print the form for reference. To open a form, display the Forms tab of the Database window, and double-click the form you want to open. You can also select a form in the Switchboard window. A typical form is shown in Figure 22-5. To change information in a field, just go to its text box and type.

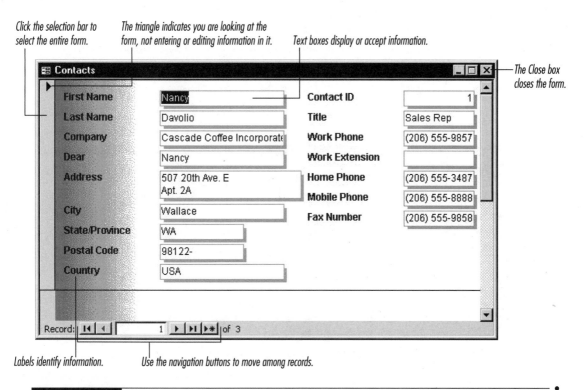

Click the selection bar to select the entire form.

The triangle indicates you are looking at the form, not entering or editing information in it.

Text boxes display or accept information.

The Close box closes the form.

Labels identify information.

Use the navigation buttons to move among records.

FIGURE 22-5 The Contacts form

The fields on a form correspond to the fields in an underlying table, although a form can have fewer fields if you only want to work with selected ones. If you change any information on the form, or add new records using a form, you are actually changing the contents of the table.

To add a new record to the table using the form, click the New Record button. A blank form appears for you to fill in. As with a datasheet, you cannot enter or edit information in an AutoNumber field.

To delete an entire record, click the Delete Record button in the toolbar. A dialog box appears warning you that the record will be deleted. Click Yes to actually delete the record. To delete every record, choose Edit | Select All Records and then press DEL.

Working with Complex Forms

Some forms contain fields from more than one table. The form shown in Figure 22-6, for example, is two forms in one. The fields on the top contain

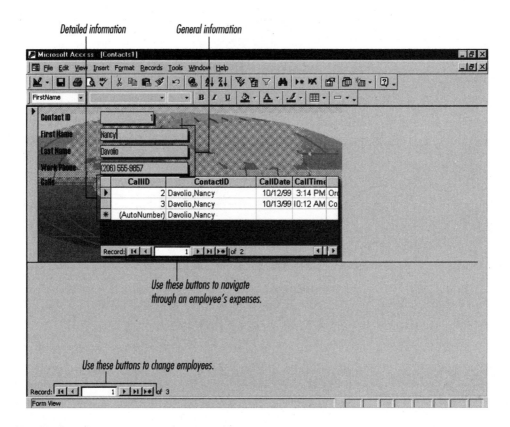

FIGURE 22-6 Forms can contain information from multiple tables

information about a contact, the fields on the bottom list information about calls with the contact. The form gets its information from two different tables.

There will be a separate set of navigation buttons for each table being represented. Use one set, for example, to select the contact you want to display or to add another contact record. When you choose a contact, his or her call information will appear in the other part of the form. Use the second set of navigation buttons to move among the contact's calls or to add another call record for that contact.

Switching Between Form and Datasheet View

When you open a form, you are in Form view, looking at your information through a form. To look at that same information as a datasheet, use the View button and drop-down arrow on the far left of the toolbar. The picture on the button represents the view you will switch to when you click the button.

BUTTON	NAME	FUNCTIONS
	Datasheet View	Displays the fields in a datasheet
	Design View	Enables layout changes in the form
	Form View	Displays the form

To display the information in a datasheet, click the down arrow next to the View button and select Datasheet View. The table that appears, however, contains just the fields that appear in the form, and in the same order in which they appear on the form, not as in the original table. So if you are working with a form that contains only three of 30 fields in the table, the datasheet contains just three fields. Any changes you make in this datasheet will still affect the table. To switch out of Datasheet view, click the down arrow and select Form View.

Sorting Records

Seeing records in a particular order can help you find and analyze information. A teacher, for example, might find it helpful to list students in grade or alphabetic order. Sort your records when you want to display them in some other order than they appear. Sorting doesn't change the physical order in which the records are stored on your disk, only the order in which they are displayed.

First, place the insertion point in the field you want to sort by. Then click either Sort Ascending or Sort Descending in the toolbar, depending on the order that you want.

SHORTCUT: You can also select Sort Ascending and Sort Descending from the shortcut menu that appears when you click the right mouse button on a field.

Access Reports

Forms are primarily designed to be viewed onscreen. When you want hardcopy, use a report. You can even perform calculations in reports for some statistical analysis, or to summarize large amounts of data.

To see a report, double-click it in the Reports tab of the Database window, or choose a report from the Switchboard. A typical report is shown in Figure 22-7.

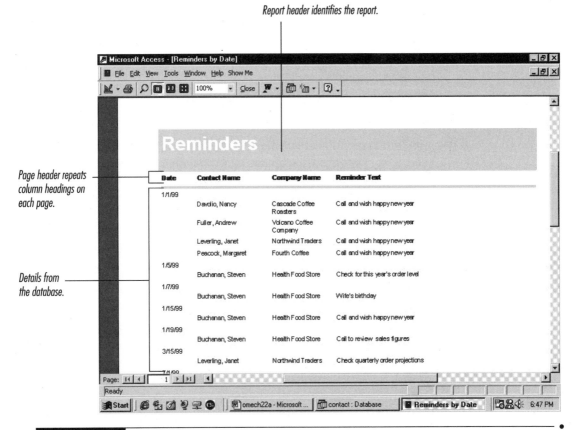

Report header identifies the report.

Page header repeats column headings on each page.

Details from the database.

FIGURE 22-7 Report in preview mode

Learning About Relationships

The relationships between tables are important when you have anything other than a simple one-table database. To see how tables are related, click the Relationships button on the Standard toolbar to display the Relationships window, shown in Figure 22-8.

If the database does not have any related tables, you'll be given the chance to select tables to be related.

The line from one table to another shows what field is used to relate the tables, and the type of relationship. The "1" indicates the "one" side of the relationship, the infinity symbol indicates the "many" side.

Each box represents a database table and lists its fields.

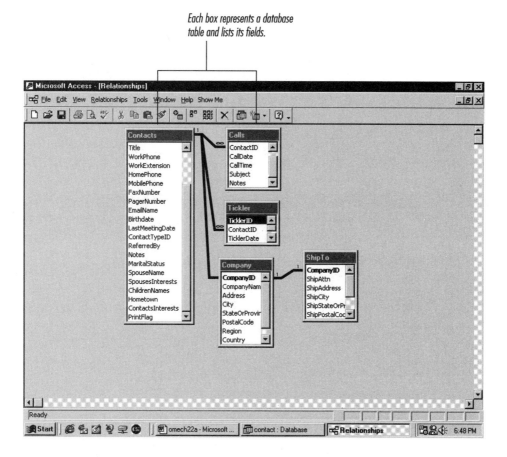

FIGURE 22-8 Relationships window showing how tables are related

Opening a Database

When you start Access, databases that you've created will be listed in the Startup dialog box. Double-click the database name, or select it and then choose Open. To see databases that are not listed in the box, click More Files.

Once you start Access, you can open a database using the File menu or the toolbar, just as you learned to open Word documents and Excel workbooks. The main difference is that you can't have more than one database open at a time. When you open or create a database, Access closes the currently open one.

Printing Forms, Reports, and Datasheets

Printing is a snap. First, select the object you want to print in the Database window, open the object, or display it in Print Preview. Then just click the Print button in the toolbar.

If you want to print specific records or pages, or otherwise control the printing process, then select File | Print to display the dialog box shown in Figure 22-9.

The options are similar to printing in Word and Excel. The Print Range section determines how many records will print. *All* prints them all. *Pages* prints just those pages designated in the From and To boxes. *Selected Record(s)* prints just the selected records.

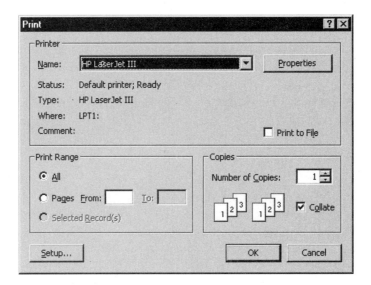

FIGURE 22-9   Print dialog box

TIP: Before printing a form, report, or datasheet, click the Print Preview button to see how the printout will appear.

Changing Page Layout

Each object in the database—each form, report, and datasheet—can have its own page layout settings. You can use one set of margins for one report, a different set for another. Either open the object you want to set the layout for, or click its name in the Database window. Then choose File | Page Setup.

NOTE: The Page Setup option will be dimmed when the Tables and Queries tabs of the Database window are displayed. To set up a page for a table or query, open the item first. The Page Setup dialog box will not contain a Columns tab.

The Page Setup dialog box has three tabs—Margins, Page, and Columns—as shown in Figure 22-10. The Margins tab lets you change the page margins and

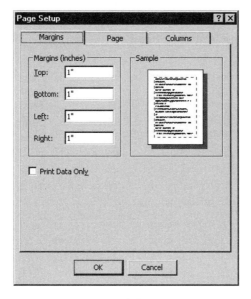

FIGURE 22-10   Margins page of the Setup dialog box

whether you want to print just the data from the form, or the data, labels, and any other text or graphics.

In the Page tab of the dialog box, you select the orientation, the page size, and source, and set a printer to be used for the current object. The settings in the Page Setup dialog box affect just the selected object in the Database window, and they are saved along with the database.

The options on the Columns tab, shown in Figure 22-11, control the layout of forms or report sections. The Grid Settings section controls how many forms print across the page, if more than one can fit, and their spacing. The Column Size section sets the size of the columns when printing multiple-column reports or labels. When Same As Detail is checked, the form will print the same size as was designed, and the same way it appears onscreen. If you enter a smaller size, some of the form will not appear on the printout.

The Column Layout section determines the order of the forms and report sections. If you select Down Then Across, Access first fits as many records as it can down the left side of the page, then continues with more records to their right. When you select Across Then Down, Access fits as many records as it can across the top of the page, and then continues in rows below them.

When you are finished with the Page Setup options, click OK to accept your changes, or click Cancel to close the box without implementing any changes.

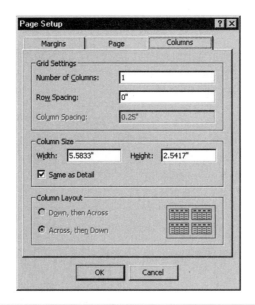

FIGURE 22-11 Columns tab of the Setup dialog box

As you develop your own database, you can customize the way it starts when you open it in Access. You can designate text to replace the words "Microsoft Access" in the Access title bar, for example, or choose a form or data page that will appear automatically.

To control setup options, select Tools | Startup, or right-click the folder bar (but not on the Objects or Groups button) and choose Startup, to see the dialog box shown here:

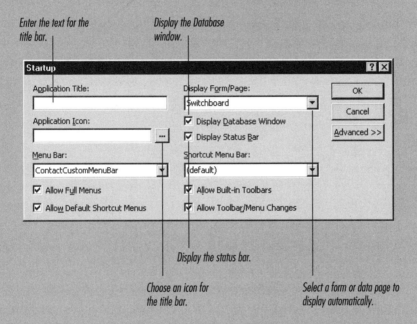

Enter the text for the title bar.

Display the Database window.

Display the status bar.

Choose an icon for the title bar.

Select a form or data page to display automatically.

Database developers and programmers use the remaining options in the dialog box to control what Access elements appear and which can be accessed. You can choose to allow the use of full menus, shortcut menus, and toolbars, and the capability to change toolbars and menus. The Advanced button displays options that let you determine what happens when an error code is encountered and the use of special keys.

- Use the Tools menu in Access to access standard Office 2000 features, such as Spelling, AutoCorrect, Online Collaboration, Customize, and Options. Use File | Send To if you want to e-mail a database object.

- To use all the default settings and fields when creating a database with the wizard, click the Finish button when it first appears.

- Entering some of the same information into a field as in the previous record? Press CTRL-' to automatically insert it.

- If you are using a database created with the Database Wizard, avoid renaming, deleting, and inserting columns. This could make forms and other features of the database unusable.

- A form can have fields that contain information calculated from other fields. Calculated fields are not part of any table; they just appear on the form to display information. You cannot enter information directly into a calculated field.

- Select File | Database Properties to enter identifying information about the database, including your name, subject, and keywords to identify the database.

- You can import Excel worksheets and databases created with other programs into your Access database. Right-click the Database window and choose Import from the shortcut menu to begin the process.

- Once you select a look for forms and reports in the Database Wizard, the same styles will automatically be selected when you run the wizard again. The wizard does not remember if you've selected optional fields, however.

- When you want to enter or edit text that doesn't fit in a column, use the Zoom box. Move to the field and press SHIFT-F2 to display a large text box that acts like a mini–word processor. As you type, your text will wrap when it reaches the right margin. To end a line manually and start another, press CTRL-ENTER—pressing ENTER by itself will close the box. Enter or edit the text as needed, and then click OK.

- You can change the way your datasheet looks by choosing a new font. Your selection affects the entire table—you cannot format individual cells, columns, or rows. Choose Format | Font, make your selections from the dialog box that appears, and then click OK.

Creating Custom Databases and Tables

23

The Database Wizard is great, but its databases certainly don't do everything you'd need a database for. You may want special fields that Microsoft never even thought of giving you, or you might want a combination of properties for controlling what the user can input. That's when you have to create your own database and tables, or at least change those created by the Database Wizard.

Creating a Database

Creating a database is about the easiest thing you can do with Access. When you start Access, select Blank Access Database. (If you select Access Database Wizards, Pages, and Projects from the startup dialog box by mistake, select the Database template in the General tab of the New dialog box.) When you click OK, the File New Database dialog box appears. Type a name for the database, and then click Create to display the Database window. That's it.

 NOTE: If a blank table appears, Access is letting you create a new table by entering data. Click the Close button on the table window. You'll learn about creating tables next.

 NOTE: If you're already in Access, select File I New or click the New button in the toolbar. In the list of templates that appears, double-click the Blank Database option.

Creating Tables

The next step is to create one or more tables for the database. There are several ways to create a table, depending on how much work you want to do. In the Database window with the Tables option selected, you can choose from these options:

- Create table in design view
- Create table by using wizard
- Create table by entering data

You can also click New in the Database Window toolbar to see the dialog box shown in Figure 23-1.

Using Datasheet View

Perhaps the easiest way to create a table with a few simple fields is to create it by entering data. Double-click Create Table By Entering Data in the Database

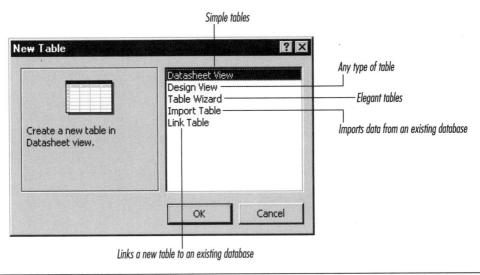

FIGURE 23-1 Creating a new table

window, or choose Datasheet View in the New dialog box and click OK. Access opens a blank datasheet with ten columns, generically labeled "Field1," "Field2," and so on.

Double-click a generic field name, type the name you want, and press ENTER.

When you've named all the fields, enter information into the datasheet. (Any generically named field that contains no information will later be deleted from the table automatically.) Click the Save button to display the Save As dialog box, type a name for the table, and then click OK.

A dialog box appears warning you that you do not have a primary key. A primary key is not absolutely necessary, but they do make things a lot easier. Click Yes to add an AutoNumber field as the first column labeled simply "ID," and then close the table.

Using the Table Wizard

The Table Wizard lets you create a table by selecting from various purposes and fields. Double-click Create Table By Using Wizard in the Database window, or choose Table Wizard in the New dialog box and click OK. Access opens the first wizard dialog box (see Figure 23-2).

Once you choose the table, you must move the fields you want to use from the Sample Fields list box, in the center, into the Fields In My New Table list box, on the right. To move an individual field, click its name in the Sample Fields list and then on the > button. If you want to use all or almost all the fields, just click >>; you can then remove the individual fields that you do not want included. To remove a field, click it in the list box on the right and then click <.

T I P : To rename a field, click it in the Fields In My New Table list, on the right, and then click the Rename Field button. Delete the old field name in the dialog box that appears, type the new name, and then click OK.

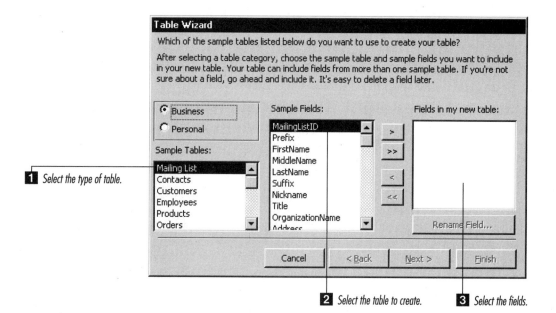

1 *Select the type of table.*

2 *Select the table to create.*

3 *Select the fields.*

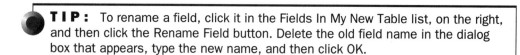

FIGURE 23-2 Select the type of table, the table itself, and then the fields

You can mix and match fields from any number of sample tables. Move the field from one table into the list box on the right, choose another table from either category, and select additional fields as you want.

When the list box on the right contains all the fields that you want, click Next. In the dialog box that appears, delete the suggested table name, type your own name for the table, and then click Next to let Access create the primary key for you. Access selects an appropriate field as the primary key field and assigns it an AutoNumber type. Click Next.

If there are already tables in the database, you'll see a dialog box asking if you want the tables to be related. If an existing table has a field that matches the primary key of your new table, Access will suggest a relationship. You can accept Access' choice, remove the relationship, or create a new one on your own.

The final wizard dialog box asks if you now want to modify the table design or enter data directly into the table using a datasheet or form.

Designing a Table

Creating a table in Design view requires quite a few steps, but it gives you the most control over your database. The techniques you use to design a table are also the same ones you'd use to change a table later on. In Design view, you not only type the names of fields, but you also must select their data types, and you have the opportunity to set their properties. Before creating a table, however, keep these three simple rules in mind:

- Never create a field that can be calculated from other fields. You can easily perform the calculations in a form or report.
- Never create repeating fields, such as Hobby1, Hobby2, Hobby3, and so on. What you need to do is to create two related tables.
- Never create a field that you know will have the same value in every record. If you are licensed to trade only with customers in Kentucky, you don't need a field called State. All your customers will be in Kentucky.

To create a table in Design view, double-click Create Table In Design View in the Database window, or choose Design View in the New dialog box and click OK, to see the dialog box shown in Figure 23-3.

You can also quickly create a field by clicking on the Build button in the toolbar. In the dialog box, select Business or Personal, choose the table containing a field you want to use, and then double-click the field to add it to your table.

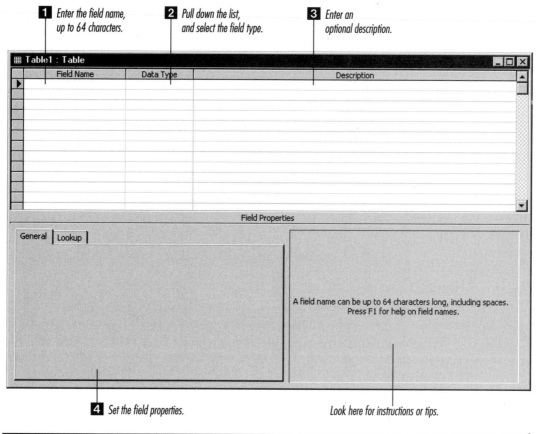

1 *Enter the field name, up to 64 characters.*

2 *Pull down the list, and select the field type.*

3 *Enter an optional description.*

4 *Set the field properties.*

Look here for instructions or tips.

FIGURE 23-3 Creating a table in Design view

When you are done creating your table, you must save it. Click the Save button and give the table a name. Then click the Datasheet View button to see the completed table.

Field Types

The field type determines what you can enter into a field and how it will be used. To designate a type, pull down the list in the type column and choose from the menu that appears. Table 23-1 summarizes the field types.

Field Properties

Field properties control what gets entered into the database or how it should appear on the screen. The properties shown in the Field Properties pane depend

FIELD TYPE	FIELD CONTENTS
Text	Use for any field that won't be used for performing calculations and doesn't fit into any of these other categories. Entries can be up to 255 characters.
Memo	Use for text up to 64,000 characters.
Number	Use only when you'll need to perform math and when you don't need it formatted as currency.
Date/Time	Use only when you need to enter dates and times. You can perform math on dates, such as calculating the number of days between two dates.
Currency	Same as Number but with a fixed number of decimal places and a dollar sign.
AutoNumber	Use when you want Access to automatically number the record for you. You can only have one AutoNumber field per table.
Yes/No	Use only when a field can be either a yes or no value, such as Paid?, High School Graduate?, Passed Inspection? The field will appear with a check box. Checked means Yes; unchecked means No.
OLE Object	Use for pictures, sound files, or graphs.
Hyperlink	Text that serves as a link to a site on the World Wide Web.
Lookup Wizard	Use to create a field that lets you select a value from a field in another table.

TABLE 23-1 The types fields for an Access table

on the data type of the selected field. To set a property, choose the field in the top of the dialog box, and then either enter specifics in the property dialog boxes or choose from their pull-down lists.

Here's a summary of the properties used by Access. Remember that not all these properties will appear for each field type.

- **Field Size** For text fields, set the number of characters that can be entered from 1 to 255. The default is 50. For number fields, choose the type of number.
- **Format** This determines how the information appears on the screen and when printed. With text fields, for example, the most common entry is >, which promotes all lowercase characters to uppercase, such as for state abbreviations.

- **Decimal Places**   This is the number of decimal places for number and currency fields.
- **New Values**   For AutoNumber fields, select either increment (1, 2, 3...) or random numbers.
- **Input Mask**   This specifies the format used when information is entered or displayed.
- **Caption**   This is a more descriptive name for the field to be used in forms and reports.
- **Default Value**   This is information that will appear in the field automatically but that you can change in the datasheet or form. If most of your clients are in California, enter **CA** as the default value in the property for the State field.
- **Validation Rule**   This is a logical expression that determines whether Access accepts your field entry. Once you assign a validation rule, you cannot leave the field blank.
- **Validation Text**   This is a message that appears if information violates the validation rule.
- **Required**   This determines if an entry must be made in the field.
- **Allow Zero Length**   This allows empty fields to be inserted.
- **Indexed**   This determines if an index will be created to provide more efficient searches. You'll learn more about indexes later in this chapter.

Input Mask

Use an input mask when you want to control the specific characters. For example, suppose your school identifies classes with a three-letter abbreviation followed by a three-digit number, such as ART102 and BIO099. You'd enter LLL000 into the input mask to ensure entries are in the proper format. This means that three letters must be entered, followed by three numbers.

 T I P : Use (999) 000-0000 as the input mask for a telephone field, and 00000-9999 as the mask for a ZIP code.

The mask characters are shown in Table 23-2. Any other character is a literal. So use the mask HRVDLLL000, for example, if you want the characters "HRVD" to appear with the field automatically.

By default, only the characters that you type in the field are saved on the disk. Literal characters, such as "HRVD" in the mask HRVDLLL000, are not saved

MASK CHARACTER	FUNCTION
0	Requires digits 0 to 9.
9	Optional digit or space.
#	Digit or space, as well as plus and minus signs.
L	Requires the letter A to Z.
?	Optional letter A to Z.
A	Requires any letter or digit.
a	Any optional letter or digit.
&	Requires any character or a space.
C	Any optional character or a space.
.	Decimal point.
,	Thousands separator.
: ; - /	Date and time separators.
<	Characters following will be converted to lowercase.
>	Characters following will be converted to uppercase (use ">LL" in a State field, for example).
!	Characters will appear from right to left, rather than from left to right. Only works when characters on the left are optional.
\	Displays the next character, even if it is an input mask character (using "\&" will actually display the & character).
"Password"	Displays an asterisk for each character typed.

TABLE 23-2 Input Mask Characters

with the entered data because the input mask displays and prints them anyway. But if you do want to save literal mask characters, add ";0" after the mask, as in HRVDLLL000;0. The characters ";1" would represent the default setting.

By default, spaces are shown as an underline character (_), so the mask (999) 000-0000 appears as (___) ___-____. To designate another character, add it to the end of the mask. For example, the mask (999) 000-0000;1;* displays (***) ***-****.

Validating Entries

Input masks help prevent errors, but errors are still possible. For example, suppose you only offer three shipping alternatives, the postal service, UPS, and FedEx. To ensure that only one of these is entered, create a Validation Rule and specify Validation Text. The validation text appears on the screen if the information entered violates the validation rule.

You enter the rule as a logical expression in the Validation Rule property text box, and enter the message in the Validation Text property text box. Using our shipping example, enter **IN("USPS", "UPS", "FEDEX")** as the Validation Rule and **Must be either USPS, UPS, or FEDEX** as the Validation Text.

General	Lookup
Field Size	50
Format	
Input Mask	
Caption	
Default Value	
Validation Rule	In ("USPS","UPS","FEDEX")
Validation Text	Must be either USPS, UPS, or FEDEX
Required	No
Allow Zero Length	No
Indexed	No
Unicode Compression	Yes

> **TIP:** Set the Format property to **>** so lowercase letters are converted to uppercase.

The validation rule for numeric values can use any of the usual operators, including >, >=, <, <=, =, and <>. For example, if you're entering information in a Wage Rate field, you'd want to be sure you wouldn't enter 95.00 instead of 9.50. To avoid this problem, use a validation rule such as <30 to ensure that only rates less than $30 can be entered. To limit values to a certain range, use the Between...And operator, as in "Between 5 And 18.25."

Keys and Indexes

When you create a table, you can also designate the primary key and create one or more indexes. The primary key maintains the order of the records and uniquely identifies each record in the table. Indexes help speed up searches and other operations.

To set the primary key, click the field that you want to use, and then click the Primary Key button in the toolbar. Access places a key symbol on the field's selector bar and sets the Index property to Yes (No Duplicates). This means that the field will be indexed and that you cannot have the same value in more than one record. The key field can be any type except Memo, OLE Object, and Hyperlink. It can be a Yes/No field, but then you could only have two records.

> **T I P :** If you want to change the primary key field, click in another field while in Design view, and then on the Primary Key button.

Creating an Index   You can also index on other fields to speed up searches and other database operations. Click the field you want to index, and then pull down the list in the Indexed property for the options No, Yes (Duplicates OK), and Yes (No Duplicates). Select Yes (Duplicates OK) when you may have the same value in more then one record.

To create an index based on more than one field, such as a combination of first and last names, click the Indexes button in the toolbar to see the dialog box shown here:

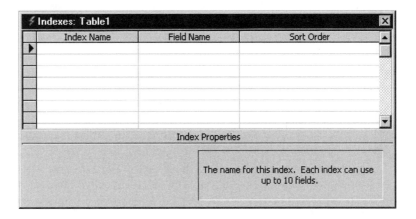

Click in the first blank row in the Index Name column, and type a name for the index.

Next designate the first field for the index. Always start with the broadest field—the one that may provide the most duplicates—and work your way to the narrowest field. Click the Field Name column in that row, pull down the list that appears to see the fields in the table, and select a field.

To add another field to the index, move to the blank row under the field you just selected, and choose another field and sort order. Do not enter an index name, because this second field is part of the same index. The index properties do not appear when you're in a row that does not have an index name. The properties are associated with the index itself, not any individual field.

Modifying a Table

All the techniques that you've just learned can be applied to changing an existing table, as well as to creating a new one. Just click the table's name in the Datasheet window and then select Design. You can then edit a field's name, selecting a new type and choosing new properties.

 To add a new field at the end of the table, just enter the field information in the first blank row. To insert a field within the table, click anywhere in the field that you want to follow the new one, and then click the Insert Rows button in the toolbar.

 To delete a field, click anywhere in the field, and then click the Delete Rows button.

To reposition a field, select it and then point to its row selector so the pointer appears like a large white arrow. Then drag the field up or down to its new position.

You can also change the field type and its properties. However, once the table has information in it, changing its type or properties could produce some unwanted results. Some information may be lost, such as characters in a text field that you are changing to a number field. If you are creating or changing a validation rule, Access asks if you want to check the existing information against the rule. If you select Yes, Access reports if it finds information that violates the rule, but it will not delete it. This lets you know that you should review your information and decide if you want to change it to conform to the new rule.

Using Lookup Fields

There may be times when you can only enter specific values in a field. Remember the example we used for a validation rule that limited entries to USPS, UPS, or FEDEX? Rather than trust your user to remember what to enter, create a lookup field. A *lookup field* displays the possible choices, so all you have to do is click the correct one. The list can be from a list that you create just for the field, or it can come from another table in the database.

For example, when creating an invoice, you probably need to insert the client's ID number in the invoice. Rather than remember the ID for every client, use a lookup list. The list can include each client's name and ID number. To insert the proper ID, pull down the list and then click the name of the client placing the order.

When you create or modify a table, add a field whose type matches the corresponding field to be looked up. Use the Number type if the matching field is AutoNumber. Pull down the Data Type list again and click Lookup Wizard to see the first dialog box with the two options as shown here:

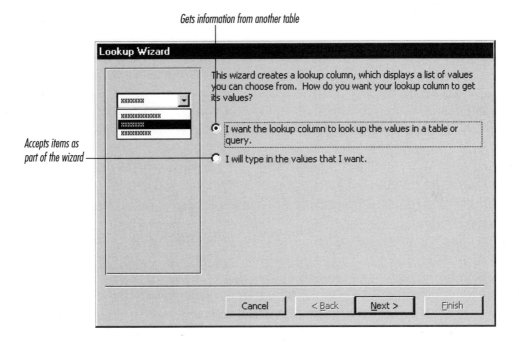

If you select to get the information from a table, the next dialog box lists the other tables in the database. Select the table containing the information you want and then click Next. The third wizard dialog box lets you select the information that you want to be listed in the lookup table.

The pull-down list that appears can contain more than one column. Information from only one column will actually be inserted into the database. For each field you want listed in the table, click it, click the > button, and then select Next. The next dialog box, shown in Figure 23-4, shows how the columns in the lookup list will appear, but the key column will be hidden. Since we want the key to appear so we can choose it when filling out the field, deselect the Hide Key Column check box. As the instructions say in the dialog box, you drag the column header buttons to adjust their width, or double-click the right edge of a column header button to fit it to the heading.

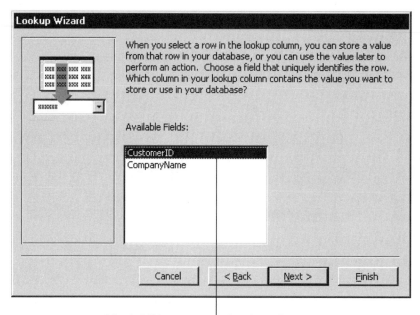

Select the field that you want inserted into the record.

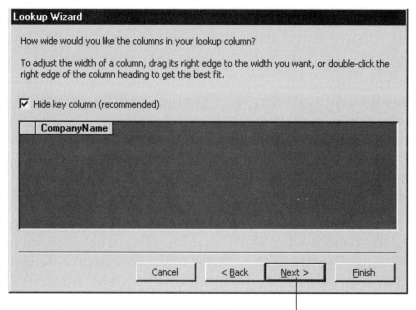

Click Next to see the wizard shown here:

FIGURE 23-4 Select field layout for lookup table

The final dialog box asks for the label you want for the field. The default will be the field name, so let's leave it that way. You can also select to display help information about formatting fields. Just click Finish and then select Yes to save the table and to create the relationship.

Finally, click the Lookup tab to see these options:

General	Lookup
Display Control	Combo Box
Row Source Type	Table/Query
Row Source	SELECT Customers.CustomerID, Custome
Bound Column	1
Column Count	2
Column Heads	No
Column Widths	0";1"
List Rows	8
List Width	1"
Limit To List	Yes

The Lookup Wizard has set these advanced options for you, but the Limit To List property is something you should check out. When this is set at No, you can type an entry into the text box that does not exist in the list. When set at Yes, you can only pick values from the list. If you created the lookup field to prevent errors, choose Yes for this property.

Building Good Relationships

When you create tables, look for candidates for a one-to-many relationship. For example, remember the rule about avoiding repeating fields, such as Hobby1 and Hobby2. If you want to store multiple sets of information like that, use two tables. One table has all the member's general information. The other table contains his or her hobbies. The two tables are related because they both refer to the member's ID number.

Without a relationship, you could delete a member from one table but forget to delete their hobbies from the other table. When you relate the tables, deleting the member automatically deletes their hobbies as well.

Open the database and then click the Relationships button in the toolbar. If you already have the database open, you'll have to return to the Database window to access the Relationships button. Access opens the Relationships window, which displays any currently related tables with a line between them.

N O T E : If the line doesn't indicate the correct relationship, double-click the line to define the relationship, as you'll soon learn.

If the tables you want to relate don't appear in the Relationships window, click the Show Table button to display this dialog box.

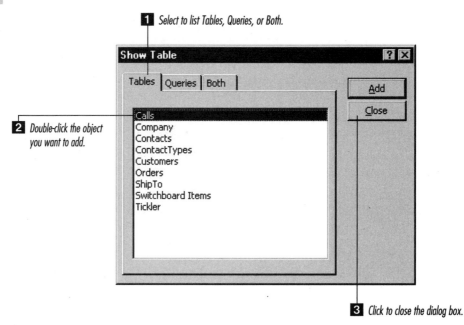

1 *Select to list Tables, Queries, or Both.*

2 *Double-click the object you want to add.*

3 *Click to close the dialog box.*

The tables will appear in the Relationships window as boxes containing lists of fields. To define the relationship, point to the field in the table that will be the "one" side of the relationship, hold down the mouse, and drag to the field in the table that will be the "many" side. When you release the mouse button, a dialog box will appear in which you define the relationship, as shown in Figure 23-5.

The Table\Query list shows the name of the field in the "one" table. The Related Table\Query list shows the name of the field in the "many" table. If either is incorrect, click the field name, pull down the list box, and select the correct field. The two fields can have different names as long as they are the same type and size. The field in the "one" table should be a primary key or a field that is indexed with no duplicates.

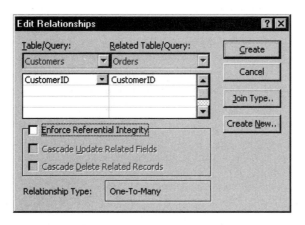

Use this dialog box to confirm the related fields and the type of relationship

 N O T E : In database-speak, the "one" table is called the *parent*, and the "many" table is called the *child*.

Next, click to select the Enforce Referential Integrity option. *Referential integrity* is what really gives the relationship its power, making sure you cannot have a "many" record that does not match a "one" record. This also lets you select the other check boxes:

- **Cascade Update Related Fields**   This will update the records in the "many" table when you change a linked field in the "one" table.
- **Cascade Delete Related Record**   This will delete records in the "many" table when you delete the matching record in the "one" table.

Now click OK. The Relationships window appears with the one-to-many relationship shown as a line from one field to the other:

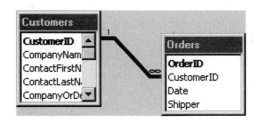

The "1" next to one table indicates the "one" side of the relationship; the infinity symbol shows the "many" side.

Here are some other ways to work with relationships:

- To delete a relationship, click the middle of the relationship line between tables and press DEL.
- To edit a relationship, double-click the middle of the relationship line to display the Relationships dialog box. Then make your edits.
- To hide a table from the Relationships display, click it and press DEL. The table will no longer appear in the window, but its relationships are unaffected.
- To redisplay all relationships in the database, click the Show All Relationships button.
- To see if a table has any hidden relationships, click it and click the Show Direct Relationships button.

- Creating a table in Design view requires the most work, but gives you the most flexibility. For maximum efficiency, however, see if there is a similar table available in the Table Wizard. Create it using the wizard, and then make any modifications to the table in Design view.

- If in doubt about which field type to select when creating a table in Design view, use the obvious—Text when you don't need to do math with the field, Number or Currency when you do, and Date/Time when you need a date or time.

- For phone numbers, dates, ZIP codes, and other common type entries, use the Input Mask Wizard rather then creating the mask yourself. Click in the Input Mask property text box, and then click the Build button on its right to begin the wizard.

- A primary key is not absolutely necessary, but you will need it if you plan to create relationships between tables. A primary key also helps keep records in order and prevents duplicate information such as an account number in a critical column.

- When designating the primary key field, make absolutely certain the contents of the field will be unique for every record.

- If you designate a new primary key when modifying a table in Design view, Access will not be able to save the changes if any duplicates exist in the new primary key field. You'll have to remove the primary key, return to the table, and correct the duplicated information before changing the primary key.

- Use =Date( ) in the Default Value property of a Date/Time field when creating or modifying a table in Design view if you want Access to insert the current date for you automatically.

- When creating a Number type field, you can select Replication ID as the Field Size property. The Replication ID is used for primary key fields with tables in briefcases. A briefcase lets you synchronize files to maintain up-to-date copies (replicas) between computers, such as your desktop and laptop.

- Use Datasheet view to create a table only when it contains a few fields or when you need to enter information quickly. You can later modify the table to change field types or properties, or to add other fields as needed.
- When creating a table in Design view, you have to balance the need to save disk space with the importance of including all necessary fields. Adding a field is usually not a problem, but changing a field or dividing it into several fields can be cumbersome. You may initially think, for example, that you can store a person's full name in one field, or use a single field for the city, state, and ZIP code components of an address. If you later decide you need a separate field for each component, you'll have to reenter a great deal of information. When in doubt, divide the information into multiple fields. You can also display the fields together by combining them on a form or report, but the structure will exist to work with them individually.

Finding Information 24

Putting information into your database is just the first step in database management. Retrieving information that you need from the database is equally important. You can scan your database in a table or form, and you can look at the information in a report. But scanning a database record-by-record, or page-by-page, is time-consuming. Fortunately, Access gives you several ways to quickly retrieve just the information you need—by using the Find command, creating filters, and building queries.

Searching Records

Access lets you easily locate information in a table, just as Word and Excel let you locate information in a document or worksheet. In fact, the techniques are similar.

If you know which field contains the information, start by placing the insertion point in that field—in any record in either the datasheet or the form. If you don't know which field it's in—or don't care—the insertion point can be in any field. Then click the Find button in the Standard toolbar to see this dialog box:

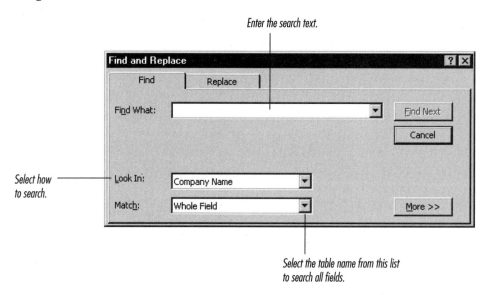

Enter the search text.

Select how to search.

Select the table name from this list to search all fields.

The Match option determines where in the field the text must be. Your choices are Any Part Of Field, Whole Field, and Start Of Field. When Match is set at Whole Field, Access only locates a record if the entire field is the same as the Find What entry. If you select Any Part Of Field, Access will locate records that contain the Find What characters anywhere in the field. If you select Start Of Field, Access will locate records that contain the Find What characters at the beginning of the field only.

Click the More button to access these additional options:

- **Search**   This lets you choose to scan *Up* through records from the current one to the first, *Down* through records from the current one to the end of the table, or *All* through all the records.
- **Match Case**   This means that the field must match the exact capitalization of the Find What text.

- **Search Fields As Formatted**   This means you must type the information as it appears onscreen to locate it. When information is entered by use of an input mask, it is stored in the database without the mask characters and spacing. It only appears formatted by the mask onscreen.

When you've specified what you want to find, and how to search the database, click the Find Next button to locate the first occurrence of the text, if any. Continue to click Find Next to locate each occurrence.

Filtering Records

While sorting changes the order in which records are displayed, scrolling through the table will still display all the records. Often, however, you'll be interested in only certain records—such as clients who owe you a lot of money, or customers who have not ordered this year. To display specific records, apply a filter. The filter hides records that you are not interested in seeing, without removing them from the table.

There are three ways to filter records—by selection, by form, and by use of an advanced filter.

Filter by Selection

In Filter By Selection, you select a field already containing the information you want to use for the condition. For example, if you want to display contacts in Washington, click any of the State fields with a "Washington" contact. Once you've selected the field, click the Filter By Selection button.

Now, only records containing the same information as in the selected field will appear—in this case records for "Washington" contacts. The record counter will show the number of records that meet the criteria, and it will remind you that you are looking at a filtered view of the table, as in:

If you now select another field for the filter, only those records from the already filtered table will be considered. This way, you can filter on the contents of more than one field—one field at a time.

To apply a new filter to the entire table, you must first remove the current filter. In the toolbar, you'll see this button pressed down:

Pressed, it is called Remove Filter; not pressed, it is called Apply Filter. Click that button or choose Records | Remove Filter/Sort to remove the filter and display all the records.

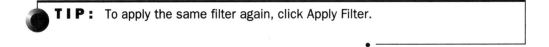

T I P : To apply the same filter again, click Apply Filter.

Using Filter For

One limitation of using the Filter By Selection button is that you must first find one record with the information you want to use for the filter. If you are looking for a contact in Margate, for instance, you first must find one such record. One way to avoid manually searching the database for a field that contains the information is to use the Filter For feature. Here's how:

1. Right-click the field that will contain the information you want to use for the filter. It does not have to contain the information you want to filter on. For example, if you want to locate contacts with the last name of Smith, right-click the Last Name field of any record.

2. In the shortcut menu, click the Filter For option. This places the insertion point in the option's text box, as shown here:

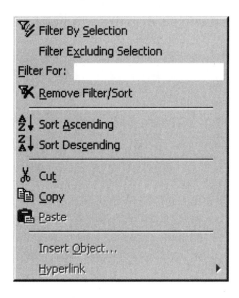

3. Type the text you want to use for the filter, and then press ENTER to apply the filter.

Filter By Form

If you want to filter a table by more than one criterion, the best way is to use Filter By Form. When you filter by form, Access displays a blank datasheet or form, depending on how you are currently viewing the table. You enter the information you want to filter by, in as many fields as needed. In fact, each field on the datasheet or form includes a list containing all the values in the field. So rather than type the information you are looking for, you can select it from the field lists.

 NOTE: The form will already contain any conditions you last used for a filter. If you just filtered the records in New Jersey, for example, "NJ" will appear in the State field.

 To start the process, click the Filter By Form button. If you are viewing a table as a datasheet, a window appears as in Figure 24-1. If you are looking at a form, a blank form appears.

When you enter information in more than one field, Access treats this as an And operation. This means that the record must match all the conditions in the form. To add an Or condition, click the Or tab at the bottom of the form. A blank datasheet or form appears—and another dimmed Or button. Enter the information for the other criteria, and then click Apply Filter.

 TIP: You can have more than one Or condition. Just click the dimmed Or button to display another form.

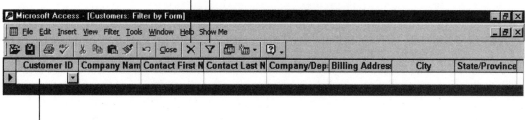

Click the Clear Grid button to remove filter criteria.

2 *Click the Apply Filter button.*

1 *Enter information you are looking for, or select it from the pull-down list.*

FIGURE 24-1 Filtering by form

Advanced Filters

The Advanced Filter/Sort command lets you filter and sort in one operation, on more than one field at a time, and using a wide range of criteria to select records. You can use the Advanced Filter/Sort command when either a datasheet or form is displayed; however, you'll notice the results more immediately in a datasheet.

With either a datasheet or form displayed, choose Records | Filter, and then click Advanced Filter/Sort to see the grid, shown in Figure 24-2. You use the

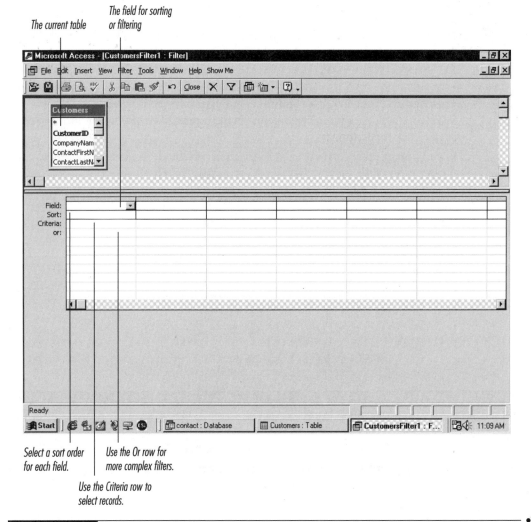

FIGURE 24-2   Advanced Filter/Sort grid

grid to determine the fields and criteria that you want to use for the filter. The table box will contain all the fields from whatever table is being used, even if not all the fields appear in the form being displayed.

You have to insert each field that you want to use for a filter or sort into the Field row of the grid. To do so, double-click the field in the table box, or drag it to the next empty cell in the Field row, or click in the next empty cell and then select the field from the drop-down list that appears. In this example, we can filter or sort on the CompanyName and Product fields.

Field:	CompanyName	Product
Sort:		
Criteria:		
or:		

> **N O T E :** To remove a field from the grid, click the gray bar above the field name and press DEL.

The next step is to specify criteria. Click in the Criteria row for a field that you want to use to select records, and enter a criterion. In this example, the criterion *coffee* will display records that contain the word "coffee" in the product field—Access enters the word "Like" and the quotation marks when you press ENTER:

Field:	CompanyName	Product
Sort:		
Criteria:		Like "*coffee*"
or:		

To sort on a field, click the Sort cell for the field, pull down the list that appears, and choose Ascending, Descending, or [not sorted]. In this example, we're sorting by the CompanyName in Ascending order, and by the Product in Descending order, as shown here:

Field:	CompanyName	Product
Sort:	Ascending	Descending
Criteria:		
or:		

Access treats criteria in more than one field—in the Criteria row of the grid—as an And operation. You can create Or conditions in a field or across fields using the Or row in the grid.

Finally, click the Apply Filter button.

NOTE: To return from the filtered datasheet to the grid, pull down the Window menu and choose the filter. It will be listed as "*Calls*Filter1: Filter," referencing the table name.

Applying a filter to a table—by selection, by form, or advanced—is treated as a change to the table layout. When you close the table, a dialog box will appear asking if you want to save the changes. If you choose to save the changes, the filter will be saved and you can reapply it when you next open the table.

Getting Answers with Queries

"Who hasn't paid their bill in over 30 days?" is a question you may ask your accountant. Each time you ask the question, you may get a different answer, depending on the status of your receivables at the time.

A *query* is a question you ask to find information in the table. In Access, you'd form the preceding question as a query that means "show me the names of clients who have unpaid invoices dated over 30 days ago." You can then save the query, not the results of what it displays, so you can run the query anytime to get the latest results. You can also perform calculations on fields and summarize information in groups.

Unlike a filter, which shows all the fields in the matching records, the results of a query show only the fields that you want to see. The query is still a datasheet of the table, however, so any changes you make to the information in the result set are actually made to the table. In fact, once you create a query, you can use it in any place where you can use a table, such as to create a form, report, or another query.

There are several ways to create a query. Using the Simple Query Wizard, you follow a series of dialog boxes to specify the fields you want to use and the type of results you want. You can also create a query in Design view, which lets you create a query manually.

Quick Queries with the Simple Query Wizard

Use the Simple Query Wizard when you want to display selected fields and summarize information in the fields, but not use criteria to select records. By summarizing information, for example, you could display the total of all orders for each client, or the averages of each student's test results.

To start the wizard, click the Queries tab of the Database window and double-click Create Query By Using Wizard. You can also click New, choose Simple Query Wizard in the New Query dialog box, and then click OK. The first wizard dialog box lets you select fields from one or more tables, as shown in Figure 24-3.

1. Select the table containing the fields.
2. Double-click an available field to add it to the query.
3. Repeat the process until all desired fields are entered.

In Figure 24-3, for instance, we've chosen the CustomerID and CompanyName fields from the Customers table, and the OrderID, Date, Shipper, and Total fields from the Orders table.

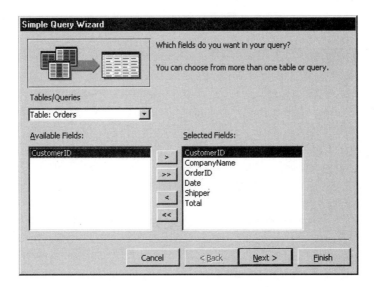

FIGURE 24-3 Simple Query Wizard

After you select the fields and click Next, Access displays a dialog box for you to choose how you want to display the records, as shown in Figure 24-4. This dialog box appears, by the way, only if you selected at least one numeric or currency field.

If you select to see all the details, the result set will list a row for each record. If you're interested in just the summary, select the Summary option and then choose the Summary Options button so you can specify how you want the information analyzed. Note that you cannot select the Summary Options button without first choosing to summarize the data.

 NOTE: If you include a date field in the query, a wizard dialog box appears asking how you want to group the dates. Options are Unique date/time, Day, Month, Quarter, and Year.

If you choose Summary Options, a dialog box appears listing the numeric and currency fields in the query and the options Sum, Avg, Min, and Max for each field. You can also choose to count the number of items for each record. To calculate the average of student grades, for example, click Avg. Click OK to return to the wizard dialog box.

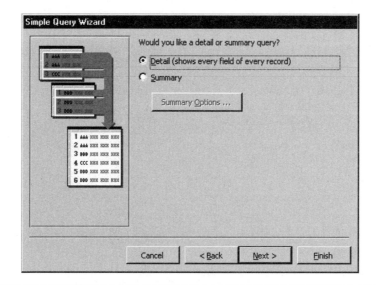

FIGURE 24-4 Choose if you want to see the details of the records or just to summarize their data

Click Next. In the final wizard dialog box, enter a name for the query. Click Finish to see the results of the query. When you're done looking at the results, close the query window. You do not have to save the query, because the wizard automatically saves it for you.

Selecting Records with Queries

In the Simple Query Wizard dialog boxes you can choose fields and perform mathematical operations, but you can't enter criteria as you can in a filter. What if, for example, you don't want to list every student in the result set, just those taking a certain course, or only those with failing averages?

Rather than use the Simple Query Wizard, create the query in Design view. To do this, double-click Create Query In Design View on the Queries page of the Database window. You can also click New, choose Design View in the New Query dialog box, and then click OK. Access displays the query window with the Show Table dialog box, as in Figure 24-5.

Double-click each table you want to use in the query, or select a table and click Add. As you add a table, it appears in the query behind the Show Table dialog box.

To use information from more than one table, make sure the tables are related. When they are related, you'll see the relationship line drawn between them in the query, connecting the linked fields.

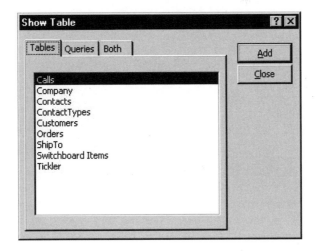

FIGURE 24-5   Selecting tables for a query

> **NOTE:** If there is no direct link between these two tables, you may need to insert another table that connects them.

When you've added the tables, close the Add Table dialog box to display the query window, which looks much like the Advanced Filter/Sort grid, as shown in Figure 24-6.

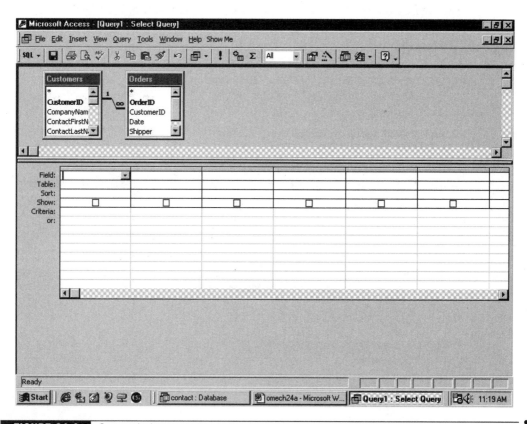

FIGURE 24-6 Query window

> **T I P :** To add a table once you've closed the Show Table dialog box, click the Show Table button in the toolbar. Double-click the tables you want to add, and then close the Show Table dialog box.

Your next step is to add the fields that you want to use for the query. To add a field to the grid, double-click it or drag it to the first blank column in the Field row. The Table row shows the table where the field information is coming from. To delete a field from the query, click the gray bar above its field name in the grid and then press DEL.

> **T I P :** You can drag columns to change their order in the query, but it's faster just to insert them in the order in which you want them listed.

You can also sort the result set in a way that makes the information more useful. To make it easier to find a specific customer, for example, click in the Sort row of the ContactLastName field, pull down the list, and select Ascending. Your other options are Descending and [not sorted].

Finally, add criteria to select records. Criteria work the same way in queries as they do in filters.

From Design view, you display the result set by clicking on either the View or Run buttons. Click View again to return to Design view. You can always click View to toggle back and forth between the Design and Datasheet views.

View

Run

Using All Fields

If you want to use all, or a majority, of the fields in a query, you don't have to bother with moving them individually. To add all the fields to the grid, double-click the table name at the top of the field list box to select all fields, and then drag the selection to the Field row. All the fields will be inserted, one per column. You can then select a sort order and set criteria in as many fields as needed.

You can also include all the fields by dragging the asterisk from the top of the field list into the grid. In this case, the individual fields do not appear in the table; just the name of the table and an asterisk appear in one of the columns. When you run the query, however, all the fields appear in the result set.

You cannot designate a sort or criterion for the column using an asterisk, because the asterisk does not represent any individual field. There's a quick solution. In addition to the asterisk, drag any individual field that you want to use for a sort order or criterion, and then make your selections or entries for it. Deselect its Show box so the field will not appear twice in the result set (once from the asterisk and again from the individual column). For example, here is a query that displays all the fields from the Customers table but only customers in France:

Field:	Customers.*	Country
Table:	Customers	Customers
Sort:		
Show:	☑	☐
Criteria:		"France"
or:		

Entering specific criteria into a query really limits it. If you change your mind and decide to list students taking some other course, for example, you can't just run the same query—it will always show students in the course you added to the criteria. To design a more general-purpose query, you enter a parameter. A parameter lets you specify the criteria each time you run the query.

Rather than type specific information in the Criteria area, enter a prompt in brackets, such as [Enter the country], as shown here:

Field:	Customers.*	Country
Table:	Customers	Customers
Sort:		
Show:	☑	☐
Criteria:		[Enter the country]
or:		

When you run the query, Access displays a dialog box prompting you for the information:

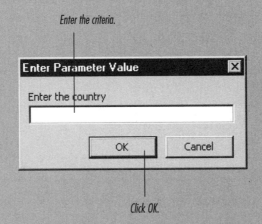

Enter the criteria.

Click OK.

Saving, Running, and Changing a Query

If you want to be able to run the same query later, click the Save button in the Standard toolbar, enter a name for the query, and then click OK. You can then close the query and run it later to display the most up-to-date results.

If you need to modify the query, select it in the Queries page and then click Design.

As with a form or report, you can open a saved query at any time. Opening a query runs the query, showing the selected records in a result set. To run a query, just double-click its name in the Queries page of the Database window.

- The Replace command on the Edit menu, and the Replace tab in the Find And Replace dialog box, work just like the same function in many word processing programs, such as Word and Excel. The only difference is that you can choose to replace text in any field, or in a specific field by placing the insertion point in it first.

- To exclude specific records from the filter, use the Filter Excluding Selection command. Right-click a field containing the information that you want to use to exclude records, and choose Filter Excluding Selection from the shortcut menu that appears.

- When designing an advanced filter, you can also use the wildcard characters * and ?, and enter comparison operators for numeric information.

- When a Filter By Form or Advanced Filter/Sort window is displayed, pull down the File menu and select Save As Query to save the filter specification as a query, or select Load From Query to use the specifications from an existing query in the current filter.

- The Crosstab Query Wizard lets you analyze information in a format resembling a spreadsheet. You select the fields to use for the row and column headings, and the fields to summarize in the body of the "spreadsheet."

- The Find Duplicate Query Wizard lets you find the records that have values in common, including duplicate records.

- The Find Unmatched Query Wizard locates records that have no matching values, such as clients who have not placed an order and therefore do not have a number that is matched in the Orders table.

- The output of a query is a special datasheet called a *result set* because it shows the results of the query, or a *dynaset* because there is a dynamic link between the result set and the underlying table.

- There are sometimes fields that you want to use for sorting or criteria, but which you do not want to actually display in the datasheet. To hide the field, turn off the check box in the Show row under the field name.

- Advanced Access users can create queries that calculate values and perform actions on a table, such as adding, deleting, or changing information.

Creating Forms, Reports, and Data Access Pages

Forms and data pages are great ways to view, enter, and edit information in your database. They're orderly and consistent, they're not intimidating, and they're easy to work with. So when you create your own table, probably one of the first things you'll want to do is to create a form or a data page. There's even one way that takes just two clicks, and you can add eye-catching charts and graphs.

Reports are designed to display information onscreen and in print. Generate a report when you want to see more than one record at a time or to summarize your database information.

Creating Forms

The quickest way to create a form is with AutoForm. You just tell Access what table you want to use and Access does the rest. Here's all you have to do:

1. Click Tables in the Database window.
2. Pull down the New Object button menu.
3. Select AutoForm.

Access creates what's called a *columnar form*, as shown in Figure 25-1. The form contains all the table's fields, and you see one record at a time onscreen. You can start using the form immediately, but you'll have to save the form before you close it. Click the Save toolbar button, type the form name, and then click OK.

N O T E: If the table used for the form has a one-to-many relationship with another table, AutoForm creates a two-part form with fields and data from both tables.

You can also use AutoForm to create a *tabular form*, which shows records in rows and columns. Click Forms in the Database window, and then click New to display this dialog box:

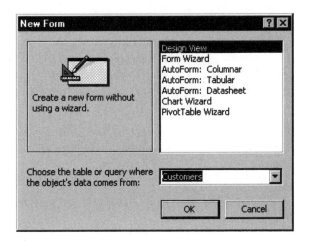

1. Pull down the list and select the table or query.
2. Choose the form style.
3. Click OK.

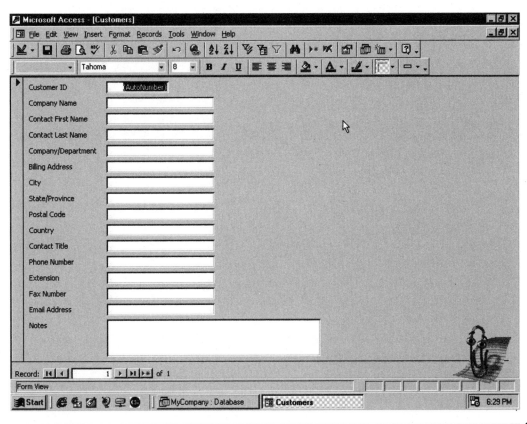

FIGURE 25-1 A columnar form lists all the fields down the screen.

In a tabular form, the fields appear across the screen like columns, so you can see more than one record at a time—although you may have to scroll left and right to see all the fields. A datasheet form looks like a tabular form with one record per page.

Using Form Wizard

AutoForm adds all the fields to a form, and you don't have the chance to mix fields from related tables. Sometimes you'll want a form that contains just selected fields, or to be able to review, edit, or enter information in multiple tables with one form. With Form Wizard you can pick which fields to use, and combine fields from related tables that have a one-to-many relationship, with referential integrity enforced.

Select New on the Forms page of the Database window, click Form Wizard, and then click OK. The first wizard dialog box (see Figure 25-2) asks you to choose the fields that you want in the form. Pull down the Tables/Queries list,

Pull down the list and select a table.

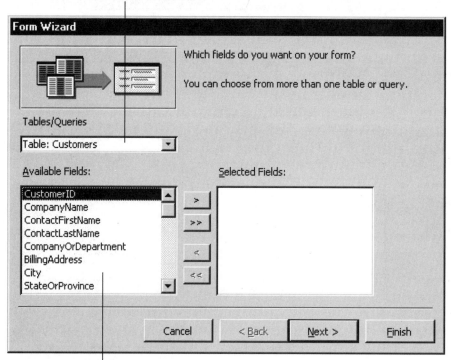

Add fields from the table to the form.

FIGURE 25-2 Choose fields for your custom form

and choose the table or query to use for the form. Then select and add fields using the > button.

To create a form using multiple tables, pull down the Tables/Queries list and select the "one" table in a one-to-many relationship. Then add the fields that you want from the table to the form. Pull down the Tables/Queries list and select the next table, the "many" side of the relationship, and add fields from it. You can repeat the process for any other tables that have one-to-many relationships. In our example, we'll use three tables:

- **Customers**   This table contains name and address information for our company's customers.
- **Orders**   This table contains information about each customer's orders.
- **Order Details**   This table contains the details of each order, one item per record.

Click Next to select how you want to view the form, as in Figure 25-3.

 N O T E : The process is similar if you are creating a form from a single table, but with fewer options and wizard dialog boxes.

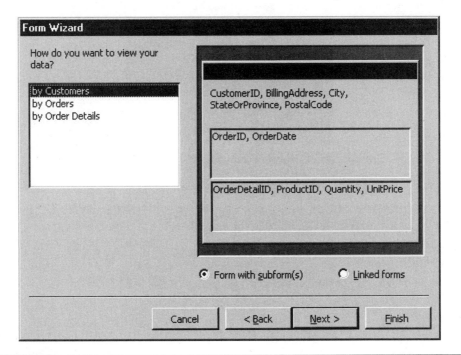

FIGURE 25-3   Choosing layout options

The suggested layout will depend on the relationships that you've created between the tables. In Figure 25-3, the form will be divided into three distinct areas, as shown in the preview panel on the right. There'll be a separate area for the fields from each of the three tables—three separate (but related) forms on the same page. You can also decide to have fewer sections or distinct form areas. If you want to combine the first two tables into one section, for example, click By Orders. There would then be just two sections—the fields from both Customers and Orders are in one section, the fields from Order Details are in the other. We don't want to do that now, so leave the selection on By Customers.

You can also select to have *subforms* or linked forms. With subforms, all the forms appear onscreen. If you select linked forms, then a button appears rather than the subforms—just click the button when you want the subform information to appear.

Click Next. You now must choose a look for each subform, either tabular or datasheet. Clicking on an option will show how it appears in the preview area. The main form is always columnar.

Click Next. The dialog box appears for you to select a style. Choose a style and then click Next. You can now name the form and each of the subforms. When you open the main form, all the subforms appear as well. The subforms will also appear listed separately in the Database window. You can choose to open the form in Form view or Design view, and to show help information. Type a form name and then click Finish to see the form. Figure 25-4 shows a sample form from three tables.

There are actually three forms displayed, each representing one of three tables. Also notice that there are three sets of navigation buttons. Each set controls one form, and thus the records in one table.

The buttons at the very bottom of the form control the main form—the records from the Customers table. As you select another customer, the customer information appears in the top of the form, and the orders appear in the Orders section. The details of the selected order appear in the Order Details section.

To see the details of another order, select it in the Orders section. To see the order for another customer, change to that customer record.

To add a new record, you first have to decide which table you want to add it to, and then choose one of the following:

- To add another customer, for example, click the Add Record button at the bottom of the form. You can also click in any of the fields from the Customers table and then use the New Record toolbar button.

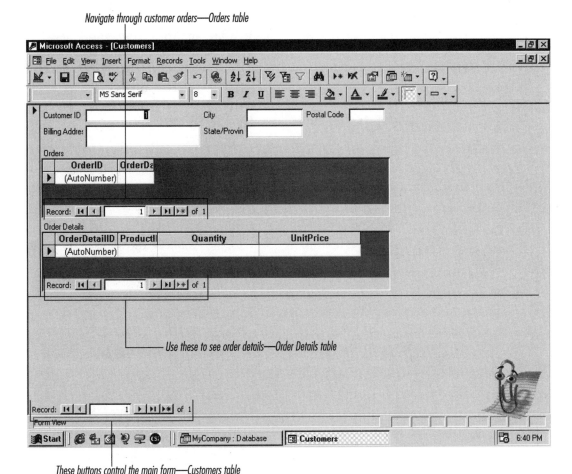

Navigate through customer orders—Orders table

Use these to see order details—Order Details table

These buttons control the main form—Customers table

FIGURE 25-4 Completed form from three tables

- To add an order, first display the customer who is placing the order, and then click the New Record button in the Order subform (or click an Order field and use the New Record toolbar button).
- To add details, make sure the focus is on the correct order as shown in the Orders section, and then click the New Record button in the Order Details section.

Use the same procedure to display or change information. Work your way from selecting the proper customer, to the order, and then to the order details. Because we did not include all the fields in the form, you will only be able to see, edit, or add partial records.

Emphasizing Information in Charts

Chart Wizard is similar to Form Wizard. You select which fields you want to include and how you want the form to appear. The difference is that Chart Wizard presents your data in a graph. Chart Wizard produces a chart that you can customize in Design view. The capabilities are much like those available in Word and Excel.

In the New Form dialog box, click New, and then click Chart Wizard. Pull down the table list at the bottom of the dialog box, choose the table to use, and click OK to see the wizard dialog box where you select fields. Add the fields that you want to chart and then click Next. You now select the type of chart and click Next. In the next dialog box, shown in Figure 25-5, you designate how you want to chart the information.

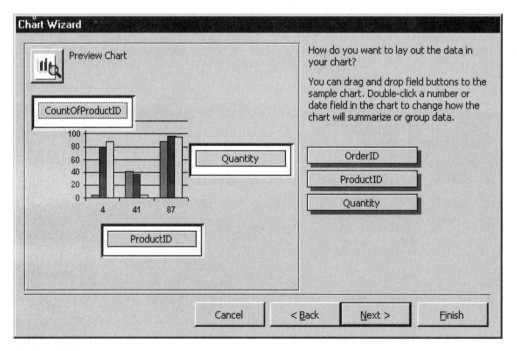

FIGURE 25-5 Designate the fields to chart and their placement

The fields that you've selected will be listed on the right. Access tries to guess how you want to create the chart, and will select an X-axis and Y-axis field for you. If the organization is incorrect:

Drag the field that contains the information you want to plot from the right side of the Chart Wizard to the Y-axis box, the one that contains CountOfProductID in Figure 25-5.

Drag the field to use for the X-axis to the box below the X-axis.

Drag the field for the series to the box on the right of the chart, the one labeled Quantity in Figure 25-5.

The notation "CountOfProductID" in the Y-axis box means that Access will summarize the data by the number of records. To change how the information is summarized, double-click the Y-axis box and choose another operation.

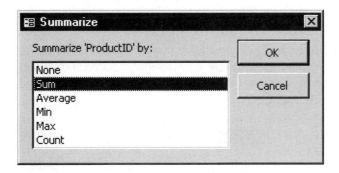

NOTE: As you move and adjust fields, the sample chart will change to reflect the new settings. However, the chart is just a rough sample of what will be created, not an exact copy.

Now click Next. In the next wizard dialog box, you enter a title for the chart and select whether you want to include a legend. You can also choose to display the chart or modify it. Type a title for the form, and then select Finish to see the completed chart. Click Save, type a form name, and then click OK.

Creating Reports

Forms are designed to be viewed onscreen. Reports are designed to be printed. You create reports just as you do forms. The only difference is that you use the AutoReport or Report options from the New Object list or select New from the Reports page of the Database window.

As with a form and a datasheet, the information you see when you open a report depends on what's in the table. Once you create a report, it will always show you the current contents of the underlying table. You only have to create a new report when you want a different layout or design.

Creating an Instant Report

To create a report in as few steps as possible, select the table in the Database window, pull down the New Object list in the toolbar, and click AutoReport.

AutoReport creates the columnar report (see Figure 25-6), showing all the record's fields in columns down the page. The report is rather sparse, with no heading, date, or page number, but it does show the contents of the table. Access will place one record after the next, but it will not divide a record between pages. If a record has more fields than can fit on one page, however, it will divide them between pages and start each record on a new page.

While the report you just created was rather plain looking, you can create better-looking AutoReports as well. Select New on the Reports page of the Database window (or choose Report from the New Object toolbar button) to see this dialog box:

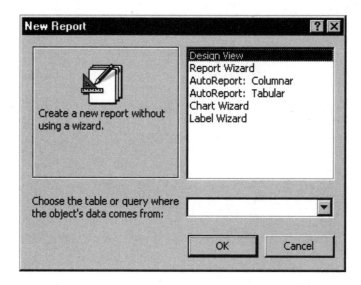

You have two AutoReport options: Columnar and Tabular. Select the type of report, and then follow the dialog boxes to design the report as you learned for

Fields are listed in a column down the page

Sparse—no heading, date, or page number

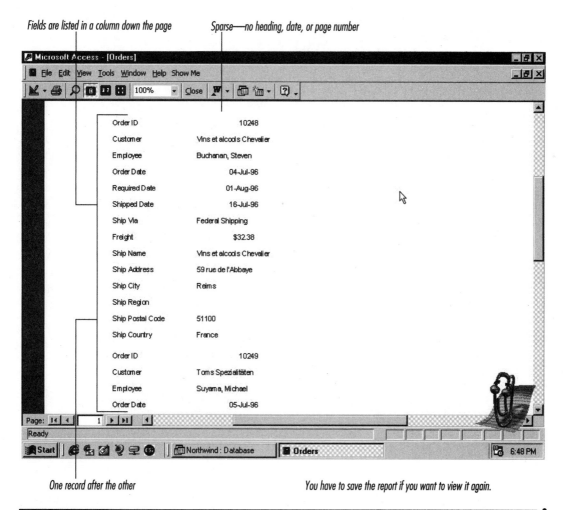

One record after the other

You have to save the report if you want to view it again.

FIGURE 25-6 Columnar report created by AutoReport

forms. In the report, the table name appears as the report heading, and the date and page number, along with the total number of pages, appear at the bottom of each page. In a tabular report, the fields are listed across the top of the page, like column headings. The report will print in landscape orientation, and Access will try to print as many fields on a page as possible, even clipping some of the field names. Extra columns will print on another page.

Using Report Wizard

If you want more control over the design of your report without getting bogged down in report design, use Report Wizard. Like Form Wizard, it lets you select fields and style options, and you can even create reports with fields from related tables.

 N O T E : Chart Wizard works exactly the same for reports as it does for forms.

To start the wizard, click Reports in the Database window, and then double-click Create Report By Using Wizard. In the first wizard dialog box, you select the fields that you want to add to the report, including fields from related tables. If you select fields from multiple tables, the next Report Wizard dialog box lets you choose their grouped arrangement, which is the same as grouping fields for forms and subforms. If you recall, this lets you select if you want the fields from each table listed separately or grouped together.

The next dialog box lets you choose if you want to organize the information by any other groups. When you do not group by a field, the records appear one after the other. Grouping by a field lets you divide the report into sections—not by tables but by the values in the selected field. You can group on more than one field. It all depends on how you want to view the records. In addition to selecting the fields for grouping, you can also select grouping options. By default, dates are grouped by month; for all other fields each unique field value is another group—each CustomerID, each Last Name, and so on. This is called *normal grouping*. Grouping lets you change what is considered a group.

With a date field, for example, you can also select to group by year, quarter, day, or some other interval. You can also select "normal" to use each unique date. For numeric and currency fields you can select normal, or by 10s, 50s, and so on. Text fields can be grouped normally, by the first letter of each value (for an index-type listing, such as A's, B's, and so on), or by some number of initial characters.

Click Next to see the Report Wizard dialog box that lets you sort on up to four fields. This same box lets you choose summary options, so you can calculate and display the sum, average, minimum, or maximum values for each group. You can also decide to show the details and summary (such as information about each specific order, as well as the count of orders), or summary information only (just the count for each customer), and you can calculate the percentage of the total for each sum. Choose a sort order if you want and then click Next.

Another Report Wizard dialog box lets you choose the layout for the details in the report, including portrait or landscape orientation, and lets you adjust field width so all fields fit on a page. Select a layout and then click Next. In the wizard dialog box, you select the overall style of the report—take your pick and then click Next. You can now enter a report title, and choose if you want it to appear in Print Preview or Design view.

Label Wizard

If you need to print mailing labels from your table, then you'll love Label Wizard. As with all wizards, you select options from a series of dialog boxes. In this case, you select the label format and the arrangement of fields on the label.

For example, to create mailing labels, select New on the Reports page of the Database window and click Label Wizard. Pull down the table list, select the table containing the name and address information, and click OK.

In the first wizard dialog box (see Figure 25-7), you must select a definition that matches the labels you are using. Select the label type (either Sheet Feed or Continuous), choose the Units Of Measure, and then scroll the list to select the specific form. For now, click Next.

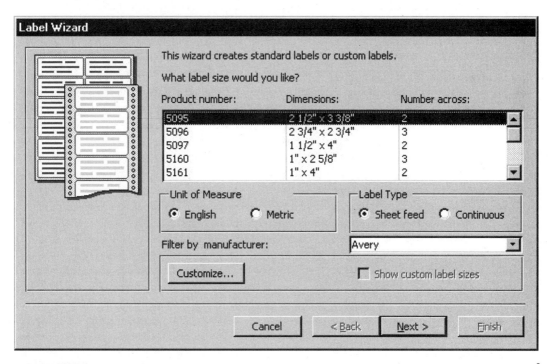

FIGURE 25-7 Choose a predefined label format or create your own

If none of the predefined labels is correct, click Customize. You'll see a dialog box where you can define your own custom label sizes. To create a new size, click the New button in that dialog box. Another box appears where you enter the specifications for your label, including its type and size, the number of labels across the page, and details about the label's spacing on the page and in relation to other labels.

 C A U T I O N : If you select a large font size, your information may not fit on the labels. For standard address labels, stick with something no larger than 12 points.

The next wizard dialog box lets you choose the font, font size, weight, style, and color for the label text. The default is Arial, 8-point, light. To change the font, for example, pull down the Font Name list in the dialog box. Make your choices from the dialog box and then click Next.

Now you must arrange the fields on the label using the dialog box, as shown in Figure 25-8. Since we're creating a mailing label, we want a standard address format. You add a field to the label in much the same way you add fields to forms and reports. Double-click a field in the Available Fields list, or click it once and then click the > button. Access moves the field to the Prototype Label box and surrounds it with braces. Press ENTER in the prototype box to start a new line, and add punctuation or text to appear on the label.

After you move a field to the prototype, the next field in the list is automatically selected. If needed, press the SPACEBAR to insert a space between the fields on the same line. Press ENTER to move to the next line in the prototype. A completed prototype might look like this:

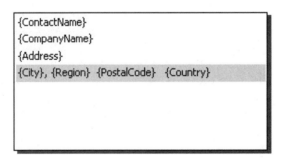

```
{ContactName}
{CompanyName}
{Address}
{City}, {Region} {PostalCode}  {Country}
```

Double-click to add a field to the prototype label.

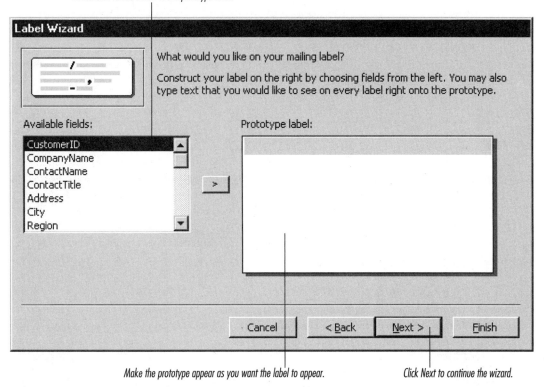

Make the prototype appear as you want the label to appear.   Click Next to continue the wizard.

FIGURE 25-8 Arrange the placement of fields on the label prototype

 N O T E : There is no < button to remove a field from the prototype. To remove a field, click it with the mouse and then press DEL.

Click Next. The next dialog box lets you select one or more fields to sort the labels by. You can use any of the fields in the table, even those not on the label itself. To take advantage of bulk rates, double-click the PostalCode field to add it to the Sort By list, and then click Next.

The final wizard dialog box asks if you want to see the labels in Print Preview or Design view. Leave the option set to the default to see the labels as they will look printed. Type a report name and then click Finish to see the labels, as shown in Figure 25-9.

Choose File | Close to return to the Database window. When you're ready to print labels, just select the report, get your labels ready in the printer, and click the Print button.

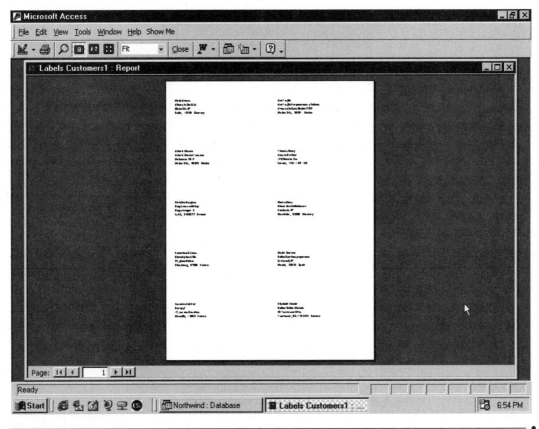

FIGURE 25-9   Labels in Print Preview

Creating Data Access Pages

A data access page is similar to a form, but it can be used to access your database from a web browser as well as within Access itself. A typical data page is shown in Figure 25-10. Like a form, it displays fields in text boxes in which you can view, edit, and add information. At the bottom of the page is a special toolbar containing the familiar navigation, Add Record, and Delete Record buttons as well as buttons to save and undo record changes, sort the table, and create and apply a filter.

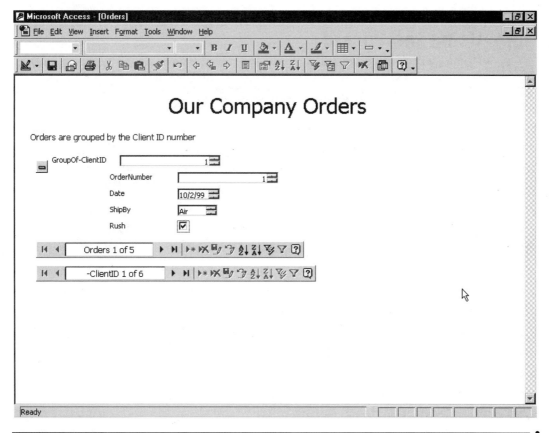

FIGURE 25-10 Data access page

When you open a data access page, you are actually looking at a web page. Right-clicking on the page displays your browser's shortcut menu rather then Access' shortcut menu.

Creating an Instant Page

To create a data page in as few steps as possible, select Tables in the Database window, pull down the New Object list in the toolbar, and click AutoPage. In the New Data Access Page dialog box that appears, type a name for the page and then click OK.

Using the Wizard

Use the wizard to create a data access page when you want more control over its design. To start the wizard, click Pages in the Database window, and then double-click Create Page By Using Wizard. The wizard is similar to the one you use for reports:

Select the fields to include and then click Next.

Select the field you want to group information on and then click Next.

Select up to four fields to use for sorting, and choose whether you want to summarize data, and then click Next.

Type a name for the page, select a theme if you want, and then click Finish.

To view a data access page on your web browser, right-click it in the Database window and choose Web Page Preview from the shortcut menu.

- You can create and modify forms, reports, and data access pages in Design view. Select the item in the Database window, and then click the Design button.
- You can quickly create a form, report, or data access page from any table using the File | Save As command. Select the table in the Database window, and then choose File | Save As. In the dialog box that appears, pull down the As list, select Form, Report, or Data Access Page, and then click OK. Use the same technique to create a report, forms, and data access pages from each other.
- To modify a chart in a form or report, open the form or report in Design view and then double-click the chart. Modify a chart just as you learned for working with charts in Word and Excel.
- Remember, you can use a query wherever you can use a table. Create a form from a query to access the fields and records that meet the query criteria.
- Use the Label Wizard for name badges, shelf labels, and other labeling tasks, in addition to mailing labels.
- The Pivot Table Wizard in the New Form dialog box lets you create a pivot table just as you learned for an Excel worksheet in Chapter 18.
- Use the Edit Web Page That Already Exists option from the Pages folder in the Database window to edit both data access pages and HTML pages from any source.
- When you create a data page, Access actually creates a number of files. There will be an HTML document containing the design of the page, and an ASP file your browser needs to add, edit, and change data on the page. There will also be a folder containing a number of supporting files and graphics. If you want to copy the data access page to your web server or copy it to another disk or folder, you have to copy all these files.
- Use caution when publishing data access pages on the Internet or intranet. Anyone with access to the page can modify your data.
- When you select an option from the list next to the New Object button on the Standard toolbar, that option becomes the new default action for the button itself. To perform the same task again, just click the button.

Microsoft Outlook

26

Microsoft Outlook is a communications and personal management program that offers something for everyone. You can use Outlook to send and receive mail over:

- **An Exchange Server network**   This consists of computers linked together through a network server, using Windows NT and running Microsoft Exchange Server to handle messages and other communications across the network.
- **A peer-to-peer Windows network**   This is made up of computers linked together without a server, using the built-in capabilities of Windows 95 and Windows 98.
- **The Internet**   This involves sending and receiving mail through a dialup Internet account.

You can also use Outlook to maintain your schedule—keeping track of appointments and meetings, the tasks you have to perform, and the people with whom you deal. In fact, you can schedule a meeting with Outlook, automatically check schedules of those you want to attend, and mail invitations all at one time.

Starting Microsoft Outlook

To start Outlook, click the Microsoft Outlook icon on the desktop, or select Start | Programs | Microsoft Outlook. If you are on a computer network, Outlook connects you to your e-mail server, such as Microsoft Exchange.

Outlook knows how to log on to your network, open your Outlook files, and how to send and receive your mail by using your *user profile*. If you have set up only one profile, Outlook automatically uses that profile. If you have several profiles, Outlook may display the Choose Profile dialog box asking you which profile you want to use. Pick the profile and then click OK.

 NOTE: If you do not have a suitable profile, you will be given the chance to create one the first time you start Outlook. You can also create or modify a profile before starting Outlook. See "Developing Your Profile" later in this chapter.

The first time you start Outlook, you may be asked to select a mail service option. Choose Corporate Or Workgroup if you are connected to a network, choose Internet Only if you are not on a network and want to use Outlook for Internet e-mail, or choose No E-Mail if you only want to use Outlook's management features.

To exit Outlook and log off the services you were connected to, choose File | Exit And Log Off. To exit Outlook without logging off from your network or Internet account, select File | Exit or click the Close button on the title bar.

Getting to Know Outlook

When you start Outlook, you'll see the Inbox folder, as shown in Figure 26-1. Outlook organizes your information in folders, so you work with Outlook by opening the folder for the type of item you want to review, create, or edit.

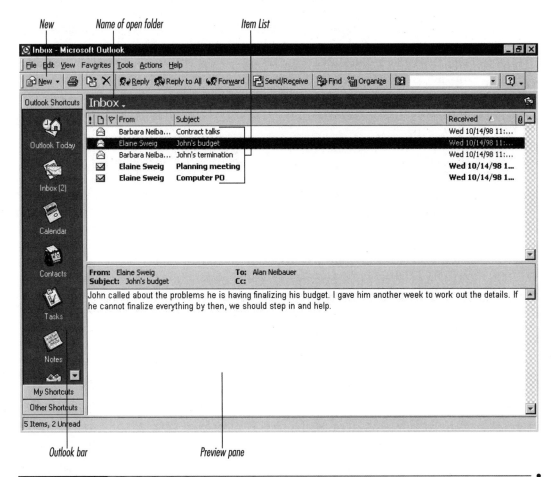

FIGURE 26-1 The Outlook Inbox

T I P : Use the first button on the left of the toolbar to create a new item for that folder. The button is named for the type of item, such as New Message, New Appointment, New Task, New Contact, and New Note. To create an item from any folder, select File | New. Then choose the type of item from the box that appears.

The Outlook Bar

Use the *Outlook bar*, which is located at the far left of the screen, to open folders, which are organized into two or three groups, depending on your setup. The groups, shown as buttons on the bar, are Outlook Shortcuts, My Shortcuts, and Other Shortcuts. The name of the open group is shown at the top of the bar, closed groups at the bottom. To open a group, click its name.

A number in parentheses next to a folder name shows you the number of *unread* messages in the folder, which is not necessarily the total number of items in the folder. To open a folder, just click it in the Outlook bar. A small down arrow at the bottom of the Outlook bar means that the group contains more folders than can be displayed. Click the arrow to scroll these folders into view.

Outlook Shortcuts Group

The Outlook Shortcuts group contains folders for all of Outlook's functions:

- The *Outlook Today* folder displays a summary of your appointments for the day, the number of unread messages in your inbox, and any tasks you have to perform. The Inbox folder contains messages you haven't read and messages you've read and haven't deleted or moved to another folder. Use the folder to read your messages and to send new ones.
- The *Calendar* folder displays a calendar of your appointments and a list of tasks you have recorded. Use the folder to schedule appointments and meetings.
- The *Contacts* folder stores names, street addresses, telephone numbers, e-mail addresses, and other information about people you might need to contact.
- The *Tasks* folder stores the tasks you have to perform and those that you have assigned to others. Use the folder to keep track of your tasks.
- The *Notes* folder contains brief reminders about anything you like.

- The *Deleted Items* folder contains Outlook items you've deleted from other folders. You can retrieve items from this folder as long as you haven't deleted them from this folder.

My Shortcuts Group

The My Shortcuts group contains copies of mail that you've created, in three folders. The *Drafts* folder stores messages that you are not yet ready to send. The *Outbox* folder contains messages you have sent but that have not yet been transferred through the mail system. *The Sent Items* folder contains copies of messages that have been mailed.

This group also includes the *Journal* folder. The Journal folder contains a record of your incoming and outgoing mail, tasks that you have created, phone calls that you initiated from Outlook, and documents you created using other Microsoft Office programs.

The My Shortcuts group also contains the Outlook Update shortcut to the Microsoft Outlook web site. Click the shortcut to launch your web browser.

Other Shortcuts Group

The folders in the Other Shortcuts group depend on how you set up Outlook. Typically, they represent folders on your hard disk or on the computer network:

- The *My Computer* folder is the same as the My Computer icon on the Windows desktop.
- The *My Documents* folder is the same as the My Documents folder (if you have one) on your disk.
- The *Favorites* folder is just like the Favorites folder on your disk, which stores links to sites on the Internet or to other folders or files.
- The *Personal* folder contains a copy of your information that's stored on the network server for use when you work by remote mail.
- *Public Folders* are stored on the Microsoft Exchange Server and can be shared by all workstations.

Displaying the Folder List

While the Outlook bar is handy, you might be more comfortable opening folders if they are displayed hierarchically, as they are in Windows Explorer.

To display folders that way, open the *Folder List* by choosing View | Folder List. (Use the same command to remove the list.) The Folder List appears like this:

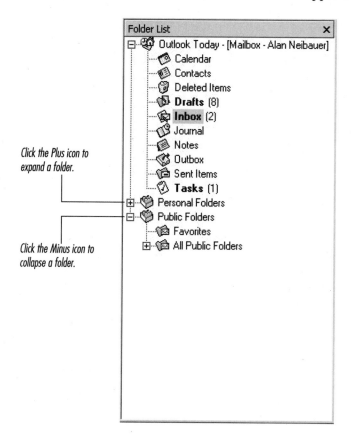

Click the Plus icon to expand a folder.

Click the Minus icon to collapse a folder.

If you want to display the list to select a folder without leaving the list on the screen, click the name of the open folder above the item list. The Folder List will appear, but will be removed as soon as you select a folder or click elsewhere in the window.

Changing Views

Each Outlook folder displays information in a certain way, which Outlook calls the *view*. Contacts, for example, are shown in Address Card view, with a sample of information from each contact's window. Other folders display items in rows and columns, like the way information appears in a worksheet.

To change the way the information in a folder is displayed, select View | Current View and choose from the options that appear. Some of the options may be common to most, if not all, of the folders. Other views are unique. When you choose a view of a group's information, such as By Category, By Sender, or By Company, information appears organized under group headers, as shown in Figure 26-2.

The Organize Pane

You can access some shortcuts and special features for working with folders by displaying the Organize pane. While the options on the pane vary with the folder, you always display it by clicking on the Organize button on the toolbar. The Organize pane for the Inbox folder, for example, is shown in Figure 26-3.

To close the Organize pane, click the Organize button again.

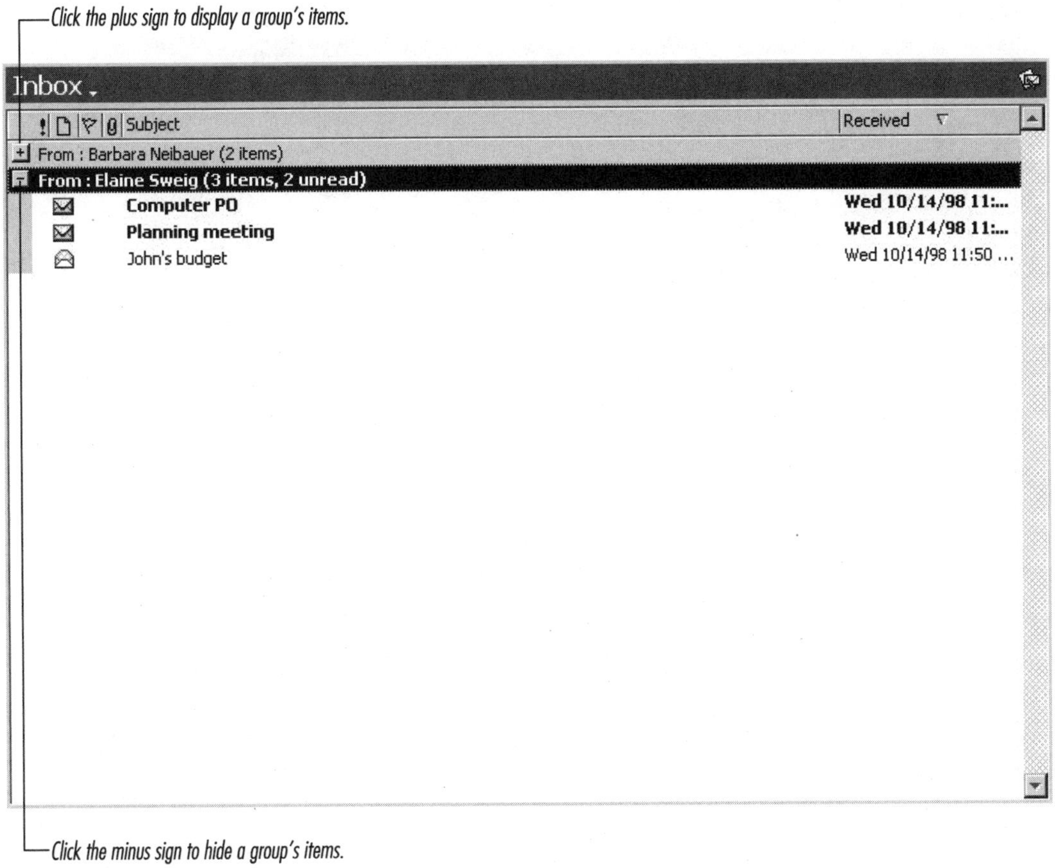

Click the plus sign to display a group's items.

Inbox ▾		
! 🗋 ▽ 🔲 Subject		Received ▽
⊞ From : Barbara Neibauer (2 items)		
⊟ From : Elaine Sweig (3 items, 2 unread)		
✉	**Computer PO**	**Wed 10/14/98 11:...**
✉	**Planning meeting**	**Wed 10/14/98 11:...**
✉	John's budget	Wed 10/14/98 11:50 ...

Click the minus sign to hide a group's items.

FIGURE 26-2 E-mail grouped by senders

Apply color to selected messages.

Move items to other folders.

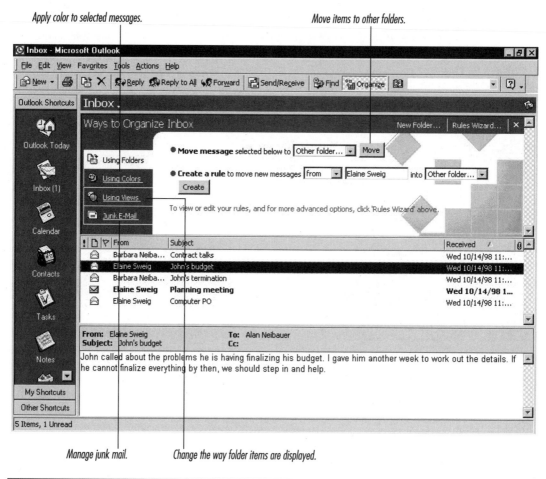

Manage junk mail. Change the way folder items are displayed.

FIGURE 26-3 The Organize pane in the Inbox folder

Organizing Your Contacts

Information about business associates and other VIPs should be stored in the Outlook Contacts folder. Click the Contacts icon to open the folder, as shown in Figure 26-4.

TIP: You can use Actions | New Distribution List to create a *distribution list*, a list of persons to whom you can send mail at one time. See "Distribution Lists" later in this chapter.

Double-click a contact name to review that person's full listing.

Click a tab to scroll to other sections of the listing.

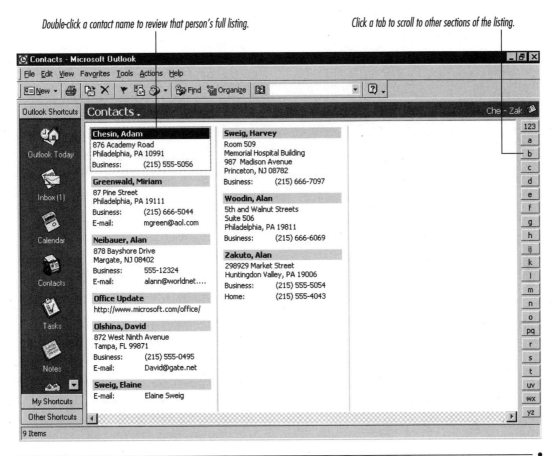

FIGURE 26-4 Contacts folder

To add a new contact, click the New Contact button on the far left of the toolbar. You should then see the Contact window, which is shown in Figure 26-5. You can also double-click an existing client entry in the Contact window to edit or review that client's information. After you complete the information, you have three options:

- Click Save And Close to return to the Contacts folder. To later edit a contact's listing, double-click the contact entry.
- Click Save And New to enter another new contact.
- Choose Actions | New Contact From Same Company to add another contact from the same company.

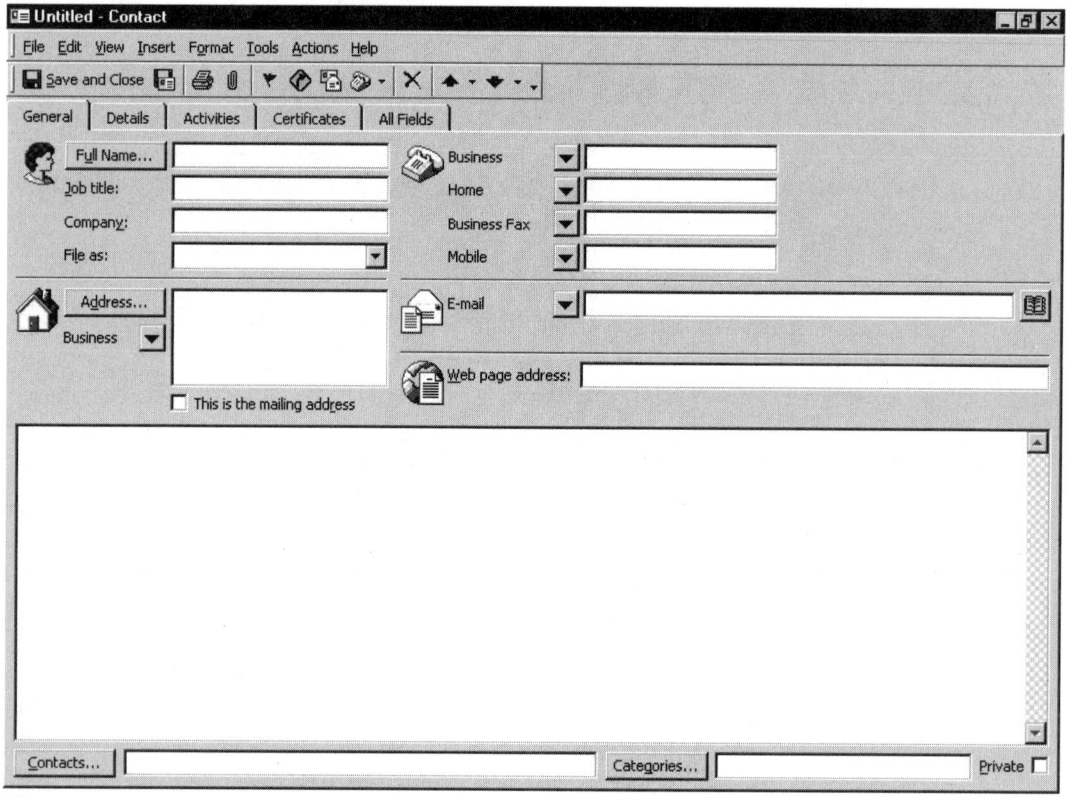

FIGURE 26-5   Contact window

The name you enter in the Full Name box, by the way, is automatically added to the File As box. Outlook uses the File As entry to determine the order of contacts in the folder. If you don't enter the full name, Outlook opens the Check Full Name dialog box so you can complete the name appropriately:

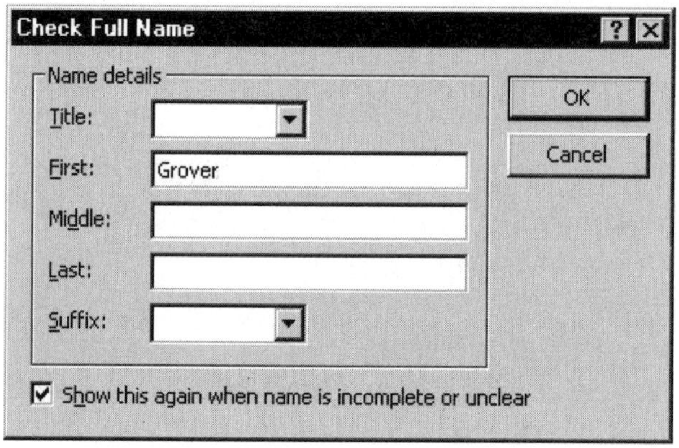

You can enter three different addresses—Home, Business, and Other—and designate one as the mailing address. Pull down the list below the Address button, and select the type of address to enter. Type the address in the text box, pressing ENTER after each line. To enter another type of address, select it from the list and enter it into the text box. Each time you choose an option from the list, the displayed address changes. Designate one of the addresses as the mailing address by selecting it from the list and turning on the This Is The Mailing Address check box. If you don't enter the full address, Outlook displays the Check Address dialog box.

Use a similar technique to enter up to four phone numbers and three e-mail addresses.

Use the large text box in the window to enter a description or notes about the contact, or to store files related to it. For example, you can attach a resume document from Word, or a worksheet containing billing information. To add a file, click on the Insert File button in the toolbar and select a file from the dialog box that appears. (You'll learn more about attaching files in the next chapter.) The files appear as icons in the window. To open an attached file, just double-click the icon.

The Categories button lets you group contacts. To assign a category to a contact, click the Categories button, and then follow these steps in the dialog box that appears:

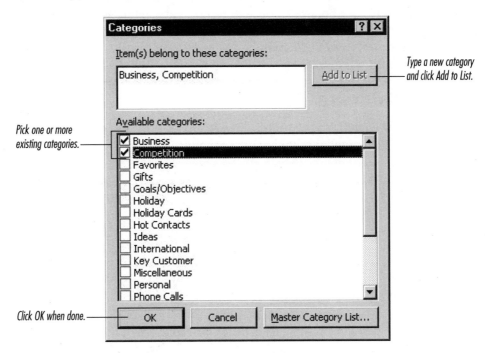

N O T E : Use the Master Category List button to delete and edit categories.

To list your contacts by their category, choose View | Current View | By Category.

When you are on a network, you may give permission to others to work with your Outlook folders. If you do not want others to have access to a particular item, turn on the Private option by selecting the Private check box in the lower right corner of the Contact window.

To send Outlook forms such as task requests and meeting notices over the Internet, enter the e-mail address and then click elsewhere. Then right-click the address and choose Properties from the shortcut menu. In the dialog box that appears, turn on the Always Send To This Recipient In Microsoft Outlook Rich-Text Format check box. This setting ensures that other Outlook users will receive task requests and meeting notices in a format that Outlook can use to update their calendar. The Details tab of the dialog box lets you enter birthday and anniversary dates. The dates will be added to the text box in the General tab as annual events. Double-click to open the calendar item. The Online NetMeeting Settings section lets you define the person's Internet call information for online meetings.

Use the Activities tab to show journal entries, a listing of activities you perform related to the contact. You use the Certificates tab to view the contact's digital IDs you have on file for sending encrypted mail. Use the All Fields tab to display all the contact's information in one location.

Outlook Address Book

For persons neither in your Contacts folder nor on your network, you'll need to add e-mail addresses to the Personal Address Book.

 N O T E : If you do not have a Personal Address Book, see "Developing Your Profile" later in this chapter.

To open Outlook's address book, shown in Figure 26-6, choose Tools | Address Book, or click the Address Book button on the Standard toolbar when any of the mail folders are open—the Inbox, Outbox, Sent Items, or Drafts folders. The address book may contain several lists of addresses, selectable in the Show Names From The list. For example, you'll have a list of persons in your Contacts folder and a Personal Address Book, and perhaps persons connected to your network.

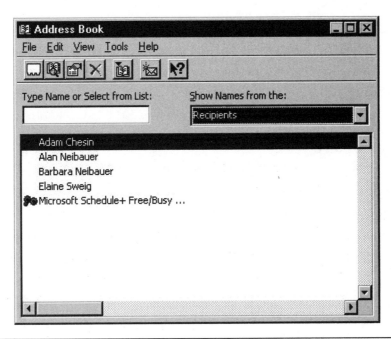

FIGURE 26-6 Address Book

To add a person to your address book, click the New Entry button on the left of the Address Book toolbar to see this dialog box:

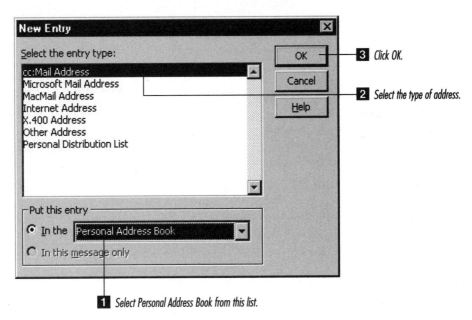

NOTE: You can choose either Internet Address or Other Address to send mail to persons on the Internet.

The next dialog box you see depends on the type of address you selected. Figure 26-7 shows the completed dialog box for the Other Address type. It is similar to Internet Address except you do not have to enter the mail type for Internet Address.

If you want to send Outlook forms, such as task assignments and meeting requests, to other users of Outlook over the Internet, turn on the box labeled "Always Send To This Recipient In Microsoft Outlook Rich-Text Format."

Fill in the other pages of the address book as desired. Only the page initially shown, however, is required. Click OK to add the listing to the address book.

To later edit the information, select the name in the address book and click the Properties button.

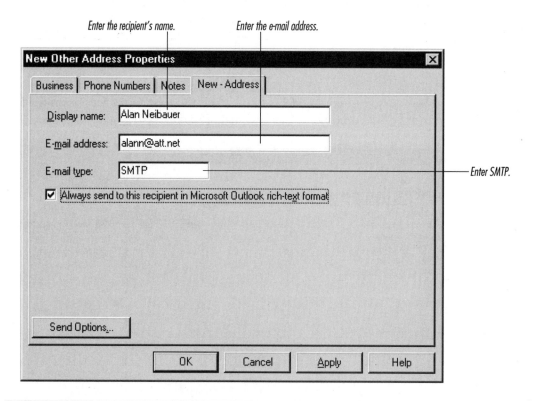

FIGURE 26-7 Entering an address

Distribution Lists

Suppose you need to send a message to a group of recipients, such as members of a project team or friends who are interested in the same subject. Rather than having to select all their names individually when you address mail, you can group them together and send mail to everyone by just selecting the group. Outlook calls this a *distribution list.*

To create a distribution list, open the address book and click the New Entry button. You can store the list in two locations, the address book or the Contacts folder. Pull down the Store This Entry In The list and choose the location. The steps to create the list now vary slightly based on the location. When you're storing it in the Personal Address Book, for example, click Personal Distribution List in the Select The Entry Type box and then click OK. When you're storing the list in the Contacts folder, the option is called New Distribution List. We'll look at using the Personal Address Book for the distribution list in this chapter, although the process is similar when storing the list in the Contacts folder.

When you select Personal Distribution List, Outlook displays this window:

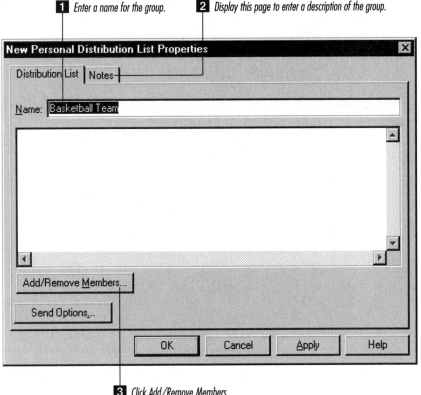

1 *Enter a name for the group.*

2 *Display this page to enter a description of the group.*

3 *Click Add/Remove Members.*

Outlook opens the Edit New Personal Distribution List Members dialog box:

5 *Double-click the names to add.*   **4** *Select the address list containing the names you want to add.*

Edit New Personal Distribution List Members   ☒

Show Names from the: Global Address List ▾

Type Name or Select from List:

[   ]

Adam Chesin	▲	Members ->		Personal Distribution List	
Alan Neibauer					
Barbara Neibauer					
Elaine Sweig					
🐾Microsoft Schedule+ Free/Bus					

◀ | ▶

New... | Properties | | Find... |

OK | Cancel | Help

● **TIP:** You can mix names from different address books.

When you're done adding names to the list, click OK to redisplay the New Personal Distribution List Properties dialog box and then click OK. The name of your group appears in the address book with a Group icon as shown here:

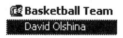

To add or remove names from an existing group, select the group name in the address book and click the Properties button. In the box that appears, click Add/Remove Members. Add members just as you did when you created the list. To remove a member, click his or her name in the list and press DEL.

Sending a Message

Sending mail with Outlook is easy. Open any mail folder, and then click the New button on the Standard toolbar to display the message form shown in Figure 26-8.

TIP: You can use Tools I Select Options I Mail Format to choose the default format for your mail. The form shown in this chapter is for Rich Text Format mail.

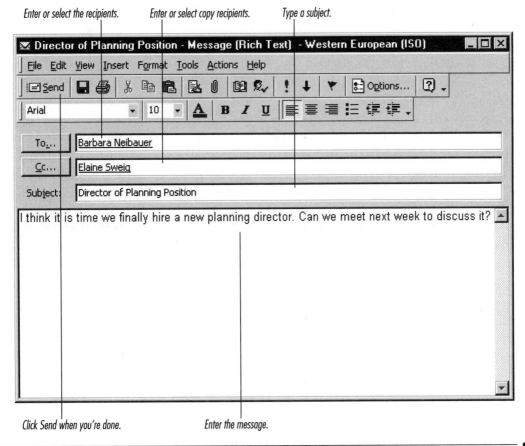

FIGURE 26-8 Composing a message

You can either type the recipient's mail address or select it from the address book. To select the name, click the To button to display this dialog box:

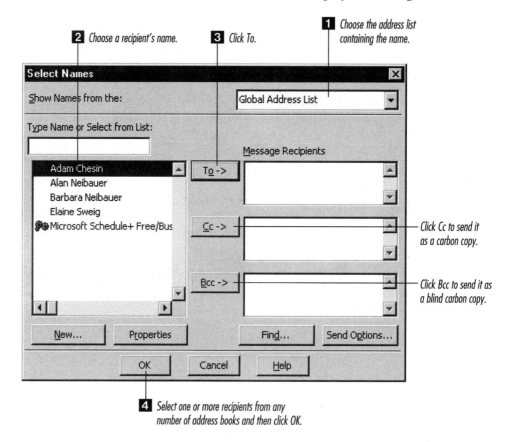

2 *Choose a recipient's name.*

3 *Click To.*

1 *Choose the address list containing the name.*

Click Cc to send it as a carbon copy.

Click Bcc to send it as a blind carbon copy.

4 *Select one or more recipients from any number of address books and then click OK.*

TIP: Exchange Server mailbox names are in the Global Address List or under Recipients under the domain name.

In the Message window, Outlook underlines the addresses that are either complete Internet addresses, valid Exchange Server addresses, or names from your Contacts folder.

When your message is ready, click the Send button. Mail to Exchange Server recipients is transmitted immediately.

Mail to Internet recipients is stored in the Outbox folder. To actually send the mail, click the Send/Receive button on the Standard toolbar. Outlook sends mail in your outbox and checks for new mail waiting for you. To send mail without getting your waiting mail, choose Tools | Send.

If you have more than one mail service in your profile, use Send And Receive to check for mail on all the services. If you want to send mail using a particular service, select Tools | Send And Receive and choose the service from the list that appears.

N O T E : Outlook automatically saves a copy of your messages in the Sent Items folder in the My Shortcuts group.

Formatting Messages

You can apply basic formats by using the options on the Formatting toolbar and on the Format menu when creating a message. Use these formats the same way you learned to format Word documents and Excel worksheets. You can also use Insert | Picture to add a graphic to the message.

Rather than design an attractive message format yourself, you can use a *stationery* design provided with Outlook. Some designs contain just background colors and graphics, while others include sample text. You can edit and format the text just as you would any text in the message.

Start a new message using stationery by choosing Actions | New Message Using. You'll see a list of any stationery designs you've already used, as well as other mail formats. If you don't want to use a stationery design listed or there are none, click More Stationery. In the dialog box that appears (Figure 26-9), choose the design you want to see a preview of, and then click OK.

If you'd like to automatically use a stationery design with every message, you can designate it as the default. Choose Tools | Options | Mail Format. Choose HTML in the Send In This Message Format list, and then choose the design from the Use This Stationery By Default list.

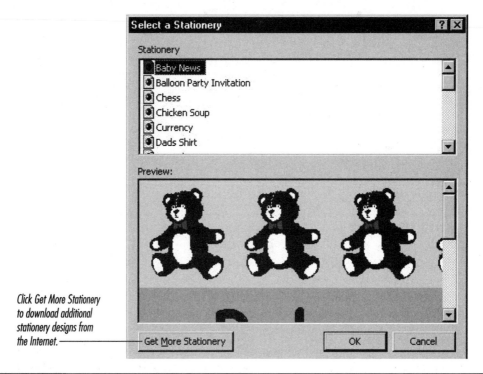

Click Get More Stationery to download additional stationery designs from the Internet.

FIGURE 26-9 Selecting a stationery

 NOTE: Not all recipients will have e-mail programs that allow them to see text formats and background stationery. In most cases, their mail server will convert the message to plain text, but they may also see the HTML tags, or codes. In some rare cases, they may not be able to read your message at all. If you have recipients with older e-mail programs, choose Plain Text as their default format.

Setting Message Options

There may be some messages that require special handling. To review some of the choices Outlook offers, click the Options button on the Message window Standard toolbar to display the dialog box shown in Figure 26-10.

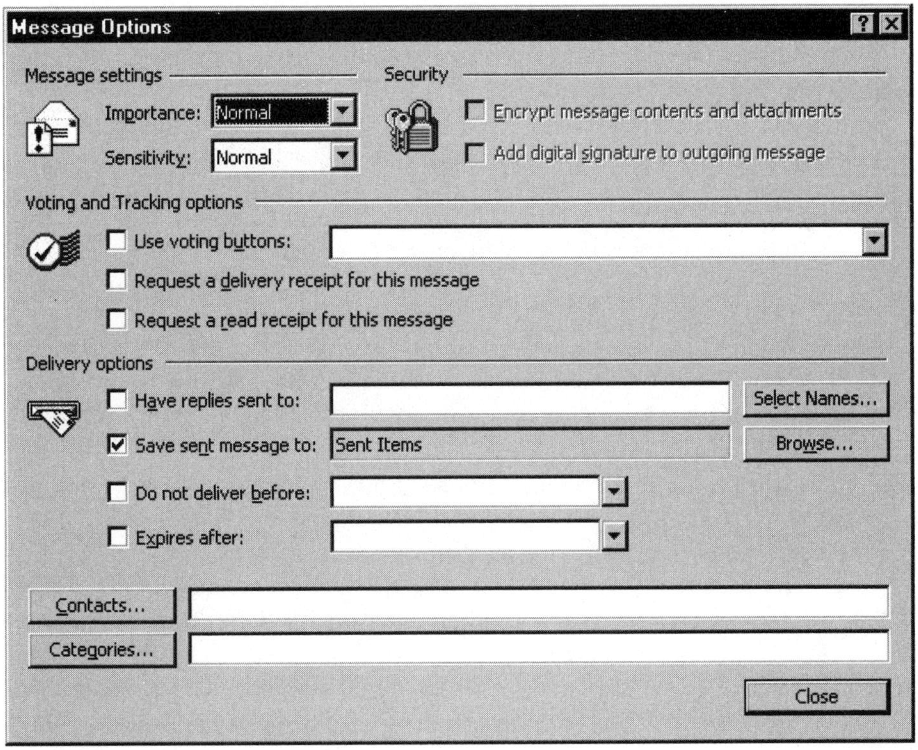

FIGURE 26-10 Message Options

Use the Importance options to show the recipient how you feel about the message. The Importance options are Low, Normal, and High. The Sensitivity options are Normal, Personal, Private, and Confidential. Your choices will appear as icons in the Importance and Sensitivity columns of the recipient's message list, if those columns are displayed, and in the Message window.

The Security settings let you encrypt the message and add your digital signature to it. To use security, you must have downloaded a digital signature over the Internet or have a security token assigned by your Microsoft Exchange Server administrator. Here's how:

1. Choose Tools | Options and click the Security tab.
2. Click Get A Digital ID.

3. If you are not connected to an Exchange Server network, Outlook launches your web browser and connects you to the site that provides information on S/MIME certificates.

4. If you are connected to an Exchange Server network, a dialog box appears where you can choose either of these options:

   • Get A S/MIME Certificate From An External Certifying Authority to obtain a digital ID for use over the Internet.

   • Set Up Security For Me On The Exchange Server if you want a digital ID to use over your Exchange Server network.

If you selected to get an S/MIME certificate, follow the instructions presented on the web site. After filling in a form, you will receive an e-mail with further instructions.

If you selected an Exchange Server digital ID, a dialog box appears in which you enter a special password, called a *token,* and a *keyset name* that you should have been given by your network administrator. When you click OK in this dialog box, a message is sent to Exchange Server requesting the ID. You will soon receive a message reporting that your security request has been granted.

The Voting And Tracking Options section helps you get responses to questions using voting buttons and asks for receipts when your mail has been delivered or read. When you turn on the Use Voting Buttons option, you can choose from three choices in the drop-down list—Approve; Reject, Yes;No, and Yes;No;Maybe. Your choice will appear as a series of buttons in the recipient's message along with the phrase "Please respond using the buttons above." When the recipient uses the voting buttons to respond, you'll get an e-mail informing you of his or her selection, and your message in the Sent Items folder will contain a Tracking tab that records a list of all recipients and the status and date of their replies.

The tracking options notify you when your message has been received or opened by the recipient. These options are mainly for use over your network and have limited function over the Internet.

The Delivery Options section determines when messages are sent, when messages expire, where sent messages are stored, where replies to messages are delivered, and which categories are assigned to the message.

The Categories option lets you associate the message with a category. The Contacts option lets you associate the message with a person in your Contacts folder.

Sending Attachments

You often may want to send a file from your disk to an e-mail recipient. Perhaps you want to share a document that you have created, or an interesting file you downloaded from the Internet. To send such a file, you add it as an attachment to a message.

To send an attachment, click the Insert File button in the message's Standard toolbar. In the dialog box that appears, select the file that you want to send, and choose the Attachment option in the Insert As section. In your outbox, the attachment appears as a Paperclip icon.

　　📧　　📎 *Barbie Neibaue... Budget*　　　　　　　　　　　　　　　　　*Mon 12/14/98 ...*

> ● **TIP:** To include the text of a plain text file in your message, select it as an attachment but choose the Text Only option in the Insert As section.

Reading a Message

Mail messages received over Microsoft Exchange Server are automatically added to your inbox. Internet e-mail is added after you connect using the Send And Receive command. Each message is shown as a message header in the inbox, along with icons representing flags and importance, as shown here:

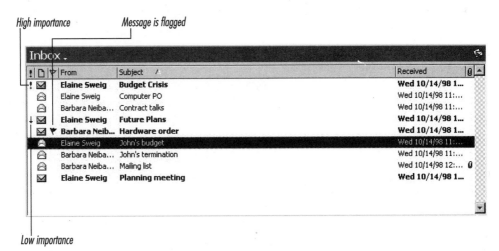

High importance　　　　　*Message is flagged*

Low importance

To read the contents of messages directly in the inbox, the Preview pane shows the contents of the message selected in the list. (If the Preview pane is not displayed, choose View | Preview Pane.) To open a message in its own window, double-click it.

If you want to respond to the message you are reading, click the Reply button on the Standard toolbar to respond just to the sender, or click the Reply To All button to send your response to everyone who received the message. A new message opens with the complete text of the original. Type your response and then click Send.

You may also decide to send a copy of the original message to someone else, which is called *forwarding*. To do so, click the Forward button on the Standard toolbar. A Message window appears with the text of the original message. Address the message as you would any other and click Send.

Reading and Saving Attachments

When you receive a message with an attachment, you can choose to either open or save the attachment. A Paperclip icon above the Preview pane indicates an attachment when you select the message. To see the names and sizes of the attachments, click the icon in the Preview pane. In this example, the message has one attachment:

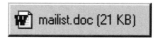

To open or save an attachment, click the attachment's name in the file list. For some types of files, the attachment will be opened immediately and displayed on its associated program, such as Word or Paint. For other types of files, you'll see the Opening Mail Attachment dialog box:

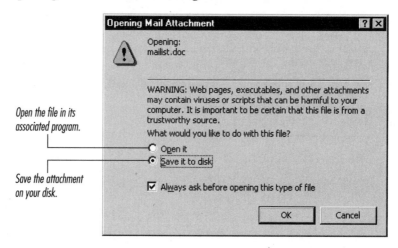

If a message has more than one attachment, you can choose to save all of them in one step. Select File | Save Attachments to see a submenu listing each attached file and the Save All option. Choose Save All to open a dialog box where you select one location for all the attachments.

N O T E : If you open a message with attachments, you'll see icons for each. Double-click an icon to open or save the attachment.

Coping with Junk Mail

If you receive mail through an Internet service provider, it won't be long before you start receiving junk mail, known as *spam*. Outlook lets you automatically delete, move, or mark junk mail using a junk mailer list that you create. It also lets you deal with potentially offensive mail using built-in rules for mail containing adult content.

If you've already received junk mail, add the sender's name to the list by right-clicking on the message in the Inbox, pointing to Junk E-Mail in the shortcut menu, and choosing either Add To Junk Senders List or Add To Adult Content Senders List.

Next you have to tell Outlook how to handle mail received from persons on the lists. From the Inbox folder, click the Organize button, and then follow the steps shown in Figure 26-11.

The folder options include Junk E-Mail, Deleted Items, or Other Folder. Choose Deleted Items if you want to delete this mail as soon as it arrives. Choose Other Folder to select any Outlook folder. If you select the Junk E-Mail folder and do not yet have one, Outlook will ask if you want to create it when you click Turn On.

N O T E : When you turn on a junk mail rule, the button changes to Turn Off. Click that button if you no longer want to channel junk or adult content mail.

If you want to leave junk or adult mail in your inbox but mark it for quick identification, choose Color rather than Move when you set up the Organize pane. You can then choose the color to display the message's header in the inbox.

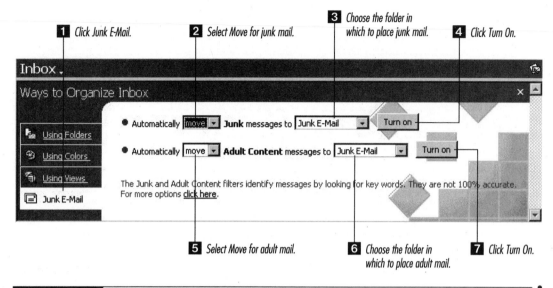

FIGURE 26-11 Dealing with junk mail

Managing the Junk Senders List

If you accidentally add a sender's name to the junk mail list, you have to remove it from the list so the mail is not treated as spam. You can also add a sender's name to the list before you receive his or her first message.

In the Organize pane, with Junk Mail selected, click the underlined words "click here" to display these options:

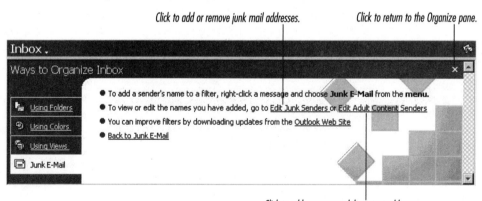

Choosing Edit Junk Senders or Edit Adult Content Senders displays a dialog box showing the senders' names. Use the dialog box to add additional names, or to edit or remove names that you've already inserted.

When you have Adult Content turned on, Outlook will automatically move some mail that contains certain words or phrases. The rules that identify adult mail are built into Outlook, but Microsoft updates them periodically. To download the most recent adult content rules, click the underlined words "Outlook Web Site" when managing junk mail.

Developing Your Profile

Your *profile* tells Outlook where to save your files and what services it can connect to for mail. If you are using a desktop computer, one profile is usually enough. When you have a laptop computer, you might want several profiles—one to use when you're at your office and connected to your network, another to use when you use the laptop at home and have to dial in to the network.

To create a profile, you use the Input Setup Wizard. Begin by selecting Start | Settings | Control Panel, and then double-click the Mail icon in the Control Panel window. In the Properties dialog box that appears, you'll see a list of the services set up for the existing profile.

Click the Show Profiles button to open the Mail dialog box. Then click the Add button to display the first box of the Inbox Setup Wizard, and use it as shown here:

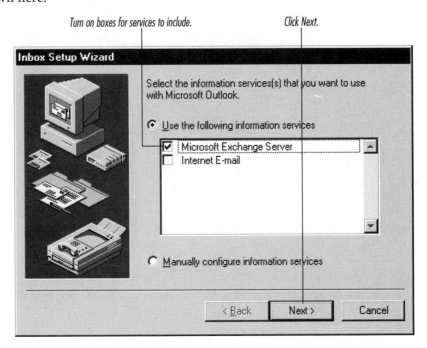

Turn on boxes for services to include.   Click Next.

The next boxes that appear depend on the services you are installing. Fill in the information requested in each box, clicking on the Next button until you get to the last box that tells you you're done and lists the services. Click Finish and then close the Mail dialog box that appears.

Editing a Profile

You may have to edit a profile. Suppose you switch Internet service providers, have to change your mailbox name on the server, or want to add faxing capabilities.

To edit a profile, double-click the Mail icon in the Control Panel window to open the Properties dialog box. You use the Services tab of the dialog box to add, delete, and change an installed service. If the profile you want to edit is not shown by default, click Show Profile, choose the profile from the list, and then click Properties.

- To add a service, click the Add button and then choose the service in the dialog box that appears, as shown here. You'll then see one or more dialog boxes that you have to complete to set up the service.

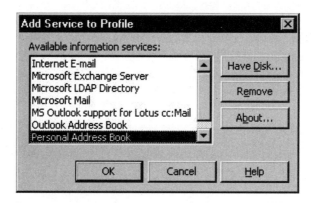

- To delete a service, select the name of the service, click the Remove button, and then click Yes in the message box.
- To review or edit a service setup, select the name of the service and then click the Properties button.

Use the Delivery tab of the Properties dialog box to change where your mail is stored and the order in which services are accessed for mail.

Use the Addressing tab of the dialog box to specify the default address list, where to save new entries in your address book, and in which order to search address lists for recipient names.

Adding a Personal Address Book

Outlook comes with an address book that automatically includes the names of persons in your Contacts folder and other users of your Exchange Server network. You'll need to add all other e-mail addresses yourself to the Personal Address Book. However, the Personal Address Book must be part of your profile.

You add this address book in the Add Service To Profile dialog box when creating or editing a profile. Select Personal Address Book and then click OK to display the following dialog box:

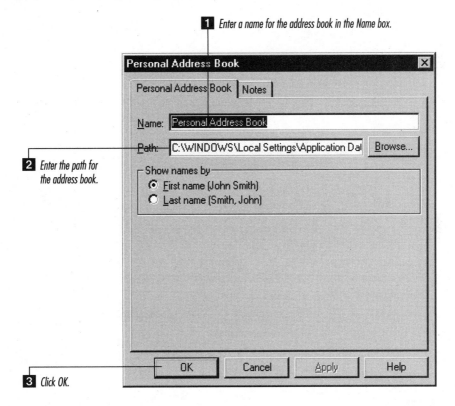

1 *Enter a name for the address book in the Name box.*

2 *Enter the path for the address book.*

3 *Click OK.*

The Personal Address Book will be available the next time you start Outlook.

- To display and print a map of an address, open the Contact item, and then choose Actions | Display Map Of Address. Outlook launches your web browser, connects to the Microsoft Expedia service, and maps the address.

- To call a contact, right-click the contact's name in the Contacts folder and choose AutoDialer from the shortcut menu.

- To send a message to a person in your Contacts folder, drag his or her name to the Inbox icon on the Outlook bar.

- If you do not complete your message, choose File | Save to store the message in the Drafts folder, and then close the message. To finish the message, open the Drafts folder in the My Shortcuts group, and double-click the message to reopen it.

- To add a group to the Outlook bar, right-click a blank area of the bar and select Add New Group from the shortcut menu. Enter the group name and then click OK.

- To add new folders to a group, right-click a blank area of the bar, and choose Outlook Bar Shortcut from the menu. In the dialog box that appears, select the folder or file to add to the bar and then click OK.

- To delete an item from the Outlook bar, right-click it and choose Remove From Outlook Bar from the shortcut menu.

- You can post messages to a public folder. Use the Public Folders icon in the Other Shortcuts group to open the folder, and then create a message just as you learned for e-mail.

- You can edit the current profile from within Outlook by choosing Tools | Services. Your changes take effect the next time you start Outlook.

- Sort messages by clicking on the header that you want to sort by, such as From, Subject, or Received.

Managing Your Schedule

27

If you only use Outlook for e-mail, then you're missing some of its best features. You can use Outlook to schedule appointments and meetings, and to keep track of tasks. You can even assign tasks to other users of Outlook, and schedule meetings by automatically checking everyone's schedule.

Managing Your Calendar

Outlook's Calendar folder lets you set up and review your schedule of appointments and meetings. In Outlook parlance, a meeting is just an appointment to which you invite others. Figure 27-1 shows a typical Calendar folder.

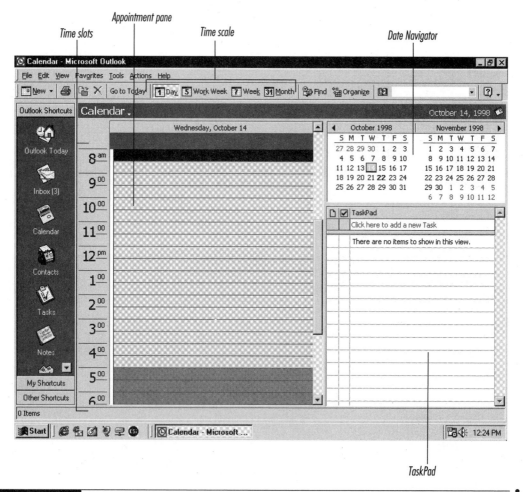

FIGURE 27-1 Calendar folder

> **T I P :** You can also schedule an *event* that doesn't have a particular time assigned to it, such as a birthday or anniversary. The event is displayed at the top of the schedule for the day you assign it to.

The time slots represent the hours of the day, divided into half-hour increments, with nonwork hours in dark gray. You can scroll the time slots to see additional times. In fact, if there is something scheduled but not displayed, you'll see a rectangle at the bottom of the time slots like this:

Appointments and meetings are shown in their appropriate time slot, with icons indicating if the appointment is a group meeting, an online meeting, a one-time or a recurring event, marked as private, and if there is a reminder set for it.

The Date Navigator is a monthly calendar showing one or more months. The dates shown in the Appointment pane, and any dates with appointments, are shown in bold. To change the date of the appointments shown, just click the date in the Date Navigator. Click the left or right arrow to scroll other months into view, or click the name of a month to also see the months before and after it, and choose the month you want. Move to a specific date by choosing View | Go To | Go To Date, enter the date you want to see, and then click OK. To go to today's date, click the Go To Today button on the Standard toolbar if it is displayed, or choose View | Go To | Go To Today.

The TaskPad shows a summary of the tasks that you have been assigned or have assigned to others. You'll learn how to work with tasks and the TaskPad later.

The default Calendar view is called the Day/Week/Month view, and it shows one day at a time. Use these buttons in the Standard toolbar to display a wider range of dates:

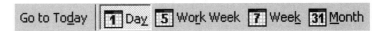

Clicking on Work Week displays the workdays for the calendar week, on Week displays the entire week (including weekends and holidays), and on Month displays the entire month.

N O T E : The Date Navigator and TaskPad do not appear when you are viewing an entire month.

Setting Up an Appointment

Outlook has two ways to set up an appointment. The first and quickest way is to display the date for the appointment, click in the time slot for the start of the meeting, and type a description of it. When you start typing, the time slot will appear in a thick border:

If the meeting is scheduled for more than a half-hour, drag the bottom border of the time slot down to the ending time. Finally, press ENTER or click outside of the time slot. Outlook removes the thick border but displays the Alarm icon, indicating that a reminder will appear onscreen 15 minutes before the starting time.

 N O T E : Outlook has to be running for reminders to appear.

If you need to change the text or times of the appointment, click its slot. To change the starting time of the appointment, drag its left borderline up or down. Dragging just the top line changes the starting time as well as the length of the meeting.

To move the appointment to another day, make sure the date appears in the Date Navigator. Then point anywhere in the time slot, and drag to the new date in Date Navigator.

Outlook's second way to schedule an appointment is more time-consuming, but provides additional detail that you may need. To schedule an appointment this way, double-click the appointment's time slot or click the New Appointment button on the Standard toolbar. Outlook then displays an untitled Appointment window in which you can add and edit the appointment details, as you'll learn next.

Editing Appointment Details

There's not much room in the appointment slot to enter details about an appointment. To completely describe an appointment, double-click on the appointment to open an Appointment window, as shown in Figure 27-2. If the insertion point is in the time slot, double-click the border around it. After making your changes, click the Save And Close button.

 TIP: To create an appointment in the window initially, double-click its time slot or click the New Appointment button on the Standard toolbar.

Set or change the starting and ending times in the appropriate boxes. To change the reminder time, select a new time from the pull-down list of the Reminder box. Turn off the Reminder option if you do not want to be reminded of the appointment.

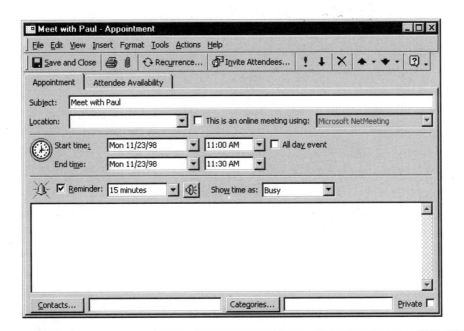

FIGURE 27-2 Appointment window

Use the large text box in the window to enter a description or notes about the appointment, or to store files related to it. To add a file, click the Insert File button in the toolbar and select a file just as you learned for e-mail messages.

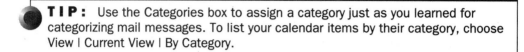

TIP: Use the Categories box to assign a category just as you learned for categorizing mail messages. To list your calendar items by their category, choose View | Current View | By Category.

When you are on a network, you can give permission to others to work with your calendar. If you do not want others to have access to a particular item, turn on the Private option.

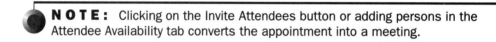

NOTE: Clicking on the Invite Attendees button or adding persons in the Attendee Availability tab converts the appointment into a meeting.

Setting Recurring Appointments

You may have appointments that you schedule regularly, such as weekly appointments with your vice president or annual appointments with your accountant. To schedule a recurring appointment, create the first of the series. Then in the Appointment window, click the Recurrence button on the Standard toolbar. Outlook opens the Appointment Recurrence dialog box, shown here:

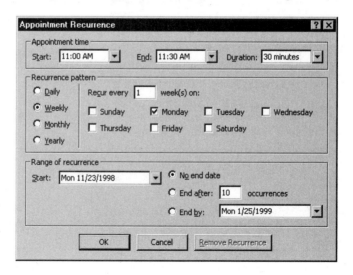

Use this dialog box to indicate when the appointment recurs, and the range of recurrences (how long the appointments will be taking place).

TIP: If you open an existing recurring appointment, you'll be asked if you want to open the one specific item or to edit the entire series.

When you select a recurrence pattern—Daily, Weekly, Monthly, or Yearly—options for that pattern appear. With a weekly recurrence, for example, you can choose the day of the week the appointment occurs and the number of weeks between recurrences. With monthly appointments, you can select the day of the month and the number of months between them, or set the recurrence by relative dates, such as the second Saturday of each month.

Dealing with a Reminder

If you have a reminder set for an appointment and Outlook is running, you'll see a dialog box like this at the reminder time:

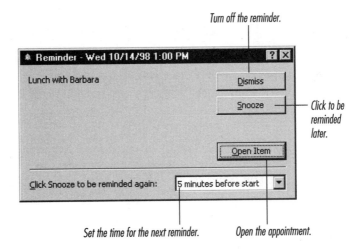

Turn off the reminder.

Click to be reminded later.

Set the time for the next reminder.

Open the appointment.

Planning a Meeting

A meeting is an appointment for which you use Outlook to invite others. To plan a meeting, select Actions | New Meeting Request to see the window shown

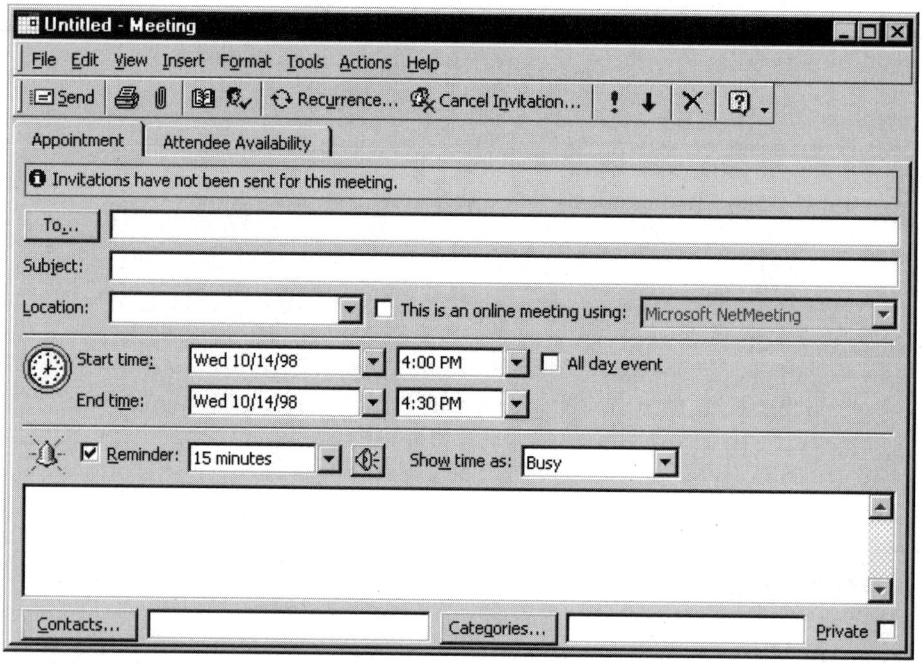

FIGURE 27-3 Planning a meeting

in Figure 27-3. Enter the subject and location of the meeting, its starting and ending times, and its reminder options.

You use the Show Time As box to indicate how the allotted time appears on your schedule when others are checking it to set up their own meetings. You can choose to show that you are busy or free at that time, have a tentative meeting, or will be out of the office.

Use the Insert File button on the toolbar to add attachments, such as a meeting agenda or background information. The attachments will be sent to invitees along with their meeting notice.

TIP: Use the Recurrence button to schedule recurring meetings.

Next, select whom you are inviting to the meeting. Click To and use the address book to select the invitees. You can designate persons as either required or optional. To invite a person not in the address book, just type his or her e-mail address in the To box.

Now click the Attendee Availability tab. If you are on Microsoft Exchange Server, Outlook checks the schedules of the invitees. Outlook maintains a special file on the server containing the schedule of those on the network. After the schedules are checked, you'll see the attendee grid shown in Figure 27-4. You use this box to change the meeting time and to review the availability of those you invited. To change the time of the meeting, for example, drag the vertical lines that indicate its starting and ending times.

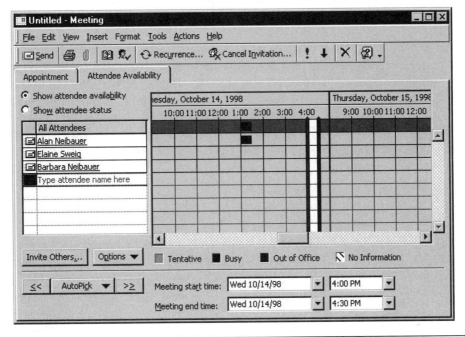

FIGURE 27-4 Checking schedules

T I P : Click AutoPick to have Outlook schedule the meeting at the next time all the invitees are free.

When you've finished creating the meeting, click the Send button. Outlook automatically sends mail messages to the people you invited. Your meeting appears in its appointment slot with this icon:

 T I P : To send meeting requests to other Outlook users over the Internet, their address must be set with the Always Send Messages In Microsoft Exchange Rich-Text Format option turned on. Right-click the address and choose Properties from the shortcut menu. In the dialog box that appears, turn on the Always Send To This Recipient In Microsoft Outlook Rich-Text Format check box.

You can change the time of a meeting by dragging it in its time slot, or by adjusting the time in the Appointment or Attendee Availability tab of the Meeting window.

If you change the meeting time in the Meeting window, click the Send Update button. Outlook will send a message to all invitees notifying them of the change. If you close the window before clicking Send Update, or change the time in the time slot, Outlook displays a dialog box asking if you want to send update notices.

To remove someone from the invitation list, delete his or her name from either the Appointment or the Attendee Availability tab. To delete all invitees, converting the meeting to an appointment, click Cancel Invitations.

When recipients respond to your meeting request, you'll receive e-mail messages indicating their plans. Open the meeting item in the Calendar, and click the Attendee Availability tab to review their responses, as shown here:

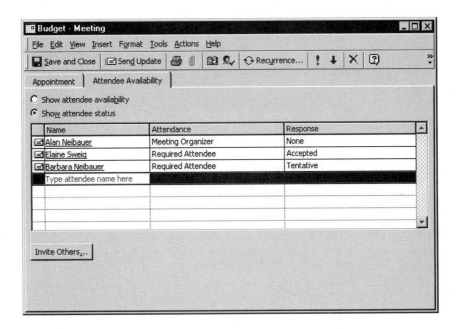

Responding to a Meeting Request

When you are being invited to a meeting and get your mail in Outlook, you'll receive a message like the one shown in Figure 27-5. You can respond by clicking the Accept, Tentative, or Decline button. A dialog box appears asking if you want to send your response immediately or to add comments to it before mailing.

N O T E : If you get mail using another program, you'll still be notified about the meeting but won't be able to respond as shown in Figure 27-5.

If you're not sure of your availability, click the Calendar button on the invitation's Standard toolbar. Outlook opens your calendar with the meeting shown in its time slot, and you can then open the item to see additional details. For example, to see who else is invited to the meeting, open the item and click the Attendee Availability tab.

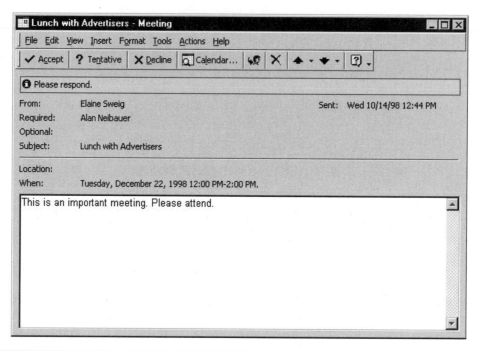

FIGURE 27-5 A meeting request

Conducting Online Meetings

An *online meeting* is one conducted over the Internet using your computer's sound and video equipment to hear and see the participants. This feature uses a program called NetMeeting that is included with Outlook. You can also use NetMeeting to chat with friends, relatives, and anyone who has the program installed on his or her machine.

The first time you run a NetMeeting, however, you'll have to set it up. Rather than wait for your first meeting, set up NetMeeting this way. Choose View | Go To | Internet Call | Internet Call, and then follow the series of dialog boxes that appears. For example, you'll be asked to enter your name and e-mail address, indicate the speed of your modem, and confirm if you have sound or video hardware installed.

Setting Up a NetMeeting

You set up a NetMeeting much the same as you do any other meeting in Outlook. However, persons you invite to attend must have some special

NetMeeting information entered into their listing in the Contacts folder. You also have to set up NetMeeting to use a *directory server*. A directory server is a computer made available by Microsoft and other companies that handles the communications between users over the Internet. Start by selecting Actions | New Meeting Request. In the meeting window that opens, enable the check box in the Appointment tab labeled This is an Online Meeting Using. If you already scheduled the meeting, open it and enable the check box to convert it into an online meeting. Outlook adds these items to the Meeting window:

Select a directory server.

Turn on to start the meeting automatically.

Enter your e-mail address.

Enter an Office document to open when the meeting begins.

If you set the meeting to start automatically, Outlook runs NetMeeting and places the Internet calls to all invitees 15 minutes before the meeting time. To start the meeting yourself, open the meeting item in the Calendar and click the Start NetMeeting button that appears in the toolbar.

TIP: If you accepted an invitation to a NetMeeting and miss the call, open the item and click the Join Meeting Now tab of the Online tab.

Persons invited to the meeting who are online and running NetMeeting will see a dialog box asking if they want to accept the call:

Running a NetMeeting

When your call is accepted, the person's name is displayed in the Current Call folder of NetMeeting, as shown in Figure 27-6, and you can start communicating. Although you can only speak with and see one person at a time, you can switch between participants by choosing their name from the Switch button on the Current Call window.

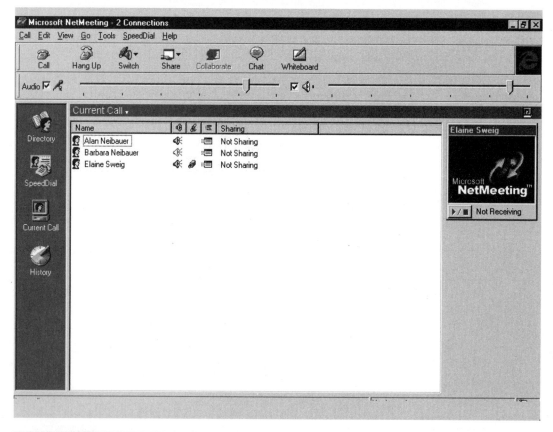

FIGURE 27-6 Conducting an online meeting

NOTE: Click Hang Up to end the meeting.

During a NetMeeting, you can use the following features:

- *Chat* lets you write messages in a window. Use it when you do not have sound equipment, or when the audio quality is poor.
- *Whiteboard* lets you and other participants draw on the screen so all can see.
- *Share* lets other participants see a program that you are using.
- *Collaborate* lets participants use a program running on another participant's computer.

Making Internet Calls

When you place an Internet call, you can communicate with other NetMeeting users around the world who are logged on to the same server. To call a contact, open the person's item in the Contacts folder, and click the Details tab. Make sure the Online Meeting Settings are complete in the Details tab, and then click Call Now. When the Contact item is open, you can also choose Actions | Call Using NetMeeting.

If the item is closed, you can initiate an Internet call by choosing View | Go To | Internet Call | Internet Call to start NetMeeting, and then click the Directory button to see a list of persons logged on to the server. Double-click the person to place the call to, or click Call on the toolbar and enter the address of the person you want to call. If the person accepts your call, the Current Call window appears and you're ready to communicate.

Working with Tasks

When you want to keep track of a specific activity you have to perform, you create a task in the Tasks folder. You can also use the folder to assign tasks to others, called a *task request,* and to track their progress.

Open the folder by clicking on the Tasks icon in the Outlook bar. Figure 27-7 shows a typical Tasks folder with several tasks already created. The icons next to each task identify its type. Overdue tasks—those that have not been completed by the due date—are shown in red, and completed tasks are crossed out. You can choose other ways to display the task list by choosing View | Current View, or by using the Organize pane.

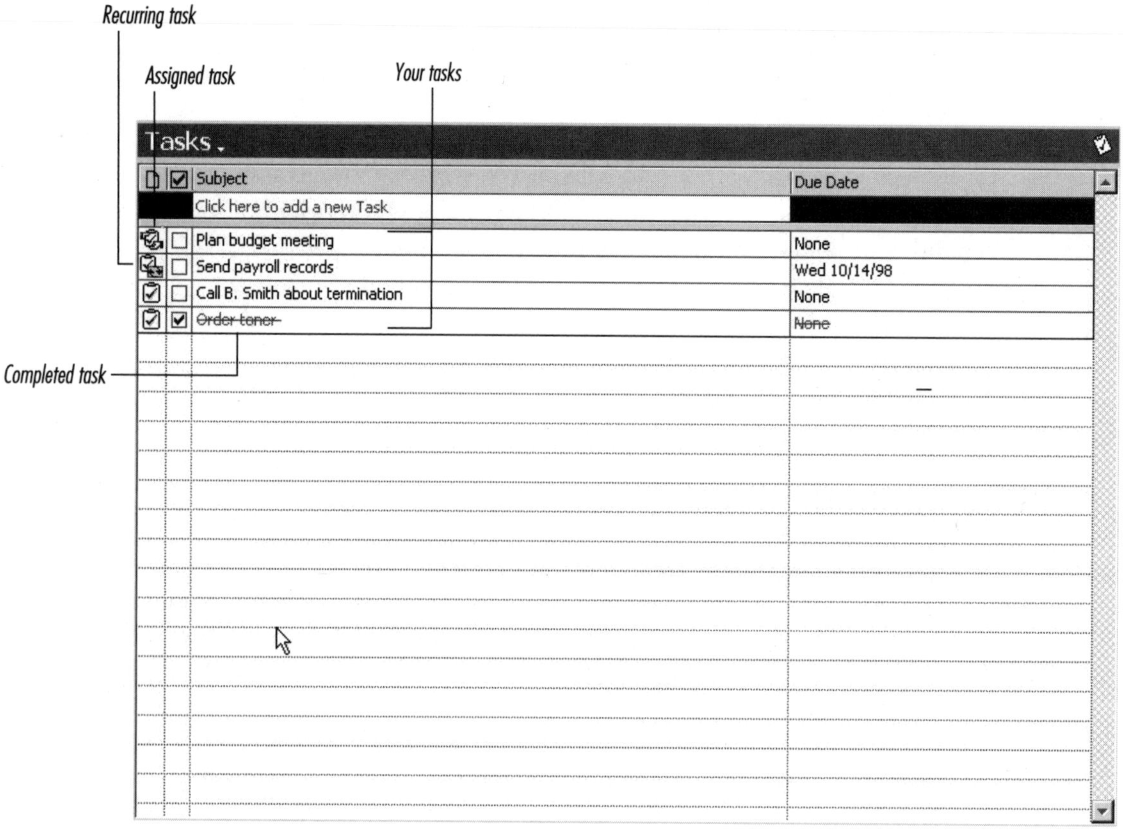

Recurring task

Assigned task   Your tasks

Completed task

FIGURE 27-7 Task folder

Creating a Task

As with setting up appointments, Outlook offers two ways to set up tasks. First, you can set up a task quickly by typing a description of it in the Task window, then adding the details when you have time. Just click where it reads "Click here to add a new Task," type the name of the task, and if desired, enter a due date in the Due Date column. To select the due date from a calendar, click the down arrow that appears next to the Due Date column, and choose the date from the calendar that appears. Press ENTER when you're done to add the task to the list.

Outlook's second way to set up a task is by double-clicking in the top row of the task list, or by clicking on the New Task button on the Standard toolbar—the leftmost button on the toolbar. Outlook then displays a Task window, shown in Figure 27-8, with two tabs—one for setting up the task, and the other for documenting the task's details. Complete the information in the window, and then click Save And Close to add the task to your task list.

 NOTE: Double-click a task in the Task folder to open its Task window to make changes.

The options in the Task window are similar to those you've seen for appointments and meetings, and they work the same way:

- Mark the task as private.
- Insert attached files.
- Categorize the task.
- Set a reminder.
- Set an importance level (priority) as you learned for mail.

You can also use the Recurrence button to create a recurring task. The Task Recurrence box, however, includes the Regenerate New Task option. Use this to set a task to recur at an interval after the previous recurrence has been

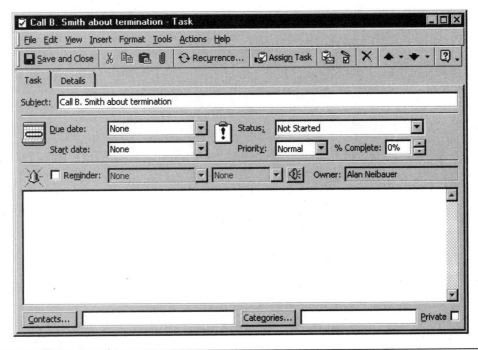

FIGURE 27-8 Using Outlook to create a Task entry

completed. For example, you can set a task to recur one week after its last occurrence was completed, rather than one week after its due date.

Special features in the Task window are Status and % Complete. Use the Status list to indicate if a task is Not Started, In Progress, Completed, Waiting For Someone, or Deferred. In the % Complete box, indicate the amount of the task that has been completed as of the current date. The two boxes are somewhat synchronized, since setting the percentage shown in the first column of this table changes the status as shown:

% COMPLETED	STATUS
0	Not Started
1–99	In Progress
100	Completed

If you change the Status to Not Started or to Completed, by the way, Outlook inserts 0 or 100, respectively, in the % Complete box.

NOTE: The Owner box shows the name of the person responsible for completing the task.

The Details tab of the Task window, shown here, lets you track progress toward completing the task and lets you record some other useful information:

Enter the date the task was completed.

Estimate the time it takes to complete the task.

Enter the actual time it took to complete the task.

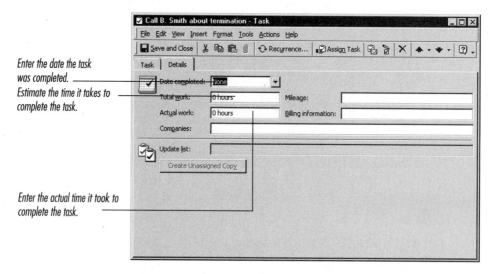

Assigning a Task

If you're an administrator, you no doubt assign tasks to other persons in your organization. You can create the task in Outlook, then mail the task to another person so it is added to their task list. This is called a *task request*.

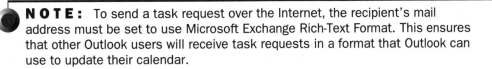

N O T E : To send a task request over the Internet, the recipient's mail address must be set to use Microsoft Exchange Rich-Text Format. This ensures that other Outlook users will receive task requests in a format that Outlook can use to update their calendar.

To create a task request, choose Actions | New Task Request or create a regular task and choose Actions | Assign Task. The Task window now appears as shown in Figure 27-9. In addition to the options you've already seen, you can click To to select one or more persons to whom you are assigning the task.

Turn off the Keep An Updated Copy Of This Task On My Task List option if you do not want the task reported on your own task list. Turn off the Send Me A Status Report When This Task Is Complete option if you do not want to be mailed a status report when the task is marked completed.

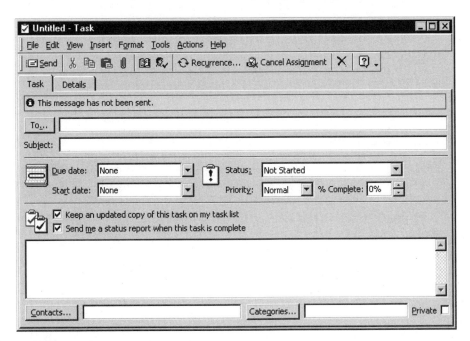

FIGURE 27-9 Task request

When you're done, click Send to mail the request.

Task requests are handled much as meeting notices. When you receive a task request, you can choose options from the mail message to accept it, decline it, forward the task to another person, or just delete it.

If you accept the task, it is added to your task list, an acceptance message is returned to the sender, and ownership is transferred to you. The original sender can no longer make any changes to it. If you decline the task, a message is sent back to the sender. The sender can then add the task to his or her own list, keep it on record as a declined task, or delete it. If you forward the task to another person, they have the same options, with notifications going to you and the original sender.

You can also delete the task request message. Outlook will then give you these options:

- **Decline And Delete**   sends a reply declining the request.
- **Mark Complete And Delete**   marks the task as completed.
- **Delete**   sends no response.

Using the TaskPad

The TaskPad in the Calendar lists your tasks much like in the Task folder but without the due date. In fact, you can use the TaskPad just as you do the task list to create new tasks, edit tasks, and mark tasks completed. Changes you make in the TaskPad are automatically reflected in the Task folder.

The Notes Folder

When you're busy working, you'll probably think of items that you want to jot down to remember. Rather than actually sticking a note on the edge of your screen, you can create a note in Outlook.

To create a note, open the Notes folder and click the New Note button on the Standard toolbar. Outlook opens a New Note window, shown here:

Click Close when done.

Type the text of the note.

10/14/98 12:45 PM

Your notes appear as icons with a preview of the text as shown here:

Call Richard for an appointment

To edit a note, double-click it. Make your changes and then click the note's Close button.

To change the note's color or assign it to a category, right-click the note when it's closed, or click the icon in the upper-left corner of the Note window if it is open. From the menu that appears, choose Color and pick a color from the list that appears, or choose Categories and assign it to a category.

 N O T E : Select Forward from the submenu to create an e-mail message with the note as an attachment.

As with all Outlook folders, you can change the way notes appear by choosing View | Current View and picking the view to display.

The Journal Folder

A *journal* is a record of your activities. In Outlook, you use the Journal folder to record your Outlook activities, such as e-mail messages and appointments, activities with persons in the Contacts folder, and your work with Office applications, such as Word documents and Excel worksheets. The journal displays the name of each document you worked on, and each call, meeting, or other Outlook activity for which you created a journal entry.

 T I P : By categorizing journal entries, you can view your work by project or by contact, to determine your progress and aid you in billing.

Setting Up the Journal

Until you set up the journal, each time you open the journal, you'll be asked if you want to turn it on so activities are recorded. You'll also have the opportunity to tell Outlook which activities to record. Click the Journal icon in the My Shortcuts group of the Outlook bar to see this dialog box:

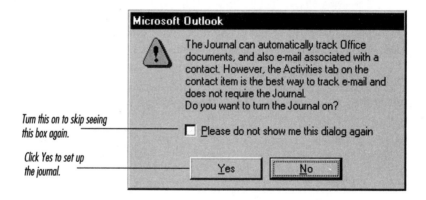

Turn this on to skip seeing this box again.

Click Yes to set up the journal.

When you click Yes, you'll see this dialog box:

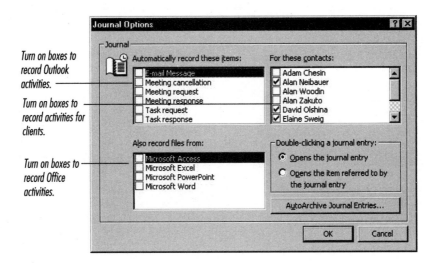

Turn on boxes to record Outlook activities.

Turn on boxes to record activities for clients.

Turn on boxes to record Office activities.

Turn on the check boxes for the activities, Office applications, and contacts whose activities you want to record in the journal. Click OK to accept your settings and to display the Journal folder.

 N O T E : You can change the settings by selecting Tools I Options I Preferences I Journal Options.

A typical Journal folder is shown in Figure 27-10. Your activities are shown with a *timeline* and grouped by activity. As with other grouped views, click the minus sign to hide a group's details, or click the plus sign to show a group's details.

You can scroll the timeline using the horizontal scroll bar at the bottom to bring other dates into view. You can also click the large bar showing the month to choose a date from a calendar like this:

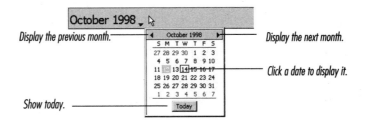

Display the previous month.

Display the next month.

Click a date to display it.

Show today.

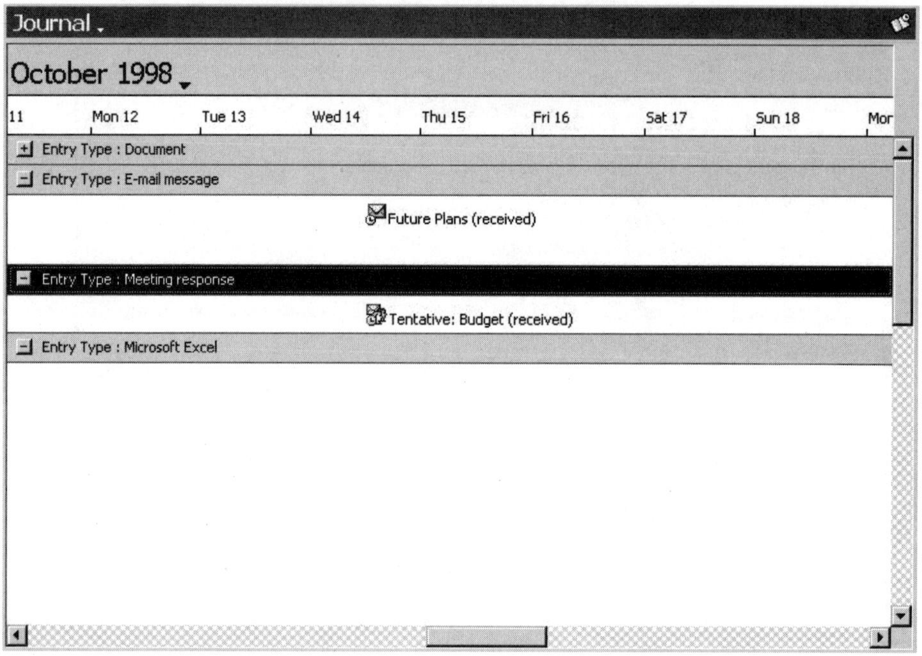

FIGURE 27-10 Journal folder

Other views of the journal let you organize activities by contact and category, or list items like a worksheet in various column orders.

Adding a Journal Entry

Not all your activities will automatically be added to the journal. If you want to record an appointment, phone call, or other activity yourself, you create a new journal entry.

Open the Journal folder, and then click the New Journal button on the Standard toolbar to open a Journal window, as shown in Figure 27-11. To start timing an activity, pull down the Duration list, choose 0 minutes, and then click the Start Timer button. As each minute passes, the time will be updated in the Duration box. Pull down the Entry Type list and choose the type of activity; then enter the information you want to record and attach any related file.

If you want the timer to continue as you work on the activity, leave the Journal window open or minimize it—closing the window records the elapsed time in the Duration box and stops the timer.

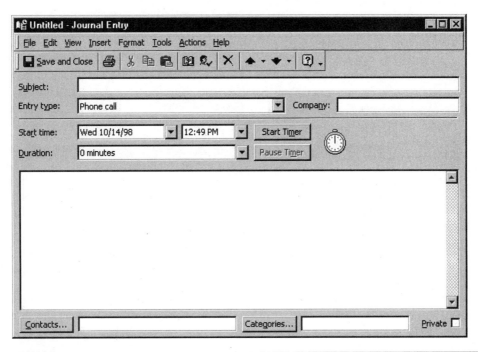

FIGURE 27-11 Journal window

Click Save And Close when you're done. The activity will appear under its related type in the Journal window. To reopen the item, double-click it.

Creating a journal item using the e-mail message, meeting, or task type will not create a corresponding Outlook item. For instance, creating a journal item of the meeting type will not actually schedule a meeting. To create a corresponding item, drag the activity from the Journal window to the appropriate icon on the Outlook bar. For example, drag a meeting activity to the Calendar folder, or an e-mail activity to the Inbox folder. Outlook opens the appropriate item window for you to complete.

Opening Journal Items

By default, when you double-click or otherwise open a journal entry, it opens the Journal Entry window. You may prefer to open the related item itself, such as a meeting window or a Word document.

To select what to open directly from the Journal window, right-click the item and choose either Open Journal Entry or Open Item Referred To from the shortcut menu.

- To change the increment of time slots in the Calendar folder, right-click anywhere in the time scale, and then choose the intervals, from 5 minutes to 60 minutes.

- To control when your schedule information is updated on the server, choose Tools | Options | Preferences | Calendar Options | Free/Busy Options. You can also use the dialog box that appears to specify a location to store schedule information on the Internet if you are not connected to a network.

- To create an appointment from any folder, press CTRL-SHIFT-A, or choose File | New | Appointment.

- You can use the Organize button to assign a category to an appointment or meeting. Click Organize on the Standard toolbar, and then click Using Categories in the Organize pane. Select the appointment, and then pull down the list next to the Add button in the Organize pane and select a category.

- You can set properties for a meeting or appointment by opening it and then choosing File | Properties. Set the levels of Importance and Sensitivity. Choose not to archive the item automatically, save a copy of sent messages, or request receipts confirming that the message has been read or received.

- Use Actions | Plan A Meeting when you want to check the schedules of invitees before specifying the details of the meeting.

- To create a meeting from any folder, press CTRL-SHIFT-Q or choose File | New | Meeting Request.

- When you are using NetMeeting, click Microsoft NetMeeting in the System Tray on the Windows taskbar and choose from the Share, Collaborate, Chat, and Whiteboard icons.

- To create a meeting from any folder, press CTRL-SHIFT-K or choose File | New | Task. Use CTRL-SHIFT-U or choose Task Request to assign a task to another person.

- To adjust the TaskPad settings, right-click any column label in the TaskPad, and choose options from the shortcut menu that appears.

Working with Outlook Express

28

BASICS

- Setting Up Mail Accounts
- Using the Address Book
- Sending and Receiving Mail

BEYOND

- Sharing Accounts
- Sharing Messages with Newsgroups

Included with Microsoft Office is a program called Outlook Express. Contrary to what the name might imply, this program is not simply a "lite" version of Outlook. Rather, it is a full-featured program for communicating over the Internet using e-mail and for trading messages with newsgroups.

Starting Outlook Express

To start Outlook Express, open its icon on your desktop or on the Windows taskbar. You can also choose Start | Programs | Outlook Express.

NOTE: If the Internet Connection Wizard begins when you start Outlook Express, then you do not have a mail account set up. Refer to "Setting Up Mail Accounts" later in this chapter.

Outlook Express stores messages in folders (much like Outlook itself) in the folder list on the left of the window, as shown in Figure 28-1. Click a folder in

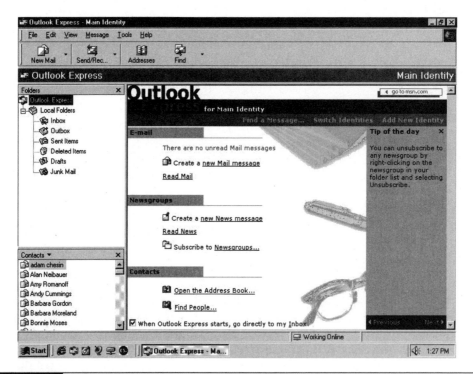

FIGURE 28-1 Outlook Express

the list to see the messages in the folder to the right. Below the folder list is a list of persons in the Outlook Express address book. While this list is called Contacts, it does not contain addresses from your Outlook Contacts folder unless you are running the Outlook Internet Only installation and sharing address books.

NOTE: If the Contacts list does not appear in the Inbox, select View | Layout, enable the Contacts checkbox, and click OK.

If your initial Outlook Express window does not show the Inbox, as in Figure 28-1, then it probably started in the Outlook Express folder. This folder offers a menu of options:

- Create a New Mail Message
- Read Mail
- Create a New News Message
- Read News
- Subscribe to Newsgroups
- Open the Address Book
- Find People

To automatically open the Inbox when you start Outlook Express, select the check box labeled "When Outlook Express Starts Go Directly To My Inbox."

To display this menu at any time, click Outlook Express in the folder list on the left.

Setting Up Mail Accounts

If you do not have an Internet mail account already set up, the Internet Connection Wizard begins the first time you start Outlook Express. Use the wizard to specify your mail server, e-mail address and password, and how you connect to your Internet provider. You can also set up a news account for sharing messages with newsgroups. If you later have to change any of the mail account information, choose Tools | Accounts to open the Internet Accounts dialog box, shown in Figure 28-2.

When the Properties dialog box opens, modify the account information as necessary, and then click OK.

You can also use Outlook Express to send and receive mail through more than one account. In the Internet Accounts dialog box, click the Add button and then choose Mail from the submenu to start the Internet Connect Wizard to create the account.

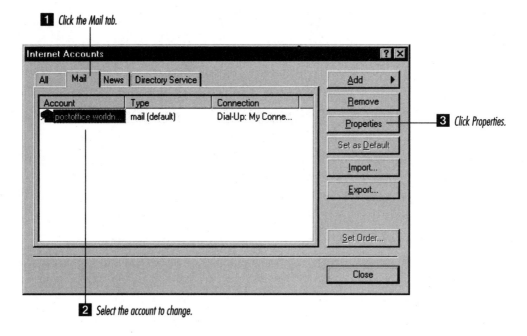

1 Click the Mail tab.

3 Click Properties.

2 Select the account to change.

FIGURE 28-2 Setting up or changing accounts

With Outlook Express, every member of the family can share one mail account and keep his or her own mail—incoming and outgoing—in separate folders. The trick is to create an *identity* for each member of the family.

To create an identity, choose File | Identities | Add New Identity. In the dialog box that appears, type a name for the identity and then click OK. You'll be asked if you want to switch to that identity. If you select Yes, a new set of Outlook Express folders appears. If you select No, then to later change identities, choose File | Switch Identity, click the identity in the box that appears, and then click OK.

For each identity, you have to create an e-mail account using Tools | Accounts. If you are sharing one e-mail account, use the same account information but type the name of the family member when the Internet Connection Wizard asks for the display name.

To choose which identity to use as the default when you start Outlook Express, select File | Identities | Manage Identities:

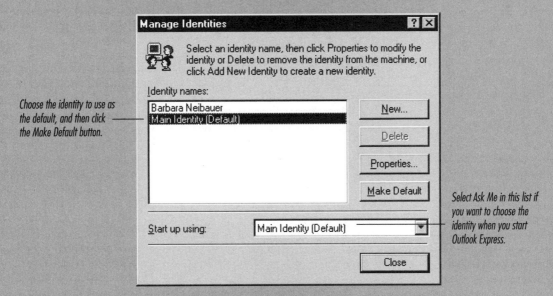

Choose the identity to use as the default, and then click the Make Default button.

Select Ask Me in this list if you want to choose the identity when you start Outlook Express.

Using the Outlook Express Address Book

To open the Outlook Express address book, click the Addresses button on the toolbar. The address book only has one address type, and you cannot access addresses on your network. To add an address, click New on the Address Book toolbar and choose New Contact from the menu.

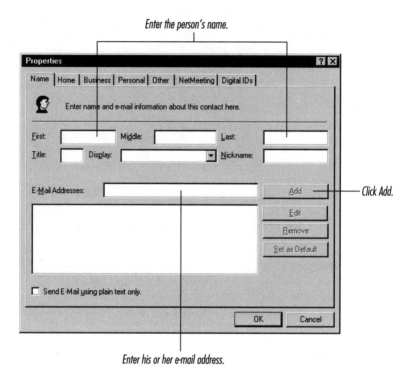

Enter the person's name.

Click Add.

Enter his or her e-mail address.

> **TIP:** Quickly create a new listing by clicking on Contacts above the contact list and choosing New Contact in the menu that appears.

When you set up Outlook using the Internet Only option, you can share its address book with Outlook Express. This way you can access the same addresses with both programs. To share the address book, open the address book in Outlook Express and select Tools | Options. In the dialog box that appears, select the check box labeled "Share Contact Information Among Microsoft Outlook And Other Applications." Finally, click OK.

Sending Mail

Before creating or sending mail, make sure you are using your own identity. Choose File | Switch Identity, click the identity in the box that appears, and then click OK.

To start a new message, double-click the recipient's name in the Contacts list to open a Message window already addressed to the recipient, as shown in Figure 28-3. If the recipient's name isn't in the Contacts list, click the New Mail button on the toolbar. You can then type the recipient's address in the To text box, or click the icon next to the To text box to open the Select Recipients dialog box, where you can select recipients from the address book.

When you click Send, Outlook Express adds the message to your Outbox. If Outlook Express isn't set up to send your mail immediately, click the Send/Rec button on the toolbar. Outlook Express dials your Internet provider, sends your mail from your Outbox, and checks for new mail. Meanwhile you'll see a dialog

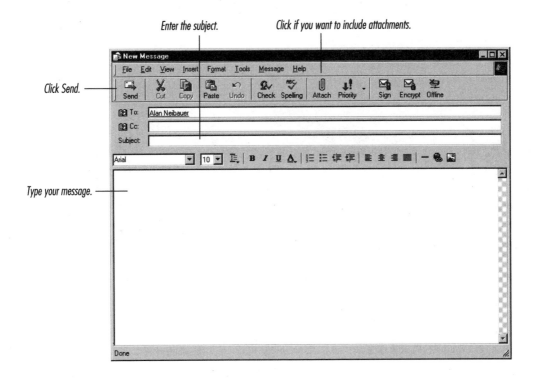

FIGURE 28-3 Outlook Express Message window

box reporting its progress, as shown in Figure 28-4. Copies of your sent messages are stored in the Sent Items folder. If you want to send mail without checking for new messages, pull down the list next to the Send/Rec button and choose Send All.

 TIP: To determine if mail is sent immediately, select Tools I Options. In the Send tab of the dialog box that appears, select or clear the check box labeled "Send Messages Immediately."

Formatting Messages

Outlook Express lets you format messages in much the same way as Outlook, using the Formatting toolbar and the Format menu. You can also choose a stationery design—Outlook Express uses the same stationery designs as Outlook. You can select stationery before or after you start a message.

Choose the Hang Up When Finished box to disconnect when Outlook Express has sent and received all your mail.

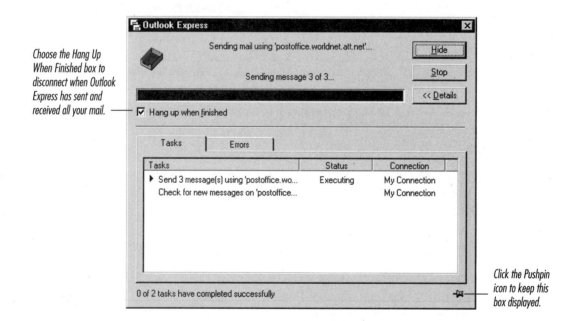

Click the Pushpin icon to keep this box displayed.

FIGURE 28-4 Sending and receiving mail

To select stationery when you start a new message, pull down the list next to the New Mail button on the Formatting toolbar, or choose Message | New Message Using from the menu.

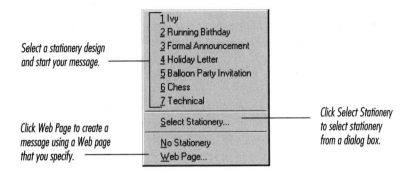

Select a stationery design and start your message.

Click Web Page to create a message using a Web page that you specify.

Click Select Stationery to select stationery from a dialog box.

If you already started a message without stationery and decide you want to add it, choose Format | Apply Stationery, and then select a stationery or More Stationery from the list.

Getting Mail

When you want to check for new mail, start Outlook Express and click the Send/Rec button to dial into your Internet provider, send any mail in your Outbox, and receive new mail. To just get mail without sending any, pull down the list next to the Send/Rec button and choose Receive All. You'll see the dialog box shown in Figure 28-5, reporting the number of messages arriving. Once the mail is downloaded, the number of unread messages appears after the name of the Inbox folder in the folder list. Click the Inbox folder to display your messages, as shown in Figure 28-5. Click a message to read it in the Preview pane, or double-click the message to read it in a separate window.

If you want to add the sender's name and e-mail address to your address book, double-click the message to open it. Then right-click the sender's name, and choose Add To Address Book from the shortcut menu.

To respond to the message, click the Reply button on the toolbar. Outlook Express starts a new message containing the text of the message you received. The reply is already addressed to the sender. Use the Reply All button to send your reply to all recipients of the original message, or the Forward button to send the message to another recipient.

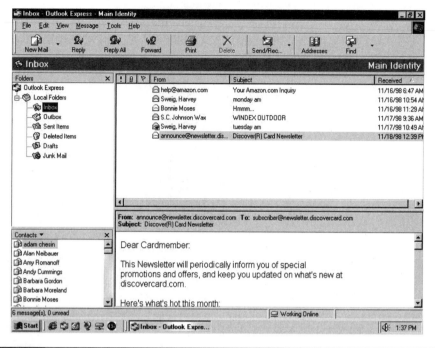

FIGURE 28-5   Inbox

Sharing Messages with Newsgroups

A *newsgroup* is a collection of persons who share messages with each other over the Internet about a common interest. There are no fees to join a newsgroup beyond what you pay for your Internet access. Most Internet service providers let you join newsgroups and handle the flow of messages between the newsgroup and your computer through a *news server*.

Setting Up for Newsgroups

Before you can access a newsgroup, you need to get the name of the news server from your Internet provider. The Internet Connection Wizard will ask if you want to set up a news account at the same time that you create a mail account. If you selected not to, you can later set up the account using these steps:

1. Choose Tools | Accounts.
2. Click the Add button and then choose News from the submenu to start the Internet Connect Wizard to create the account.

NOTE: To modify a news account, click the account in the News tab of the Internet Accounts dialog box and click Properties. Each identity can subscribe to individual newsgroups.

Downloading and Subscribing to Newsgroups

When you close the Internet Accounts dialog box after setting up a news account, you'll be asked if you want to download the names of the newsgroups. Click Yes to be connected to your news server and to download the group names. Some servers track thousands of newsgroups, so the process may take some time, but when they are downloaded, their names appear as shown in Figure 28-6. To send and receive messages from a newsgroup, you have to subscribe to it, as shown in the figure.

Newsgroups

You can later display this dialog box again by clicking on the news server name in the News Reader window, and then clicking on the Newsgroups button on the toolbar.

The newsgroups that you subscribe to will be listed in the folder list below the news server name. If there is a plus sign next to the news server name, click

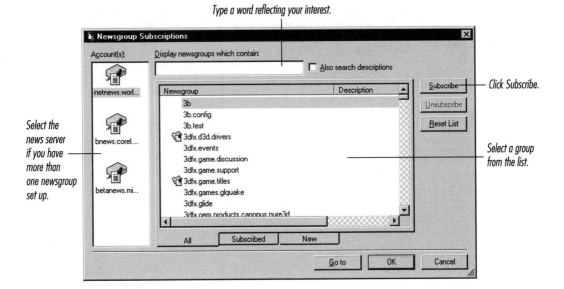

FIGURE 28-6 Subscribing to newsgroups

it to list the groups. You'll also see the newsgroups listed to the right, showing the number of unread and total messages, as well as the synchronization status, as shown in Figure 28-7.

Getting Messages

To save you connect time, the news reader normally downloads just *message headers*—the subject of each message—not the complete text of the message. In the folder list, click the newsgroup name that you want to read. Any message headers you already downloaded will appear in the message list. Messages that you have not yet read appear in bold. The list has eight columns, although you may have to scroll to see them all. The first four columns contain icons indicating whether the message contains an attachment, is flagged for your special attention, is marked to be downloaded, and is set to be watched or ignored. The other columns contain icons for Subject, From, Sent, and Size.

The news reader will then download up to 300 new message headers showing the number of message headers being received on the left of the status bar.

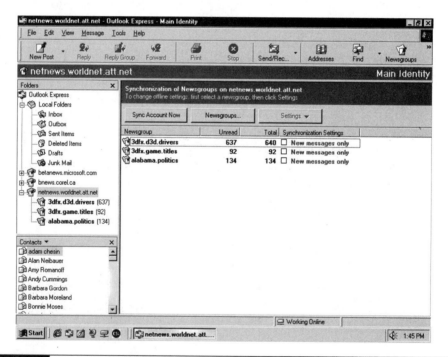

FIGURE 28-7 Subscribed newsgroups

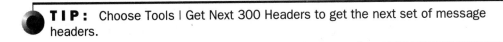

> **TIP:** Choose Tools | Get Next 300 Headers to get the next set of message headers.

Reading Messages

If you are not online, Outlook Express may connect when you click a newsgroup name and download the list of new message headers. If it does not connect, you can download the headers by selecting Tools | Synchronize, or by clicking on the Sync Account Now button that you saw in Figure 28-7.

You're now ready to read messages that interest you. When you are connected and online, clicking on a message header will retrieve the message and display it in the Preview pane for you to read. Double-clicking on the header opens the message in its own window. Both methods also store a temporary copy of the message on your disk in the *cache*.

> **NOTE:** If messages do not appear in the Preview pane, choose Tools | Options, click the Read tab, and then turn on the Automatically Show News Messages In The Preview Pane option.

Many messages are replies to others. The original message and its replies represent a conversation about a specific topic. In newsgroup parlance this is a *thread*. All the messages in the thread are kept together to make it easy to follow the conversation.

When a plus sign or a minus sign precedes a message, the message represents the start of a thread—a message to which replies have been sent. Usually, the default setting shows just the initial messages in the thread, like this:

⊞ 📝 **Manifesto of the National Trevourist Party**	Noxvomica	11/14/9
📝 **Politicians----The Finest Money Can Buy**	R. Patrick Pugh	11/13/9
📝 **Celebrate America Recycles Day**	sroberts@4env.com	11/13/9
⊞ 📝 **Re: Liberal definition..**	Wesley	11/12/9
📝 **Re: Fob's hunting and fishing trip**	yogijr@snowhill.com	11/11/9

Click the plus sign to expand the thread, showing replies to it. The replies are indented and usually have the same title, but starting with "Re:," as shown here:

⊟ 📄 **Manifesto of the National Trevourist Party**	**Noxvomica**		11/14/9
📄 **Re: Manifesto of the National Trevou...**	**Randy**		11/14/9
📄 **Politicians----The Finest Money Can Buy**	**R. Patrick Pugh**		11/13/9
📄 **Celebrate America Recycles Day**	**sroberts@4env.com**		11/13/9
⊞ 📄 **Re: Liberal definition..**	**Wesley**		11/12/9

Click a minus sign to collapse a thread, hiding the responses to it. As long as one message in the thread is unread, the message starting the thread will be bold.

In some cases, replies are sent in response to other replies. In this case, you'll see several levels of indentation, and messages that begin threads within threads:

⊟ 📄 **Re: Founding Fathers & 2nd Amendment**	**Robert Forkner**	11/8/98
⊟ 📄 **Re: Founding Fathers & 2nd Amendm...**	**Mark A. Fuller**	11/9/98
⊟ 📄 **Re: Founding Fathers & 2nd Ame...**	**Tony Minkoff**	11/10/9
⊟ 📄 **Re: Founding Fathers & 2nd A...**	**Mark A. Fuller**	11/10/9
⊟ 📄 **Re: Founding Fathers & 2nd ...**	**Tony Minkoff**	11/11/9
📄 **Re: Founding Fathers & 2...**	**Mark A. Fuller**	11/11/9
📄 **Re: Founding Fathers & 2...**	**Paul Schauble**	11/18/9
⊟ 📄 **Re: Founding Fathers & 2nd Ame...**	**Michael R. McAfee**	11/11/9
⊟ 📄 **Re: Founding Fathers & 2nd A...**	**Mark A. Fuller**	11/11/9
📄 **Re: Founding Fathers & 2nd ...**	**Polar Bear**	11/12/9

N O T E : If your messages are not organized by threads, choose View | Sort By | Group Messages By Subject.

If you are offline, clicking on a header will only show the message if it is still in the cache, or if you downloaded the full text of the message. If you want to read messages after you log off, you can set up your news reader to download the full contents of all messages automatically, or you can mark and download selected messages.

To mark a newsgroup for automatic downloading, follow these steps:

1. Click the news server name in the folder list.
2. Click the newsgroup you want to set for offline reading.
3. Pull down the Settings list and choose what you want to download—All Messages, New Messages Only, or New Headers Only.

Now when you want to download the newsgroup items, click the Sync Account Now button or chose Tools | Synchronize.

To download a specific message, click it in the message list, and then choose Tools | Mark For Offline | Download Message Later. Then to get the messages, choose Tools | Synchronize.

Sending Newsgroup Messages

Now it's your turn. You can send a message to the entire group, or reply to a message. You can choose to send the reply so everyone can read it, or send it as a personal e-mail to the sender.

When you send a new message to the newsgroup, you are *posting* it so it is available to everyone within the group. To post a message, click the newsgroup where you want to send the message in the folder list, and then click the New Post button to open the New Message window:

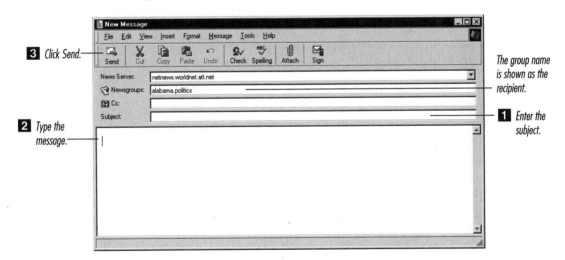

When you click Send, your message is inserted in the Outbox. Click the Outbox folder in the folder list, and then click the Send/Rec button.

To reply to a message so it is sent to everyone in the group, click the message in the message list, and then click the Reply Group button. A Message window appears addressed to the group, with the subject line filled out (adding "Re:" to the original subject) and the text of the message to which you are replying:

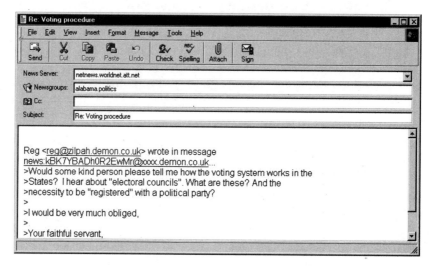

Type your own message in reply. You can leave or delete the text of the original message, it's up to you. Since your message will become part of a thread, readers will know what it is in response to. However, after some time, very old messages will be deleted from the news server and may not appear in the thread. While it is your choice, protocol calls for only sending the text of the previous reply. If you see a long list of replies, consider deleting some of the older ones. When you're ready to send the message, click Post. Next click the Outbox, and then the Send/Rec button.

If you want to reply to a message but not have your reply shown to everyone in the group, click the Reply button. In this case, the sender, not the entire group, will be shown as the recipient. Enter your reply and then click the Send button (you are sending, not posting a message). Click the Outbox, then on Send/Rec.

Finally, to forward a message by e-mail, click Forward. In the message box that appears, enter the recipient's e-mail address and your message. Click Send, the Outbox, and then on Send/Rec.

- Use Tools | Options to customize Outlook Express.
- When composing a message, choose Format | Plain Text if the recipient cannot receive formatted mail.
- If you do not complete a message, choose File | Save to add it to the Drafts folder. You can later open the message in the Drafts folder to complete it and then click Send.
- To choose default stationery, select Tools | Options and click the Compose tab. Turn on the Mail check box for a default mail stationery, or the New check box for new stationery. Click the Select button to the right of the check box, and choose the stationery from the box that appears.
- Use Tools | Message Rules to create rules for automatically moving or deleting mail, and for sending automatic replies.
- To print a message, right-click it in the message list and choose Print from the shortcut menu.
- Choose Edit | Find Message to search for messages based on the sender, recipient, subject, text in the message, or date received.
- Use the Maintenance tab of the Options dialog box to determine how long downloaded-and-read newsgroup messages are retained.
- To unsubscribe from a newsgroup, right-click it in the folder list, and choose Unsubscribe From This Newsgroup from the shortcut menu.
- If you share your computer with children, watch for inappropriate content in newsgroup messages.

Index

• Z